The Oil Cringe of the West

J. B. Kelly being greeted by Sheikh Rashid of Ajman in 1957

The Oil Cringe of the West

The Collected Essays
and Reviews
of J.B. Kelly
Vol. 2.

edited by S.B. Kelly

Published by New English Review Press
a subsidiary of World Encounter Institute
PO Box 158397
Nashville, Tennessee 37215
&
27 Old Gloucester Street
London, England, WC1N 3AX

Cover Art and Design by Kendra Adams

ISBN: 978-0-9884778-9-6

First Edition

NEW ENGLISH REVIEW PRESS
newenglishreview.org

To David Pryce-Jones
for *Arabia, the Gulf and the West.*

Acknowledgements

I t would not have been possible to put this this collection together without the help and co-operation of a number of people and organisations. I am grateful to the following publishers and their editors for permission to reprint my late father's articles, letters and book reviews: John Wiley & Sons (for Chapters 10 and 25), *The Middle East Journal* (for Chapter 2), Taylor & Francis (for Chapters 1, 3, 4, 6, 7, 8, 12, 18, and 20), Cambridge University Press (for Chapter 15). Although JBK owns the copyright for the remaining chapters, I would like to credit the following for having published them originally: *The Times Higher Educational Supplement* (Chapters 9, 11, and 29), *Commentary* (Chapter 14), *The Times Literary Supplement* (Chapters 16 and 22), *The Daily Telegraph* (Chapters 13 and 21), *The Sunday Telegraph* (Chapters 17, 19, 23, 24, 26, 27, 28, 30, 32, and 34), *The New Republic* (Chapters 31 and 36), *Encounter* (Chapters 33 and 35), *Survey* (Chapter 37), *National Review* (Chapter 38) and *Quadrant* (Chapter 39).

I owe a debt of gratitude to Karen Crouch for so willingly giving of her time to type up quite a few of the longer chapters. My thanks to Professor Edmund Bosworth, John O'Sullivan and David Pryce-Jones, who all knew my father, for reading and commenting on the manuscript. Above all, Hugh Fitzgerald and Rebecca Bynum have been the moving forces behind this endeavour. It has been a great pleasure to work with so efficient an editor as Rebecca. I can highly recommend her to any prospective author with the New English Review Press. The *NER* should be cherished and supported by all right-thinking men and women. It is one of the few champions of intellectual freedom left in the West. As such, my father would have been one of its greatest supporters.

Contents

Introduction: Macaulay's New Zealander   13

1 - Shades of Amber   25

2 - British Policy in the Arab World   42

3 - Middle East Record   48

4 - 'TLS' In the Desert   56

5 - The Slave Trade of the Indian Ocean and the Red Sea   84

6 - The Middle East in Revolution   122

7 - Nationalism in Asia and Africa   135

8 - Political Dynamics in the Middle East   140

9 - Towards Fanatic Rule   144

10 - Arabic Political Memoirs   147

11 - Tales of Arabian Knights   150

12 - Middle East Survey   154

13 - The Shah and the Gulf   165

14 - Oil & the West   169

15 - Britain, India and the Turkish Empire   176

16 - In the Middle East Labyrinth   180

17 - Farce in the Bazaar   185

18 - The Experience of Revolution in South Arabia   188

19 - Such Decent Chaps, the Arabs   213

20 - Philby of Arabia   215

21 - OPEC Should Be Put In Its Place 220

22 - Diplomacy Among the Derricks   224

23 - Lament for the Lebanon   229

24 - Time To Fold Those Tents   231

25 - Kuwait Oil   234

26 - Seeking Refuge in the RAF   237

27 - Trying, Egypt, Trying   239

28 - Suez: A Story of Sabotage   241

29 - A Damning Indictment of a Repressive Ruler   244

30 - What the Editor Saw   251

31 - Militant Islam   253

32 - Acute Triangle   260

33 - Of Valuable Oil and Worthless Policies 262

34 - A Time for Toughness in the Gulf   274

35 - The Kremlin and the Gulf   277

36 - Saudi Censors   290

37 - Great Game or Grand Illusion?   296

38 - Yamani's Book of Revelations   316

39 - The Oil Cringe of the West   321

About the Author   341

Index   347

Introduction:
Macaulay's New Zealander

We have already noted (in volume 1) the amusing literary parallels between the great nineteenth century Whig historian, Thomas Babington Macaulay, and his late modern incarnation, the historian of Arabia and the Gulf, J. B. Kelly (JBK). Grounded in a common classical education, seduced by science at university, and then finding their more natural metier in historical studies, both men were consummate stylists of English prose. There was a mutual passion, deriving from their similar temperaments, for 'straight, unhesitating phrasing', for a cold mastery of facts and tight reasoning in their argumentation, often laced with a deadly mocking humour, barely concealing scorn and contempt, all leading to the utter annihilation of their chosen targets: the ignorance, cant and prejudice of contemporary and historical figures.[1] One can share in, and appreciate, the sheer pleasure they must have had in demolishing the myths and misconceptions of their respective ages. The brio with which they wrote their histories was also informed by their contact with the reality of politics, Macaulay as a member of parliament and cabinet minister, and Kelly as an advisor to Arab shaikhs, and British and American politicians.[2] They were

---

1 See Pieter Geyl, *Debates with Historians* (London, B.T. Batsford Ltd., 1955), p. 29.

2 In 1970, J.B. Kelly not only helped establish the Abu Dhabi Documentation and Research Centre in the old palace, but acted for the Ruler Shaikh Zayid ibn Sultan Al Niyayan in trying to persuade the new Conservative government in Britain to stay in the Gulf, thus reversing the decision to withdraw made by the previous Labour government. It involved meetings in London in 1970-71 with Julian Amery, M.P., who was to become a minister of state at the Foreign and Commonwealth Office in 1972. By then, the permanent officials of 'the Office' had persuaded the politicians to withdraw from the Gulf, a decision the dire consequences of which JBK was to chronicle in the next decade. As will be seen in the next volume, American politicians were more alive

also zealots (as the great Dutch historian Pieter Geyl said of Macaulay) 'for public virtues and for progress and for the cause of liberty.'[3]

Whereas Macaulay concentrated on political reform in Britain and India, Kelly exposed the complicity of successive British governments, riddled by appeasers, in propping up their enemies, some of the most repressive regimes in the Middle East, and betraying Britain's real friends among the peoples and rulers of the region. A native of New Zealand, Britain's most loyal dominion, JBK felt keenly this sense of betrayal. It was embodied not only in Britain abandoning her responsibilities in Arabia and the Gulf between 1967 and 1971 (chronicled in this and the previous volume), but in Britain's turning her back on New Zealand, and other Commonwealth countries, by entering the European Economic Community in 1973. It meant that, following his return to London from the United States in 1970 with his family, JBK now found himself an alien in a once familiar land, his continued residence dependent on the sufferance and whim of Her Majesty's Immigration Service. This enforced sense of his being an outsider was only increased by his exclusion from British academe because of the unpopularity of his views on the Middle East. Undaunted, and now with an independent income (courtesy of the hard work and thrift of his recently-deceased mother), he could afford to sit, contemplate and comment on the unfolding political scene before his eye, perched as he was in his eyrie of a house on Primrose Hill, with its sweeping views of London. He had, perforce, become that mythical traveller from New Zealand, whom Macaulay had portrayed at some point in the future standing 'on a broken arch of London Bridge to sketch the ruins of St. Paul's.'[4] This image (immortalised by Gustave Dore in 1872) was misinterpreted in the nineteenth century as a terrible warning by Macaulay that the fate of Victorian Britain and its empire would be that of ancient Greece or Rome. Instead, as has been pointed out, Macaulay was in 1840 'asking for recognition that, although Britain seems to have reached a state of power and prosperity unparalleled in the history of the world, it is in the nature of things to be impermanent. The New Zealander is less a harbinger of doom than a prompt to self-awareness and self-criticism. This is the function of

---

to the growing threats to Western interests in the Gulf and more receptive to JBK's arguments.

3 Geyl, p. 29.

4 'Von Ranke.' (October,1840) in *Critical and Historical Essays* contributed to the *Edinburgh Review* by Lord Macaulay. New Edition in Three Volumes, Vol. III (London, Longmans, Green and Co. and New York, 1891), p. 101.

the historian when he plays the role of superior journalist.'[5]

This was, indeed, the role that JBK assumed in London during the 1970's, before he returned once again to the United States in 1980. Although the British Empire had to all intents and purposes become as 'one with Nineveh or Tyre'[6], he was fearless in his pursuit of the often uncomfortable reasons for its demise and its consequences for post-imperial Britain. Above all, he attributed it to the illusions and failure of will of the British ruling class. As the decade advanced (and as this volume will show) he became increasingly concerned about the implications of these failures, especially in the Middle East, for the security of Britain and the West in the face of a combined onslaught from the East, represented by a resurgent Islam and an increasingly malevolent Soviet Union. He was not only determined to highlight this threat in his various writings but to sound a call to arms, to rally the forces of light against those of darkness. That he was to succeed in his quest, with the coming to power of the Reagan Administration in 1981 (which will be shown in the next volume), was due not only to his own unswerving perseverance but also to that small band of like-minded men and women who encouraged him and shared his appreciation of the seriousness of the situation.

Without doubt, the most important member of that select band of doughty friends and fighters was Elie Kedourie, professor of politics at the London School of Economics and Political Science. Kedourie had been, since his student days at Oxford in the 1950's, the scourge of the British Arabo-phile establishment in his various writings and his editorship of *Middle Eastern Studies* (to such an extent that he was unjustly deprived of his DPhil by the Laudian Professor of Arabic at Oxford, Hamilton Gibb).[7] When in 1970 Kedourie published his collection of essays entitled *The Chatham House Version and Other Middle Eastern Studies*, which included a sober, scholarly, critique of Arnold Toynbee and the baleful influence which he had had, not only on historical studies but on British official attitudes and policy towards the Arab states, he was met, not with counter-argument but rank innuendo from the anonymous reviewers of his work in *The Economist* and *The Times Literary Supplement* (*TLS*). Whereas the for-

---

5 David Skilton, 'Tourists at the Ruins of London: The Metropolis and the struggle for Empire', *Cercles*, 17, pp. 116-117.

6 Rudyard Kipling, 'Recessional', *Rudyard Kipling's Verse*. Definitive Edition (Hodder and Stoughton, London, 1940), pp. 328-9.

7 Kedourie published his D.Phil. as *England and the Middle East: The Destruction of the Ottoman Empire, 1914-1921* (1956). It was reprinted in 1978 and again in 1987 with a new introduction, which explains the Oxford cabal against him.

mer made a gratuitous reference to Professor Kedourie's origins: '[he] was born in Baghdad and is of Jewish descent', the latter reviewer labelled him: 'a leading member of the Zionist demolition squad.' JBK was so outraged by these racial and religious slurs, masquerading as informed criticism, that he wrote stinging letters of reproach to the literary editor of *The Economist* and the editor of the *TLS*. As he pointed out to the former: 'I am not aware that being born in Iraq and being Jewish by religion disqualified one from acceptance as a serious and reputable scholar of Middle-Eastern history. (If such is the case, then I must assume that because I was born in New Zealand and am a Christian my antecedents deprive anything that I might write on British Imperial history of academic respectability.)'[8] When the same illogical slur was again levelled at both Kedourie and P. J. Vatikiotis, another professor of politics at the University of London (at the School of Oriental and African Studies) in December 1971 in an anonymous review of the latters' book, *Conflict in the Middle East*, JBK returned to the attack against the notion that only Muslim Arabs and the Englishman that had ruled over them 'were capable of balanced judgements on Arab politics' because of the sympathetic feelings which existed between them.

Undismayed by the refusal of either *The Economist* or the *TLS* to publish his letters, on the grounds they were 'expressions of opinion', JBK expressed to the editor of the *TLS* his 'progressive dissatisfaction with the quality of [its]reviews of books dealing with modern Arab history and politics… [which seems] to have become the preserve of a clique, whose touchstone in apportioning praise or blame to an author is whether or not he identifies himself with the "Arab cause", "Arab aspirations", or any of the hundred-an-one catch-phrases commonly applied to the elusive phenomenon generically termed "Arab nationalism".'[9] The *TLS*, in the shape of its assistant editor, denied the existence of such a clique or the need for Kedourie, and Vatikiotis for that matter, to be defended by Kelly. He must have later regretted this faint riposte, for it only served to spur JBK to write his famously damning indictment of the indefensible policy of anonymous reviewing which still prevailed at the *TLS* (see chapter 4, '"TLS" in the Desert'). Refused for publication by Melvyn Lasky of *Encounter*, on the grounds that it was libellous, and Leopold Labedz's *Survey*, it was eventually published in 1973 by the editor of *The Journal of Imperial and Commonwealth History*, Trevor Reese, who was an old friend of my father's from student days in London. Welcomed by distinguished literary

---

8 J.B. Kelly Papers, 'TLS' in the Desert file, Kelly to The Editor, *The Economist*, 22 April 1970.

9 Kelly to Editor, The *TLS*, 10 January 1972.

and historical scholars alike (including professors Frank Kermode, F.W. Bateson, C.D. Cowan, Bernard Lewis, William Norton Medlicott, Hugh Seton-Watson, Hugh Trevor-Roper and Malcom Yapp), it was to lead to the abandonment of this policy by the editor-in-chief of *The Times*, Denis Hamilton, the early retirement of the editor of the *TLS*, Arthur Crook, and his replacement by John Gross. It was also to bring JBK to the attention of Fleet Street, which was to provide him with a platform to promote an alternative view of the Middle East to the educated British public.

JBK was soon reviewing books on the Middle East for not only *The Times Higher Educational Supplement* (see chapters 9, 11, and 29) but even the *TLS*, and under his own name! (see chapters 16 and 22). But he found a spiritual affinity with the extraordinary group of journalists who then worked for and ran the editorial and literary pages of T*he Daily Telegraph* and *The Sunday Telegraph*, namely Colin Welch, Frank Johnson, John O'Sullivan, Duff Hart-Davis, Nicholas Bagnall and Peregrine Worsthorne. This is reflected in the slew of reviews which he wrote for them between 1976 and 1979 (see chapters 17, 19, 23, 24, 26, 27, 28, 30, 32, and 34). The tone was set from the first review, in *The Sunday Telegraph* on 22 February 1976 (see chapter 13), which spoke of Elie Kedourie's *In the Anglo-Arab Labyrinth*, which exploded the myth of the British betrayal of the Arabs, as guiding 'us with unfaltering sureness through the labyrinthine intricacies of negotiation and elucidation, [where] we find ourselves in the middle of a bizarre farce (or perhaps more aptly, a farcical bazaar) of oriental haggling, British ineptitude, Arab importunity, and individual delusion, self-serving and deceit.'[10] The partnership between Kelly and Kedourie was to endure, and prove a productive one. Not only did JBK review regularly for Kedourie's *MES* (see chapters 1, 3, 6, 12, 17, 18) but he reviewed Kedourie's works in other publications (see chapters 7, 10 and, of course, 17). They were a formidable duo, often working out their tactics for refuting in the press the continued sleights and slurs against them by shadowy journalistic figures, whilst walking at the weekend on Hampstead Heath or Primrose Hill, near their respective homes. When again, in 1979, *The Economist* gave space to an attack from two of their correspondents on 'western Islamists [sic], many of whom dislike the men and faith they study…'[11], later identified by a member of CAABU

---

10 JBK was quick to counter a quibbling review of *In the Anglo-Arab Labyrinth* by Professor Briton Cooper Busch in *The Middle East Journal* in the winter of 1977/78, which sparked off a further correspondence with Professor Tareq Ismael and Professor A.L. Tibawi on the interpretation of the infamous Hussein-McMahon correspondence.

11 Kelly to Editor, *The Economist*, 22 October 1979 (the original), published in

(the Council for the Advancement of Arab-British Understanding) as 'a so-called "London school"' (comprising Kedourie, Lewis, Vatikiotis, and Kelly, who were associated with *MES*), they denied the existence of any 'such cabal', or 'wicked Gang of Four'.[12] Again, as earlier in the decade with *The Economist* and the *TLS*, Kelly and Kedourie were concerned with countering 'the wholly untenable proposition that sympathy for a subject was an indispensable prerequisite for its study…', and exposing the refusal or inability of such correspondents to engage in discussion of 'matters of substance relating to Islamic history or Middle Eastern politics…' Instead these individuals resorted to 'the arid pursuit of name-calling, of accusing people of bias and labelling them "anti-Arab" or "anti-Muslim" simply because they do not share [the same] predilections or loyalties…'[13] Kelly was to return to the charge when he reviewed in *The New Republic* in January 1980 the book which had sparked the latest encounter in *The Economist* (chapter 31). It was not to be the last such contretemps, as JBK was to clash again with *The Economist*, and its editor Andrew Knight, in September 1980 on William F. Buckley's T.V. programme *Firing Line*, following the publication of JBK's attack on the extortionate oil price rises by Arab states and the craven Western response in his *Arabia, The Gulf and the West*.

In a sense it can be said that the 1970's represented 'the letter-writing years' as far as JBK was concerned. He directed his gaze, in particular, at those British institutions which fell far short, in his view, of the required standards of political impartiality and even freedom of speech. One after another he took them on and exposed their biases and hidden agendas. We find him bearding B.B.C. T.V. in 1972 for their series on the British Empire with its 'surfeit of glib, partial and sniggering pseudo-examinations of serious subjects, inadequately researched and sensationally presented.'[14] As if to counter this tendency, he wrote a long and learned essay in 1973 on 'The Slave Trade of the Indian Ocean and the Red Sea', which was intended for publication in a two volume collection of essays on 'the African Diaspora' to be published by Harvard University Press. In the event only one volume was published and JBK's essay was not included, presumably for reasons of space (it is here published for the first time as chapter 5).[15]

---

amended form 3 November 1979.

12 See Kelly to Editor, *The Economist*, 6 and 31 December 1979 (not published), but see correspondence from Vatikiotis and Kedourie in *The Economist* for 8 December 1979.

13 Kelly to Editor, *The Economist*, 31 December 1979.

14 Kelly to Editor, *The Times*, 2 February 1972.

15 See Martin L. Kilson and Robert I. Rotberg, eds., *The African Diaspora. Interpretive Essays* (Harvard University Press, Cambridge, MA, 1976).

It was difficult in the climate of Western appeasement of Arab and African states alike in the 1970's for JBK to obtain a hearing for his work on the Arab slave trade in East Africa. The B.B.C. was happy, though, to give a platform in the annual Reith Lectures in 1980 to Professor Ali Mazrui for a:

> diatribe against the West for the slave trade, in which he confines his attention solely to the Atlantic trade. There is not a whisper, not a syllable, about the Arab slave trade, which had gone on for centuries before the first Portuguese navigator ever ventured south of the Equator and which has continued up to our day. It is all very strange, especially for a man who bears the same name as the Mazrui of Mombasa, who were among the principal slave dealers on the African coast in the nineteenth century. (At the time the coast lay under the dominion of the sultanate of Oman, and later that of Zanzibar, after the division of the sultanate in 1861.) The Mazrui came originally from Oman. The name is the singular of Mazari'.

> It is equally strange, particularly for one who is (from his name) presumably a Muslim, that he should never at any stage in his six lectures examine the pertinent question why it was that no movement for the abolition of slavery and the slave trade, comparable to that which arose in the Christian world, ever arose of its own accord in the Islamic world; why it was that Muslim rulers and their subjects only desisted from trafficking in slaves when they were compelled to do so by the Christian powers of Europe, and by Britain in particular. Could it possibly be that the East African slave trade, a trade conducted by Arabs (with the assistance of Africans), financed by Indians and suppressed by the British, doesn't fit into his thoroughly perverted interpretation of European activities in Africa?[16]

The next year, 1974, saw JBK castigating the British government for breaking ranks with its European neighbours and the United States by acceding so readily to the 'astronomical increases in the price of oil imposed by the Shah of Iran and the Arab oil-producing states' and concluding separate barter agreements with Iran and Saudi Arabia. 'If we go on like

---

16 J.B. Kelly Papers, 'Mazrui: Reith Lectures.' A short letter with regard to the origins of Mazrui's name was sent to the editor of *Encounter* on 3 June 1980.

this [with trade deficits in 1974 of $50-60,000 m.]...we shall repeat the grim pattern of the thirties and find ourselves, one day, keeping an appointment, not in Riyadh or Tehran, but in Samarra.'[17] In January 1975, we find JBK writing to *The Daily Telegraph* attacking the 'received opinion of the day as propounded by politicians, financiers and others anxious for one reason or another, and few of them creditable, to get their hands on Arab oil funds', concerning 'the readiness of the Arabs to invest wisely in the West and to co-operate for the general economic good.' On the contrary, as JBK pointed out, there were 'substantial grounds for believing that the motive behind the excessive prices now being charged for Middle-Eastern oil is political and religious rather than economic, and is designed to redress the balance between the Islamic countries of the Middle East and Western Europe, which has been tilted in favour of the latter for two centuries or more.'[18] It was summed up by the exclamation from one Arab oil state official in December 1973: "It is our revenge for Poitiers!" (a reference to Charles Martel's defeat of the Arab armies in France in 732).[19] Commenting a few days later on a disparaging review in the *TLS* by Alastair Buchan (the son of the novelist and Montague Burton Professor of International Relations at the University of Oxford) of a book by Edward Luttwak (who was to become a much weightier authority on defence matters than Buchan), JBK revealed Buchan as being one of the 'sages... who counsels abject surrender as the sole possible response to OPEC's extortions.'[20] The following month *The Times* refused to pub-

17 Kelly letter to *The Times*, 8 February 1974. 'The Appointment in Samarra' is a reference to W. Somerset Maugham's retelling of an old story (which can be found in the Babylonian Talmud, Sukkah 53a), in his play *Sheppey* (1933). The speaker is Death: 'There was a merchant in Bagdad who sent his servant to market to buy provisions and in a little while the servant came back, white and trembling, and said, "Master, just now when I was in the marketplace I was jostled by a woman in the crowd and when I turned I saw it was Death that jostled me. She looked at me and made a threatening gesture, now lend me your horse, and I will ride away from this city and avoid my fate. I will go to Samarra and there Death will not find me." The merchant lent him his horse, and the servant mounted it, and he dug his spurs in its flanks and as fast as the horse could gallop he went. Then the merchant went down to the marketplace and he saw me standing in the crowd and he came to me and said, "Why did you make such a threatening gesture to my servant when you saw him this morning?" "That was not a threatening gesture", I said, "it was only a start of surprise. I was astonished to see him in Bagdad, for I had an appointment with him tonight in Samarra."' This inspired John O'Hara to take it as the title of his novel (1934).

18 Kelly to Editor, *The Daily Telegraph*, 21 January 1975.

19 J.B. Kelly, *Arabia, the Gulf and the West* (London, Weidenfeld & Nicolson, 1980), p. 423.

20 Kelly to Editor, *TLS*, 24 January 1975.

lish his critique of the 'rapturous account' in that paper on 4 February by Lord Chalfont (a former Labour minister of state at the Foreign and Commonwealth Office from 1964-1970) of his 'audience of the Shah'. JBK observed that this was 'becoming the established canon of newspaper reporting these days. *Autre temps*...A few years ago we had "the interview with Nasser", and before that "the interview with Hitler". They certainly confirm one item in Lord Chalfont's eulogistic litany—the pusillanimity of the West when confronting its enemies.'[21] Unphased, JBK turned a few months later to *The Daily Telegraph* to publish his assessment of the true motivations of the Shah in the Gulf (see chapter 13).

JBK was critical of the Western media's unbalanced coverage of the Lebanon's descent into civil war from the mid-1970's (see chapter 23). He took to task the editorial team of *The Times* for blaming the French, in creating the Grand Liban in 1920, and:

> the Maronite community for wanting to preserve the Christian position in the country and to assert the sovereignty of the Lebanese state over the Palestinians... What has brought this sorry situation to pass is the presence in the Lebanon of the Palestinians, whose leaders, acting not only from their own ideological and religious compulsions but also as the adjuncts of the radical Arab states, now threaten the very survival of the Lebanese state. The motives which impel the radical Arab regimes to interfere in the Lebanon (they are reported to have poured in some $600 million in the past few months to fuel the conflict there) are as much religious as they are political. It is not just Lebanon's parliamentary institutions, its capitalist economy and its political independence that they find irritating; they look even more balefully upon the special position which the Christian community occupies in the life of the country and its strong links with the West. To minimise the part played by militant Islamic feeling in the exploitation of the Lebanese conflict is seriously to misjudge the realities of contemporary Arab politics. For Western Christendom to ignore, or affect to ignore, as it seems bent upon doing, the fate of the Lebanese Christians is worse than a misjudgement: it is a shameful dereliction of Western responsibilities.[22]

---

21 Kelly to Editor, *The Times*, 4 February 1975 (unpublished).
22 Kelly to the Editor, *The Times*, 29 January 1976.

It is clear from his letters to the newspapers and monthly political journals (especially to *Commentary* in 1975, see chapter 14 and also chapter 21), that JBK was becoming increasingly concerned in the 1970's by the deleterious effects that the steady haemorrhaging of Western wealth to the East, through extortionate oil price rises by OPEC as a form of *Danegeld*, was having on the fabric of Western civilization. He was the first commentator to highlight the fact that Islam was wielding the oil weapon by way of revenge against Western Christendom and that this had been made possible by Britain's craven abdication of her responsibilities by withdrawing from the Gulf in 1971, and thus relinquishing some control over the supply of the black lifeblood of the industrialised world. He warned that the Soviet Union had gained from Western appeasement of Arabs and Persians, by installing herself in Iraq, South Yemen (thereby securing control of the Bab al-Mandab strait and the southern entrance to the Red Sea), by attempting to subvert the sultan of Oman (in order to gain control of the Strait of Hormuz) and from 1978 moving on Afghanistan. The fall of the Shah at this time seemed to open up infinite possibilities for Russia to achieve her age-old strategic ambition to control Persia and the Gulf. This was all laid out in a series of articles for various key publications in both Britain and the United States in 1979 and 1980 (see chapters 33, 34, 35, 37, and 38). These were precursors, or tasters if you like, of his major work, *Arabia, the Gulf and the West*, which was published in June 1980 in the UK by Weidenfeld & Nicolson and in September in the USA by Basic Books (JBK had travelled to New York City to secure this contract through Midge Dector and Norman Podhoretz; he went on to Australia to promote the book there as well, hence the extract entitled 'The Oil Cringe of the West' published in *Quadrant* in July 1980, see chapter 39). That *Arabia, the Gulf and the West* appeared at all was largely due to the encouragement of David Pryce-Jones (and it is most suitable, therefore, that this present volume of JBK's collected works should be dedicated to him).

Given how critical JBK had been in the 1970's of the British Establishment's craven reaction to the crippling oil price hikes of OPEC, orchestrated by Shaikh Yamani of Saudi Arabia, it is not surprising that on the whole the British media should give *Arabia, the Gulf and the West* a decidedly cool reception. The common tactics employed by those journalists that reviewed the book was to either dismiss it as an anti-Arab polemic, written in venomous or Macaulayesque prose (*The Times, Financial Times, Middle East International, New Society*, BBC World Service), or to so delay the review (seven months in the case of that 'old anonymous friend',

The Economist, and eight months by *The Observer*) as to ignore it.[23] It was left to the academics to assess the real worth of the book and its place in the canon of works not only in Middle Eastern, but British history. The Stevenson Professor of International History at the London School of Economics and Political Science, D. Cameron Watt, had no doubt that future students of British historiography would observe that 1980 was the year in which was launched 'the revisionist counter-attack' against the orthodox version of Britain's retreat from empire (including the withdrawal from Arabia and the Gulf), and that it was a New Zealander, JBK, who 'pulled the firing lanyard'. Watt also warned that 'the liberal orthodoxy' prevailing in Western universities and the 'obsequious contortions' of British, French and American officials and politicians would try to 'isolate' JBK and attempt to 'discredit his scholarship'.[24] To a larger extent this was the case in the UK, though attempts were made by JBK and Elie Kedourie (who wrote the copy on the jacket of the book) to counter this by a direct approach to the new incumbent of 10 Downing Street, Margaret Thatcher.

The response in the United States was of a different order altogether. The fall of the Shah, the Soviet invasion of Afghanistan and the onset of the Iran-Iraq War, and the floundering of the Carter Administration in its dying days, all called for 'Action this Day', Churchill's administrative watchword during the Second World War. It was clear that whoever won the 1980 Presidential election would have to deal with the fall-out for US national security of the complete and utter failure of U.S. and Western policies in the Gulf, embodied in the misnamed 'twin-pillars' strategy of relying on Iran and Saudi Arabia to safeguard the West's oil supplies. The Iranian pillar had fallen, the Saudi one was left isolated and vulnerable, surrounded as it was by the new, revolutionary Shi'a regime in Tehran and the Soviet surrogates in South Yemen and Iraq, and further afield in the Horn of Africa and Afghanistan. The U.S. Government needed a new

---

23 Reviews appeared in the *Evening Standard*, 22 May 1980, *The Daily Telegraph*, 29 May 1980, *The Daily Express*, 29 May 1980, *The Sunday Telegraph*, 1 June 1980, *The Times*, 5 June 1980, *New Society*, 12 June 1980, *Oxford Times*, 20 June 1980, *NOW*, 20 June 1980, *Jewish Observer*, June 1980, *Manchester Evening News*, 26 June 1980, *Sunday Mail Glasgow*, 29 June 1980, *The Guardian*, 10 July 1980, *Financial Times*, 12 July and 27 December 1980, *Middle East International*, 18 July 1980, *Jewish Chronicle*, 25 July 1980, *Britain & Israel*, September/October 1980, *The Economist*, 13-19 December 1980, with letter from Lionel Bloch, *The Observer*, 11 January 1981, BBC World Service, Arab Topical Programmes, 21 March 1981.

24 D. Cameron Watt, 'In Ignominious Retreat', *TLS*, 18 July 1980. See also the reviews by Professor Lukasz Hirszowicz in *THES*, 25 July 1980 and Professor Malcolm Yapp in the *Bulletin of the School of Oriental and African Studies*, Vol. 44, No. 2, (1981), pp. 378-379.

vision and strategy for the Gulf. One lay readily at hand in JBK's *Arabia, the Gulf and the West*, which was published only two months before the November 1980 U.S. elections. As the campaign team of the Republican presidential candidate Ronald Reagan geared itself up for power, it cast around for a strategy in the Gulf. JBK was soon at hand to help out in Washington, as the next volume will detail.

S.B. Kelly,
King's College, London.

1
Shades of Amber[1]

Shades of Amber: a South Arabian Episode, by Sir Kennedy Trevaskis. Pp. xvi + 256, illustrations, map, index. Hutchinson.
South Arabia: Arena of Conflict, by Tom Little. Pp. xii + 196,
maps, bibliography, index. Pall Mall Press.
Having Been a Soldier, by Lieut.-Col. Colin Mitchell. Pp. viii +
248, illustrations, maps, index. Hamish Hamilton.

I t is curious how little notice is taken nowadays of the affairs of
South Arabia in contrast to the volume of reportage, special
pleading, and plain propaganda which was poured out in the months and
years up to November 1967 over the question of Aden and the South
Arabian Federation. One would expect that, at the very least, those who
had argued so strenuously for the ending of British rule, and who had so
ardently echoed the demands of the South Arabian nationalists to be rid
of their traditional rulers, would have shown some interest in how their
erstwhile proteges were faring. But, alas, they have, as would seem to be
their wont, long since moved on to fresh fields in their constant quest
for sins of palaeo- or neo-colonialist complexion which cry out for expia-
tion. The reluctance of those politicians and officials in Westminster and
Whitehall, who were charged with the direction and conduct of British
policy in Aden and the Protectorates, to examine the consequences of their
decisions and indecision is perhaps more understandable, if scarcely more

1 From *Middle Eastern Studies*, Vol. 7, No. 1 (Jan., 1971), pp. 111-121. Published by
Taylor & Francis, Ltd. Reproduced by permission.

admirable. It is not a reluctance, however, which is peculiar to them, nor is it limited solely to the subject of the breakdown in Aden. Rather is it part of a general disinclination at present, on the part of those sections of British society which are by habit and tradition concerned with Britain's relations with the rest of the world, to dissect too nicely the conduct of British foreign and imperial policy in the decades since the Second World War. While much of the disenchantment can be ascribed to a feeling of impotence engendered by Britain's diminishing power and authority in the world, part of it is also attributable to the distaste aroused by the manner in which British governments of late have been resigning their imperial responsibilities. Practitioners of the art of self-exculpation (which qualifies as a 'growth industry' in certain circles in Britain today) try to connect the one with the other, to the exclusion of other contributory causes; but it is not a sufficient explanation of the sombre spectacle provided by recent British colonial leave-takings. A better explanation is to be found in Disraeli's warning of a century ago against leaving 'the destinies of the British Empire to prigs and pedants'. Nowhere is this better illustrated than in the melancholy history of the Federation of South Arabia which forms the subject of the three books under review, the first by a former High Commissioner to the Federation, the second by a journalist with long experience of the Middle East, and the last by a soldier whose professional career ended shortly after the withdrawal from Aden.

If Sir Kennedy Trevaskis's book holds the greatest interest for the reader, it is not because the other two lose from comparison—far from it—but because it derives from a much longer acquaintance and involvement with south-western Arabia, and because it is written from a higher level of authority. Trevaskis's connection with Aden and the Protectorates began in November 1951, when he was posted from Northern Rhodesia to the Western Protectorate as Assistant Political Agent. He found there a wild and savage country whose inhabitants led lives as harsh and brutal as the landscape around them. What order existed was enforced by hereditary rulers and tribal councils, or *dolas*, whose chief characteristics seemed to be inefficiency, corruption, and capriciousness. At first Trevaskis was appalled that so little had been done by Britain to improve the governments of the various shaikhdoms, sultanates and amirates in the century during which she had extended her protection to them; but as he grew to know the Protectorate better he came to the conclusion that there was some system to the apparent anarchy which prevailed, especially in the rudimentary protection and patronage which the *dolas* provided for the tribesmen. Since no political institutions other than the *dolas* existed in the territory, the only way in which the condition of its inhabitants could be improved was to improve the quality of the *dolas* by political advice and economic aid. Advisory treaties with some of the rulers had been concluded during the 1940s, on the model of those concluded by Harold Ingrams in the Eastern Protectorate in the previous decade. They had been objected to by the Imam of the Yemen as altering the status quo in the Western Protectorate, and the question which had to be decided in 1951-52 was whether to go on with the policy at the risk of antagonizing the Imam further, or whether to abandon the policy and thereby expose the Protectorate to possible conquest from the Yemen. Sir Tom Hickinbotham, who had recently been appointed Governor of Aden, decided to go on, and to try to bring some semblance of order, coherence and internal security to the Protectorate states.

Progress was slow, and the principal effect of the forward policy seemed to be to lead the Imam to stir up trouble in the tribal areas adjacent to his frontier. The need to counteract the danger from the Yemen, and to facilitate economic co-operation and advancement among the treaty states, led Hickinbotham and Trevaskis (now Political Agent for the Protectorate) to propose to the Colonial Office in 1953 that the rulers of the states be invited to combine in a federation. The Colonial Office agreed, but the plan which it evolved and which was put before the rulers in January 1954 envisioned the setting up of an administration of the type which had developed in British colonial dependencies, and which was entirely unsuited to South Arabia. Though the rulers naturally rejected this particular plan, the idea of some kind of association among them did not entirely die, and the events of the next two years lent it an increasing attraction. Not only did the subversion from the Yemen continue but it was supported from the latter months of 1954 onwards by Egypt. Britain's agreement with Nasser in the autumn of that year to evacuate the Canal Zone was interpreted and broadcast by Cairo Radio as evidence of British weakness and the prelude to a British withdrawal from the Middle East as a whole. When the Protectorate rulers expressed alarm at this possibility, which would leave them and their people at the mercy of the Imam, they were explicitly assured that nothing of the kind was in contemplation. Indeed, the Minister of State at the Colonial Office, Harry Hopkinson, was sent out in January 1955 to convey the assurance in person. Trevaskis has an amusing description (p. 66) of Hopkinson's meeting with Sharif Husain of Baihan, who, after Hopkinson had pointed to the investment of several million pounds in the new oil refinery at Aden as confirmation of Britain's intention to remain, asked him innocently, 'How many million pounds have the British Government invested in the Suez Canal?'

One thing was certain about the rebellion which the Yemen and Egypt were stirring up among some of the Protectorate tribes, and this was that, whatever Cairo or San'a might claim to the contrary, the tribes were not fighting for union with the Yemen or in the larger cause of Arab nationalism. What was it, then, that they were rebelling against? Trevaskis thought initially that under the stimulus of nationalist propaganda the tribesmen were revolting against the incompetent and arbitrary rule of their shaikhs, sultans and naibs. But then he noticed that the two states in which the British had interfered least in an effort to stimulate political reform and material progress, the Upper Aulaqi and Audhali sultanates, were those which were coping best with tribal revolt and subversion from the Yemen. The explanation, it seemed to him, lay with the rebel tribesmen themselves, who, for all their parrotting of the 'soiled catch phrases of Cairo' about colonial oppression (which they had never experienced), were actually protesting against interference, however, well-meaning, with their traditional way of life. It was a life dominated by fear, cupidity, and xenophobia (not nationalism), and no matter how corrupt the *dolas* might be, however grasping and despotic a ruler might appear (at least, to European eyes), they were also for the tribesmen the source of patronage, largesse, and, most important of all, protection. The realization of this situation led Trevaskis and other political officers to two general conclusions: one, that British interference with traditional, tribal institutions should be tempered with discretion; the other, that the British government had a responsibility, not only as every civilized government had, but also as the most powerful *dola* in South Arabia, to protect their subjects from their enemies, *i.e.* the Yemen and Egypt. It also underlined the fact that, since normal British colonial administration was unsuited to South Arabia, any move towards a federal system would have to be initiated by the Protectorate rulers themselves and its form dictated by their traditions and experience. This conclusion was accepted by the Colonial Office in January 1956.

Federation, of course, even in prospect, raised the question of the future status of Aden colony and its relationship to a South Arabian federation. Up to this time, Aden, with its mixed population of Arabs (Adeni and Yemeni), Indians, Somalis, and Europeans, had preserved a faintly ridiculous sense of self-sufficiency and importance. 'British colonial rule had converted Aden into an island which might have been separated by a hundred miles of ocean from the South Arabian mainland. As a consequence, the old-established families had cultivated the kind of oyster-like introversion sometimes found amongst the inhabitants of small and remote islands' (Trevaskis, p. 94). But even in Aden the first stirrings of Arab nationalism had been felt, more decorously among the old-established Arab merchant class and more vehemently by the young Adenis whose fathers had migrated to Aden from the Yemen in the 1930s. Mostly clerks and students who looked with envy upon the comparatively well to-do foreigners and older Adenis, and whose political and economic ambitions had been fired by the revolutionary nationalism being preached from Cairo, they formed themselves into a political party, the United National Front, in 1955. At hand they had a ready-made 'street' for the implementation of their political aims in the shape of the thousands of Yemeni labourers who had come to the colony to work, and whom they sought to control through the Aden Trades Union Council. Tom Little in his book (pp. 50-1) gives the impression that the Aden T.U.C. was founded independently of the United National Front, but Trevaskis says (p. 98) that 'the A.T.U.C. had been forged as the industrial weapon of the U.N.F.'. One thing at least is certain, and this is that the Aden T.U.C. bore little resemblance to the trades union movement in Britain, however much politicians and journalists in London might draw bland comparisons between the two. Nor is there doubt about the real nature of the U.N.F.'s leaders and their plans: they were Yemeni nationalists and their goal was the eventual union of Aden and the Protectorates with the Yemen, after the Imam Ahmad had been swept away by the tide of revolutionary Arab socialism. Both Trevaskis and Little believe that the U.N.F.'s thunder could have been stolen, and Aden set on the road to union with the impending federation, if Aden had been granted a firm assurance of early self-government in the spring of 1956. As Trevaskis writes (p. 99): 'By granting Aden early self-government with the prospect of independence, when a federation of the hinterland states had come into being and when the two had agreed to unite, we could, I believed, have solved it [the challenge of Yemeni nationalism] there and then.' Instead, Lord Lloyd, the Under-Secretary of State for the Colonies, visited Aden in May 1956 and declared that 'the importance of Aden both strategically and economically within the Commonwealth is such that they [H.M. government] cannot foresee the possibility of any fundamental relaxation of their responsibility for the Colony'. Although neither Trevaskis nor Little pays as much attention as perhaps they might to the wider considerations of British defence and foreign policy which influenced the British government's decision at the time, it would be difficult to fault the judgment which they both reach independently, *viz.* that a great chance was missed in 1956. Little puts it succinctly (p. 35): 'As a statement of policy it [Lloyd's declaration] was already verging on the unreal, for the planning of a federation of South Arabia was underway and was firmly fixed in many minds as the next stage of development. It was hardly possible that a federation could exist without Aden, and it was equally unlikely that Aden could remain a colony or constitutional advance be unduly delayed if it joined.'

Contrary to much that has been written on the subject, there was, as Trevaskis makes clear, no great opposition in Aden or the Western Protectorate to a merger of the two. The seeds of dissension lay rather in the differing views of the form that the merger should take, the area it should embrace, and the distribution of authority within it. The radical nationalists of Aden wanted power, first in the colony and later in the Protectorate, to be followed by union with a Yemen purged of the evils of theocratic rule. Above all, they wanted nothing to do with any British plan of federation, nor any connection with Britain in the future. Their antipathy towards a British-sponsored federation was shared by the Sultan of Lahej, 'Ali ibn 'Abdul Karim, who saw himself as the Nasser of South Arabia and his principality as the Prussia of a new empire which would embrace Aden and all the Protectorate states, but not the Yemen. He posed as the patron of the South Arabian League, a political party established in Lahej in the early 1950s and having as its object a united and independent South Arabia. In the heady atmosphere of 1956 and 1957, when Britain was being anathematized by Arab nationalists everywhere, the slow process of constitutional advance to federation and self-government was not a glittering enough guerdon for Sultan 'Ali and the South Arabian League to strive after; so in the early months of 1957 they set out, with money and arms supplied by Egypt and the Yemen, to force the Protectorate rulers to fall in behind their standard. The union of Egypt and Syria in the United Arab Republic early in 1958 seemed, at first glance, to strengthen their hand, for it made federation as a political device respectable in Arab eyes. But, in fact, it dealt their efforts a mortal blow, for Cairo soon made it clear that only federations of Egyptian manufacture would be tolerated in the Arab world; and the admission of the Yemen into political association with the United Arab Republic in the incongruously named 'United Arab States', at a time when the Imam was doing his best to subvert the authority of the Protectorate rulers over their subjects, only served to increase their suspicions and fears of Cairo and San'a. Sultan 'Ali and the South Arabian League strove desperately to recover the initiative by intensifying the campaign of intimidation which they had begun earlier, and by plotting to renounce Lahej's treaties with Britain and to proclaim the sultanate's adhesion to the United Arab States. Their gamble failed, primarily because of the firm action taken against them by the Governor of Aden, Sir William Luce. The leaders of the S.A.L. fled to the Yemen and later to Egypt to avoid arrest, while Sultan 'Ali went to London to complain to the Colonial Secretary. Towards the close of the year he was deposed, and he subsequently took his burden of woes to Cairo where he hoped to receive a more sympathetic hearing.

The Federation of Arab Amirates of the South was inaugurated in February 1959 and was immediately condemned by devout anti-colonialists everywhere as a sinister device to keep South Arabia in subjection, as the perpetration of feudalism, as a barrier to Arab unity, and as a crime against Arab nationalism. None of the criticism was particularly enlightened or well-informed: most of it derived more from the personal and political compulsions of the critics than it did from an understanding of the realities of Arabia. Trevaskis is scathing in his comments upon the 'higher wisdom' dispensed by Labour M.P.s and leftwing journalists in Britain about how Aden and the Protectorates should have been governed. The constitution of the new federation, for instance, was strongly criticized because it made no provision for election to the legislature. But the federation, as he points out, had to build upon whatever political tradition actually existed in South Arabia and not upon the mythical figure of the democratic tribesman who beguiled the imagination of contemporary Rousseaus. The only basis of authority which existed in the Western Protectorate, 'the only element of stability offered by an endemically unstable society' (in Trevaskis's words), was the tribal *dola*, and its power was circumscribed by custom and prescription. 'To anyone who has worked with South Arabian tribesmen', Trevaskis writes (p. 145), with a justifiable note of scorn, 'it would be hard to imagine any people less amenable to authoritarian government or one upon whom any dictatorship could be less easily imposed. With bullets in their cartridge belts they had the most effective means of influencing their rulers and so long as tribalism persists and they have guns in their hands, they are unlikely to be converted to unintelligible principles of the ballot box and the majority vote.' Nor were the *dolas* the ramshackle, decrepit, and irrelevant instruments of government which their distant critics made them out to be. Still less were the federal rulers the unregenerate, ignorant, and corrupt petty tyrants which it pleased the anti-colonialist lobby to portray them as. Such portraits are simply caricatures, bearing no resemblance to the men who pass through Trevaskis's pages, many of whom were superior in moral worth and practical ability to the great majority of the nationalist politicians who coveted their positions and authority. If they are to be criticized, they must be criticized individually, and not condemned wholesale in an access of pseudo-plebeian righteousness merely on account of their birth. How, for instance, can one equate Sharif Husain of Baihan, whose acumen, wit, courage and steadfastness illuminate the pages of *Shades of Amber* and throw into drab relief the mean and shabby manoeuvrings of the Yemeni-Adeni nationalists, with the Naib of Lower Yafa, Muhammad Aidrus, who thought he saw a quick and easy path to power by embracing the revolutionary nationalist cause, went on to accuse the British of exploiting the people of Lower Yafa by manipulating the finances of the Abyan Cotton Board, and finally absconded to the Yemen in 1957 with funds appropriated from the board and a further £10,000 from the Lower Yafa treasury, a feat which Cairo and San'a radio stations glorified as a 'noble resistance to colonialism'? It is the one serious defect of Tom Little's book that he seemed to accept the comfortable canard about the Protectorate rulers, which is all the more surprising since he is far from being an armchair journalist and has visited South Arabia several times. On the other hand, his disenchantment with the nationalists, as revealed in the pages of his book, is complete, and it is upon them that he lays the major share of the blame for the failure and collapse of the Federation in the years after 1959.

Aden's constitutional advance from representative government of the crown colony variety to responsible government was complicated by the development of Aden in the early 1960s as the main British base in the Middle East. Sir William Luce's last act as Governor, before he left in the autumn of 1960 to become Political Resident in the Persian Gulf, was to recommend to the Colonial Office that Britain should grant autonomy to Aden and allow it to negotiate its way into the Federation. In London's eyes, however, the retention of British sovereignty over the colony was essential to the security of the base. It was left to Sir Charles Johnston, Luce's successor, to devise a compromise formula in March 1961, whereby Aden would stand in much the same relationship to the Federation of South Arabia (as it was now to be called) as Singapore did to the Malayan Federation. The possibility of Aden's eventually attaining full self-government under a regime dominated by the Yemeni *Uitlanders*, who would undoubtedly seek to establish a link with the Yemen, was not to the liking of the Federal rulers, and so a further compromise was worked out at a constitutional conference held in London in the summer of 1961, by which full self-government for Aden was made conditional upon its entering the Federation.

A predictable outcry arose from the leaders of the Aden T.U.C. Not only had no provision been made for the enfranchisement of the transient

Yemeni labourers in Aden, who represented their only means of gaining power in the colony, but the insistence that the merger with the Federation precede self-government blighted their hopes of eventually dominating the Federation. A campaign was immediately initiated against the merger, on the grounds that it would subordinate the progressive, dynamic, modern and enlightened inhabitants of the colony to the arbitrary and archaic rule of the backward shaikhs and sultans of the Protectorate. It was an argument calculated to awaken an instinctively sympathetic response in liberal circles in Britain. The cry for Aden's separate development towards independence was echoed by the British Left with an eagerness and a vigour which must have surprised as much as it delighted Yemeni-Adeni nationalists. For their goal was not and never had been an independent Aden. As 'Abdullah al-Asnaj, the secretary-general of the Aden T.U.C., had publicly avowed in February 1960, their goal was 'one nation, one Yemen and one struggle only. No North, no South, but one Yemen. No Legislative Council. No Federation ... There is only one Yemen, the occupied part of which must be liberated' (Trevaskis, p. 157). Independence for Aden was merely a sham: the colony could not, nor was it desired that it should, remain separate from the Protectorates. No one in Aden in the last decade of British rule there wanted independence for Aden alone. The demand for independence put forward by the radical Adeni nationalists was merely a tactical move: once independence had been gained they would join forces with the Yemen and, supported by Egypt, set out to crush the rulers of the Federation.

One reason why their supporters and apologists in Britain failed to grasp their true purpose was, as Trevaskis points out with some asperity, that the Aden T.U.C. was regarded benignly at Transport House and elsewhere as a normal trades union movement and 'Abdullah al-Asnaj as a kind of jolly Ernest Bevin. It was, of course, nothing of the kind, and its alter ego, the People's Socialist Party, which usurped the centre of the political stage from the United National Front in 1962, was indistinguishable from it in leadership, membership and programme. Indistinguishable, that is to say, to anyone resident in Aden, but not apparently to visiting Labour M.P.s, two of whom, George Thomson and Robert Edwards, were invited to Aden in June 1962 by the Aden T.U.C., were paraded around the colony by their hosts, gave speeches to the Yemeni workers, and finally were taken surreptitiously across the frontier into the Yemen to meet a genuine nationalist hero, Muhammad Aidrus, the 'patriot' of Lower Yafa. As Trevaskis comments laconically (p. 174), 'this public exhibition of British parliamentarian sympathy with the opponents of the Federation had, as its authors intended, a powerful effect on Aden's public.'

Three months later the Imam Ahmad died, the republican revolution was proclaimed in San'a, and the Egyptians began their long and bloody campaign to bring the enlightenment of Cairo's 'new order' to the Yemen. With indecent haste the People's Socialist Party in Aden threw off the mask of pseudo-reasonableness and prophesied the coming of the revolution and the liquidation of its enemies in the Colony and the Federation. Four of its leaders flew off to San'a to become ministers in the republican government. From this moment forward the future of South Arabia depended upon the outcome of the contest between British efforts to integrate Aden with the Federation, and to strengthen that organization sufficiently to enable it to stand upon its own feet, on the one side, and, on the other, the determination of the Yemeni-Adeni nationalists to bring Aden to its knees by chaos and bloodshed and, with Egyptian help, to destroy the federal structure in the Protectorate. Two conditions were vital to the Federation's survival: one was adequate financial aid, the other was effective protection from its external enemies. Neither was immediately forthcoming in the months following Aden's formal accession to the Federation on January 1, 1963, mainly because the Colonial Office was lulled into a torpid sense of security by the initial setbacks suffered by the Egyptians in the Yemen, and by the consequent dying-down of disruptive activity by the P.S.P. in Aden. Outside Arabia, however, the campaign against the Federation was growing in viciousness and intensity. Trevaskis, who succeed Johnston as High Commissioner in August 1963, went over the heads of the permanent officials at the Colonial Office to the Colonial Secretary, Duncan Sandys, and persuaded him that the only means by which the enemies of the Federation could be baulked of their objective was by ceding sovereignty in Aden and beginning negotiations on South Arabia's independence. British strategic interests could be protected by the retention of sovereignty over the base areas.

It was the culmination of all that Trevaskis and others had aimed and worked for over the previous decade, and, what is more, it was a remarkable act of far-sightedness, trust, and generosity on the part of Sandys himself. If self-government and national independence were the true goals of the Adeni nationalists, their shouts of triumph should have echoed from the walls of Crater to the mountains of Radfan. They did not. 'Abdullah al-Asnaj and others might have been willing to accept the decision, at least for the moment, but they were no longer, and especially after al-Asnaj's visit to Cairo earlier in the year, in control of events, or even themselves. Sandys' decision was greeted by a strike and by an attempt upon Trevaskis's life as he was about to board an aircraft at Khormaksar airport, with the Federal and Adeni delegations, to attend the constitutional conference which was being convened in London to fix a date for independence. It would appear from the account given by Trevaskis of the grenade attack upon him, which killed George Henderson, his assistant, and an Indian woman, that al-Asnaj had a hand in it; although Little suggests that the attack might have been the work of the National Front for the Liberation of South Yemen (N.L.F.), which had lately been set up in San'a under Egyptian patronage to direct terrorism in Aden and the Protectorates. The outcome of the incident was that the plan to surrender sovereignty over Aden and to grant independence to the Federation was shelved for the time being, and a state of emergency was declared in the colony. This action was naturally greeted by a calculated and well coordinated outcry from the usual quarters abroad, and it also brought a delegation of Labour M.P.s to Aden as guests of the P.S.P. to protest against the detention of political prisoners and the suppression of democratic rights. The M.P.s refused to accept Trevaskis's patient explanations that these were dangerous times, and that not even a Nasser could rule South Arabia without the power of preventive detention (he could not rule even Egypt without it). The High Commissioner's knowledge and experience apparently counted for nothing in the eyes of his inquisitors, although as he himself ruefully reflected at the time, it was hardly likely that they would tolerate his telling them in return how to run the Union of Shop, Distributive and Allied Workers. There was a bizarre sequel to the attempted assassination of Trevaskis when, the following October, elections were held in Aden for a new legislative council, following the agreement reached at the delayed constitutional conference held in London in the summer of 1964 that a new Aden government should negotiate with the Federation and the British government for the transfer of sovereignty and independence by 1968. One of the candidates put up by the P.S.P. was the man accused of throwing the grenade at Khormaksar airport. The case against him had failed because the chief witness for the prosecution had fled to Cairo. He was, however, still being held in detention under the emergency regulations. Despite, or rather because of, this, he was elected to the Aden legislature, and a clamour quickly arose for his release. Trevaskis refused to heed it, but the new Colonial Secretary, Anthony Greenwood (who, Trevaskis notes sardonically, was also Vice-President of the National Society for the Abolition of Cruel Sports), thought that it would be a gracious gesture of goodwill on the part of the new Labour government if the accused murderer were to be released. He was released.

With the advent to power of the Labour government the last and bloodiest chapter in the history of the South Arabian Federation began. Trevaskis warned Greenwood that there would be three contenders for power in South Arabia when independence came—the Federal Government, Nasser, and anarchy. The British government, he said, had only two choices before them: they could support the Federal government to the hilt or they could attempt, in that fine, old, tried and trusted phrase, 'to come to terms with Nasser'. Greenwood thought he saw a third choice, 'to come to terms' with the P.S.P. and al-Asnaj, in whom he discerned the lineaments of another Archbishop Makarios. Believing, with sublime simplicity, that all Aden's troubles sprang from the 'unnatural' alliance of the colony with the Federation, and from the 'unrepresentative' character of the Aden legislature, he set out to woo the P.S.P. and the Aden T.U.C. Because Trevaskis had not the stomach for such a policy, which, he was certain, could only result in victory for the third contender for power, anarchy, Greenwood sacked him at the close of 1964. The Colonial Secretary's foolish delusions about the reasonableness and devotion to democratic ideals of al-Asnaj and the other P.S.P. leaders persisted for several months through a barrage of insults and humiliations from the nationalists. What he could not, or would not, grasp was that they had no interest whatever in peaceful and constitutional progress to independence or in sharing power with the Federal rulers. What they wanted was what they had wanted all along, *viz.* to destroy the rulers' authority and that of the *dolas* and to rule the whole of South Arabia. Furthermore, they knew very well that if their rule was ever to be accepted by the people of South Arabia, and to receive the imprimatur of nationalist legitimacy from the revolutionary Arab regimes, their coming to power would have to be preceded, if not accomplished (for in these matters the appearance is all), by an armed struggle, as decreed by the established canons of the anti-colonialist movement. Practically, too, armed resistance was necessary if Cairo's support, in money, arms and propaganda, was to be ensured.

A pathetic endeavour by Greenwood in August 1965 to persuade al-Asnaj and his friends to tread the path of moderation by inviting them to a working conference in London ended in al-Asnaj's going off to Cairo to take direct charge of the Organization for the Liberation of the Arab South, which he had formed earlier in the year by amalgamating the P.S.P. with the South Arabian League, the better to wage guerrilla warfare. In Aden the nationalists celebrated the failure of the conference by murdering the speaker of the legislative assembly and the superintendent of police. All that Greenwood could do in response was to suspend the constitution and reimpose direct British rule upon the colony, to the delight of the nationalists and the dismay of the Federal rulers, who rightly saw their only hope for the future in the immediate cession of British sovereignty over Aden colony and the imposition by them of a settlement along Arab lines. Little sums up the implications of Greenwood's blunder well (p. 146): 'In choosing to impose direct rule, the British had, in effect, admitted their open confrontation with their extreme opponents, and there could be no turning back short of complete victory or complete defeat.'

There was worse to come, much worse. In January 1966 an all-out campaign of terrorism was initiated by the formation of the Front for the Liberation of South Yemen (F.L.O.S.Y.) by a merger of al-Asnaj's organization with the N.L.F. under the leadership of Qahtan al-Sha'abi, which up to date had been the chief instrument of Egyptian subversion in the Federation. (The South Arabian League had by this time been expelled from the nationalist camp as being too 'bourgeois'.) A month later the British government announced that they were withdrawing their base from Aden by the end of 1968, and that no defence treaty would be concluded with the Federation on independence. It was total abandonment—of past undertakings, of responsibility, of honour. Shocked by the betrayal of trust, Trevaskis went to see Denis Healey, the Secretary of State for Defence. He was told politely that the decision was irrevocable: neither the British government nor the people of Aden wanted the base. 'Surely I must see', Trevaskis records of his conversation with the Secretary of State, 'that to undertake a defence commitment which had only been proposed by Sandys as a complement to a British base would be nonsensical? I did not. I saw only a long line of Arab friends whom I, and others, had led up the garden path' (p. 238). It is a path that stretches back a long way.

Having delivered the Federation over to its enemies within and without, the British government were now without a policy except to await the day of release at the end of 1968. All that they could do was to carry on a running fight with the terrorists in the streets of Aden and to grasp spasmodically at any straw which seemed to offer a hope of escape from their tribulations. George Brown, the Foreign Secretary, wrote cajoling letters to Nasser, appealing to his better nature for help in keeping the peace in South Arabia, while George Thomson, who had got on so well with the nationalists in 1962, flew back and forth between Aden and London to try to salvage something from the wreck. They had no more success with their colonial difficulties than their Hanoverian namesake. The final ignominy was reached when the British government appealed for help to the United Nations Committee on Colonialism, a body whose mischievous and malicious interference in the past had contributed not a little to their present-woes. The committee's efforts lent a touch of farce to a tragic situation. A delegation of three commissioners, which arrived in Aden in March 1967 determined to boycott the Federal government, was itself boycotted by the nationalists and left in a huff. The incident, however, did not prevent the British government from running to the U.N. Committee a second time.

Meanwhile the mantle of power in Aden was being fought over by F.L.O.S.Y. and the N.L.F., whose fragile alliance had collapsed soon after its formation, F.L.O.S.Y. was now being supported by the Egyptians and the N.L.F. by the terrified merchants of Aden. Around and between them the British Army battled to afford to the dwindling ranks of moderate Adenis some measure of the protection which it is the duty of a civilized government to accord to its subjects, even those whom it is shortly to forsake. How gallantly and valiantly the Army performed this duty throughout the summer and autumn of 1967 is admirably related in Lieutenant-Colonel Colin Mitchell's autobiography, *Having Been a Soldier*. Mitchell had his first experience of war as a young lieutenant of the 8th Battalion Argyll and Sutherland Highlanders in the closing stages of the Italian campaign in 1945, and after service in Palestine with the 1st Argylls in the last two years of the British mandate, he went to war again with the 1st Argylls in Korea in 1950. His active service thereafter, in common with that of his battalion, was spent in the thankless and wearisome task of suppressing disorders in British colonies and territories in the throes of pre-independence rebellion or post-independence turmoil. By the time he arrived in Aden in June 1967, as commanding officer of the 1st Argylls, Mitchell had learned much about the theory and practice of terrorism in Palestine, Cyprus, Kenya and Borneo, and his battalion was probably the most experienced in the British Army in the mounting and maintenance of internal security operations.

Within days of Mitchell's arrival in advance of his battalion a mutiny broke out in the South Arabian Army, upset by the recent disturbance of the tribal balance in its ranks caused by the merging of the old Federal Army with the Federal National Guard, and sullen over the defeat of the Arab armies by Israel earlier in the month. On the morning of June 20 the mutineers ran amok in their cantonments and ambushed a truck carrying British soldiers, killing eight of them. Word of the mutiny quickly reached Crater, where a state of high hysteria, brought on by the terrorists' campaign and the humiliation of of Arab arms by Israel, already reigned—to such a degree, in fact, that patrolling by British troops in the town was kept to a minimum, lest it provoke F.L.O.S.Y. and the N.L.F. to greater violence. The armed police in Crater threw in their lot with the South Arabian Army mutineers on the morning of June 20, and announced that they would fire from their barracks on any British troops which ventured near them. Unaware of the threat, two patrols of the 1st Battalion Royal Northumberland Fusiliers and the 1st Argylls entered Crater that day. They were ambushed outside the police barracks and slaughtered. No attempt was made to rescue them when they failed to return, and the bodies of the slain soldiers and their officers were only recovered by permission of the police mutineers.

Mitchell was sickened and enraged by the episode. 'Crater was now in the hands of the enemy. This fantastic, nightmarish situation, where in the middle of a British Colony in peacetime the rule of the Queen is abandoned, had actually taken place. And worse, it was about to be condoned by Her Majesty's Government with 22 dead British soldiers to prove it' (p. 13). If his political masters were so fearful of international opinion as to let the defeat go unavenged, and to leave Crater's inhabitants at the mercy of the terrorists, Mitchell was not. From the moment that the Argylls assumed responsibility for security in Crater from the Northumberland Fusiliers, he was determined to reassert British authority in the town, and he proceeded to do so despite the qualms of some senior officers in Aden and the peevish reproaches of progressive politicians in England. For the latter's automatic protestations of distress at the use of force to restore order in a British possession Mitchell had nothing but scorn. Past experience had convinced him that 'firm, tough, efficient military action, if taken quickly enough, can effectively prevent a really terrible blood-letting. Methods which may appear ruthless to politicians at home are only the way of saving lives. In any case, what do politicians know of the cruel, hard facts of life when civil disorders has broken out?' (p. 113). What was remarkable was that, despite all the tremulous predictions of a blood bath in Crater if British control was reasserted there, there was only one casualty, a suspected Arab terrorist, when the Argylls occupied Crater on July 3 and 4. Mitchell's calculation, that the wail of the pipes would suffice to frighten 'a lot of third-rate, fly-blown terrorists and mutineers' (p. 179), proved perfectly correct.

For the next four months the Argylls kept the peace in Crater while the representatives of the British government scurried backwards and forwards between F.L.O.S.Y. and the N.L.F., frantically trying to decide to which of these rival gangs of armed thugs they should transfer the symbols of authority and sovereignty over Aden. In the end their choice fell upon the N.L.F. 'When it happened', Mitchell recalls (p. 220), 'I reminded myself of what Nelson had said about the Neapolitans and how well the quotation fitted Harold Wilson and his Government: "God knows they had little enough honour to lose, but what little they had, they lost!'" Harsh words, but not entirely undeserved of a government which, while evading its responsibilities to its colonial subjects and flinching from its enemies in Arabia, could still be magnificently petty in its treatment of its own servants. When the list of honours and awards for the Aden campaign was published Colonel Mitchell's name was conspicuously absent. He and the Argylls had embarrassed Westminster and Whitehall by showing them where their duty lay and how it should be performed, and now they had to be punished. In July 1968 the Ministry of Defence announced that the Argylls, the original 'thin red line' of the British Army, were to be disbanded as a regiment.

Mitchell has some sharp things to say (pp. 153-4) about the Secretary of State for Defence, Denis Healey, which merit quotation both for their relationship to the comment by Kennedy Trevaskis quoted earlier and for their wider significance:

> Denis Healey was an interesting person. He generated confidence. He was erudite, a brilliant lecturer, well-briefed, and he mastered and marshalled his facts with don-like precision. Personally kind and pleasant, he was extraordinarily acceptable in all societies, particularly in the Services, and I believe he was the only Labour Minister the Arab up-country rulers trusted.

> Yet in my view he was a shadow without substance. He had all the apparent qualities, the appearance and the methods of a statesman. But I suspected he was entirely dominated by his colleagues in the Socialist Cabinet and their useless dogma, later demonstrated by his series of utterly contradictory defence policies. There must have been a terrible cynicism in him to be party to the Labour Government's fundamental allergy to monarchical institutions in the Middle East whilst having the intelligence to realize that the only long-term alternative was for South Arabia to look towards Egypt and Russia for support.

It is doubtful whether, in the entire history of the British Empire, there has been such a shameful end to British rule over a colonial territory as that which overtook Aden in November 1967. Yet it was not for the want of ability, experience or dedication in the political agents, advisers and governors who served Britain in Aden and the Protectorates in recent times that British rule in South Arabia foundered. Rather was it the lack of resolution on the part of successive British governments. A sequence of remarkably able governors and high commissioners was appointed to Aden in the thirty years between 1937 and 1967, and if their masters had been as true to them as they were to their commissions, British rule might have ended in a different manner from what it did. For Trevaskis, the relating in *Shades of Amber* of the unhappy course of events in South Arabia over the past decade must have been a painful experience—almost as painful as the witnessing of them—but he shows little trace of rancour, although he does not mince words or hesitate to deliver some hard judgements when the occasion calls for them. His book is a graceful lament for what might have been, and it is this quality of personal engagement, as remarked earlier, which puts it into a different category from Tom Little's book. Little on the whole is fair and balanced, though he seems somewhat distant from his subject and there are moments when the air seems redolent with the scent of the press cuttings' library at Chatham House. Towards the close of his book, as he describes the last months of British rule and the emergence of the new Republic of South Yemen, a note of bewilderment creeps into his narrative—as well it might. But the bewilderment has a source apart from the hurly-burly in Aden at the close of 1967: it arises also from the clash between reality and the approved attitudes which he occasionally reflects, as when he remarks near the end of his book (p. 184), 'that one primary problem had been removed by the defeat of the tribal rulers'. Surely the prime result of the destruction of traditional authority in South Arabia has been to unleash the tribal Caliban? Or as Trevaskis has it in his closing sentence, 'The oldest traditional ruler of all, Anarchy, was back on his throne'.

2
British Policy in the Arab World[1]

Foundations of British Policy in the Arab World: The Cairo Conference of 1921, by Aaron S. Klieman. Baltimore: Johns Hopkins Univ. Press, 1970. xiv + 322 pages. Illus. Maps. Appen. Bibl. Index.

E arly in his book Dr Klieman quotes a remark made by Arthur Balfour in August 1919 about the various written engagements entered into by the British, French, Arabs and Zionists during World War I with respect to the future disposition of the Arab provinces of the Ottoman Empire.

> These documents are not consistent with each other; they represent no clear-cut policy; the policy which they confusedly adumbrate is not really the policy of the Allied and Associated Powers; and yet so far as I can see, none of them have wholly lost their validity or can be treated in all respects as of merely historic interest. Each can be quoted by Frenchmen, Englishmen, Americans, and Arabs when it happens to suit their purpose. Doubtless each will be so quoted before we come to a final arrangement about the Middle East (p. 21).

The number of times since 1919 that the Sykes-Picot agreement, the Husayn-McMahon correspondence and the Balfour Declaration have

---

1 From *Middle East Journal*; Fall 1972; 26, 4, pp. 446-448. Reproduced by permission.

been quoted and misquoted, analysed and annotated, must be legion; yet there is still uncertainty in the minds of many about their true import and a corresponding reluctance to accept that these engagements had a limited intent and application. Dr Klieman has no fresh theory or explanation to offer about them (or any obvious scholarly or political axe to grind), being concerned simply to describe, in somewhat prosaic fashion, how Great Britain attempted to make "a final arrangement" for the Arab Middle East after the allocation of the mandates for Syria, Iraq and Palestine at San Remo in 1920.

Responsibility for the implementation of the mandates for Palestine and Iraq, and for the care of British interests in Arabia (except the Hijaz), was entrusted at the close of that year to a new Middle East Department set up within the Colonial Office and staffed primarily by officials from the Foreign Office, the India Office and the Treasury. The Secretary of State for the Colonies was Winston Churchill, and it was on his initiative that a conference was held at Cairo in March 1921 to try to devise solutions to the several problems of government which confronted Great Britain in the Arab lands which fell within her Middle Eastern sphere of influence. Everyone who was anyone among British representatives in the Middle East at that time converged upon the Semiramis Hotel in the second week of March, among them Churchill himself, Percy Cox, Arnold Wilson, Gertrude Bell, Lawrence, Herbert Samuel and Hubert Young. Their deliberations over the next fortnight are invested by Dr. Klieman with considerable significance, and he quotes Lawrence in support of his judgment. "It made straight all the tangle, finding solutions fulfilling (I think) our promises in letter and spirit (where humanly possible) without sacrificing any interest of the peoples concerned." But Lawrence is hardly an authority to be relied upon, and Dr. Klieman bears unconscious witness to this (and tends to confound his own judgment) by devoting fewer than thirty pages, less than a tenth of his book, to the actual conference and its doings. The fault lies not in himself, however, but in his stars; for they formed such a galaxy of talent, knowledge and experience that he, like others before him, feels bound to conclude that what they accomplished in concert could not have been less than spectacular. It was, if the truth be faced, a good deal more ordinary, and Dr. Klieman's own book, perhaps undesignedly, bears this out. Every event of any moment which occurred in the Middle East before or after the conference occurred in spite of it; indeed, as if it had never been held. For all the real decisions had been taken elsewhere before it convened, and of those reached through its instrumentality many had later to be modified or abandoned.

Much of what Dr. Klieman has to say himself about the years 1919-1922 (as distinct from his recording of what others said or did at the time) reflects received opinion of the most arid kind, especially about the frustration of Arab ambitions at the Paris Peace Conference and afterwards.

> Those Arabs of the Fertile Crescent and Arabia who were politically alert looked to the conference as an international forum prepared to acknowledge their contribution to the war and qualified to approve their aim of independence. But as the months passed, and as what President Wilson termed 'the whole disgusting scramble' for territory became apparent in the Arab provinces, disillusionment set in and moderation yielded to militancy (pp. 33-34).

> ….It became apparent that the Arabs, contrary to their expectations, were to be regarded as supplicants rather than as equal members of the victorious coalition and that the Sykes-Picot agreement remained very much an obstacle to Arab self-government (p. 35).

> The Arabs, who began by seeking the aid of the European powers, faced the new year alienated from France and disappointed with Great Britain. Thus the year 1919 left the Arab goal of independence and unity more remote than it may have seemed in 1914, the Anglo-French alliance seriously weakened, and the principle of self-determination virtually inapplicable to the Fertile Crescent (p. 42).

Disillusion normally presupposes the existence of illusion. President Wilson's pieties notwithstanding, did the Arabs' contribution to the war warrant their being placed on a level with the principal Allied Powers? Was there an actual, as distinct from an assumed, basis for Arab unity and independence in 1919 and therefore for the later reproaches that their achievement was selfishly blocked by Britain and France? The short answer to the last question, and the one sanctified by usage and the passage of time, is that the Arabs were given no chance to prove that there was substance beneath their rhetoric. But to reason thus, and to rebuke Britain and France for subordinating Arab interests and ambitions to their own, is to engage in apologetics, to act the moral philosopher rather than the historian. The wearisome clamor which has gone on for decades about the wrongs done the Arabs after World War I has all but drowned the sombre, distant echoes from Gallipoli and Kut, from Gaza, Beersheba and Megiddo. Far off though those campaigns and battles may be now, it is worth reminding ourselves occasionally by whose arms the Ottoman Empire was defeated, just as fifty years ago Winston Churchill reminded an Arab delegation at Jerusalem, after it had harangued him at length about Britain's ingratitude to the Arabs for their help in the war and her iniquity in partitioning the Arab lands afterwards. "I thought," Churchill said, "when listening to your statements, that it seemed that the Arabs of Palestine had overthrown the Turkish Government. That is the reverse of the true facts. It has been the armies of Britain which have liberated these regions. You had only to look on your road here this afternoon to see the graveyard of over 2,000 British soldiers, and there are many other graveyards, some even larger, that are scattered about this land. The position of Great Britain in Palestine is one of trust, but it is also one of right."

If Dr. Klieman had exercised greater independence of judgment instead of submitting to the conventional constraints when writing about Arab nationalism, British imperialism, self-determination, and other sacred topics, he would have produced a better book and certainly a less colorless one. As it is, all that can reasonably be said of his study is that he has made competent use of his sources, which are principally the Foreign Office and Colonial Office records. There are some curious omissions in his account of the formulation and execution of British Middle Eastern policy in the years 1920-1922. Was Curzon as Foreign Secretary as aloof from the goings-on in Iraq, Palestine, Transjordan and the Hijaz as would appear from his occasional appearances in Dr. Klieman's narrative? Did the Government of India have nothing to say about events in Iraq? (Did Ibn Sa'ud?) Why is there so little expression of Arab views other than those emanating from the Sharifians? Why, in an historical episode dominated by personalities, does everyone appear flat and two-dimensional? Were there no knaves, fools or heroes? Churchill is characterized (p. 247) by a remark of Milner's (".... his weakness is that he is too apt to make up his mind without sufficient knowledge"), which Dr. Klieman then uses as a justification for accusing Churchill of adopting "a simplistic approach to the Palestine problem" and of applying to the Arabs "his preconceived notions about the relationship of an imperial power to its subject peoples," an accusation which Dr. Klieman goes on to document by quoting Churchill's thoughts in 1921 about how the 'Iraqis should be governed.

There is no doubt that these turbulent people are apt to get

extremely bored if they are subjected to a higher form of justice and more efficient administration than those to which they
have for centuries been accustomed. At any rate we have re-
verted perforce, and by the teaching of experience, to more
primitive methods (p. 248).

What in essence, one might ask, is the logical relationship of an imperial power to is subjects? Fundamentally and ineluctably it is that of ruler to ruled. Whether that rule is exercised with justice, firmness, patience,
humanity, moderation or restraint is secondary to this basic principle.
Would the principle have appeared strange in 1921 to the great majority
of Arabs, a people accustomed for centuries to offer unquestioning obedience to their rulers? How otherwise would they have expected an imperial
power to conduct itself? As for Iraq, would Dr. Klieman, after reflecting
briefly upon the methods by which successive 'Iraqi governments have
ruled in the years since the end of the British mandate, really disagree with
Churchill's assessment?

Finally, on the subject of "preconceived notions," what of Dr.
Klieman's own contentions put forward in the conclusion of his book that
Arab nationalist resentment of Britain in the interwar years and since dam-
aged "the cause of democracy" in the Arab countries?

Those tenets and institutions introduced with the mandates
gradually were overthrown as disillusionment with Europe led
to a rejection of its forms of government. Equality and freedom
were viewed as incompatible in the framework of Arab politics.
Representative government, parliamentary bodies, political
parties – those were abused and eventually repudiated. Barriers
against intervention by the military were torn down in country
after country by those very armies brought into existence by
Great Britain in the 1920s (p. 243).

Was it disillusionment with Europe which caused the destruction of
parliamentary government and constitutional rights, or was it something
deeper within the Arab character, within Islamic society, and within the
political tradition of the Middle East? After all, parliamentary government
is not all that long established in Europe itself: in some countries it is less
than a century old, and even in Britain universal suffrage has existed for
barely half that time. Why then should parliamentary institutions have
been expected to take root in the Arab states after 1918? As for those

armies which of late years have usurped the civil power, their officers had no need for the pretext of disenchantment with European-inspired political institutions to do what military commanders have been doing in the Middle East for a thousand years, and doubtless will continue to do for another thousand.

3

Middle East Record[1]

Middle East Record, Vol. 1, 1960 edited by Yitzhak Oron. Jerusalem: Weidenfeld & Nicolson, 1965, for the Israel Oriental Society, Reuven Shiloah Research Centre, Tel Aviv University. Pp. xxii, 584, maps, tables, indexes.
Middle East Record, Vol. 2, 1961 edited by Yitzhak Oron. Jerusalem: Tel Aviv University, 1967. Pp. xxv, 800, maps, tables, indexes.
Middle East Record, Vol. 3, 1967 edited by Daniel Dishon. Jerusalem: Israel Universities Press, 1971. Pp. xxx, 638, maps, tables, indexes.

N ormally the reviewing of handbooks, surveys, and similar compendia is a pretty tedious business, almost as arid a pursuit in its way as seeking enlightenment in the memoirs of contemporary politicians. One tends to glance at the list of contents and to leaf listlessly through the pages of text, pausing now and then to read a passage which promises a brief moment of instruction or entertainment before arriving, after an indecently short interval of time, at the index, which one then, in a sudden access of energy brought on by guilt for one's earlier *flânerie*, examines sternly to see whether it has been compiled with any thought or is merely a limp succession of proper names. Guilt assuaged, one is now in a position to rattle off cheerfully the usual pieties associated with reviewing of this

1 From *Middle Eastern Studies*, Vol. 9, No. 1 (Jan., 1973), pp. 111-115, Published by: Taylor & Francis, Ltd. Reproduced by permission.

kind ('invaluable aid', 'store-house of information', 'abundant data', 'useful maps', 'attractive format', 'cheap at the price') laced with the obligatory prim reproaches ('awkward arrangement', 'inconsistent terminology', 'erratic choice', 'inadequate tables', 'poorly produced', 'much too expensive'). It is all something of a game, and so long as the players know the rules and stick to them it affords a certain measure of innocuous enjoyment to all concerned.

A prefatory passage such as this, tacked to the head of a review, is a none too subtle warning that the rules are about to be broken in some caddish way. However, this is not quite the case here, because the customary rules simply do not apply to the *Middle East Record*. It is so far ahead of the ruck of Middle Eastern surveys and handbooks as to be in a field all by itself. There has not been anything like it before in modern Middle Eastern studies, and if Chatham House, whose own *Survey of International Affairs* seems to be moribund, wants to revive its flagging sense of purpose it could not do better than to move its research department to the Shiloah Research Centre at Tel Aviv University for a year or two and learn all over again how a survey of international affairs is assembled and written. For the *Middle East Record*, so far as is humanly possible in the febrile and clamorous atmosphere of contemporary Middle Eastern politics, is irreproachable—cool, detached, and strictly factual, as its editors and contributors doubtless knew full well it would have to be if it was to stand the close scrutiny which its antecedents and provenance were bound to invite.

The *Middle East Record* originated in the political survey of Middle Eastern affairs which *Hamizrah Hehadash* (*The New East*), the quarterly journal of the Israel Oriental Society, began publishing about twenty years ago. The decision to enlarge the survey and publish it as a separate annual volume was taken in the early nineteen-sixties, and the first volume, covering the year 1960, was issued in 1965 under the title, *Middle East Record*. A second volume, covering the events of 1961, appeared in 1967, but publication was then suspended for a time and the next volume (for the year 1967) was not published until 1971. The nature and aims of the survey are fully explained in the preface to the volume for 1960:

> The aim of this work is to present the facts in full detail and from the widest possible variety of sources. Where the facts are disputed—and that happens frequently enough in the Middle East—all available versions are quoted, precedence being given to official statements. When it is a matter of underlying motives and causes, or the significance and consequences

of events, both official statements and unofficial comment are treated as facts to be recorded. In compiling MER, over 200 newspapers, periodicals and official publications have been regularly scanned and many additional publications consulted. As far as possible, official publications have been used, but the overwhelming majority of items included are Press reports and monitored broadcasts. For maximum accuracy, these have been cross-checked as far as possible and early reports have been corrected by later, more accurate ones.

Perhaps the most distinctive of the several features which mark the *Middle East Record* out from other publications of this nature is the copious quotation from sources, not only from government documents, which is normal practice, and from Western newspapers and periodicals, which is of mixed usefulness, but also and more interestingly from the Arabic press and radio. It is doubtful whether monitored broadcasts have previously been put to such pertinent use in the compiling of a chronicle of political events as they have here. Distance, the filtering of news through so many intermediate channels, and the habitual tendency to discuss and interpret Middle Eastern politics in the political terminology of the West, have all contrived to impart a certain blandness to the reporting and analysis of Middle Eastern affairs in Western countries. It is highly salutary (and also slightly unnerving) to be reminded so bluntly by the extensive quotation from the Arabic press and radio in the *Middle East Record* of the language, tone and manner in which political debate is customarily carried on in the 'progressive' Arab states. To read, for instance, the extracts from the Cairo and Baghdad press and radio in the volumes for 1960 and 1961 is to open a window upon a strange and desolate landscape, strewn with weird, amorphous shapes cryptically inscribed 'imperialist plot', 'Zionist crime', 'Western exploitation', 'socialist solidarity', 'people's justice', 'brotherhood', 'nationalism', 'liberation', 'vile conspiracy', 'unending struggle', 'immortal leader', 'the glorious revolution', 'the undefeated revolution', and 'the revolution betrayed'. Around and among these enigmatic structures, curious figures, like so many mythical beasts, caper and cavort—'enemies', 'traitors', 'stooges', 'hyenas', 'puppets', 'lackeys', 'feudalists', 'gangsters', 'tyrants', 'criminals', 'oppressors', 'plotters' and 'deviationists'.

There are sideshows, too, promising light relief, booths labelled 'Casablanca Conference', 'Kuwait Crisis', 'Break-up of the UAR', and, more splendid than most, 'Belgrade Conference of Non-Aligned Countries', from which float sounds of harmony and discord, lamentations and vociferations, murmurings, chuckles, whispers, and caterwauls. It is all rather like a monstrous playing board for some grotesque and sinister game, in which the snakes are all hydras, the ladders have no rungs, and the dice are blank.

Now and again, browsing through these volumes, one comes across a refreshing reminder that sense, proportion and reality can and often do assert themselves in the Middle Eastern political arena. On the very eve of the Belgrade Conference, which opened on September 1, 1961, the Soviet Union announced the resumption of nuclear testing, an action which, in view of the fears and pretensions of the leaders of the 'non-aligned' countries represented at the conference, was almost a calculated gesture of contempt for their susceptibilities. The only man who protested against the Soviet action on the opening day of the conference, and who did so with vigour, was Gamal 'Abdul Nasser. On another occasion, earlier in the year, Anwar al-Sadat gave a spirited reply (though admittedly by letter and not in person) to a hectoring lecture delivered by Nikita Khrushchev to the delegation from the UAR which Sadat had led to Moscow in May. Communism, Khrushchev had declared, was a superior economic system to capitalism, and furthermore. it would eventually triumph over nationalism as the principal driving force in the Arab world. Sadat in his reply observed that, to judge from the standard of living it provided for its people, capitalism was economically far in advance of communism. As for Khrushchev's second boast, Sadat said that he himself did not subscribe to the belief that history progressed 'along a blind alley of which capitalism is the beginning and communism is the imperative end'.

The tone of the Belgrade Conference, however, was not set by Nasser's protest at the outset. For the leaders and representatives of the 'progressive' states criticism of the Soviet Union formed no part of the doctrine of 'non-alignment', which pertained exclusively to Western imperialism. 'In every single case', President Sukarno of Indonesia earnestly informed his fellow conferees, 'the cause of international tension is imperialism and colonialism and the forcible division of nations'. Hashim Jawad, the foreign minister of Iraq, fervently agreed. Western imperialists, he said, were utilizing 'the fraudulent pretext of collective security against the so-called communist conspiracy to dominate the world' to retain their own flabby grip on the under-developed countries. The assertion must have caused a slight bewilderment to some of the delegates present, especially those from the Arab states. Two months earlier, at the outset of the Kuwait crisis, Cairo Radio had accused General Qasim of bringing about the 'imperialist' intervention in Kuwait by allowing himself to be duped by the British; while Hassanein Heykal, the editor of *Al-Ahram*, declared that Qasim had paved the way for the British to remain in Kuwait for ever. Not to be outdone, the Baghdad press had responded with the accusation that the UAR, by allowing British warships to pass through the Suez Canal on their way to Kuwait, was working hand in glove with the imperialists. Perhaps it was the difficulty of determining exactly who it was that was collaborating with the imperialists which persuaded the participants at Belgrade to exclude the Kuwait affair from their deliberations; or perhaps the issue simply lacked those elements of cultural and ideological antipathy which lent charm to most conflicts of interests with the West. Whatever the reason, Iraq looked in vain at Belgrade for support for her claim to Kuwait, and at the close of 1961 Qasim was still grumbling that his 'sacred mission' to 'liberate' Kuwait was being frustrated by the continued presence in the amirate of the Arab force which had earlier taken over from the British. 'These traitors, calling themselves Arab forces, do nothing more than serve the imperialists, but they will be thrown out too,' Qasim threatened over Baghdad Radio in late December. Imperialism in 'the usurped province of Kuwait' would be defeated, 'just as the Indians have done in Goa'.

The Indian invasion of Goa in December 1961 was a nosegay of non-alignment proffered by Pandit Nehru to the confraternity of Belgrade, which in its closing declaration had called for the 'immediate, unconditional, total and final abolition of colonialism' in Asia, Africa, and Latin America. Its fragrance was less appreciated by Western nostrils, which detected in it a strong whiff of humbug, to which its recipients were either oblivious or indifferent. This particular odour still hung in the air some half-a-dozen years later, in October 1967, when Nehru's daughter, Mrs Indira Gandhi, conferred with President Nasser in Cairo after the Six Days' War, and publicly reaffirmed with him her faith in 'non-alignment and the right of all sovereign states to preserve and strengthen their political and economic independence without any outside pressure or interference', adding, with enviable insouciance, that they both also adhered to the principle enunciated at Belgrade 'that the use of force to achieve territorial or political gains is impermissible'. Earlier in the year Mrs Gandhi had joined with the foreign minister of Iraq, 'Adnan Pachachi, on the occasion of his visit to Delhi in March 1967, in declaring that India and Iraq were as one in their devotion to the policy of non-alignment, and in their steadfast opposition to colonialism, foreign intervention, racialism, and 'military pacts and other alliances which impede international co-operation'. Mrs Gandhi's further peregrinations and declarations are doubtless awaited with the keenest interest in Moscow.

One of the most valuable services performed by the *Middle East Record*, as may be gathered from these not entirely objective remarks, has been to separate and treat as a whole the various activities of the 'non-aligned' states in relation to the Middle East, whether by direct involvement or through the medium of the UN. Viewed like this, they assume much more definite shape and purpose than is discernible when they are regarded merely as adjuncts to the actions of the Middle Eastern states themselves, or to the policies of the Western and communist blocs in the region. Among the many fresh impressions gained by this approach is that of the blatant opportunism and capacity for mischief-making of President Tito's policies. For many a long year now the West has patiently endured his homilies on its wicked and reprobate ways, delivered either solo or in trio with his fellow troubadours of non-alignment, Nehru and Nasser. For years, too, we have been vouchsafed the inspiring sight of his successive 'initiatives for peace', undertaken in a variety of causes. It is only when one stands back a short distance and allows a little scepticism to intrude between the spectacle offered and one's own beguiled vision that the realization dawns that what one has been watching all these years is one of the greatest producers of humbug in the history of political confectionery.

Whether by design or accident (and the evidence points more to the former than the latter) Tito has played a major role in bringing the 'progressive' Arab states within the Soviet orbit. The climax of his efforts to bolster and encourage Nasser in his ambitions came in May 1967, when the Egyptian president moved his army into Sinai and demanded the evacuation of the UN force from the peninsula. Even before the secretary-general of the UN had had time to consider the demand fully, let alone to act upon it (and he acted upon it, it will be recalled, with astonishing alacrity), Tito had agreed to withdraw the Yugoslav contingent with the UN force. With equal precipitateness Mrs Gandhi signified her readiness to withdraw the Indian contingent. Unfortunately for Tito's calculations, and even more unfortunately for Nasser's, the result was the overwhelming defeat of the Egyptian army three weeks later. Tito went some way towards atoning for his error in the months that followed by increasing the flow of Soviet arms through Yugoslavia to Egypt, and by undertaking yet another 'mission of peace' to several Arab states to exhort their governments to be of good cheer. On his return to Belgrade he treated a grateful world to a further selection from his *pensées*. Yugoslavia's activities in the Middle East, he announced in October, had not been motivated by

some megalomaniac, grandiose and delusive obsession to ...

play a starring role on the world stage ... but by way of her humane, peace-loving and friendly policies towards all people in general and towards those people who used to be or still are enslaved by colonialists in particular.... The Israeli aggression hit us also because the Arab countries are close friends of ours, especially the UAR.... We are interested in a solution to the crisis in the Middle East, particularly as it lies very near. Naturally, for the Imperialists it would be extremely important to compel the Arab countries to capitulate. Then they would set up governments there which would suit them, and ... which would threaten the entire Mediterranean region.

For connoisseurs of the absurd in international affairs, it must by now be apparent, the three volumes of the *Middle East Record* offer rich pickings. For those who take a more serious view of Middle Eastern politics they provide a narrative and documentation of events for the years 1960, 1961 and 1967 which could hardly be bettered. In some instances, *e.g.* the description of the struggle for power within the Sa'udi ruling house in 1960-61, the information supplied is much more comprehensive than anything published hitherto. There is an excellent section in the volume for 1961 on the break-up of the UAR which is full of absorbing incidental detail, not least in the explanations offered afterwards by the parties concerned of the reasons for the break-up. (Those wicked souls who take perverse delight in seeing oracles confounded will relish the considered judgement of *The Times* on the durability of the union, delivered on the morning of September 28, 1961, when the Syrian army was busy expelling the Egyptians. 'There is no reason to suppose', *The Times* declared, apropos of the resignation two days earlier of the Syrian vice-president', Abdul Hamid Sarraj,' that the latest change will weaken the structure of the UAR.') Half-forgotten and almost unreal episodes like Egypt's adventure in the Congo in 1960, are brought to light again in these volumes; and absurd or sinister figures, who perhaps are best forgotten, strut once more before our eyes, like Colonel Mahdawi of fragrant memory, the president of the special military tribunal in Baghdad in 1959-60, whose total vocabulary ran the brief gamut from vulgar to obscene.

The antecedents, course and aftermath of the Six Days' War are recounted with almost painful objectivity in the volume for 1967, as if the authors were over-sensitive to the possibility that the impartiality of the volume as a whole would be judged on this section alone. They have little cause for apprehension: justice has been done to all sides, especially in the quotations from government documents, official statements and press and radio comment. If there is a flaw in the volume for 1967 it lies not in its objectivity but rather in its authors having partly yielded to the temptation to construct a narrative of events rather than a chronicle, as the volumes for 1960 and 1961 had been. The change may have increased the volume's readability (although it would be difficult to improve on the literary quality of the earlier volumes, which is greatly superior to that of most annual surveys), but the compression which it has necessitated has tended to transform factual information into exposition, with a consequent reduction in the survey's value as a source book. Next to the scrupulous care with which the *Middle East Record* has been compiled, its principal distinction, as remarked earlier, is the great volume and variety of quotation which it supplies. It would be a pity if editorial policy were now to decree that this practice, by which the *Middle East Record* makes its singular contribution to Western understanding of Middle Eastern politics, should be altered.

4
'TLS' In the Desert[1]

There are two passages in David Pryce-Jones's recently published book on the Palestinian refugees and guerrillas, *The Face of Defeat*, which refer to the way in which the guerrilla movement was taken up after the Arab-Israeli war of 1967 by the radical-chic set. They read in part:

> In the mournful years of exile the Palestinians had been neglected or at best patronized, but now supporters fell upon them from all sides. The Fatah and PFLP and PDF offices in Amman were faced with difficulties which would have confused far more experienced politicians; how to take advantage of being so fresh yet so stale a cause, and how to deal with the kind of fad which rides upon the back of the mass media....

> Revolutionary romanticism—a flower from Asia shipped via South America—attracted some students and they spent a season or two camping out with the *fedayeen*.... Such fans arived to promote victory after the resistance movement had suffered already the one defeat which counted, on the West Bank. The *fedayeen* did not have to let themselves be driven either into more posturing or into a showdown with the Jordanian army which was certain to be bloody and final.... Secrecy and diplomacy could have given them the necessary options. With publicity, with the party line, they ceased to be Palestinians in need of justice, they become mascots for the causemongers over their shoulders, for the cinema teams of modish young bullies

1 From *The Journal of Imperial and Commonwealth History*, 1:3, 1973, pp. 357-379. Published by Routledge. Reproduced by permission.

with fierce hair and girls in tailored denims, for the anonymous promoters who ride in cars with CD plates....

The first of these passages was quoted in a notice of the book which appeared in the *Times Literary Supplement* of 1 December 1972. Interestingly enough, the second and more telling passage was omitted. Perhaps it was its pertinence which made it unwelcome, especially as the same page of the journal carried a review of three books on the Middle East, the greater part of which was given over to an excursus upon Palestine, the Jews, the Arabs and the British, along the following lines:

The main burden of responsibility for the confusion reigning throughout the Arab world lies with the major powers, whose ambitions continued to bedevil the Arabs at a time when they were fighting for independence.

Theodor Herzl [was] a Zionist who welcomed antisemitism as a force impelling the Jews to leave Europe and form a nation in the Levant. Herzl's book *Der Judenstaat*, Zionist determination, Weizmann's devious stratagems, Lloyd George's romantic interest in the Old Testament and ignorance of foreign affairs—as disastrous in Turkey as in Palestine—Balfour's sybilline Declaration of 1917, which he wilfully misinterpreted, and the refusal of the United States to welcome Jewish immigration following the terrible Nazi massacres, showed that Herzl's "propellent" of antisemitism was still a force; all such factors combined to create confusion, injustice, hatred, misery and warfare.

The documents have been drawn on before by various authors, but, concentrated as they are in this book [Palestine Papers, 1917-1922], they build up to an extraordinary and dramatic and humiliating story of ignorance, dishonesty and cynicism. Britain and France were working to a plan for self-determination for all former territories of the Ottoman Empire and promised the Arabs independence. Balfour rejected these promises for Palestine, where 90 per cent of the population was then Arab, and welcomed the Zionist plan.... He believed, or made out, that the Jews had historical rights to Palestine. Curzon, who had succeeded Balfour as Foreign Secretary in

1919, was emphatic that the Jews had no such rights.... Curzon realised how unjust and dangerous it was that the British Government, given the Mandate for Palestine, should be inveigled into accepting the Zionist interpretation of the Balfour Declaration, but he allowed himself to be overruled.

These statements are representative of an attitude towards a particular phase of recent British imperial history, *viz.*, British relations with the Arabs and Zionists during and after World War I, which has been fashionable in some quarters, not least in the columns of the *TLS*, for so long that it has acquired the standing virtually of a genuine historical interpretation. That it is in reality nothing of the kind may readily be discerned by looking more closely at the major propositions advanced in the above extracts. The first, that the ambitions of the major powers (presumably Britain and France) 'continued to bedevil the Arabs at a time when they were fighting for independence', will surprise anyone who has read the Foreign Office papers on the Arab revolt. These reveal quite clearly that the rebellion of the Sharif of Mecca against the Turks in 1916 was far from spontaneous, and that if it had not been for British encouragement, and British gold and British arms, the rebellion would probably not have occurred. Originally, the Arab revolt was conceived (or, at least it was represented to the Foreign Office and the cabinet in London by British officials in Cairo) as a means of harrying the Turks. Very quickly, however, and well before it had started, its advocates on the British side reversed their argument and took the line that the war with Turkey was being fought to achieve independence for the Arabs. Far from rebelling against the Turks on his own initiative and reckless of any support that might be forthcoming from outside Arabia, the Sharif of Mecca, well before he renounced his allegiance to the Ottoman Sultan, sought and obtained assurances not only of British help but also of the recognition of his independence after the war. So also did Ibn Sa'ud, the ruler of Najd, who thereafter confined himself to campaigning against his hereditary enemy, Ibn Rashid. Not once during the war did he take the field against the Turks. The Arabs of Syria and Mesopotamia did not revolt against the Turks, although some were executed for treasonable activities or for cherishing nationalist ambitions.

Much the same objections can be raised to the assertions in the third of the extracts quoted. Far from 'working to a plan for self-determination' for the former Ottoman territories, the British and French governments regarded self-determination as a chimera. Acrimony, not harmony, distinguished their post-war discussions on the settlement in the Middle East.

The only 'plan' to which they might have worked was the so-called Sykes-Picot agreement of 1916, and it had been eviscerated by British attempts from 1917 onwards to back away from the undertakings which had been entered into in the agreement. France certainly never 'promised the Arabs independence', and British promises to the Sharif of Mecca were imprecise and hedged with considerable reservations. Palestine was not included in the area recognised in the exchanges with the Sharif as constituting the territory of a future Arab state or states. On the contrary, as the Foreign Office papers make plain, it was excluded from the very first, even by the most sedulous proponents of the Arab cause among the British officials in Egypt; and the prime consideration in the discussions about its status after the war, whatever may have been contended since by interested parties, was not whether Palestine should be independent under an Arab government but whether it should come under French control or British control or that of an international administration.

If such are the facts ascertainable from the historical evidence, how is it that the conclusions formulated by the reviewer in the *TLS* of 1 December 1972 are so much at variance with them? For an answer one might look to a tendency of late years among *TLS* reviewers of books on modern Arab history and politics to concern themselves less with the critical evaluation of scholarship than with the expounding of a body of received doctrine on the subject of Britain, the Arabs and Israel. A survey of the reviews of books on Britain and the Arabs, and Israel and the Arabs, published in the *TLS* since the beginning of 1968—a fatiguing exercise, not to be recommended—indicates the existence of a deep-seated irritation with Israel on the part of the reviewers, as much for the fact of her birth as for the manner of her growth; while on British relations with the Arabs they are wont to wax alternatively poetic and evangelical: one moment lyrically extolling the charms of Arabism, the next insistently proclaiming the gospel of British wickedness. So intense is their ardour, so fierce their sense of apostolic mission, that they seem to deny to anyone who has not travelled the penitential road to the new Damascus the right to comment upon Arab affairs. To say this is to exaggerate only slightly; for the Arabophile school has long made it clear that it regards the question of Anglo-Arab relations as pertaining less to the mundane affairs of men and governments than to the most solemn matters of faith and dogma—of British guilt and Arab innocence and the doctrine of redemption through vicarious atonement. Debate consequently tends to assume the character of theological disputation, revolving around a kind of Damascene creed constructed from revelation, ideology, and sacerdotal pronouncement. It runs, briefly, thus:

Britain promised independence to the Arabs during World War I and betrayed that promise afterwards. The worst act of betrayal was the Balfour Declaration which led to the formation of the state of Israel. Arab unity was stultified by British obstinacy in propping up reactionary regimes and opposing revolutionary movements. Although Britain has at last seen the error of its ways and has left the Arabs alone, it still bears the stigmata of past misdeeds. Until these have been erased and the guilt purged, the Arabophile order must toil at its penitential labours, ritually flogging the irreverent and ceaselessly chanting the orisons of repentance. These, as they appear in the columns of the *TLS*, assume the form of a primitive dialectical shorthand—Arabs good, British bad—Aden sad, Suez mad—Nasser angelic, Eden diabolic—revolution righteous, royalism rotten. And so on.

The first to feel the lash in the expiatory exercises of the 1970 season was Elie Kedourie, a professor of politics at the University of London, who early in the year published a collection of essays entitled *The Chatham House Version and Other Middle Eastern Studies*. These, among other things, subjected the formation and conduct of British policy towards the Arabs during and since the First World War to a close and unsentimental scrutiny, particularly in the title essay, which was an examination of the links which might be discerned between Arnold Toynbee's historical thinking, the fostering of guilt feelings about the Arabs at Chatham House while he was director of studies there, and the influence which this sentiment may subsequently have exerted upon British policy towards the Arab states. Kedourie was plainly treading upon holy ground. Moreover, he was doing so with a sureness of step which could only derive from scrupulous research and irreproachable scholarship. Faced with such a formidable challenge to the orthodoxy, the reviewer chosen by the *TLS* to deal with the book reached for the literary weapon which is the resort of those who shrink from forthright critical attack—the innuendo.

The review which appeared in the TLS of 14 May 1970 opened with the standard apology for the sins of the West against the peoples of Asia and Africa before rounding upon Kedourie and branding him 'the Zionist historian who is now Professor of Politics at London University', and 'a leading member of the Zionist demolition squad'. The reviewer accused him of traducing Toynbee, misrepresenting Chatham House, and distorting history in the Zionist interest:

As the latest instruments of Western expansion the Zionists may well feel aggrieved by a revolutionary dissent which they once shared but which has now turned against them. Like other conquerors they are busy substituting their own versions of history for those which went before. The creation of a heroic legend requires that the ladder be kicked down, their helpers on the road discredited, the defeated and now subject enemy annihilated with the pen. The Arabs, as Arabs, never existed, nor did a Palestine problem. Britain is called to account not for having been imperialist but for having been so half-hearted and incompetent about it.

It need hardly be said that this is not the language of the scholarly critic. It slanders Kedourie and it slanders the University of London. Phrases like 'Zionist demolition squad' disgrace the pages of what the *TLS*'s editor is pleased to call 'the only truly international literary journal'. Those who employ them, moreover, as often as not lack the courage to defend them. When Kedourie wrote to the *TLS* coldly asking for an explanation of these remarks, the reviewer hastily withdrew them and fell to mumbling about 'beasts beneath the skin' and other horrors which beset him from the dark Mesopotamian past. It was a deplorable episode, yet it was no more than an extreme example of a technique that was becoming standard in the *TLS* for the reviewing of books on modern Arab history and politics whose conclusions a reviewer might find unpalatable but which he was unable to refute, *viz.*, to vilify the author, impugn his intentions, and dismiss his labours as futile or perverse. It is the resort of Yeats's 'Leaders of the Crowd':

> They must to keep their certainty accuse
> All that are different of a base intent....

Since the school of history which Kedourie represents is obviously not to the taste of the *TLS* reviewers, which school, it is legitimate to ask, do they admire? A fair answer is to be found in a review in the issue of 3 December 1971 of a book by an American professor, Briton Cooper Busch, entitled *Britain, India, and the Arabs, 1914-1921*. Its subject is the formation and execution of British policy towards the Arabs during and immediately after the First World War, and the book itself is based largely upon a reading of the pertinent Foreign Office and India Office files. These, according to the reviewer 'are so voluminous that any scholar should be glad of a guide through their mazes'. Busch's book, we are told, 'may be too overloaded with fact for the casual reader, but it is good reading for any student of modern Middle Eastern history, or of the British machinery of policy-making two generations ago'. The main topics treated are the British negotiations with Sharif Husain of the Hijaz and the Amir Ibn Sa'ud of Najd; the British campaign in Mesopotamia and the uprising in that country in 1920; various disagreements between the Indian and home governments over the conduct of political and military affairs in the Middle East; the Arab revolt of 1916; Anglo-French relations in the Middle East during after the war; the dismemberment of the Ottoman empire; the peace conference; and the post-war settlement in the Arab world. 'The diplomatic historian who is confronted with the huge documentation on these subjects', writes the *TLS* reviewer, 'has his work cut out.'

> Is he to give his scholarly reader confidence by copious quotation, or to summarize minutes with his nose in the files, or to look up every now and then at what was happening elsewhere in the world, and put his detail into the context of war and peace-making? All told, Professor Busch strikes a happy balance between these choices: his quotations are lively and his comment keeps his reader's eye on the main points, and the results, of the muddles that he retails.... Some may find his treatment breezy, but it is seldom wide of the mark.

The reviewer concludes with a further encomium:

> Professor Busch is said to be preparing a . . . volume on British policy over the successive peace treaties with Ottoman and with Kemalist Turkey. If so, his will be the first books, based on all the documents, to fill a gap so far covered only by eyewitnesses such as Harold Nicolson and the writers of memoirs; other contemporary scholars who have combed the Public Record Office have confined themselves to small sectors of the picture. Sir Steven Runciman, when tackling the Crusades as a whole, once wrote that scholars are too apt to take refuge in "small fortresses that are easy to defend from attack" and too fearful of "attempting to describe in one sweeping sequence" a broad spectrum of events that have swayed human destinies. Professor Busch's description of the destinies meted out to the Arabs aims straight at the Runciman goal. Any sweeping statements are offset by a good bibliography and minutely detailed footnotes....

How deserved is this praise, especially in contrast with the opprobrium meted out by *TLS* reviewers to other scholars of Arab history and politics? 'Breezy' is not the word which naturally springs to mind to describe Busch's style. 'Careless', perhaps, or 'infelicitous'—either of these would be more appropriate to a text which abounds in sentences of the order of 'From the India Office, and India, Montagu did resign in 1922 and died only two years later', and 'he [Sir Arnold Wilson] became "missing believed killed" as an R.A.F. gunner over France in 1940 (surely the only gunner with a name preceded by "Sir" and followed by K.C.I.E., C.S.I., C.M.G., D.S.O., M.P.)'. Busch's delight in titles and decorations (not an official makes his entrance unless bedecked with the initials of his orders) is matched by his enthusiasm for identifying every proposal, shift and expedient of British policy as being put forward in a dispatch, a telegram, a minute, a memorandum, a letter or a note. His way with quotations, however, which his reviewer finds 'lively', might strike others as a trifle perverse. Chapter seven of his book begins with the couplet:

> For forms of government let fools contest;
> Whatever is best administered is best...,

which Busch attributes to Sir Michael O'Dwyer in his book, *India as I knew It, 1885-1925*.

These, however, are peccadilloes. What Busch may properly be charged with (again *pace* his reviewer) is that he never gets to grips with the fundamental reasons for the various disagreements over policy which plagued British relations with the Arabs from 1914 onwards, or with the characters and passions of the individuals responsible for these disagreements. If the Arab revolt be taken as central to the book's theme, then the correspondence which passed between Sir Henry McMahon, the British high commissioner in Egypt, and the Sharif Husain ibn Ali of Mecca in 1915-16 is central to the revolt itself and to its aftermath. Busch's treatment of the origins and nature of the McMahon correspondence can only be described as muddled and inadequate. He does not examine the letters thoroughly, or decide for himself what they mean, and he does not determine what the several British authorities concerned in their composition and transmission had in mind as their purpose. The Husain-McMahon correspondence has been at the very heart of Anglo-Arab relations (and even more of Anglo-Arab legends) for the past half-century: as such it positively cries out for careful and detailed analysis. Busch seems deaf to its appeal, just as he is blind to that other aspect of the Husain-McMahon negotiation which is such a vital and integral part of it, *viz.*, the character and ambitions of the Sharif of Mecca. In place of the close examination which these call for, we get owlish remarks of the type: 'Husain was interested in getting on with the revolt'. Nothing could be further from the truth. The first British approach to the Sharif was made in October 1914; he did not proclaim the revolt until June 1916. In the interval he sat on the fence, watching the progress of the war between Britain and the Ottoman empire and haggling with the British authorities in Cairo over the price of his co-belligerency. What Busch insufficiently appreciates is how Husain's ambitions rapidly expanded as he realised the gullibility of those with whom he was treating. At the outset he looked only for recognition of his independence as ruler of the Hijaz. His position there in 1914-15 was unsteady: the Turks controlled Madina, several tribes and districts rejected his authority, and he was fearful of the growing power of Ibn Sa'ud to the east. When the British began talking not merely of the independence of the Hijaz on the conclusion of the war but also of the reversion of the caliphate of Islam to 'a true Arab born of the blessed stock of the Prophet', and of the independence of the other Arab provinces of the Ottoman empire, Husain could scarcely believe his eyes or his ears. Splendid horizons now beckoned, and he spurred towards them gleefully.

Because Busch takes too little notice of Husain's actual situation in 1914-15, and because he only imperfectly understands, as the little he has to say on the subject in his book makes clear, the nature of the caliphate as an Islamic institution, he fails to accord this critical question the attention it deserves and which it received at the Foreign Office and India Office between 1915 and 1924, particularly as it was closely linked with the settlement with Turkey and the sentiments of Indian Muslims. The sensitivity of Indian Muslims about the war with Turkey, the Ottoman caliphate, and the possibility of its replacement by an Arabian caliphate found active and potentially dangerous outlet in the *khilafat* (caliphate) movement in the Indian empire. It is a topic one might rightly expect Busch to discuss at length in his book, especially in view of its title. Despite this, and despite the claim in his preface that he accords to India's role 'the separate treatment its influence warrants' but which 'it has never received', he has nothing of substance to say about the *khilafat* movement or about the repercussions of the war in the Middle East in India in general. Instead, he offers banalities such as: 'There can be no question of the significance of the *Khilafat* movement for internal Indian politics, as a review of the literature on the subject makes clear.' It would be interesting to learn what is meant by 'the literature on the subject'. To the present writer's knowledge no proper study of the *khilafat* movement has ever been published. What has been published, and what is well known to students of modern Middle Eastern history, is a study of the caliphate by the late Sir Thomas Arnold (C.I.E., Litt.D., etc.), based upon the memoranda and comments which he supplied to the India Office during and after the war, when he was called in to help clear up the misunderstandings over the nature of the caliphate which existed in that department and even more at the Foreign Office. Arnold does not appear in Busch's book, nor is his work on the caliphate included in the list of 254 books and articles, many of them, it would seem, with only a tenuous connection with his subject, which constitute Busch's bibliography of published sources.

Sharif Husain's principal rival for supremacy in Arabia was the Amir Abdul Aziz ibn Sa'ud of Najd. In December 1915 Ibn Sa'ud concluded a treaty of protection with the British government that was to have an important bearing upon his future position in Arabia and especially upon his relations with Husain and the British. Busch's account of the treaty and its negotiation is hasty and superficial, even misleading. He writes of 'the failure to designate any boundaries to Ibn Sa'ud's area', whereas article 1 of the treaty lists Ibn Sa'ud's territories and provides for the subsequent definition of their frontiers by the British government. Busch doubts whether the treaty was later communicated to Sharif Husain: in fact, it was. He speculates on the reasons why Ibn Sa'ud, late in 1917, demanded a large increase in the subsidy being paid him by the British government. Speculation is unnecessary: he was advised to raise his price by H. St. J. B. Philby who was then on a mission to his court. The information is all in the 'maze' of Foreign Office and India Office files, through which, so our *TLS* reviewer informs us, Busch is such an expert guide. When fighting broke out between followers of Husain and adherents of Ibn Sa'ud at the village of Khurma on the borders of the Hijaz in 1918, Ibn Sa'ud refused, Busch tells us, to entertain the idea of a British boundary commission to determine the Hijaz-Najd frontier. On the contrary, he asked for such a commission, invoking in support of his request article 1 of the 1915 treaty. As for the Khurma dispute itself, the importance of which may be judged from the fact that it led, six years later, to Husain's abdication and the conquest of the Hijaz by Ibn Sa'ud, what Busch has to say about it is valueless, since he is obviously unfamiliar with its origins and nature, despite his having had the advantage, so he intimates, of seeing in advance of publication an article in the new edition of the *Encyclopaedia of Islam* which touches upon the Khurma affair, and which proves on examination (it has since been published) to get much closer to the heart of the matter than ever he does.

In May 1917 Sir Mark Sykes (who is described by Busch in one particularly memorable phrase as a 'free-lance operative') and M. Georges Picot of the French foreign ministry visited the Hijaz to discuss with Sharif Husain the implementation of the agreement bearing their names for the division and administration of the Arab provinces of the Ottoman empire when the war had ended. Busch writes: 'Whether Husain was given the details of the Sykes-Picot Agreement at this time remains an open question'. It is scarcely that—except to the exponents of the 'betrayal' theory of Anglo-Arab relations, one of whose basic propositions is that Sharif Husain was kept in ignorance of British and French plans for the future government of the Arab provinces. Busch does not go so far as to endorse this proposition completely, but he expresses more doubt about what Sykes and Picot told Husain than is justified by the information available in the Foreign Office records that he has used. He has ignored also the evidence of Husain's knowledge of the details of the Sykes-Picot agreement contained in a book and an article by Elie Kedourie, although he lists both in his bibliography.

There is no more satisfaction to be gained from Busch's treatment of the disagreements which arose between the British and French governments at the close of the war as a consequence of Britain's arbitrary abandonment of the Sykes-Picot agreement. Although he pays great attention to the comings and goings of statesmen and officials and to the drafting of statements and protocols, he ignores the actual condition of the Arab territories and fails to address himself to the basic question whether purely Arab governments could feasibly be established in them. He describes at length the uprising in Iraq in 1920 without making a measurable effort to discover its real causes, although he informs us that the committee appointed to suggest a constitution for the country included 'Sir E. Bonham-Carter (K.C.M.G., C.I.E.), Lieutenant-Colonel E. B. Howell (C.S.I., C.I.E., I.C.S.), Lieutenant-Colonel F. C. C. Balfour (C.I.E., M.C.), and Major H. F. M. Tyler (C.I.E., I.C.S.)'. Such seem to be the preoccupations of an historian who, in the judgment of the *TLS* reviewer, is not content simply 'to summarize minutes with his nose in the files', or to lurk fearfully in tiny strongholds of expertise, but ventures bravely out to assault 'a broad spectrum of events that have swayed human destinies'. One of Busch's bolder sallies is to inform us early in his book that the Indian army was actually controlled by the government of India and the India Office and not by the War Office. Apprehensive, however, that he may have been over-venturesome, he hurries to buttress this bold assertion with a footnote citing sixteen authorities.

How did this very indifferent work come to be so warmly commended by the *TLS* reviewer, especially as it is so obvious that its author knows little of the British, even less of the Indians, and nothing at all of the Arabs? Only two explanations suggest themselves. One is that he pays the proper deference to the orthodox Arabophile contentions concerning British and French behaviour towards the Arabs during and after World War I. The other is that the reviewer was incapable of judging the book's worth, a conclusion which every line of his review reinforces. Experienced diplomatic historians do not prattle about 'mazes of voluminous files' and 'combing the Public Record Office'. Nor are they awed by the presence of footnotes, however 'minutely detailed'. These are the expressions of the bogus scholar, or of the type of journalist who drifts occasionally into the Public Record Office to see whether any newsworthy items have been brought to light lately by the operation of the thirty-year rule. What saves this particular reviewer from the humiliation of seeing his pretensions publicly exposed, just as it enabled the reviewer of Kedourie's collection of essays to indulge his malice with impunity, is the protection afforded by the tradition of anonymity in *TLS* reviewing.

In the introduction to the first volume of the *History of 'The Times'* published in 1935, its authors rejected the charge which had been made at various times that the anonymity of the newspaper's correspondents all too often conferred impunity upon them. 'The impunity', they said, quoting the greatest of the early editors, Thomas Barnes, writing a hundred years earlier,

> is purely nominal: for though the writer in a newspaper is obliged by a bond of honourable confidence not to claim even the honour due to his own writings, he is sufficiently known to be subject to all the usual responsibilities and penalties for any violation of social decorum. The public is a gainer because it obtains a full and free discussion without any mixture of that egotism and self-intrusion which are almost inseparable from the compositions of any individual writer in his own personal character.

The practice of anonymity extended to the literary supplement of *The Times* and it was continued when the *TLS* in due course acquired a separate existence. Its desirability in a learned journal was not seriously questioned until 1957, when F. W. Bateson, writing in the October number of the quarterly, *Essays in Criticism*, took issue with both the tone and the intent of several of the reviews of works of literary history and criticism which had appeared in the *TLS* between 1955 and 1957. 'A fundamental critical principle', Bateson believed, was involved in the identification of a reviewer:

> This is because a reviewer, by the nature of his trade, can only present the reader with part of the evidence from which he has reached his conclusions. In the *TLS* where most of the reviews are comparatively short, the reader does not really expect much more than the reviewer's considered opinion. But the worth of an opinion varies with the degree of respect we have for the holder of the opinion....In other words, *the reviewer's name is an essential part of the meaning of the review.*

Bateson went on to argue that anonymity raised an even more important issue of principle than the quality of a review: 'Why on earth should the relationship between reviewer and reviewed be subject to a different morality from that which rules in every other public relationship in a democratic society?' He developed the argument in a letter to the *TLS* some weeks later:

> In our more or less Christian society an institution of the eminence and far-flung influence of *The Times Literary Supplement* is reasonably required to respect the commonplaces of Christian morality. If I circulate anonymous libels about my neighbour the first thing the rest of you will do to protect *him* is to identify *me*. Why should your realistic anonym enjoy the anomalous immunity?

Ruffled by Bateson's article and also by a letter from Professor Hugh Trevor-Roper in the first week of November 1957 (protesting against the derogatory remarks passed by the reviewer of his volume of *Historical Essays*, and demanding to know 'who he is and what authority he has to justify such smug postures'), the editor of the *TLS* set out to defend the rule of anonymity in a leader on 22 November 1957. Conceding that 'the sound of a superior and disembodied voice can easily grate on the ear', and even that the occupant of the editorial chair might occasionally 'be overtaken by some extension of his normal incapacity and allow among the anonymous pages an example of undetected malice, bias, or sheer silliness', he nevertheless remained firm in his belief in the virtues of anonymity, which, he said, had withstood the test of time and of changed conditions. Furthermore, he maintained, scholarship had benefited because the anonymous reviewer was not tempted to seek notoriety through his reviews. 'His criticism will be wholly disinterested, since the general public will not know he has written it.' The leader concluded: 'The signed review keeps its place because it satisfies human curiosity. The unsigned review holds an audience because it may, with luck and skill, achieve a cooler detachment.'

A flurry of letters followed in the next few weeks, some echoing or embroidering the theme of contentment, others, particularly from Bateson and Trevor-Roper, tearing it to shreds. '... With no signatures to guide them', Bateson asked on 29 November 1957, 'how can nonspecialist readers hope to distinguish between the comments of your many experts and those of a clever amateur who knows how to put a bold face on his half-knowledge?' Trevor-Roper rejected the claim that had been made that *TLS* reviewers were better scholars than those to be found reviewing elsewhere over their own signatures, and declared on 3 January 1958: 'If there are scholars who will only criticize when they are themselves immune from criticism, I find it difficult to respect either them or their judgments.' Somewhat taken aback by this brusque rejection of his graceful defence of anonymity, the editor of the *TLS* discarded the urbane tone of his original response and became waspish.

Bateson and Trevor-Roper, he wrote on 10 January 1958, 'like... to know where they are. They bring out their slide-rule at the sight of a signature, and then, by nice calculation, decide whether there has been any sense in the prose equations which precede it.' This was not the way of the *TLS*, which aspired to loftier things:

> . . . In a world where the exhibition of personality for its own sake has become a hallmark of the age, there is something to be said for the display, as a change, of corporate personality, for the merging of the individual name, famous or no, into a collegiate entity.

To identify every reviewer would be to deface the journal's pages with 'a rash of signatures'; worse still, it might compel the *TLS* to bid a regretful farewell to 'those of our contributors who prefer the penumbra of anonymity'. For 'it may look as though the mere addition of a signature to each review involves no very great complication. Yet, for each case where such an addition might be easy, it would be necessary to postulate another where the signature, for compelling reasons, would be withheld.' On reflection, the editor concluded, he remained unrepentant.

> . . . So long as we feel assured that in the main our college makes its weekly contribution in the spirit of equity and objective truthfulness, we shall not be tempted to tear down its walls.

There have been no further *ex cathedra* pronouncements on the subject from the *TLS* in the fifteen years which have elapsed since the promulgation of these (to use a phrase of Bateson's) 'sophisticated irrelevancies and/or ingenious sophistries'. Slight though they are, they provide a measure by which the conduct of the body of reviewers here under consideration may be judged. Thomas Barnes's reassurance that anonymity conferred no real impunity upon a contributor ('he is sufficiently known to be subject to all the usual responsibilities and penalties for any violation of social decorum') may have sufficed in an age when reviewers were chosen from the limited number of people really competent to review a given book, and when they in turn were restrained in the performance of their critical duties by a sense both of scholarly responsibility and of gentlemanly conduct. It offers scant protection today against those who reject all such restraints and abuse the privilege accorded them by the rule of anonymity in the *TLS*.[2] There are certainly 'compelling reasons' for the withholding of the names of the reviewers of books on modern Arab history and politics from the public eye; for if they were known, as the quality of their reviews makes abundantly clear, they might well be recognised as persons of little consequence and less reputation in the field of scholarship in which they profess to review. They bring to mind the Duke of Wellington's reported response on being informed of the composition of the administration formed by the Earl of Derby in February 1852. 'Who?' Wellington kept asking, with mounting disbelief and a growing conviction that his deafness was preventing him from hearing aright as one lustreless name after another was recited to him, 'Who? Who?'

Some prime examples of 'Who? Who?' reviewing in the *TLS* are to be found in the notices of books on Arabia, which would appear, if one may 'by indirections find directions out', to be from the one hand. One

---

2 The only other weekly periodical published in London which practises anonymity in its book reviewing is the *Economist*, which raises the interesting possibility that there may have been occasions when the same reviewer, unknown to either the one editor or the other, has reviewed a book in both the *TLS* and the *Economist*. Such, however, are the hazards of anonymity as a reviewing policy.

example has already been given, the review of B. C. Busch's *Britain, India, and the Arabs, 1914-21*. To take another from the five years under consideration, a notice in the issue of 4 April 1968 of *South Arabia* by Tom Little. The book, an unremarkable exercise in the conventional wisdom (Arabs relentless, British stupid; Nationalism natural, Federation naughty; Traditionalism reprehensible, Terrorism inevitable), is predictably though somewhat cursorily praised, the reviewer being more anxious to exploit the opportunity offered by the review to parade his own opinions on the subject and to heap veiled derision upon the former British administration in Aden. Commiseration is offered the British government for allegedly being handicapped in their efforts to create the South Arabian Federation (against 'irresistible force—Arab nationalism as preached from Cairo') by way of a suggestion that 'some of the servants whose advice they took knew Somalia better than they knew Cairo'. This is an unpleasant reference to, among others, a former governor, Sir Kennedy Trevaskis, whose own book on his experiences, *Shades of Amber*, although it appeared at the same time as Little's and was a much more important, valuable, and thoughtful work, was not reviewed in the *TLS*.

The style affected by this particular reviewer (tough, slangy, knowing) is as consistent as the sentiments that pervade his reviews—a contempt for any British official, especially of the old Indian political service, who served in Arabia and who did not embrace the orthodox doctrines concerning British villainy and Arab rectitude, and an intense dislike of traditional rulers, whether shaikhs, sultans, amirs or imams. If the sentiments seem to conflict, they do no more than reflect the confusion present in the reviewer's mind about the history of Arabia, the administration of the former British government of India, and the policy it pursued in the Arabian peninsula. A further example will perhaps suffice to illustrate the approach, a review on 25 June 1970 of Sir Gilbert Clayton's *An Arabian Diary*, edited by Robert O. Collins. It is a book, according to the reviewer, 'of real value both to the specialist and the general reader'. Besides the diary there are 'two admirable introductory essays and a wealth of scholarly annotation' contributed by Professor Collins. Obviously a work deserving of close consideration. The diary turns out to be Clayton's personal record of his mission to Ibn Sa'ud and the Imam Yahya of the Yemen in 1925 and 1926 to attempt to secure their agreement to the definition and policing of sections of their frontiers. A good quarter of it is made up of chit-chat whose interest for the general reader cannot be very great, however much Collins embellishes it with his scholarly annotations. To illustrate:

Clayton: 'Cairo, 2nd October, 1925—Friday. I then went to Davies Bryan's and bought some bedding, towels, and various other necessaries, while George Antonius ordered a reserve store of food and drink from Fleurent.'

Collins: 'Davies Bryan was a men's general outfitters in Cairo which catered to English residents. Fleurent was a superior grocer's shop that stocked English and European brands.'

Clayton: 'Port Sudan, 8th October—Thursday. I did a little shopping in the forenoon, buying some stores (soda water, etc.) from Lorenzato's and a deck chair, I also had my hair cut.'

Collins: 'Lorenzato's was a well-known bar in Port Sudan, situated in the Lorenzato building opposite the Ottoman Bank and the old National Bank of Egypt, now the Bank of the Sudan. Here the European community would gather for a "sundowner" and to purchase supplies.'

Collins is no more able to resist a C.M.G. or K.C.I.E. than is his fellow countryman, Busch, and to help us over the hurdles of abbreviations and acronyms which bestrew his pages he has provided us with a list explaining among other things, that 'H.M.G.' stands for 'His Majesty's Government', 'H.Q.' for 'head-quarters', 'M.P.' for 'Member of Parliament', 'n.c.o.' for 'non-commissioned officer', and 'R.A.F.' for 'Royal Air Force'. The most useful annotations which Collins has to make are those he has culled from Clayton's official reports of his missions—which raises the question whether it might not have been better to publish the reports and annotate them from the diary.

The greater part of Collins's main introductory essay (the second is very brief) is taken up with a survey of British policy in Arabia before, during, and immediately after World War I, the burden of which is that few British officials at the time recognised the importance of Ibn Sa'ud or judged correctly the direction in which the tide of events in the peninsula was flowing. Instead, most of those responsible for the conduct of policy believed Sharif Husain of Mecca to be the stronger and the worthier of the two, and they continued to support him despite the growth of evidence to the contrary. The thesis is not novel, and its restatement here, unsupported by fresh evidence and marred by several factual errors and misconceptions, does not advance scholarship very far. The rest of the introduction consists of a short biography of Clayton himself, from his early days in the Sudan, through the war years, when he was successively director of military intelligence for the Egyptian Expeditionary Force and chief political officer with Allenby's army in Palestine, down to his post-war career as adviser to the Egyptian ministry of the interior and chief secretary to the government of Palestine. It would appear from what Collins has to say that Clayton never uttered an unwise word or did a foolish thing, a portrait which hardly accords with the impression of the man gained from a reading of the Foreign Office and India Office records for the period of World War I and afterwards.

Clayton's political vision was narrow, his judgment too often was unsound, and he frequently allowed partisanship to override commonsense. Collins criticises Sir Archibald Murray, the G.O.C. of the Egyptian Expeditionary Force, for being sceptical of the value of the Arab revolt. Even if the criticism were justified—and it is not certain that it is—Murray was far from being alone in his scepticism: the government of India, the India Office, and the Indian political service, all looked with scorn upon the extravagant fancies of the Arab Bureau and the scurryings to and fro between Cairo and the Hijaz. Collins never asks the critical question whether Clayton was perspicacious enough to see that the future in Arabia lay with Ibn Sa'ud rather than with Sharif Husain. He is silent about Clayton's infatuation with the Sharifians and about his refusal to acknowledge the power of Ibn Sa'ud until the latter had finally triumphed over the Arab Bureau's protege. Instead, he makes the astonishing assertion that Ibn Sa'ud trusted Clayton more than any other Englishman he had encountered, a statement which is manifestly unfair to Sir Percy Cox, the civil commissioner in Iraq, whom Ibn Sa'ud had known, liked and admired for years before he ever set eyes upon Clayton. Moreover Collins's claims regarding Ibn Sa'ud's trusting faith in Clayton makes odd reading when set beside the following telegram, which is typical of those Clayton sent to the Foreign Office on the subject of the Husain-Ibn Sa'ud feud in the early months of 1919: 'In my opinion the time has come when we must take a definite side in this dispute. I consider we must back King Hussein against Wahabi encroachment and show Bin Saud clearly we are doing so.' Ibn Sa'ud was not a fool, he was certainly not without means of ascertaining what various British officials thought of him, and he took the measure of Clayton quite easily, as the latter's own reports of his mission in 1925 reveal quite clearly, if all unwittingly.

Does the *TLS* reviewer make any of these points? He does not. There are the customary genuflexions in the direction of 'scholarship' and 'research', *penates* which he apparently feels obliged to propitiate while entertaining some doubt about their actual significance; and he gives Collins a pat on the head, presumably for saying all the right things about Clayton,

Storrs, Lawrence, Wingate, and the other founder-members of the Arabophile order. For the rest, the book merely provides the reviewer with yet another opportunity to entertain us with his own quaint interpretation of Arabian history between the wars. Thus:

> The area enclosed by the routes to India, the vast neutral desert lying between the Euphrates and the Red Sea, exploded into question-marks as Ibn Saud launched his drive towards empire. His conquering *Ikhwan* pressed hotly on the frontiers of two British mandated territories, Iraq and Transjordan, and dominated the Hejaz. Having briskly exploited the disarray of their wartime instrument King Hussein of the Hejaz, by annexing to Transjordan the whole northern province of his kingdom, including the useful port of Aqaba, the British Government sent Clayton to negotiate with Ibn Saud a definition of frontiers acceptable to British imperial interests. These dictated the denial to the new Lord of Arabia of direct access to Syria or of any other right of way across the Transjordan-Iraq line.

> The collapse of the Ottoman Empire and the postwar Balkanization of Arab territory ended one precious Arab liberty: that of travel, without nonsense of passport or customs-control, anywhere in the Peninsula and beyond. Familiar oases and wells were suddenly put out of bounds by accident of cartography. Ibn Saud detested this new constraint, and only his basic goodwill towards Britain, the fruit of tactful handling by British Residents in the Persian Gulf and of his own appreciation of the British imperial achievement, enabled his signature of the two Treaties which gave Britain the frontiers it wanted and left Ibn Saud master in his own house. The Imam of the Yemen, who had similar frontier disputes with Aden, also argued for a fluid 'tribal" frontier; but he had other and equally inacceptable demands, and that part of Clayton's mission ended in apparent failure.

The reviewer's own notice ends on a familiar note:

> One could have wished that Professor Collins might have extended his Epilogue to bring his story up to date. He writes: "The mission was over, but the result endures." Not much en-

dures today of the Zaidi Imams of Sanaa, with their addiction to kat and their alleged esoteric knowledge. And Ibn Saud himself lived long enough to stab an angry finger at those detested lines on the map with which, once his British friends had shuffled off their mandatory responsibilities, his dynastic enemies still hemmed him in: those Hashemite princes in Amman and Baghdad whose territories, when he still talked with Clayton, Ibn Saud had stood poised to invade.

What on earth is one supposed to make of all this?

1. Britain did not exploit, 'briskly' or otherwise, the disarray of King Husain by annexing the northern Hijaz to Transjordan. Husain had abdicated and left the country by July 1925 when this step was taken. It was Ibn Sa'ud who had cause to complain about the truncation of his conquests, and he reinforced that complaint by refusing to recognise the existence of any frontier between Aqaba and a point 180 miles due east of it—as the Hadda agreement, concluded by Clayton on 2 November 1925 and reprinted by Professor Collins in his book, makes perfectly clear.

2. To contend that the Hadda agreement and the Bahra agreement, the second of the two instruments negotiated by Clayton and one which provided for the policing of the Najd-Iraq frontier, denied to Ibn Sa'ud 'direct access to Syria or . . . any other right of way across the Transjordan-Iraq line' is to misunderstand the character of those agreements. Ibn Sa'ud had conquered and annexed Jabal Shammar, to the north of Najd, only four years earlier; and his *Ikhwan* did not begin raiding up the Wadi Sirhan in the direction of Amman for another couple of years. To imply that these raids entitled Ibn Sa'ud to 'direct access' to southern Syria, four hundred miles to the north-west of Jabal Shammar across the vast stretches of the Great Nafud, is ridiculous. Britain, as the mandatory power in Transjordan, was anxious to curb the *Ikhwan* raids, prevent the forcible proselytism of the Ruwalla and Bani Sakhr tribes by Ibn Sa'ud's agents, and preserve a common frontier between Transjordan and Iraq. What the reviewer means by saying that Ibn Sa'ud was denied 'any other right of way across the Transjordan-Iraq line' is unclear. One assumes that he is referring to the frontier of Najd with Transjordan and Iraq, not to the Transjordan-Iraq frontier. But what he intends by 'any other right of way' is a mystery. The question is not worth pursuing, beyond remarking that the Hadda and Bahra agreements were designed to regulate and not prohibit the movements of tribesmen on their lawful occasions across the Najd frontier.

3. It is foolish to talk of 'familiar oases being put out of bounds' and

of 'the precious Arab liberty of travel without passport or customs-control anywhere in the Peninsula or beyond' being ended by the frontier settlement after World War I. The only oases of any consequence affected by the frontier agreements were the Qaf group in the Wadi Sirhan, which Ibn Sa'ud bamboozled Clayton into handing over to him by the terms of the Hadda agreement. The Qaf oases continued to be frequented after 1925 by the tribes which had previously been accustomed to use them, just as the other watering places along the Najd frontier continued to be used by nomads following their usual grazing pattern. Elsewhere in the peninsula there wasn't a single fixed frontier, if one excepts the Kuwait frontier and the attempts made in 1934 and 1936 to define portions of the Yemen-Aden and Yemen-Sa'udi Arabia borders. Tribes and individuals roamed as they had always roamed, the only variations in their movements deriving, as they had normally derived, from considerations of prudence and the vagaries of fortune.

4. Were the Zaidi Imams of San'a addicted to qat and was their esoteric knowledge only alleged? Without some elaboration of these charges by the reviewer and more evidence about the personal lives and religious attainments of past Zaidi rulers than is at present available to us, it would be impossible to supply an answer. The longest lived of recent Zaidi Imams was Yahya ibn Muhammad, who ruled from 1904 to 1948. According to Harold Ingrams, a well-known authority on the Yemen, Imam Yahya was a ruler of considerable distinction:

> His power was founded in Zeidi zeal, the native pride of the Yemeni mountaineer and in long isolation from outside influence. The Imam exemplified these things: he was pious and orthodox, secure in the prestige of two lineages, one ancient and native, that from the Tubbas of Himyar, and one sacred, that from the Prophet. No ruler of importance could have so personified isolation. He had never been out of his country, nor seen the sea; he had always lived in the highlands. Nevertheless, he attracted much respect in the Arab world in the 1920's, not only for his ancient lineage and his reputation for piety and religious knowledge, but mainly because of his uncompromising stand for Arab independence. (*The Yemen*, London, 1963, pp. 63-64.)

5. Finally, did Ibn Sa'ud actually 'stab an angry finger' at his frontiers with Iraq and Transjordan after the British 'had shuffled off their manda-

tory responsibilities'? The mandate for Iraq was terminated in 1932. Two years earlier, after the British government had made known its intention to end the mandate, Ibn Sa'ud had concluded an agreement of *bon voisinage* with King Faisal of Iraq that implicitly accepted the existing frontiers and the standing arrangements for their policing. In 1936 the friendly relationship was confirmed by a treaty of alliance between the two countries. Again, the established frontier was not an issue. Britain relinquished the mandate for Transjordan in 1946. Despite Ibn Sa'ud's dislike for King Abdullah he never threatened the Jordan frontier, even though he did not abandon his claim to Aqaba. His son and successor, King Faisal, eventually acknowledged Jordan's right to Aqaba in 1965, when the final stretch of the Sa'udi Arabia-Jordan frontier was defined. The only area, in fact, where Ibn Sa'ud challenged the British government's conception of his frontiers was where those frontiers were never established and where Britain was never a mandatory power, *viz.*, along the Arabian littoral of the Gulf.

All too often, as with these Arabian confections, the 'Who? Who?' reviewers of the *TLS* give the impression that their sole acquaintance with the subject under discussion derives from the books they are reviewing. Perhaps this is why they are afforded such a singular degree of editorial protection in comparison with reviewers in other fields. Very few letters critical of reviews of books on modern Arab history and politics (or on the Middle East in general) appear in the correspondence columns of the *TLS*. It is odd that so important an area as the Middle East should provoke no correspondence other than occasional letters from authors defending themselves against intemperate or incompetent reviewers. Enquiry reveals, in fact, that a number of letters on Middle Eastern subjects, some from distinguished scholars, have been sent to the *TLS* in recent years, only to be rejected for publication with the explanation that while the editor was prepared to accept letters correcting factual errors made by reviewers, it was not his policy to publish letters merely expressive of a difference of opinion. It may not be; but as even the most cursory examination of the correspondence columns of almost any issue of the *TLS* will show, it is a policy honoured as often in the breach as in the observance. Nor does it apparently exclude the advocacy of causes by interested parties. The issue of 1 December 1972, for instance, contains a letter putting the case for the publication of pornography from the editor of *Curious* magazine.

The protective concern exhibited by the *TLS* for its reviewers of works on modern Arab history and politics is matched in turn by the deference displayed by the reviewers themselves towards the countries and regimes which are the subjects of these works. Egypt is the country upon which the

'Who? Who?' reviewers lavish the most sympathy, and about which they write with perhaps more partisanship, inaccuracy and downright foolishness than any other. A reader unfamiliar with modern Egyptian history would gain the impression from *TLS* reviews over the past five years that repression, injustice and ineptitude first made their appearance in Egypt on the heels of the British occupation in 1882, and that they made an instantaneous exit with the revolution of 1952. He would also learn, perhaps to his surprise, that the grossest act in the calendar of human crime was the British invasion of Egypt in 1956 in association with the French and the Israelis. A specimen of this type of thinking is a review in the issue of 27 October 1972 of Egypt: *Imperialism and Revolution* by Jacques Berque. It opens with some characteristic flim-flam about Egypt, India, the Raj, and the imperial heyday, then plunges into a eulogy of Berque for having written what the reviewer evidently believes is a triumphant evocation and mystical celebration of the Egyptian people:

> It is a great book, among the greatest to be written about Egypt in a European language: a work almost of genius, certainly of passionate insight. Its immense size and density should not deter even the casual reader, for the work develops with its theme, and what seems to begin as an academic thesis concludes as a deeply moving testament of love, wisdom and conviction.

There is a slight flaw in the book, the reviewer concedes, but it is insubstantial: 'The thought is often opaque, at least in translation, and sometimes apparently meaningless.' (To set his mind at rest: it is meaningless in the original, also.) But what does a fault like meaninglessness matter when it occurs in the context of Berque's majestic denunciation of the period of British supremacy in Egypt? How pathetically irrelevant, declaims the reviewer, the British presence now seems! 'How superficial its concerns appear set against the antique convictions of Al Azhar, or the unwritten atavisms of the fellahin!' Summing up, he declares unequivocally:

> The British cannot as a whole take much pride in their Egyptian record.... Great works of engineering were completed, a degree of order was momentarily imposed, the economy was temporarily rescued from disaster. But the motives were dubious, the methods were often shifty, the relationship was soured by the arrival of great British armies in two world wars, and in Egypt as in most of Africa British imperialism fell below its

own best standards, leaving us with an aftertaste less of defiance than of regret.

Perhaps the most striking demonstration of the preoccupation of these reviewers with the defence of regimes which they admire rather than with their critical duties is afforded by a review which appeared on 5 March 1971 of a book entitled *Islam in Egypt Today*. According to the reviewer, it was 'mistitled' and 'simple to the point of banality when not actually misleading'. The major questions . . . are virtually ignored.' The author, Morroe Berger, a professor of sociology at Princeton University, had very little to say, and that unilluminating, about the political and social contexts of contemporary Islamic belief and practice'. Such remarks lead one naturally to assume that the reviewer must be an Islamicist of the very first rank to be in a position to condemn a work by a leading American scholar so utterly and finally. Unfortunately this initial impression begins to fade when one looks at the book itself. It turns out to be a competent and useful work of scholarship, describing in straightforward and factual terms (there are twenty-six pages of statistical information in a book of 130 pages) the administration of Egyptian mosques, aspects of the organisation of sufi orders and benevolent societies, and, for about twenty pages, the policy of the Egyptian government towards these bodies. The book is based upon research carried out in Egypt at various times, and much of the information it supplies was not previously available to Western scholars.

Why, then, had the *TLS* reviewer misrepresented the book's qualities and its author's intentions and capacities? The answer is supplied by the closing sentences of his review:

> The book is consistently both directly and implicitly antipathetic to the post-1952 government of Egypt which is referred to throughout as 'the military regime.' Its reforms are brushed aside and its actions presented as an attempt to take over religion for nationalist and socialist purposes in the face of what one is led to believe is popular alienation and suppression. This tone of disapproval is irritating and one wonders what kind of freedom and progress Dr. Berger thinks the mass of the Egyptian people enjoyed before 1952.

Such, however, was not the reaction of Egyptians to the book; when it appeared it was favourably reviewed in *Al Ahram*, Egypt's leading newspaper.

It is not often that the reigning prejudice emerges like this from behind the customary arras of euphemism and innuendo. But it was to do so again on 17 December 1971 in a review of a book, *Conflict in the Middle East*, by P. J. Vatikiotis. The only factual criticism which the reviewer had to make of the book (concerning the Senussi connection with the Asir) revealed his own knowledge to be at fault. Factual criticism, however, it soon became evident, was less the object of the review than the taking of Vatikiotis to task for the frank opinions he had expressed of Arab political habits and traditions. After quoting some of these opinions the reviewer went on to declare:

> It is unfruitful and misleading to discuss the political changes of the last twenty-five years, even more so their justification or otherwise, without at least trying to assess their effects on the standards of living of the masses in the countries concerned. For Egypt, Professor Vatikiotis does briefly suggest that the revolution has benefited the townsfolk more than the peasants; for Iraq and Syria, even such easy generalizations are omitted. But once economics are taken into account, it is not really possible to maintain, as he does, that the military regimes conceive politics much as their predecessors did. The old rulers valued power largely for its material perquisites, while the soldiers are after power for its own sake and not infrequently for genuine patriotic or ideological reasons.

An earlier book by Vatikiotis, *The Modern History of Egypt*, had been greeted rapturously by the *TLS* when it appeared. 'A scholarly work of first-class importance', ran the review in the issue of 11 September 1969. 'It has breadth of horizon, an authoritativeness, a continuity of theme, and a reflective and sympathetic approach to its subject matter.... Certainly the best general history of modern Egypt available in English...' What had happened in the intervening two years to bring about such a fall from grace? Why had Vatikiotis committed these doctrinal errors which the reviewer now felt under an obligation to correct? The answer was readily forthcoming:

> The bibliography pays special tribute to Dr. Elie Kedourie, and the two writers have something in common—because, perhaps, both were born into non-Arab, non-Muslim minorities in the Middle East (Jews in Baghdad, Greeks in Palestine), without

being associated with the then privileged class of resident Englishmen. The resulting lack of sympathy for both Muslim Arabs and the Englishmen who handed over to them is less obvious in the case of Professor Vatikiotis, but one might ascribe to it, perhaps, such things as his statement that President Nasser aimed before 1967 to destroy Israel....

Another 'beast beneath the skin' had been discovered, requiring the restatement in emphatic terms of the law governing the *index librorum prohibitorum Arabicorum*. Sympathy with (*aequat* identification with) the object of study is a *sine qua non* of scholarship, and a deficiency of it a crippling impediment. Only Englishmen previously resident in the Middle East, or their spiritual heirs, are capable of sympathising with their Muslim Arab constituents. By extension, therefore, only they are capable of arriving at balanced judgments respecting them and their affairs. Scholars like Vatikiotis and Kedourie are obviously precluded by their origins from writing judiciously on Arab politics, and their scholarship must consequently be regarded as suspect.

In a letter published in the *TLS* of 31 December 1971 Vatikiotis exposed this law for the ass it is; and the reviewer reacted by disclaiming by verbal legerdemain the opinions he had so boldly put forward in his review, disavowing any intention of maligning Vatikiotis, and apologising archly for having bracketed him with Kedourie. The original offence against the latter was allowed to stand; and it appeared that it did so with editorial acquiescence, for letters from several scholars protesting against the slur were rejected for publication. It was more difficult, it would seem, for the editor to refuse a letter from Kedourie himself, for one appeared in the issue of 14 January 1972 asking how it was that the reviewer in question could discourse with such glib assurance upon his (Kedourie's) motives in writing Middle Eastern history. Such assurance could only derive from intimate knowledge of the person concerned, and the quality of mind displayed by the reviewer, Kedourie pointed out, was not such as to have led him to cultivate his acquaintance or admit him into his intimacy. Put to flight yet again, the reviewer offered a limp apology:

I certainly did not 'design' my remarks to discredit his work: I should have thought that my tribute to his writing would have shown him—and other readers—that I admire it.

What, in sum, has been the effect of this ill-informed and tendentious reviewing in the TLS over the past few years? Whether it has gained any adherents to the cause espoused by its practitioners is open to doubt. That they have damaged the reputation of the *TLS* and debased the standards of scholarly criticism in the field of modern Arab history and politics is certain. To look over the reviews of the years 1968-72 and to note the books which have been praised or damned according to the degree of their authors' subservience to the dictates of the Arabophile school, is to be struck by the shallowness and capriciousness of the reviewers' judgments. Ephemera from journalists, pulp from vulgarisers, tracts from political panders, apologia from guiltridden ex-diplomatists, gauche and fumbling theses from American Ph.D.-mills—all are indiscriminately enthused over while serious works by reputable scholars are treated to a cursory notice, a flippant aside, a cheap sneer, or a testy rebuke for not being written in a more elementary style, more to the taste and comprehension of the 'Who? Who?' reviewers.

In the issue of 8 January 1971 the better part of half-a-page is devoted to praise of yet another journalistic account of the Suez campaigns, while in the issue of 4 February 1972 the *Cambridge History of Islam*, a two-volume work edited by three prominent British orientalists and numbering among its contributors some of the most distinguished Islamicists in the Western world, was disparagingly noticed in a bare third of a page, most of which was given over to the reviewer's own reflections upon the antipathy felt for Islam by Christianity and the West in past centuries. Half-a-page was expended in 1968 on a denunciation of an 87-page booklet on the Balfour declaration, even though the reviewer declared it had 'little new to add'; while later in that year three scholarly works of modern Middle Eastern history, totalling nearly 2,000 pages and presenting a great deal of new information, were accorded no more space. (As the review plumbed new depths of ineptitude the brevity was perhaps merciful.) They fared somewhat better, however, than a work on Arab politics by a leading Arab scholar, Majid Khadduri, which was relegated to the 'Books Received' section of the issue of 26 November 1971 and curtly dismissed as being 'of some interest'. A final illustration of this lack of proportion is afforded by the page given over on 21 January 1972 to three books, one an encomium of Nasser, another a study of the British in Egypt, and a third on the Trucial States. The first two are by journalists as well known for their admiration of the late Egyptian leader as they are for their shame over Britain's record in the Middle East. Their books are variously described as 'authoritative', 'professional', 'superbly detailed and clear', 'valuable to the expert', and of 'scholarly interst'—phrases conspicuously lacking in most

TLS reviews of books by academics and scholars who do not engage in the standard apologetics for Arabism. The third book, by a diplomatist, is described as 'indispensable' and as 'the first generally accessible account' of the history of the Trucial States. It is neither of these things. Nor does it, as the reviewer claims, relate that history 'with scrupulous care'.

With reviewers such as these it is little wonder that the *TLS* prefers to retain the rule of anonymity; it is even less a cause for wonder that the reviewers themselves should prefer its penumbra. What is greatly to be regretted is that by their acclamations of the glib and the meretricious, and by their denigration of true scholarship, they have lowered the level of informed criticism in the journal to which they contribute. It is even more regrettable that the *TLS* of late years, in contradistinction to its declarations of 1957-58 about 'a cooler detachment', 'wholly disinterested criticism', and 'the spirit of equity and objective truthfulness', appears to have acquiesced in the misappropriation of its columns to fashionable or contrived political causes. When F. W. Bateson in 1957 accused the *TLS* of partisanship, cliquishness and intellectual dishonesty, the editor laughed the accusation off with the comment that 'the concept of a commando-group... reckless, shameless, nameless, raiding campus and quad alike, is one associated almost entirely with signed reviewing'. Could the same confident reply be made today, especially about the reviewing of books on modern Arab history and politics? And if it were, would it be too much to ask that the veil of anonymity be lifted so that the rest of us could share the joke? After all, *The Times* itself, now replete with 'a rash of signatures', has already given a lead in this direction. If the *TLS* were to follow, not only would the critical air be cleared but the Arabs themselves would surely benefit from learning the identities of those self-appointed advocates of their cause who have done them so much disservice and dishonour.

5

The Slave Trade of the Indian Ocean and the Red Sea[1]

B lack slaves have been a commodity in the commerce of the Indian Ocean, the Red Sea, and the Persian Gulf since the beginning of recorded time. They were obtained in the main from Abyssinia, from the Horn of Africa, and from the coast and hinterland of East Africa, as far south as present-day Mozambique. The civilisations which flourished in South Arabia in the first millennium B.C. controlled the trade of the African coast opposite, and they were the principal suppliers of the marts of India, Mesopotamia, and Persia with the staples of that trade—ivory, tortoise-shell, myrrh, frankincense, cinnamon, and slaves. The South Arabian kingdoms also controlled the trade routes running up through western Arabia to Syria and Egypt, and there are sufficient references in the works of the classical authors to indicate that slaves formed part of the customary traffic along these routes. A direct trade in slaves and ivory between east Africa and India existed in ancient times. Dravidian vessels made the passage across the Indian Ocean to Africa in the first millennium B.C., and Indian settlements were established on the African coast as early as the 6th century B.C. These early Indian mariners knew the use of the monsoons, and it was from their experience that the Arabs later learned how to sail for east Africa on the north-east monsoon and to return before the onset of the south-west monsoon.

The slave trade from the African coasts of the Red Sea and the Indian Ocean in classical times was directed both northwards to Egypt, western

---

1 A previously unpublished chapter for JB Kelly's collection on the slave trade, 1973.

Arabia, and the Mediterranean, and eastwards to India, Persia, eastern Arabia, and Mesopotamia. *The Periplus of the Erythraean Sea*, a sailing guide to the western Indian Ocean and its shores, written by a Greek mariner of Berenike, on the Red Sea coast of Egypt, in the first century A.D., refers, in the course of describing the ports of the Somali coast (the 'Land of Punt' of the ancient Egyptians) to 'a market-town called Opone [Ras Hafun, about 90 miles south of Cape Guardafui], where the greatest quantity of cinnamon is produced, and slaves of the better sort, which are brought to Egypt in increasing numbers'.[2] By 'slaves of the better sort' the author of the *Periplus* probably means Abyssinians, since the slave trade of the Red Sea with Egypt, western Arabia, and the Mediterranean was primarily in Abyssinians, not negroes. Most of the black slaves known to the Mediterranean world of classical antiquity were Nubians, brought down the Nile to Egypt. Black slaves for the markets of India, Persia, Mesopotamia, and eastern Arabia, on the other hand, were obtained from the east African coast south of Mogadishu, those desert tracts beyond the equator which were known to the ancients as 'the Courses of Azania' and to the Arabs, in a derivative form of the word, as 'Zinjibar', 'the land of Zinj' or 'land of the blacks', and as 'Zanzibar' or 'Zanquebar' to the later European world.

In the early centuries of the Christian era Arab colonies were established along the east African coast, at Mombasa, Malindi, Pangani, Lamu, Zanzibar, and elsewhere. After the advent of Islam their growth was assisted by the periodic influx of refugees from wars or sectarian struggles within the Muslim dominions to the northward. It was also helped by their control of the slave trade to India and the 'Abbasid empire, where Africans were in demand both as laborers and as soldiers. A bloody uprising of these slaves against the 'Abbasid caliph in the ninth century A.D., and its equally bloody suppression, acquired fame in Muslim history as 'the revolt of the Zanj', and a similar story was enacted in Bengal in the last two decades of the fifteenth century. The arrival of the Portuguese in east African waters in the early sixteenth century did not break the grip of the coast Arabs on the slave trade. Instead, the Portuguese obtained what slaves they needed from Arab and Afro-Arab slavers, as did the French later, when they took possession of the Mascarenes and needed slaves to work their plantations. In the late seventeenth and early eighteenth centuries the Ya'ariba rulers of 'Oman drove the Portuguese from their strongholds north of Cape Delgado and exerted their authority over the Arabs of the coastal settlements. From this time onwards the east African slave trade became a monopoly

---

2 *The Periplus of the Erythraean Sea*, translated and annotated by Wilfred H. Schoff, New York, 1912, p. 27.

of the Muscat Arabs, and it remained so despite the decline and fall of the Ya'ariba dynasty shortly afterwards and the reassertion of their independence by the coastal Arabs. A nominal suzerainty was exercised over them by the *saiyids* of the Al Bu Sa'id dynasty, who came to power in 'Oman in the mid-eighteenth century after the fall of the Ya'ariba; but it was not until the early decades of the nineteenth century and the accession to power of Saiyid Sa'id ibn Sultan, the greatest of the Al Bu Sa'id line, that 'Omani control over the east African coast was made a reality and the slave trade became a prime source of revenue for the Muscat treasury.

Because east Africa lay off the normal shipping tracks between Europe and the East, so that few European vessels ever ventured into its waters, little was known in Europe of the scope and operation of the Arab slave trade until well into the nineteenth century. Before that time the only contact which Europeans had had with the trade had been at its northern end, at Muscat and in the ports of the Persian Gulf. Muscat was the chief emporium of the trade in Arabian waters, just as Zanzibar was the great clearing house in east Africa. Every year, at the outset of the north-east monsoon in late October or early November, *dhows* from Muscat set out for Zanzibar with cargoes of dates, spices, cloth, drugs, and manufactured goods, both Indian and European, to barter for ivory, copal, and slaves. Their return voyages were made after the turn of the year and before the south-west monsoon set in sometime in April. Some of them shipped slaves direct from the coastal settlements but most obtained them from Zanzibar Island, to which the bulk of the slaves procured up-country had previously been transported.

The organisation of the trade at the mainland ports was in the hands of Arabs and local African magnates, who in turn relied upon tribal chieftains in the interior to maintain the supply of slaves and ivory. Financially, the entire trade was under-written by *banians* (traders from western India, and from Gujerat in particular, found in the ports of Arabia, the Red Sea and east Africa) resident at Zanzibar and in the coastal towns. Customs duty usually of one Maria Theresa dollar a head, was levied upon slaves exported from the mainland ports, and a further duty of $MT1.00 was imposed upon slaves imported into Zanzibar. Normally, the customs of Zanzibar and the mainland ports, including the duties on slaves, were farmed by the ruler of Muscat to one or other of the leading *banians* of Zanzibar. Captain Atkins Hamerton, the first British consul appointed to Zanzibar, reported in 1842 that the customs were then farmed for the sum of $MT155,000 per annum. He also described the workings of the slave trade from the mainland.

They [the slaves] are procured chiefly by the banian brokers. On the chiefs coming to the coast, these brokers go from Zanzibar to the different ports under the dominion of H.H. the Imam[3] and procure the slaves in the following manner. The Tribes from the interior who bring down the ivory and gum copal have it all carried by the people they from time to time take in war, and they always barter the slaves along with the articles they have carried from the interior to the coast. Money is not given either for the slaves or for the articles they bring: it is a barter trade. American cloth, beads, muskets and powder are the chief articles given in exchange for the slaves, ivory and gum copal....... The business is chiefly carried on by banians and Indian Mohamedans, and the slaves from the time they come into the hands of the brokers are kept at the least possible expense. They barely receive as much food as will keep them alive until they reach the market in Zanzibar.[4]

The first European to supply a written description of the slave market at Zanzibar was Captain. T. Smee of the Bombay Marine (the armed branch of the English East India Company's maritime service), who visited Zanzibar in the cruiser *Ternate* in 1811 in the course of a reconnaissance of the east African coast. Smee wrote:

The show commences at 4 o'clock in the afternoon. The slaves, set off to the best advantage by having their skins cleaned and burnished with coconut oil, their faces painted with red and white stripes which is here esteemed elegance, and their hands, noses, ears and feet ornamented with a profusion of bracelets of gold and silver and jewels, are ranged in a line commencing with the youngest and increasing to the rear according to their

---

3 Generally speaking, the ruler of 'Oman was known to his subjects by the title of imam, to which office he was traditionally elected by those 'Omani tribes which professed the Ibadi interpretation of Islam. Although the first two rulers of the Al Bu Sa'id line had been imams, neither Sa'id ibn Sultan (regn. 1806-1856) nor his immediate predecessors bore the title. Instead they styled themselves 'saiyids', in its temporal sense of 'lord'. Europeans, however, persisted in calling Saiyid Sa'id 'Imam' to the end of his days. His successors at Muscat and Zanzibar were with equal arbitrariness accorded the title of 'Sultan'.

4 [India Office Records, Foreign and Commonwealth Office, London] *Enclosures to Secret Letters from Bombay*, vol. 44, enclose. 3 to Sec. Letter 43 of 30 April 1842, Hamerton, no. 2 Pol. Dept., Zanzibar, 2 January 1842.

size and age. At the head of this file, which is composed of all sexes and ages from six to sixty, walks the person who owns them. Behind and at each side two or three of his domestic slaves, armed with swords and spears, serve as a guard. Thus ordered, the procession begins and passes through the market-place and principal streets, the owner holding forth in a kind of song the good qualities of his slaves and the high prices that have been offered for them.

When any of them strikes a spectator's fancy, the line imme-diately stops, and a process of examination ensures which for minuteness is unequalled in any cattle-market in Europe. The intending purchaser, having ascertained there is no defect in the faculties of speech, hearing, etc., that there is no disease present, and that the slave does not snore in sleeping which is counted a very great fault, next proceeds to examine the per-son: the mouth and teeth are first inspected, and afterwards every part of the body in succession, not even excepting the breasts, etc. of the girls, many of whom I have seen handled in the most indecent manner in the public market by their pur-chasers: indeed, there is every reason to believe that the slave-dealers almost universally force the young females to submit to their lust previous to their being disposed of. The slave is then made to walk or run a little way to show there is no de-fect about the feet; after which, if the price is agreed to, they are stripped of their finery and delivered over to their future master. I have frequently counted between twenty and thirty of these files in the market at one time, some of which contained about thirty [slaves]. Women with children newly born hang-ing at their breasts and others so old they can scarcely walk are sometimes seen dragged about in this manner. I observed they had in general a very dejected look; some groups appeared so ill fed that their bones appeared as if ready to penetrate the skin.[5]

Indolence and avarice, in the view of Captain Hamerton, who spent fifteen years of his life at Zanzibar and died there in 1857, were the twin pillars of the Arab slave trade.

---

5 Captain T. Smee, 'Observations during a Voyage of Research on the East Coast of Af-rica from Cape Guardafui south to the Island of Zanzibar', *Transactions of the Bombay Geographical Society*, vi (1844), 44-46.

The meanest of the Imaum's subjects in Oman, Zanzibar, and on the coast of Africa, whether an Arab or a half-caste Arab or a freed man being a Mussulman, never dreams of doing any sort of labour when he has once got together sufficient money to purchase a slave or a number of slaves; after which he lounges about from place to place with a sword under his arm, and calling himself an Arab, appears content to subsist on whatever his slave or slaves may by their labour, or frequently by robbery, procure for him. He has but one care on earth, how to procure the means of obtaining slaves. Female slaves are rarely kept for any length of time by the subjects of the Imaum. They, in consequence of the facility of procuring female slaves in the bazar of Zanzibar, have the opportunity of indulging to the fullest extent their love of variety in women. The meanest ruffian frequently buys a number of young girls in the slave market with an understanding between him and the broker from whom he buys them that on their being resold within a given time – when he has satisfied himself – should there be a deficiency on the girls being resold, the buyer is to sustain the loss. These girls are always sold again for exportation to the Persian Gulf, Red Sea and Coast of Arabia. A great number die from the little care taken of them from the time they are brought from the coast of Africa until they are resold – generally between the months of February and April, when the vessels coming from the northward leave Zanzibar.

The male slaves on their arrival at Zanzibar are sold by the people who buy them to the different Shambas or farms all over the island; until the time arrives when their owners sell them as they require and retain as many as are necessary for domestic servants or labourers on the farms. Some are brought up to trades as blacksmiths, carpenters, etc. Their masters receive whatever they may earn. The only article of food given to the slaves by their masters is dried shark fish and mahogo (cassava), and for clothing as much coarse American cloth as is sufficient to hide their nakedness. Yet notwithstanding all this the slaves appear happy and contented. Excepting a total want of care of them, the people do not treat their slaves ill. They seldom or never flog them, but the master has little control over his slaves.[6]

There is no way of knowing, and there never will be, how many Africans were shipped as slaves from the coasts of Africa to the marts of Asia over the centuries. All that can be said is that the scantiness of the population of east Africa in relation to its resources, which the first European explorers to penetrate the interior all remarked upon, indicates that the figure must have been of great magnitude. When the trade was at its peak in the middle decades of the nineteenth century it was estimated that some 40,000 slaves annually were shipped from the mainland to Zanzibar, half of them being absorbed within the island and half being re-exported to the Arab lands to the northward.[7] There are indications, however, that this estimate is exaggerated, and that the true figures are more like 20,000 annually imported into Zanzibar, 5,000 – 10,000 absorbed into the island's economy, and 10,000 – 15,000 shipped northward. Possibly between 1,000 and 2,000 of these *sidis* (as the African slaves were called) were shipped each year to the ports of southern Arabia and, to a lesser degree, the Red Sea, but most were carried to Muscat or to Sur, a port on the coast of 'Oman south of Muscat, which by the middle of the century had become the principal slave emporium of eastern and southern Arabia. Anything from 5,000 to 8,000 *sidis* were sold annually in 'Oman and the neighbouring shaikhdoms of the Pirate Coast, or Trucial Coast, as it later came to be called. A further 3,000 – 5,000 were re-exported from Muscat and Sur to the ports of the upper Gulf – Bahrain, Bushire, Kuwait, and Basra – either in 'Omani vessels or in *dhows* from the Trucial Coast. As the century wore on the 'Omani monopoly of the carrying trade from Zanzibar was gradually eroded, as more and more ships from the Trucial Coast, Kuwait, Bahrain, and the Persian ports of Bushire and Lingah made the voyage to east Africa to obtain slaves direct and so deprive the 'Omani merchants of their profits as middlemen.

The purchase, shipment and sale of slaves took place within the seasonal cycle of trade in the western Indian Ocean, and the slaves themselves were regarded as little more than an ordinary constituent of this trade. Ev-

---

6 Hamerton's report of 2 January 1842, above.

7 For the difficulties in interpreting the available statistics, see J.B. Kelly, *Britain and the Persian Gulf 1795-1880*, Oxford, 1968, pp. 414-17. Captain Hamerton, in his report cited above, states that the average number of slaves shipped every year through the customs-house at Zanzibar between 1837 and 1841 was 15,000. 'But', he adds, 'it is to be observed that a vast number are imported for whom no duty is paid. For instance, the boats of H.H. the Imaum and those of his sons pay no duty on the slaves imported in them from the coast of Africa, and the number imported is very great.'

ery year, in the late summer, after the conclusion of the pearl fishery in the Gulf, *dhows* from most of the ports of eastern and southern Arabia and a fair number of vessels from western India, sailed for Basra for the date harvest. In return for Indian cloths and metalware, spices, drugs, specie and slaves, they obtained cargoes of dates and goods of European manufacture. The larger Arab *dhows*, or *baghalahs*, began leaving Basra and the Shatt al-Arab in early October, bound for the Arabian Sea and the Indian Ocean, where the north-east monsoon would carry them to Zanzibar and east Africa, the Horn of Africa and the Red Sea. Some set course first for the ports of western India, while Indian vessels from these same ports sailed on the monsoon for Berbera, on the Somali coast of the Gulf of Aden, and for Mocha, Hodeida and Jeddah on the Arabian coast of the Red Sea. Nearly every one of these vessels, Arab and Indian, returned with slaves, either Africans purchased at Zanzibar and the nearby mainland ports or Abyssinians purchased at Berbera and, more particularly, at Mocha and Hodeida, where the trade in slaves rivalled in importance that in coffee.

A good proportion of these slaves was smuggled or shipped openly into the ports of Sind, Kutch, Kathiawar, and the Bombay Presidency. The earliest attempt to estimate the size of the traffic, made by Bombay government officials in the late 1830s and early 1840s, put the number imported at 1,500-2,000 per annum, 500-600 of whom were Abyssinians purchased in the ports of Yemen. Most of the vessels engaged in the trade were of Arab, Turkish or Persian registry, hailing mainly from Bahrain, Kuwait, Basra and Bushire. The rest were vessels of Indian registry. As early as 1805 the importation of slaves into the Bombay Presidency had been forbidden by proclamation, and the prohibition was reinforced by a further regulation in 1813. Enforcement, however, was lax and slaves continued to be smuggled into Bombay and other ports with ease. The political resident in the Persian Gulf reported in 1841, after talking to some of the *nakhudas*, or masters, of Gulf *dhows* trading to India:

> So far as I can learn, the manner in which slaves are introduced into our Indian possessions is by the males being classed on board the Arab vessels on which they are embarked as part of the crew, while the females are passed off as their wives. As a large proportion of the crews of native boats is frequently composed of negroes, it must of course be extremely difficult, if not impossible, for any examining officer to examine whether the Africans on board are bona fide seamen or brought for sale. I am told, moreover, that so little repugnance is in general enter-

tained by the negroes themselves to be sold out of the vessels bringing them, that both males and females readily join in the deception, and, if interrogated, seldom if ever fail to corroborate the statement of the Nakhoda, or commander, as to their composing part of the equipage of the vessel or boat.[8]

The principal markets in India for Abyssinian and negro slaves were in Oudh, Hyderabad and the Deccan, where they were employed as domestic servants or as soldiers in the service of rulers and nobles.

Hadramis from southern Arabia, employed by successive Nizams of Hyderabad as mercenary soldiers, were heavily involved in the smuggling of black slaves across the East India Company's territories in western India to Hyderabad and neighbouring states, and they were also implicated in the complementary, though very much smaller, trade in Indian girls, who were bought or kidnapped for sale in the Gulf or at Zanzibar.

The demand for slaves in Muslim lands was not dictated by a need for plantation slave labour to cultivate extensive agricultural holdings. On the contrary, slave labour had been found both impracticable and uneconomic for this purpose. Slaves were required primarily for domestic service and for concubinage, and it was for such employment that the great majority of the slaves shipped from Abyssinia, Zanzibar and east Africa to Arabia and the Gulf were destined. The men were also employed as sailors, fishermen, and pearl divers. The condition of their lives and the treatment they received were not unduly harsh: indeed, their lives differed little, if at all, from the life of the ordinary Gulf tribesman. Lieutenant Arnold Kemball, the assistant political resident in the Gulf in 1842, observed in the course of a lengthy report on the Gulf slave trade:

> The treatment of the slaves is at no time either severe or cruel, but they are [at] most compelled to rough it during the sea voyage, when they are very scantily clothed and supplied with but sufficient food, and that coarse, to keep them alive. From the moment of purchase at their eventual destination, however, their condition is materially changed for the better, the purchasers in general feeding and treating them almost as kindly as the members of their own families; they in return work hard, willingly and well, and appear to be happy and contented – unless indeed they become the property of other slave merchants

---

8 [I.O.] Enclos. To Sec. Letters from Bombay, vol. 38, enclose. 6 to Sec. Letter 97 of 30 November 1841, Captain S. Hennell, no. 101 Pol. Dept., Kharg Island, 31 August 1841.

from the interior, when their condition remains much the same. In travelling from one place to another they are supplied with mules. In the boats they are not bound or manacled.

The *sidi* men are employed in hard or outdoor work, the women in cooking, bringing water, etc., and, but very rarely, as concubines, except by the poorer and lower classes. Children born in bondage are free but are nevertheless provided for by the owners of their parents, and with them entitled to the same rights and privileges.

The Hubshee [*habashi,* i.e. Abyssinian] slaves of both sexes are at all times much cared for, well clothed and well fed. The males are early sent to school, and having learnt to read and write, are employed in the performance of house duties, etc., and very frequently, if intelligent, in the most trustworthy situations, as supercargo of ships, stewards, and superintendents. The females are most generally retained as concubines, or employed in the lightest duties, as attendants in Harems, bringing Calleoons [water-pipes], etc. The intelligence and honesty of Hubshee slaves are almost proverbial. The children by these concubines are heirs equally to the estate of the Father with his legitimate offspring.

Nubian and Hubshee eunuchs are very highly prized, and only to be seen in the service of the King [of Persia], nobles, and very rich merchants.[9]

There was no vital or fundamental economic interest at stake, as there was in the Americas, in the perpetuation of slavery in the Muslim world. The institution was as old as the Middle East itself, and the Koran both acknowledged its prescriptive nature and endowed it with religious

---

9 [Public Record Office, London] Foreign Office series 84 (Slave Trade), vol. 426, Lieutenant A.B. Kemball to Lieutenant-Colonel H.D. Robertson (Officiating Resident), Kharg Island, 8 July 1842, enclosed in Lieutenant-Colonel Justin Sheil (H.B.M. charge d'affaires, Tehran), no. 54, Tehran, 1 September 1842. Lady Sheil made a similar observation in her memoirs some years later. 'It is believed that in general, cruelty, or even harshness, is rarely practised towards slaves in Persia. Their customary treatment is similar to that of the other servants of a family, or even something better, particularly when they happened to be Nubees [Nubians] or Habeshees.' (*Glimpses of Life* and *Manners in Persia*, London, 1856, p. 244.)

sanction. The *shari'ah*, the law of Islam, recognized as lawful both the retention in servitude of the offspring of slave parents and the enslavement of infidels captured in the holy war (*jihad*). At the same time, however, the Koran enjoined upon Muslims the humane treatment of their slaves, and it recommended their emancipation as an act of exceptional merit. The practice of manumission, whether by the outright grant of freedom by master to slave or by a contract between them for the slave to purchase his freedom, inevitably created a need for the constant replenishment of the slave population; and the need was reinforced by the widespread application of the provision in Muslim law that the child of a female slave and a free-born master should be regarded as free. The supply of slaves, therefore, had to be maintained by *jihad* on the frontiers of Islam or by their commercial acquisition under the fiction of *jihad*, *i.e.* obtained from foreign lands (*dar al-harb*). Muslim jurisprudence (*fiqh*) recognised as lawful the enslavement of infidel captives and of Muslims who were already slaves at the time of their capture. A free-born Muslim could not, in theory, legally be made a slave, although there have been several instances in Muslim history where the members of a fanatical Muslim sect have enslaved other Muslims on the grounds that they were not true believers but infidels (*kafirs*). There was, however, no clear denunciation in *fiqh*, backed by systemtic sanctions, of the kidnapping and sale, as opposed to capture in war, of free persons (*hurr*), whether Muslim or non-Muslim, thus leaving legal loopholes for the enslavement, for example, of Somalis, who were Muslim and *hurr*, or of Abyssinians, who were Christian and *hurr*. Similarly, although the castration of young slaves to meet the demand for eunuchs (*tawashi*) was deplored in principle, the practice was unrestrained by legal penalties.

A slave was regarded by the *shari'ah* both as a chattel and as a person. He could be bought, sold, jointly owned, hired out, given away or inherited. According to the classification of property in *fiqh*, he ranked with livestock and the new-born infants of slave mothers, other than those fathered by their Muslim masters, were regarded, like the progeny of animals, as the property of their parent owners. Yet there were important provisions in *fiqh* for the consideration of slaves as persons. As one leading authority has expressed it, 'The Islamic law of slavery is patriarchal and belongs more to the law of family than to the law of property.'[10] All four Sunni law schools evolved elaborate codes of embodying the rights and responsibilities of slaves and their masters. These regulated the personal life of the slave, defined his religious status, determined his judicial standing and competence, and stipulated the limits within which he was entitled to

10 Joseph Schacht, *An Introduction to Islamic Law*, Oxford, 1964, p. 130.

marry, raise children, and hold property. The rights and duties of masters were likewise elaborated, especially with respect to female concubinage which was in most cases the principal purpose for which slaves were acquired. The structure of Islamic Law pertaining to slavery, therefore, was complex, yet for all its complexity it could not obscure the presumption which underlay every aspect of it, *viz.* that the slave was, in fact, inferior to the free man, whatever spiritual equality he might theoretically possess in the brotherhood of Islam.

The legality of slavery as affirmed by the *shari'ah* was much used in argument by Muslim rulers in the nineteenth century to justify the continuance of the institution in their dominions and to reject representations from the European powers for its abolition. Thus in 1846 Muhammad Shah of Persia met a request from the British minister at his court for the closing of his ports on the Gulf to the slave trade with the reply: '....The purchase and sale of negro men and women are sanctioned by the precepts of our resplendent faith, and we cannot therefore issue commands to the people of Persia that that which is lawful by the law should be unlawful to them.'[11] When the minister, Lieutenant-Colonel Justin Sheil, pointed out that the slave trade was abominated by all the civilised powers of Europe, the Shah remarked: 'If according to their religion the traffic is considered an abominable practice, in our religion it is lawful; why then should the things our Prophet has made lawful to us be imputed detestable?'[12] Sheil did not raise the matter again until the spring of 1847, by which time he had fortified himself with a legal opinion obtained from six of the leading Shi'i divines, or *mujtahids*, of Tehran to the effect that the slave trade was 'an abomination' and that the Prophet himself had declared 'the seller of men to be the worst of men'. The Shah reputed this argument with the simple assertion that 'proselytism overcame every other consideration'. To prohibit the slave trade, he said, would be contrary to the sacred law, 'in as much as multitudes of people would be prevented from becoming Mussulmans, the penalties of which violation of the law equalled the rewards of those who obtained converts to Islam.'[13] Support for his view was afforded by the chief *mujtahid* of Najaf, the holy Shi'i city in Iraq, to whom the British consul-general at Baghdad had applied, at Sheil's request, for an opinion on the legality of the slave trade. Although the slave trade, the *mujtahid* explained, might be regarded as an 'unbecoming' activity, there was 'no warrant in Mohammedan law for sanctifying or even for pronouncing

---

11 [P.R.O.] F.O./84/647, Sheil, S.T. no. 2, Tehran, 31 December 1846, and enclosures.
12 *Ibid.*
13 [P.R.O.] F.O.84/692, Sheil, S.T. no. 4, Tehran, 27 April 1847.

commendable the prohibition of an act to which is merely attached this qualified condemnation'. The transport of slaves, he went on, 'is nowhere condemned, or even reprobated, in the Koran or Traditions. All acts are lawful except those which are condemned on revealed authority. The temporal power cannot forbid a lawful act, consequently the prohibition in question would be illegal'.[14]

There was, of course, more than a pinch of sophistry present in such arguments, and even more so in the uses to which they were put. The cure of souls was not the prime motive for the procurement of slaves by Persians, Turks and Arabs, however much Muslim jurists might profess it in their discourses. The real purpose was much less noble, as the British vice-consul at Jeddah had occasion to point out with some asperity in 1878. The vice-consul, A.B. Wylde, had been asked by a Persian army officer visiting the Hijaz for the *hajj* (pilgrimage) for a certificate of attestation that three slaves which he had recently purchased—an Abyssinian girl of fourteen and two Sudanese eunuchs aged thirteen and fourteen respectively—were in fact domestic servants travelling with him. The officer, a certain Ardashir Khan, intended to sail from Jeddah for Bushire on the Austrian Lloyd steamer *Arethusa*, and he wanted the certificate as a safeguard lest the steamer be stopped and searched *en route* by a British cruiser on anti-slave-trade patrol. 'I consider this transaction', Wylde observed,

> as one of the very worst type, namely the traffic in mutilated human beings, purchased for servants of the harem, or for the worst of immoral crimes ....It may be said and argued by those interested that Arda Sheer Khan only bought these slaves for philanthropic motives to improve their condition. This I do not believe. What can a man of his standing [his father was a general in the suite of the shah] want with these slaves? And if the slaves wish to stay with him it will only be encouraging others to run human beings from the opposite coast to satisfy the wants of wealthy people and foster the Slave Trade in its most degraded form.[15]

There were even worse degradations arising from the commerce in human beings, which no amount of casuistry could explain away. Captain

---

14 Same series and volume, Lieutenant-Colonel T. Farrant (charge d'affaires), S.T. no.2, Tehran, 18 December 1847, enclosing Major H.G. Rawlinson to Sheil, Baghdad, 8 November 1847.
15 [P.R.O.] F.O.84/1510, Wylde, S.T. no. 3, Jeddah, 26 February 1878.

Hamerton, the British consul at Zanzibar, told an officer of the Bombay Marine in 1843 that when he had taken up his appointment two years previously he had found that it was the practice for dying slaves to be thrown onto the beach in front of the town, there to be devoured by dogs.

> He one day came upon a scene which aroused every feeling of his mind: four dogs were devouring a young female who had died in child-birth. Parturition not having been effected, the dogs were completing it, two wallowing in the womb, and two tearing the breasts away. The Mahomedans look on with perfect indifference at such a scene. 'She is only a slave,' they say. They are accustomed to such sights ....[16]

Hamerton protested in the strongest terms to the ruler, Saiyid Sa'id, against this shocking incident, and secured from him a promise that in future all slaves should receive burial at their deaths.

The first move towards restricting the slave trade from east Africa was made by Great Britain after the Napoleonic Wars. Mauritius (Île de France), the principal island of the Mascarenes, had been occupied by British troops in 1810, and it was formally ceded to Britain by France at the peace settlement. A flourishing trade in slave labour for the plantations of Mauritius and the neighbouring island of Bourbon (later Réunion), which France had retained, had been carried on for some years with Madagascar and, to a lesser extent, Zanzibar. The importation of slaves into British possessions and the participation of British ships and subjects in the slave trade had been declared illegal by acts of parliament in 1807 and 1811. The slave trade was also forbidden to French subjects and territories by acts of the French legislature in 1817 and 1818. A concerted drive by the French and British governors of Bourbon and Mauritius against the slave trade from Madagascar after 1817 brought this branch of the traffic to a halt; but slaves continued to be smuggled from Zanzibar into the two colonies by French and Arab slavers. To cripple this trade the governor of Mauritius proposed in 1821 that the ruler of Muscat and Zanzibar, Saiyid Sa'id, should be asked to conclude a treaty forbidding both the sale of slaves in his dominions to Christians and their transport in Arab vessels to

---

16 [I.O.] Enclos. To Sec. Letters from Bombay, vol. 60, enclose. 5 to Sec. Letter 54 of 18 August 1843, Lieutenant W. Christopher to Captain Stafford Haines (Political Resident, Aden), no. 7 of 10 May 1843.

European possessions. The proposal was accepted in London and a treaty embodying the governor's suggestions was concluded at Muscat in September 1822 by Captain Fairfax Moresby of the Royal Navy. Arab vessels engaged in the slave trade were required, on passage from Africa to Arabia, to keep to the west and north of a line drawn from Cape Delgado on the African coast to a point two degrees east of the island Socotra and thence to Diu Head on the coast of Kathiawar. Any vessel found with slaves on board to the east or south of this line, unless driven there by stress of weather, would be seized by ships of the Royal Navy and subjected to the penalties prescribed for British ships found engaged in the trade.

While the Moresby treaty was effective in reducing the slave trade from east Africa to the Mascarenes it did little to hamper the operations of the trade elsewhere in the Indian Ocean. Ships of the Royal Navy rarely visited African or Arabian waters, and what few could be spared for anti-slave-trade patrolling duties were allocated to the west African station. Only the cruisers of the Bombay Marine frequented the Arabian Sea with any regularity, a fact of which Saiyid Sa'id had not been unmindful when he restricted to the Royal Navy the grant of the right of search and seizure of 'Omani *dhows* found to the east of the Moresby line. The British authorities in India were well aware of the largely ineffectual nature of the treaty but they were reluctant to seek to amend it lest they offend Muslim opinion unduly and thereby endanger the political foothold which they had acquired in the Persian Gulf during and since the Napoleonic Wars. Their reluctance was increased rather than decreased in the late 1820s and early 1830s when Russia began to exert pressure upon both the Ottoman and Persian empires in an apparent endeavour to obtain an outlet to the Mediterranean and perhaps the Persian Gulf. Fears of an eventual Russian threat to the British dominions in India led Britain in these years to evolve a policy of upholding the political and territorial integrity of the Ottoman and Persian empires as a barrier to the southward advance of Russia, and as a safeguard to both the 'direct' route to India through Turkish Iraq and the Gulf, and the 'overland' route through Egypt and the Red Sea. The policy required that nothing should be done to weaken the governments of the sultan and the shah, least of all by interfering with long established social and religious institutions, and this requirement was observed, by and large, throughout the 1830s. With the resolution in Britain's favour of the great eastern crisis of 1839-40, which had been precipitated by the revolt of the powerful viceroy of Egypt, Mehmet 'Ali Pasha, against the Sultan, the constraint was to some degree lessened; and the British foreign secretary of the day, Lord Palmerston, who had been the architect of Mehmet 'Ali's defeat and the subsequent diminution of Russian influence at Constantinople, now felt himself able to proceed with the accomplishment of a task which had already become, and would remain, a dominant passion in his life – the destruction of the slave trade wherever it might be found.

There were, unfortunately, large and numerous obstacles in the way of the fulfilment of this noble aspiration, especially in the Ottoman empire. When Palmerston instructed the British ambassador to the Sublime Forte, Lord Ponsonby, towards the close of 1840 to press the sultan to end the slave trade throughout the empire, Ponsonby replied:

> I have mentioned the subject and I have been heard with extreme astonishment accompanied with a smile at a proposition for destroying an institution closely interwoven with the frame of society in this country, and intimately connected with the Law and with the habits and even the religion of all classes, from the Sultan himself down to the lowest peasant.

> The Sultans for some centuries past have never married, and the Imperial Race is perpetuated by mothers who are slaves. In all other families, slaves may be, and often are, the mothers of legitimatized children who are in all respects as much esteemed as those of legal wives.

> The Admirals, the Generals, the Ministers of State in great part have been originally slaves. In most families the slaves enjoy the highest degree of confidence and influence with the head of the house.

> To carry what your Lordship desires into execution, it will be necessary to limit the law of succession to the Crown and alter the policy that has so long guided the Sultans in that respect, and also to change fundamentally the political and civil institution and laws and domestic arrangements of the people. Universal confusion would perhaps be the consequence of such violent changes, and probably those persons intended to be most benefited by them would be the greatest sufferers....

> I think that all attempts to effect your Lordship's purpose will fail, and I fear they might give offence if urged forward with importunity.

The Turks may believe us to be their superiors in the Sciences, in Arts, and in Arms, but they are far from thinking our wisdom or our morality greater than their own.[17]

Ponsonby's remarks applied only to the trade in Circassians and Georgians, the white slave trade, but there were political objections also to any drastic interference with the black slave trade in Africans and Abyssinians. Lord Auckland, the governor-general of India, summed them up early in 1842:

.....The British Government, if with a view only to the eventual suppression of all trade in slaves between the coast of Africa and India and the countries bordering on the Persian Gulf and the Red Sea, must shape its measures in such a manner as not to enlist against its cause the whole of the maritime tribes in those quarters, and thereby destroy its own influence for the gradual promotion of this and other objects of enlightened policy; and must trust to time and favourable circumstances for the accomplishment of its humane views, rather than to a course of violent and arbitrary proceedings which would unite against us the interests, habits and feelings of all the states and communities along the shores of the Gulf. Other Powers are ready to take advantage of the prejudices against us which the belief of our resolution everywhere to suppress slavery is calculated to excite among the tribes of eastern Africa and Arabia; and ..... the existence of our influence among them is liable to be endangered by such a belief; ..... the delay of a few years in the final extinction of this traffic is a far less evil than the annihilation of that political influence by which the British Government may fairly hope to effect so much for the cause of humanity in the vast uncivilized regions of eastern Africa.[18]

The idea of delay, however, was not to Palmerston's taste, nor to that of his successor as foreign secretary, Lord Aberdeen, who at the close of 1841 instructed Captain Hamerton at Zanzibar to inform Saiyid Sa'id

---

17 [P.R.O.] F.O.84/333, Ponsonby, S.T. no. 1, Therapia, 27 December 1840.

18 [I.O.] Enclos. To sec. Letters from Bombay, vol. 43, enclose. To Sec. Letter 29 of 30 March 1842, Secy. To Gov.-Gen., Fort William, to Pol. Secy. To Govt., Bombay, no.110 Sec. Dept., 28 February 1842.
[P.R.O.] F.O.84/444, Hamerton, no. 5 Sec. Dept., Zanzibar, 5 January 1842.

that the British government were determined to bring an end to the slave trade from east Africa. When Hamerton conveyed the message to Sa'id he was thunderstruck by it. 'Now all is over!' he exclaimed. 'This letter and the orders of Azrael – the angel of death – are to the Arabs one and the same thing!'[19] He and his subjects in both 'Oman and east Africa, he declared, would be economically ruined, and he himself would incur the abiding hostility of his fellow Muslim rulers. Confident that the British would relent if they were made to understand fully the consequences of what they were proposing, Sa'id sent a personal envoy to London in 1842 to plead his case. It was to no avail, and in October 1845 he was made to affix his signature to a treaty prohibiting the export of slaves from Zanzibar and his possessions on the African mainland. A concession was made over the importation of slaves from the mainland into Zanzibar after Sa'id had pleaded, and had been reluctantly supported in his plea by Hamerton, that the sudden deprivation of labour for the island's agriculture would virtually destroy it.

To stop the trade at its northern end required the co-operation of the Trucial shaikhs, the shah of Persia, and the Ottoman sultan. Engagements had already been taken from the five Trucial shaikhs in 1838 and 1839 to respect the Moresby Line when transporting slaves from Africa, and to desist from kidnapping and enslaving Somalis. Eighteen months after the conclusion of the treaty with Saiyid Sa'id the shaikhs, along with the ruler of Bahrain, agreed to prohibit their subjects from engaging in the slave trade and to grant rights of search and seizure of their *dhows* to the ships of the Bombay Marine and the Royal Navy. The sultan and the shah proved less tractable. An approach was made to the sultan, 'Abdul Nejid, in January 1847 to ascertain whether he would consent to the closing of the Turkish ports in the Gulf to the trade. The timing was deliberate, since the sultan had that very month ordered the closure of the public slave market in Constantinople. Now he felt constrained by this action to agree to the dispatch of a *firman* or imperial rescript, to the *vali* (governor-general) of Baghdad forbidding the transport of slaves from east Africa, by Turkish subjects or in Turkish ships, to the ports of Turkish Iraq, and granting to British ships of war rights of search and seizure, on condition that any vessels detained should be handed over to the Turkish authorities at Basra for condemnation. However, the sultan stipulated that the *firman's* existence should be kept secret, lest the Russians should use it to demand an end to the trade in Circassians. The *firman* was, for all practical purposes, worthless. It did not ban the actual importation of slaves into Turkish Iraq, and

19 [P.R.O.] F.O.84/444, Hamerton, no. 5 Sec. Dept., Zanzibar, 5 January 1842.

the only vessels under Turkish colours involved in the trade came from Kuwait, whose exact relationship with the Ottoman empire was obscure. Most slaves, moreover, were brought up to Basra in Arab or Persian *dhows*.

Similar difficulties were encountered at Tehran when Muhammad Shah was asked to prohibit the slave trade at Persia's ports in the Gulf. The shah's objections, as noticed earlier, were primarily religious in nature, and two years were consumed in argument before he eventually agreed, in June 1848, to issue a *firman* closing his ports on the Gulf to the trade. Three years later his son and successor, Nasir ud-din Shah, conceded to British ships of war the right of search and seizure of Persian vessels implicated in the trade, on condition that Persian officers accompanied British cruisers on anti-slave-trade patrols, and that any Persian vessels seized should be handed over to the governors of the Persian ports for trial and condemnation. As with the sultan, it was the presence of Russia in the background which determined the nature of the condition attached by the shah to the concession. Some years previously the Russians had used the pretext of suppressing piracy and slave raiding by the Turcomans along the shores of the Caspian Sea to extend their influence into Persia's northern provinces; and it was a further infringement of Persian sovereignty, under the same pretext, in the summer of 1851 which led the shah to offset Russia's new gain in the Caspian by a further concession to Britain in the Gulf.

None of these agreements had any real effect upon the slave trade from east Africa. Although slaves could no longer be sold legitimately at Zanzibar for shipment abroad, they could be, and were, smuggled out of the island, and mainland ports opposite, on much the same scale as they had been legally exported earlier. Saiyid Sa'id made a creditable effort to honour his undertakings in the 1845 treaty, as creditable as could be expected from a ruler to whom these undertakings were as repugnant on personal and religious grounds as they were subversive both of his country's well-being and of his own authority over his subjects. Neither the Ottoman sultan nor the shah made a comparable effort to meet their obligations under the treaties they had concluded, which was hardly surprising [nor should it have been an occasion for surprise that they did so]. An institution as venerable as slavery, so inextricably bound up with religious sentiment and so much a part of the fabric of Muslim society, could not be lightly tampered with by a Muslim ruler, even if he had the desire to do so. And while slavery endured, so, too, would the slave trade. On occasions Muslim authorities did co-operate with British naval or political officers in the Gulf and the Red Sea, particularly in the apprehension of slavers, but they were, as a rule, motivated less by considerations of humanity or regard for the sanctity of treaties than by a desire to mollify the representatives of a power, whose occasional eccentricities, however illogical or baffling they might seem, did not detract from its weight and influence in the politics of Asia.

Calculations of a similar kind influenced the Trucial shaikhs and the ruler of Bahrain in their observance of their engagements, together with the knowledge that they were more vulnerable to naval retaliation should they fail to honour their obligations than were the sultan and the shah. Naval resources, however, were what the British, in fact, lacked when it came to enforcing the slave-trade treaties. It was a rare occasion when a cruiser of the Bombay Marine, still less a ship of the Royal Navy, could be spared for exclusively anti-slave-trade duties. Indeed there were barely half-a-dozen instances, in the twenty years following the conclusion of the 1845 treaty with Muscat, of a ship being detached to cruise against the trade. Perhaps the only real and permanent success gained after 1845 was the virtual annihilation of the slave trade to India, and this was accomplished, not by naval patrols or by the co-operation of the signatories of the treaties, but by the abolition of the status of slavery throughout British India in the great legal reforms of the early 1840s, and by the extension of British rule over Sind and other territories which had hitherto lain outside the Company's borders. As time wore on, it became all too obvious that the Palmerstonian policy of treaty-making backed by naval patrolling, well-intentioned though it was, had been a failure; not so much because of the non-fulfilment by the Muslim states of their undertakings, common failing though it was, or because of the lack of ships to enforce the treaties at sea, but because the slave trade could only be destroyed, as several British political and naval officers with experience of African and Arabian waters had pointed out at the very outset of the campaign in 1840-41, by striking at its source – and its source lay not in Persia, Arabia, India or Turkey but in East Africa and Abyssinia.[20]

The slave trade of Abyssinia, as in most of Africa, had its origins in innumerable wars among its tribal inhabitants, in outbreaks of famine and disease, and in the migrations of racial groups and offshoots to which these disasters gave rise. Slavery itself was endemic in Abyssinian society although its incidence and nature varied in the northern, western and

---

20 For a fuller description of the diplomatic and naval campaigns of the 1840s and 1850s, see Sir Reginald Coupland, *East Africa and Its Invaders*, Oxford 1938, chapter xvi, and Kelly, *Britain and the Persian Gulf*, chapter xiii.

southern parts of the country. Tigré and Gondar were not in the strictest sense slave states, although in Tigré captives taken in war (mostly pagan Shankalla, a Nilotic people) were made to labour seven years according to the Mosaic law. The southern kingdom of Shoa, on the other hand, was intrinsically a slave society, the consequence, to a great extent, of its long and ultimately debasing contact with the Galla peoples and the Muslim slavers of the coast. Pagan Galla tribes from the south had been migrating northwards and eastwards since the sixteenth century, warring on the one side with the Abyssinian Christian kingdoms, and on the other with the Somali, a kindred people, by whom in the course of time they were defeated and scattered and driven from their lands. The Somali conquest did not cease until the third quarter of the nineteenth century, by which time they had subjugated the whole coastal region north of the Tana River. The Galla warred as much among themselves as they did with others, and their conflicts after a while acquired a fanatical tinge as some of them were converted to Christianity, and others to Islam, while the rest remained pagan. A predominantly nomadic people, with little but cattle and grain to exchange for merchandise, they early fell into the habit of selling captives taken in war.

It was through these interminable wars of the Galla, particularly in the country south of Lake Zwai and the Kaffa region further westward, that the supply of slaves for the Shoan market was kept up. Captives obtained by war or barter were taken up to the Shoan capital, Ankobar, or to Debra Libanos, to be disposed of on the domestic market or sent down to the coast for sale to Arab or Dankali slavers, who were in turn financed by *banians* resident in the coast towns. There were three main routes from the highlands to the coast: one ran from Ankobar north-eastwards through the Aussa country to Tajura and Zeila; another ran through the Dankali country to Rahitha, Assab and Bailul; while the third ran northward through the country of the Wollo Galla and along the flanks of the Tigréan highlands to Massawa. There was also a direct route from the Enarya country, south of Shoa, to Harar and on to the coast at Berbera.

Although Tigré and Gondar were not slave societies they nevertheless participated in the traffic and profited from it, through the imposition of transit dues on slave caravans and, in the case of Gondar, by conducting slave raids into the Shankalla country east of the Nile. These activities were curbed to some extent by the occupation of Sennar in 1820 by the expedition sent into the Sudan by Mehmet 'Ali Pasha to hunt for slaves; but considerable numbers of slaves still continued to pass along the route from Sennar to Gondar, and on through Tigré to Adowa and Massawa. There was another route from Sennar which ran through Gedaref and Kassala, along which Nubians, procured in Kordofan and Darfur, were taken to the Red Sea coast at Suakin. Wars among the tribes, especially in the south between the Galla and the Danakil, often cut one of the routes for a season or two, but the trade never suffered any serious disruption for any length of time.

Most of the slaves who travelled by the northern routes came from tribes to the east of the Nile. The greater part of those who came through Shoa were pagan and Christian Galla, Shankalla and others, from the regions of Enarya, Guragué, Sidama, Ludama and Kaffa. Males were classified for purposes of sale as *baligh* (post-pubescent), *khumasi* (about 3ft. 9ins. tall), *sudasi* (about a foot taller), and *tawashi* (eunuchs). Females were divided into *baligh*, *murahakah* (near puberty), and *mas'ha* (flat-breasted). The greater part of the trade was in children. The slave *kafilahs*, or caravans, from Ankobar and Debra Libanos normally did not start for the coast until the appearance of the new moon in September, on the eve of the opening of the trading season in the Red Sea and the Gulf of Aden. They were escorted by Dankali tribesmen, most of whom were nominally Muslim and who acted as brokers for the coastal traders. As well as slaves, the *kafilahs* brought down gold-dust, ivory, ostrich feathers, senna, madder, civet, gums, myrrh, frankincense, grains, honey, hides and cattle.

A typical slave *kafilah* was described by Captain W.C. Harris of the Bombay army, who led a British mission to Shoa in 1842-43, as follows:

Nine-tenths were females varying in age from 6 to 13 years, but chiefly very young. They were uniformly attired in dirty smocks of Abyssinian manufacture, sometimes adorned with cuffs of blue calico. Their long raven tresses, elaborately greased, were plaited into cords with tassels at the extremity, and interwoven about the head with a band of coloured thread to which were suspended clusters of cowry shells. Bead necklaces, pewter earrings, bracelets and anklets decorated the persons of most; and these forming the stock in hand of the trader are invariably resumed on each bargain effected, to be transferred to some victim hereafter to be purchased.

Each slave carried a large gourd as a water flagon, and walked the entire distance with a cheerfulness and display of endurance that was truly surprising in children, especially of such tender years. A very few only became weary or footsore, when they were mounted either on mules or camels, or provided with rude sandals of ox-hide which sufficiently protected their tender feet against the sharp lava boulders. The males, chiefly boys, were entrusted with the charge of camels, and not only readily engaged in the work but generally rendered themselves extremely useful to their owners; whilst the females, some few of whom occupied the position of temporary mistresses, either led the camels on the line of march or fetched wood and water on arriving at the halting ground.

The food consisted of four large handfuls daily of parched grain, comprising a mixture of wheat, maize and grain [sic]. No meat was ever given, even when most abundant, in consequence of all being alike unaccustomed to such diet. Each drove slept huddled together on mats upon the ground, the charge of them being vested in the most intelligent of either sex who was held responsible for the rest. During the entire march only one effected escape. This was an adult Shankalla who contrived to abscond unobserved during the night, and was supposed to have carried to the neighbouring tribe of Galla an intimation of the foray meditating against them on the part of the warriors of the caravan.

Although the greater number of these slaves were so young – and many of them extremely pretty – they did not excite that interest which might have been anticipated. Children accustomed to bad fare and harsh treatment in their own country, they very readily adapted themselves to the will of their new masters, whose obvious interest it was to keep them fat and in good spirits. In general there was nothing but singing, dancing, and romping, and even after the longest and most trying march, the greater number were in the most exuberant spirits and might rather be conjectured to be proceeding on a party of pleasure than bending their steps forever from their native land.

There were of course some surly old drivers who preferred the application of the whip to the more gentle persuasion of words, but the chastisement inflicted was generally deserved for some duty neglected, and was never very harsh or severe. There was

nothing to remind the spectator of the horror of slavery as wit-
nessed in the western world. Not a single casualty occurred,
although few caravans ever traverse the deadly Adel plains
without losing some slaves at least – by the wanton spear of the
Galla and still more by the severity of the climate.[21]

Slaves brought down by the Danakil were mostly taken to Tajura for
sale. Those brought by the route through Harar, usually by Shaikash tribesmen, were taken to Zeila or Berbera, where a great trade fair was held every
year from October to April. Slaves were one of the principal commodities
bartered at the fair, whose scope and importance may be gauged from this
description of it by an officer of the Bombay Marine in 1848:

.... The place from April to the early part of October was utterly deserted, not even a fisherman being found there; but
no sooner did the season change, than the inland tribes commenced moving down towards the coast, and preparing their
huts for their expected visitors. Small craft from the ports of Yemen, anxious to have an opportunity of purchasing before vessels from the gulf could arrive, hastened across, followed about
a fortnight to three weeks later by their larger brethren from
Muscat, Soor, and Ras el Khyma, and the valuably freighted
Bagalas from Bahrain, Bussorah, and Graen [Kuwait]. Lastly,
the fat and wealthy Banian traders from Porebunder, Manda-
vie, and Bombay, rolled across in their clumsy Kotias, and with
a formidable row of empty ghee jars slung over the quarters
of their vessels, elbowed themselves into a permanent position
in the front tier of craft in the harbour, and by their superior
capital, cunning, and influence soon distanced all competitors.

During the height of the fair, Berbera is a perfect Babel, in
confusion as in languages: no chief is acknowledged, and the
customs of bygone days are the laws of the place. Disputes between the inland tribes daily arise, and are settled by the spear
and dagger, the combatants retiring to the beach at a short distance from the town, in order that they may not disturb the
trade. Long strings of camels are arriving and departing day
and night, escorted generally by women alone, until at a dis-

21 [I.O.] Enclos. To Sec. Letters from Bombay, vol. 58, enclose. To Sec. Letter 37 of 20
May 1843, Harris, no. 10 Sec. Dept., 6 April 1843.

tance from the town; and an occasional group of dusky and travel-worn children marks the arrival of the slave Cafila from Hurrur and Efat.

At Berbera, the Guragué and Hurrur slave merchant meets his correspondent from Bussorah, Baghdad, or Bunder Abbas; and the savage Gidrbeersi, with his head tastefully ornamented with a scarlet sheepskin in lieu of a wig, is seen peacefully bartering his ostrich feathers and gums with the smooth-spoken Banian from Porebunder, who prudently living on board his ark, and locking up his puggree, which would infallibly be knocked off the instant he was seen wearing it, exhibits but a small portion of his wares at a time, under a miserable mat spread on the beach.

By the end of March the fair is nearly at a close, and craft of all kinds, deeply laden, and sailing generally in parties of three and four, commence their homeward journey. The Soori boats are generally the last to leave, and by the first week in April, Berbera is again deserted, nothing being left to mark the site of a town lately containing 20,000 inhabitants, beyond bones of slaughtered camels and sheep, and the framework of a few huts, which is carefully piled on the beach in readiness for the ensuing year. Beasts of prey now take the opportunity to approach the sea; lions are commonly seen at the town well during the hot weather; and in April last year, but a week after the fair had ended, I observed three ostriches quietly walking on the beach.[22]

A good deal of confusion existed in these years over the exact nature and extent of the jurisdiction exercised by various rulers and states over the western shores of the Red Sea and the Gulf of Aden. The Ottoman Turks, since their conquest of Egypt and the Hijaz in the early sixteenth century, laid claim to sovereignty over both shores of the Red Sea as far as the Straits of Bab al-Mandab, but their authority on the African side, at least, was no more than nominal. Massawa was administered as part of the pashaliq of Jeddah, and its governor was appointed by the pasha; but real power in the hinterland behind Massawa was wielded by successive *naibs* (deputies) of

---

22 Lieutenant C.J. Cruttenden quoted in Richard F. Burton, *First Footsteps in East Africa*, London, 1856, pp. 408-10.

Arkiko, who had received an annual stipend from the Turks since the original conquest in the sixteenth century. When Mehmet 'Ali of Egypt was invested with the governorship of the Hijaz after his defeat of the Wahhabis in the second decade of the nineteenth century, Massawa passed under his control. He lost it in 1840-41, when the settlement of the eastern crisis of those years divested him of the governorship of the Hijaz, only to regain it in 1847 when he managed to persuade the Sublime Porte to transfer the town to the vilayet of Egypt. Two years later, on Mehmet 'Ali's death, Massawa was re-attached by the Porte to the pashaliq of Jeddah.

To the south of Massawa the coastal plain of Abyssinia, the inhabitants of which, in the main, were Arabicized and Islamicized, was controlled by a number of petty though grandiosely titled 'sultans' and 'amirs'. Beyond, in the highlands, the Christian kingdoms of Tigré, Gondar and Shoa held sway. As Massawa was Tigré's natural outlet to the sea, so Zeila, on the Gulf of Aden, was the natural outlet of Shoa. In the early decades of the nineteenth century Zeila was a dependency of Mocha, in the Yemen, as doubtless it had been for the greater part of its existence. The *Periplus of the Erythraean Sea*, for example, records that in the first century A.D. Mocha controlled the coast opposite, both within and beyond the Straits of Bab al-Mandab.[23] The tiny sultanate of Tajura, to the west of Zeila, was in turn a dependency of Zeila. By the early 1840s the ruler of Berbera, Shaikh 'Ali Shermakhi, had come to wield authority over Zeila, the revenues of which he farmed from the Sharif of Mocha. The Sharif himself was nominally subject to the Zaidi Imam of San'a.

Possibly as many as 2,000 slaves were shipped from Zeila and Tajura each year in the middle decades of the nineteenth century, and almost half as many from Berbera. Most of those sold at Berbera were shipped in Arab and sometimes Indian vessels to the ports of the Hadramaut, the Persian Gulf and western India. Those exported from Zeila and Tajura were carried in small craft (*sambuqs*, etc) manned by Arabs, Danakil and Somalis, up the coast to Rahitha, just inside the straits, from which point they are run across to Mocha and Hodeida. Slaves brought down from the highlands, to the number of perhaps 2,000 per annum, were also shipped direct from Rahitha and other ports to the southward, like Bailul and Amphilla, to the Yemeni coast. A duty of $MT1.00 a head was levied upon slaves exported from Zeila and Tajura, and import and export duties of a dollar and half-a-dollar respectively were imposed at both Mocha and Hodeida.[24]

23 *Periplus*, p. 16.
24 Most of the above information has been derived from Captain Harris's report on the slave trade of Abyssinia and from reports and dispatches written in the 1840s by

Hodeida was the chief slave mart for the southern half of the Red Sea. About half the slaves landed there were sold within the Yemen (a report in 1869 estimated that of the 3,500-4,000 slaves imported from Zeila that year 2,000 remained in the country), while the other half were re-exported, mainly to Jeddah. Slaves were also shipped directly from the Abyssinian coast to ports in the Hijaz, principally Luhaiyah, Qunfidhah and Lith, from which they were later brought up to Jeddah for sale. Several hundred of the slaves re-exported from Hodeida were purchased by Arabs from the Persian Gulf, Muscat, the Hadramaut and Zanzibar, and by Indian merchants and seafarers trading to Berbera and the Yemen. The importation of Abyssinians into Muscat and the Gulf ports before 1840 was reckoned at between 700 and 1,000 per annum, and a further 500-600 were smuggled into Bombay and other Indian ports for eventual sale to buyers from Oudh and the Deccan. The trade, as elsewhere, was mainly in girls and boys, for use as concubines or household servants. The demand for eunuchs was small and confined mainly to Persia. Occasionally Somalis were kidnapped from the environs of Berbera by Arabs from the Gulf, usually Qawasim from Ras al-Khaima, even though, as seen earlier, the enslavement of free Muslims ran contrary to Islamic law.

The prices paid for Abyssinians, or *habashis*, depended as much upon their age and sex as upon the distance they were transported for sale. A young girl purchased in the markets of Shoa for $MT10-20, or at Massawa for $MT40-70, would fetch $MT85-120 at Mocha, Jeddah, Muscat or Bushire, and exceptionally attractive girls could bring anything up to $MT300 at these ports. Generally speaking, boys were sold for half the price paid for girls, although as much as $MT150-200 was obtained for young eunuchs. These prices obtained in the Arabian ports of the Red Sea throughout the greater part of the nineteenth century, and they only began to increase towards its close, partly because of the declining value of the Maria Theresa dollar, and partly because of a falling-off in supply. There

---

Captain Stafford Haines, the Political Resident at Aden, and by Lieutenants Christopher and Cruttenden of the Bombay Marine, especially those in [I.O.] Enclos. To Sec. Letters from Bombay, vols. 34, 61, 87 and 91, enclose. To Sec. Letters 59 of 17 July 1841, 59 of 26 August 1843., 48 of 11 May 1847, and 8 of 11 February 1848. See also reports by the C.M.S. missionary, J.L. Krapf, from Ankobar in January and February 1840, in the same series, vol. 24, enclose. To Sec. Letter 65 of 28 July 1840; and by Lieutenant Christopher of 7 March and 2 October 1842 in [P.R.O.] F.O.84/444. There is also an excellent report by J. Hunter, the assistant Political Resident at Aden, dated 1 November 1877, in [Parliamentary Papers] Accounts and Papers, 1878, C.2139, 'Correspondence with British Representatives and Agents Abroad, and Reports from Naval Officers, relating to the Slave Trade' (S.T. no. 3, 1878).

was, however, no spectacular or even steady rise in prices in the closing years of the century to offset the reduced numbers of slaves coming into Arabia. At Hodeida in 1875 and 1876 *habashi* boys were sold for $MT50-100 each and girls for $MT75-130. Twenty-five years later they were being sold at Jeddah for $MT80-125 and for half as much again at Mecca and Madinah. In the Persian Gulf prices remained steady until the late 1860s, when the policy of suppression adopted by the British began to take effect. A male or female *sidi* purchased at Zanzibar for $MT20-35 fetched $MT25-40 at Muscat in the 1830s and $MT40-50 at Bahrain or Bushire. Thirty years later, as Arab slavers became less and less willing to run the risk of interception by naval patrols, the numbers of slaves dwindled and prices rose steeply.[25]

Jeddah was the main port of entry for Abyssinian slaves destined for the Meccan and Madinan markets and the interior of Arabia. They were either brought up from Hodeida, Qunfidhah, Luhaiyah and Lith, or they were shipped direct from Suakin and Massawa. Most of the Nubians came through Suakin, those from the basin of the Blue Nile being brought by way of Katarif and Kassala, while those from Darfur and Kordofan were marched to Dongola or Berber on the Nile, and thence to the sea. The slaves taken down to Massawa by way of Asmara and Adowa were mainly Galla, from the south. Figures for the trade at both Suakin and Massawa are hard to come by, but 1,400-1,600 slaves were said to have been shipped from Massawa in the 1842 season.[26] A few figures are available for the slave trade of Jeddah but not enough to form a coherent pattern. The annual importation before the 1860s was said to be about 2,400, while another estimate puts the figure for the early 1860s at 12,000-15,000, and for the latter years of the decade at 2,000-2,500. Estimates made in the mid-1870s put the total number of slaves shipped across the Red Sea to the Yemen and the Hijaz as high as 30,000 annually. Up to the early 1870s some

---

25 The figures quoted, both for numbers and for prices, are derived mainly from:- [P.R.O.] F.O.84/387, Report on the Gulf slave trade by Dr T. Mackenzie (acting Political Resident), 6 October 1840; F.O. series 78 (Turkey), vol.5327, Report on the slave trade of Jeddah by Dr Abdur Razzack (vice-consul, Jeddah), 12 June 1894; same series and volume, Report on the slave trade of Jeddah by J.G. Lang (U.S. consul-general, Cairo), 27 June 1901; [Parl. Papers] Accounts and Papers, 1878, C.2139, 'Correspondence …… relating to the Slave Trade' (S.T. no. 3, 1878), report by Hunter, 1 November 1877; and Accounts and Papers, 1881, C.3052, 'Correspondence ….relative to the Slave Trade' (S.T. no.1, 1881), T.S. Jago (vice-consul, Damascus) to Sir Henry Layard (H.B.M. ambassador, Constantinople), 10 February 1880; [P.R.O.] F.O.84/1144, G.E. Stanley (consul, Jeddah), S.T. no.1,

26 [P.R.O.] F.O.84/444, Lieutenant W.C. Christopher to senior naval officer, Aden, 7 March 1842

500-600 slaves were re-exported from Jeddah to Egypt each year, although as a general rule slaves for the Egyptian market were brought down the Nile. Another 400-500 were taken to Syria with the returning *hajj* caravan every year. Most of the slaves imported into Jeddah were run across in the six weeks following the end of Ramadan, the month of fasting, so as to arrive in time for the *hajj*. Exposed for sale in the markets of Jeddah, Mecca and Madinah, they were bought in their hundreds by pilgrims from Persia, Syria, Iraq, India, and from other parts of Arabia, in particular, Najd, Kuwait and 'Oman.

The lot of slaves in Arabia, once purchased, was by no means intolerable. Wylde, the British vice-consul at Jeddah, wrote in 1877:

The evil of the slave trade is not within Hedjaz or Yemen, although these places are partly the cause of the trade. The life of the slave commencing from entering Arabia is nearly devoid of hardship, cruelty by the master to the servant is nearly unknown, and considering the enormous number of slaves, crime and cruelty compare favourably with the list of offences against law in the most civilized countries. The slave in Arabia is not looked upon as a beast of burden, he is well treated and well fed. Many of the merchants of Jeddah and Mecca were originally slaves. They fill posts of trust and their origin is no cause of reproach.[27]

Much the same conclusion was reached by the German naturalist, Wilhelm Schimper, who spent several years in the middle of the nineteenth century travelling in Arabia and Abyssinia.[28]

Up to the middle of the nineteenth century the Sublime Porte showed no disposition to interfere with the Red Sea slave trade, nor was there any good reason why it should. As Lord Ponsonby had pointed out in 1840 slavery was an intrinsic element of Ottoman society: its continuance was not only sanctioned by religion but it was also bound up with the perpetuation of the dynasty. Although preliminary enquiries into the Red Sea trade had been initiated by Palmerston in 1840-41 (one of the purposes of the mission under Captain Harris to the court of Sahela Selassie of Shoa in 1842 was to investigate the extent of the Abyssinian slave trade), there

27 [P.R.O.] F.O.84/1482, Wylde, S.T. no. 2, Jeddah, 29 May 1877.
28 [P.R.O.] F.O.84/1304, Memo. By Schimper, Adowa, 25 August 1868.

was a reluctance on the part of the British government to proceed further, partly because of the jurisdictional confusion prevailing in the lower half of the Red Sea, but also because of the need to avoid giving offence to Muslim religious feeling in the most sacred of all Islamic lands—the Hijaz. Thus the only step taken against the Red Sea trade after 1841—the securing of the firman of 1847 forbidding Turkish ships and subjects to import slaves into the ports of Turkish Iraq—only affected it at a far remove.

It was not until after the outbreak of the Crimean War that the British broached the subject again at Constantinople. In October 1854 the British ambassador to the Porte, Lord Stratford de Recliffe, suggested to the sultan that he should forbid the taking of women and children from Georgia as slaves, and that Circassians should be dissuaded from selling their own children and stealing those of others for sale. The sultan accepted the suggestion and issued a *firman*. The trade, however, continued much as before, for reasons which another British ambassador, Sir Henry Elliot, was to explain some years later:

> I trust not to be taken as an apologist for this detestable institution if I observe that in the White Slave Trade it is found in its mildest form. The slaves are seldom taken by fraud or by force, a greater number of them being bought as children from parents who sell them with the sincere intention of bettering their condition.

> Monstrous and unnatural as this is, the parents are right in believing that it ensures for their children a position far above their own in the social scale; they generally receive the best education that is given to Turkish girls and become eligible as wives not only for the greatest Pashas but for the Sultan himself..........

> Their condition does not in this country bear with it the slightest stigma of degradation, and I believe that it may truly be affirmed that the social distance between the Turkish Slaves and their mistresses is not so great as it is between the free servants and mistresses in Christian countries.[29]

The trade in black slaves, however, was another matter, and one

29 [P.R.O.] F.O.84/1305, Elliot, S.T. no. 16, Therapia, 27 October 1869.

which the British government felt less inhibited in attacking, especially after the critical period of the Crimean War had passed. At the close of 1856 Palmerston, who was now prime minister, instructed the British ambassador to the Porte to bring pressure upon the sultan to ban the shipment of black slaves across the Mediterranean and their importation into the Ottoman dominions. A *firman* along these lines was issued in January 1857. Its purpose was primarily to suppress the traffic in black slaves through Egypt, but at the close of 1857 the Porte sent a vizirial letter to the pasha of Jeddah instructing him to apply the ban to the Red Sea trade. When the sultan's *firman* was read publicly at Mecca a riot broke out, and the *qadi* (judge) who had read it was murdered by the mob along with several other Ottoman officials. Thereafter the *firman* remained a dead letter in the Hijaz, except when a conscientious *vali* made an occasional quixotic attempt to enforce it at Jeddah.

The Porte was far from being dishonest in its professions of good faith about ending the black slave trade, but it was helpless against the extent of religious feeling surrounding the trade, and against the insubordination of so many Ottoman officials in distant places who were themselves, as often as not, implicated in it. Moreover, the growing incidence of manumission in Turkey proper, praiseworthy though it might have been, created a continual shortage of slaves for domestic work and a consequent need for their replacement. The predicament was summed up in a dispatch from Sir Henry Elliot to the Foreign Office in 1869.

> Here it is usual to give the slaves their freedom after about seven years' service, and the number of children born of slaves, and so slaves by birth, is comparatively very small; but this practice of manumission (however creditable to the humanity of the Turks) by leading to the necessity of their introduction from Africa, and to all the accompanying horrors of the slave hunts, causes far more suffering than if the women were kept in their domestic slavery and became the mothers of children who would succeed them in the service of their masters.[30]

The first determined attack upon the Red Sea slave trade came about as a consequence of the campaign undertaken by Britain in the 1870s to put an end, once and for all, to the trade from east Africa. Muscat and Zanzibar had been separated from each other in 1861 by the so-called

---

30 Same series and volume, Elliot, S.T. no. 2, Therapia, 10 June 1869.

Canning Award, which followed the government of India's intervention in the contest for the succession to the sultanate after the death of Saiyid Sa'id in 1856. Influenced more by calculations concerning the suppression of the slave trade than by considerations of strict legality and equity, the governor-general of India, Lord Canning, decreed in 1861 that the sultanate should be divided between two of the surviving sons of Saiyid Sa'id, that Muscat and Zanzibar should henceforth constitute separate and distinct sultanates, and that Zanzibar should pay an annual subsidy to Muscat as compensation for the loss in revenue which it would suffer from the cutting-off of its African possessions. The separation of Zanzibar from Muscat did little of itself to diminish the slave trade from east Africa. While slaves could still be shipped freely from the mainland ports to Zanzibar Island under the terms of the 1845 treaty, and while no British ships of war were regularly assigned to patrol east African coastal waters, there was nothing to prevent Arab slavers from the north from taking on cargoes of slaves from these ports or, indeed, from Zanzibar itself. Majid ibn Sa'id, the new sultan, had neither the strength nor the stomach to deal with the fierce northern Arabs who descended upon the island every season, to buy, barter for, or, preferably, steal slaves for sale in the Gulf and south Arabia. Few, if any, of these northerners, who came mainly from the Trucial Coast, 'Oman and the Hadramaut, felt themselves restrained by the undertakings given by their chiefs regarding the slave trade, nor were they in any way deterred by the fear of interception at sea by British cruisers; for the Royal Navy simply did not have the ships to patrol the vast stretches of water between Ras al-Hadd, the easternmost point of 'Oman, and the Straits of Bab al-Mandab, as between Cape Guardafui, the easternmost corner of the African continent, and the Mozambique Channel. Throughout the 1860s at least 10,000 *sidis* a year were shipped northwards from Zanzibar and the mainland ports, most of them bound for the Gulf; and a further 2,500 *habashis*, it was reckoned, were imported into the Gulf every year in defiance of every undertaking given by the Persian, Turkish and various Arab governments.[31]

The only effective way to stop the trade was to strangle it in African waters, and so in June 1873 the sultan of Zanzibar, Barghash ibn Sa'id, who had succeeded his brother Majid in 1870, was made to conclude, under some duress, a new treaty abolishing the export of slaves from his

---

31 See [Parl. Papers] Accounts and Papers, 1870, C.209, 'East African Slave Trade: Report addressed to the Earl of Clarendon by the [interdepartmental] Committee', Foreign Office, 24 January 1870; and Captain P. Colomb, *Slave Catching in the Indian Ocean*, London, 1873, pp. 47-51.

mainland possessions to Zanzibar Island or anywhere else, and closing the public slave markets. The price of his compliance was the assumption by the British government of responsibility for the payment of the annual subsidy to Muscat. Fresh undertakings were secured from the sultan of Muscat, the Trucial shaikhs, and the sheikh of Bahrain to prohibit the slave trade to their subjects, and in March 1882 a new convention was concluded with the shah of Persia confirming both the closure of his ports to the trade and its interdiction to Persian subjects and ships. The rights of search and seizure granted to British ships of war thirty years earlier were also reaffirmed. A man-o'-war was permanently stationed in Zanzibar waters from 1873 onwards to prevent the smuggling of slaves from the mainland, and after a series of grim and protracted struggles with the northern slavers, lasting the better part of a decade, the seaborne trade from the Zanzibar dominions was virtually extinguished. It was still carried on to some extent from a few ports in Mozambique, despite the best efforts of the Portuguese, in collaboration with the British, to suppress it; while further north slaves were conveyed overland to the Somali coast beyond Chisimayo, for clandestine embarkation in *dhows* from Arabia and the Red Sea.

For a number of reasons a comparable diplomatic and naval offensive could not be simultaneously mounted against the Red Sea slave trade. The opening of the Suez Canal in 1869 had enabled the Porte for the first time in many decades to make its authority felt along the Arabian coast of the Red Sea. Turkish administration of the Hijaz was tightened, and Turkish control was reasserted over the seaports and hinterland of the Yemen in 1871-72. At the same time the Porte put forward claims to suzerainty over the greater part of Arabia, claims which derived largely from the sultan's titular role as caliph of Islam, upon which increasing emphasis was being laid at Constantinople. Inevitably these activities generated a certain degree of friction with the British where their spheres of interest and influence met and overlapped those of the Porte, notably on the borders of the Yemen and the Aden protectorates, and in the Persian Gulf, where the Turks in 1871 occupied and subdued al-Hasa, the coastal region lying between Qatar and Kuwait. The atmosphere, then, in the early 1870s was not conducive to co-operation between the two governments over measures to suppress the Red Sea slave trade, especially as these measures would have required the Porte, on the one hand, to affront Muslim sentiment at a time when it was engaged in furthering the sultan's caliphal pretensions, and, on the other, to swallow its pride to the extent of allowing British warships to search vessels flying the Turkish flag and to seize any found engaged in slaving.

On the African shore of the Red Sea the Porte's activities had stirred the ambitions of the Khedive Isma'il of Egypt, who began to have Pharaonic dreams of an empire embracing the southern Sudan, the coastal lowlands of Abyssinia, and the Horn of Africa. Isma'il had in 1866 secured the transfer of Massawa (and Suakin) to the viceroyalty of Egypt, and in 1870-71 an Egyptian gunboat raised the Turkish flag over Berbera. Five years later, in August 1875, Isma'il was invested by the Porte with the governorship of Zeila and Tajura, and in November of that year Egyptian troops occupied Harar. For a time the Egyptian expansion raised British hopes that a crushing blow might soon be struck at the Abyssinian slave trade, for Isma'il had frequently professed himself opposed to slavery, and he had directed Sir Samuel Baker, at the time of appointing him governor-general of the Sudan, to apply his energies to the suppression of the slave trade. But in October 1875 an Egyptian force dispatched inland from Massawa against the Abyssinians was badly defeated on the road to Adowa, and the following month a second expeditionary force, starting from Zeila, was cut to pieces by Dankali tribesmen near Aussa on the Awash River. Though the Egyptians were to linger on at Massawa, Zeila, Tajura and Berbera for some years to come, Isma'il's African empire was now seen to be, if it had ever been other than, a mere sham.

Since the chances of stifling the Red Sea slave trade at its source now seemed remote, British efforts against it in the late 1870s were concentrated upon its Arabian outlets, and particularly upon Jeddah. For some years British representation at the port had been limited to a native agent, but in 1874 the consulate was re-established on a regular basis with a European consul and vice-consul. One of the first acts of the new consul, Captain G. Beyts, was to ask the governor to comply with the letter and spirit of previous instructions from the Porte and to close the public slave market. The governor complied, but chiefly as a means of ensuring that the consular authorities should discover as little as possible about the workings of the trade. As Jeddah was a walled town, slaves could only be brought in through one of the town gates, and it had been the practice for longer than anyone could remember for them to be landed at the customs-house gate on the seaward side. Following the closure of the slave market they were put ashore from boats some distance from the town and smuggled in through one of the gates on the landward side, to be sold clandestinely in private houses. Nearly everyone in Jeddah knew what was going on, and that the officials and guards at the gates were bribed to turn a blind eye to the traffic. Even if the governor had been disposed to clamp down on it, commercial interest married to religious sentiment would have secured its continuance. The British consul, who as a Christian and a European was an object of suspicion and dislike to the inhabitants of Jeddah, stood even less of a chance of curbing the traffic.

The only hope lay with the Porte, and so, in the spring of 1877, following the proclamation the previous December of the Ottoman constitution, with its provisions concerning the liberty of the subject, and under the shadow of Russia's declaration of war upon the Ottoman empire, the British ambassador at Constantinople persuaded the new sultan, 'Abdul Hamid, to issue an edict declaring an end to the black slave trade throughout the empire for all time. In the next three years the Porte made a real effort to enforce the ban. It bore some fruit in the Hijaz where the public slave markets at Mecca and Madinah were closed, and in Syria, where the returning hajj caravan in 1880 brought back only sixteen slaves; but as in the past it was largely frustrated by the reluctance of local officials to excite Muslim-Arab passions, and by the Porte's own inability to act against the trade at sea. After a series of protracted negotiations the Ottoman and British governments concluded a convention on the slave trade on 25 January 1880, the first such convention concluded between them on the subject. Its principal value was to grant reciprocal rights of search and seizure to British and Turkish ships of war in the Red Sea, the Persian Gulf, and adjacent waters. These rights were not extended to the Mediterranean and Black Seas, it being understood though delicately not alluded to, that the surreptitious traffic in white slaves was not to be interfered with, the exemption applying to both the traffic to Turkey proper and to Egypt, where the *khedive* and his mother were the principal slave owners, their personal households alone containing over 400 white slaves. To stop the abuse of the *hajj* for slave trading, the treaty specified that bona fide domestic black slaves accompanying their masters on pilgrimage should be issued with passports specifying their status. Any black slaves brought back from the *hajj* who did not possess such passports would be immediately freed and their possessors prosecuted for slaving. Ratification of the convention was delayed for a time as the Porte sought to amend some of its provisions, and a final version was not agreed until March 1883. Even then the Turks were slow to give it effect, and it was only in December 1889 that an edict was finally issued putting its provisions into operation throughout the empire.[32]

In practice, the regulation concerning domestic slaves making the *hajj* did little to hamper the purchase of fresh slaves by pilgrims to the Hi-

---

32 For details of the negotiations, see [P.R.O.] F.O.84/1658; and for the *khedive*'s slave-holding, F.O.84/1305, Elliot, S.T. no. 6, Therapia, 18 August 1869.

jaz. The trade was too lucrative, and too long established, for those involved in it to abandon it lightly. Instead, to get around the regulations, use was made of a stratagem whereby newly purchased slaves were equipped with certificates of manumission, issued by a *qadi* and attested by an Ottoman official or foreign consul, which enabled them to accompany their new masters on their homeward voyage and be passed off as bona fide domestic servants (in attendance upon them), should the vessel on which they were travelling be stopped and searched by a British warship. Though the British consular authorities in the Hijaz were well aware of this ruse, they were reluctant to complain about it, not only because genuine confusion could easily arise over the status of slaves but also because disputes about them between Christians and Muslims could quickly arouse religious animosity. As Wylde, the vice-consul at Jeddah, put it:

.... To interfere with slavery as recognized by their religion in their Holy Land, to prevent domestic slaves being shipped with their masters while travelling will only tend to alienate the present good feeling existing between Arabia and the English nation, and will not put a stop to the trade which can only be put an end to by preventing the importation..... To separate master from wife or servant when the Mohamedan religion justifies the purchase of slaves for wives or servants, and preventing them from keeping what is their rightful property; separating persons that have been married according to Mohamedan law, or boys that have been bought or who have a chance of filling posts of trust as many slaves do, hardly tends to bear out our reputation for justice.[33]

The death knell of the Abyssinian and east African slave trade was sounded by European penetration and occupation of eastern and northeastern Africa in the closing decades of the nineteenth century and the early years of the twentieth. The British occupation of Egypt in 1882 enabled more positive effect to be given to the convention concluded with the *khedive*'s government five years earlier, on 4 August 1877, imposing an absolute ban upon the importation of slaves into Egypt by land or sea and forbidding the transit of slaves through Egyptian territory. Slaving revived in the Sudan during the regime of the Mahdi and his successor, but it was brought to an end in the years following the defeat of the Mahdist forces

---

33 [P.R.O.] F.O.84/1482, Wylde, S.T. no. 2, Jedah, 29 May 1877.

in 1898 and the setting-up of the Anglo-Egyptian condominium in 1899. The establishment of Italian, French and British control over the African littoral of the Red Sea and the Horn of Africa at the turn of the century greatly reduced the volume and scope of the slave trade from Abyssinia. German occupation of the east African coastline north of Cape Delgado in the 1880s, and the assumption of a British protectorate over Zanzibar in 1890, sealed the ports through which slaves were being smuggled abroad; and the subsequent opening-up of the interior made the operations of the slavers increasingly precarious.

The task of suppression at sea suffered a setback in the late 1890s when 'Omani *dhows*, equipped with French flags and papers, began running illegal cargoes of slaves from the African coast across to Sur and other 'Omani ports. From 1899 to 1905 the Admiralty suspended patrolling against the trade in Arabian waters while the British and French governments argued over the question. It was eventually submitted for arbitration to the International Court of Justice at the Hague, which in August 1905 handed down a decision of an equivocal nature, unsatisfactory to both parties. Gradually, however, in the next few years, the granting of French colours to 'Omani vessels was discontinued and the Admiralty resumed anti-slave-trade patrolling.

Slavery as an institution was abolished in British East Africa in 1907, and two years later it was abolished in Zanzibar by decree of the sultan. Any infringement of the liberty of an individual had been made a criminal offence in Egypt in 1895, and a similar provision in the Ottoman constitution of 1876 was brought into operation by the Young Turks in the revolution of 1908. Neither the Germans in east Africa nor the rulers of the Arabian peninsula chose to follow suit in the years before the First World War. Slavery persisted throughout Arabia (with the exception of the British colony of Aden) and with it the slave trade, even though it was now greatly attenuated. Its persistence was made possible largely by the continued readiness of African to sell African, by the torpor of some governments, and by the indifference, and, in some cases, corruption, of their officials. Probably the worst offender in this respect was the government of Abyssinia, a Christian state which nevertheless tolerated slavery within its borders and was indifferent to the transport of its subjects beyond them, to be sold into servitude in the Hijaz and the Yemen and other parts of Arabia. An equally degenerate traffic went on in African converts to Islam, poor and simple creatures who set out from as far away as Nigeria or Senegal to make the pilgrimage to Mecca, and who, on reaching the Hijaz weary and destitute, months of even years later, fell easy victims to unscrupulous fellow Muslims who sold them into slavery.

Much has happened in the last half-century to reduce this sordid commerce in human beings. Since the Italian conquest of Abyssinia in the 1930s the slave trade from that country has shrunk to a trickle, while on the other side of the Red Sea the states of Arabia have found themselves forced by outside opinion to make placatory gestures towards its prohibition within their borders. But whether an institution such as slavery, sanctified by thirteen centuries of religious doctrine and condoned by social custom and convenience, can be eradicated by mere pronouncements, or whether the seaborne slave trade, suppressed by the diplomatic and naval exertions of Great Britain, will find new life now that British power has waned and the Royal Navy has withdrawn from Arabian waters, are questions that only a future generation of historians will be able to answer.

6

The Middle East in Revolution[1]

The Middle East in Revolution by Humphrey Trevelyan, pp. xii
+ 275, index. London: Macmillan 1970.

Lord Trevelyan's book is an account of his service as British ambassador to Egypt and Iraq and as the last high commissioner of
the short-lived Federation of South Arabia. It is, he says, 'a personal record,
based on accounts written, in each case, soon after the event . . .' He has
tried 'to be as objective as possible and serious students can treat it as evidence to be accepted or rejected, as they please'. It is because it is historical
evidence that this is an important book, and we can be doubly grateful to
Lord Trevelyan not only for affording us a glimpse of the private thoughts
of a British diplomat about events in which he has recently been involved
in an official capacity, but also for telling us something about the attitudes and assumptions current among senior officials of the Foreign Office
('This book is as much their story as my own') concerning the nature and
purpose of British policy in the Middle East in the past two decades.

The Middle East in Revolution covers the years 1955-56 in
Egypt, 1958-61 in Iraq, and 1967 in South Arabia. It is a period, Lord Trevelyan writes, which is sometimes regarded as a
period of failure in British foreign policy in the Middle East.
It should more properly be considered to have been a period

1 From *Middle Eastern Studies*, Vol. 9, No. 3 (Oct., 1973), pp. 363-370. Published by:
Taylor & Francis, Ltd. Reproduced by permission.

of difficult readjustment to changing conditions in the Arab world and changing power relationships. Those who consider it to have been a period of failure are the sentimentalists who do not understand why things should not have gone on as they were before. A more correct judgement is that though we made mistakes like everyone else involved, we have so far come through an unusually difficult and complex period without more damage to our real interests in the Middle East than was inevitable as a result of the fundamental changes in world conditions which have taken place since the end of the German war.

Sir Humphrey Trevelyan, as he then was, succeeded Sir Ralph Stevenson as British ambassador in Cairo in August 1955. His thoughts at the time about Anglo-Egyptian relations and British relations with the Arab states in general ran as follows:

We could not ignore Arab nationalism. It was strongly backed by the Afro-Asian world, which regarded itself as the anti-colonial front, by the Communists intent on winning Arab friendship and, up to a point, by the Americans, mainly for historical and sentimental reasons. The general trend of British policy in bringing colonial territories to independence was to put the nationalists into power and to make terms with them. We had either to fight it successfully, which in the long run we could not do, or to try and make such terms with it as would safeguard our real interests at a time when we had lost our old paramountcy in the Arab world . .. At the same time we had to try and get on terms with the new Egypt. Nasser might go, but the old Egypt would never come back.

'Getting on terms with Egypt.' Like the title of an old pop song it brings back memories of the 'fifties, the honeymoon period after the conclusion of the Anglo-Egyptian agreement of July 1954 which provided for the evacuation of the Canal Zone by British troops. Lord Trevelyan catches the mood well:

Evacuation was an inevitable retreat in the face of Egyptian nationalism, which grew stronger as our power in the world diminished. We did not take our Forces away from Egypt in order to strengthen our position in the Middle East, nor out of any excessive expectation of fruitful anti-Communist cooperation with Nasser, though we may have persuaded ourselves that this was a possible outcome of our action. We took them away because we could not keep them there much longer. We were only retreating from positions which had already been lost.

Unfortunately, questions kept arising between the British and Egyptian governments to disturb the harmony which Lord Trevelyan was endeavouring to create - over the Sudan, the supply of arms, the High Dam, the Suez Canal, Israel, the Baghdad Pact, and so on. To each of these subjects Lord Trevelyan allots a short chapter, so enabling him to convey more clearly to his readers an understanding of the Egyptian government's position on these various issues, its fears, its ambitions and its frustrations. His own understanding led Lord Trevelyan to sympathize with the Egyptian government in its difficulties, even when these were largely of its own making. The officers of the military regime were, after all, he explains, contending with problems which were in the main a legacy of past misrule, and their occasional headstrong acts could be attributed to their inexperience and to the humiliations which they and their fellow countrymen had formerly suffered, especially at the hands of the British. Lord Trevelyan tried hardest of all to understand Nasser, and he spends pages of his book analyzing the Egyptian leader's character, his motives and his actions. He feels that too much fuss has been made about Nasser's habitual use of subversion to attain his ends in the Arab world:

> It would be a mistake, however much we deplore in principle this generally wasteful and inefficient method of conducting international affairs, to regard his actions as a black spot in an area of purity. They should be judged in the light of a climate of opinion which considered subversion and conspiracy as a normal method of governmental operation and only condemned it when it was unsuccessful.

The policy which Lord Trevelyan believed should be pursued towards Nasser, and which he urged upon the foreign secretary, Mr Selwyn Lloyd, during the latter's visit to Cairo in March 1956, was that of 'striking a bargain' with him:

> We could not expect genuine co-operation from him in return

for it. We should have to look out for Egyptian attempts to injure our interests elsewhere in the Arab world, but we might be able to take the edge off Nasser's hostility and arrive at a modus vivendi of a sort. The alternative was to adopt a thoroughly tough policy against him. We must then expect unrelieved hostility from him. We knew that he had the power to hurt our interests. If we decided on this course, we must hit hard and accept all the serious international consequences which would follow. I recommended that we should try the first course.

Lord Trevelyan persisted in this advice in the face of increasing Egyptian hostility in the next few months.

We should not fall between two stools. We could adopt a really tough policy against increasing pressure from world opinion, or we could be cautious, keep our relations with Egypt at a low level, and try and avoid violent hostility on either side.

Although, as he concedes, the 1954 agreement was by now 'really in ruins', he insisted that the evacuation of the last British troops from the Canal Zone should be effected by the date originally agreed upon, June 18, 1956.

We had an agreement and had no valid reason for not carrying it out. [Any delay] would be immediately observable to the Egyptians, who would retaliate by again unleashing their Commandos on British troops, and we should be back to the worst days of the troubles before the 1954 Agreement, without any reasonable excuse. The Egyptians could make life impossible for the [Canal Zone] contractors. In any case, it was too late.

For all Lord Trevelyan's efforts at understanding and his hopes of an accommodation, Nasser continued to disappoint him. In a most affecting passage Lord Trevelyan describes how, in the early summer of 1956, he urged Nasser to show a more friendly countenance to Great Britain.

I argued that it was ridiculous that our public relations should be so bad. For the first time in modern history there was no specifically Anglo-Egyptian dispute. The Sudan and the Base were out of the way. The Base Agreement was being carried out harmoniously . . . Our quarrels were all on matters outside

Egypt . .. It was all very well for Nasser to say that he only reacted and never acted. That was not true. He often acted against us and we reacted ... Why could we not have a period of quiet on both sides? The British had an excellent record in dealing with territories dependent on them. They were responsive to political developments and had succeeded in adjusting their relations with many countries in Asia and Africa ... Why did he order such virulent propaganda to be put out against us? How could he hope for good relations with us if he acted like this? He accused us of being insensitive to Arab opinion. But we had a public opinion too and he was grossly insensitive to it ... Could he not make a gesture of friendship.. . ? Could we not gradually get onto better terms again?

But Nasser refused to be swayed, even by such plangent appeals as this, and Lord Trevelyan never held another conversation of any substance with him until the Suez crisis broke at the end of October.

Lord Trevelyan was shocked by the British ultimatum of October 30 and even more by his government's readiness to use force against Egypt after he had earlier warned against it, especially in view of the danger to which it would expose British subjects in Egypt. He writes:

The British Community knew well enough that the only threat to their lives and property would come from British action, which would result in the breakdown of the Egyptian Security Services ... A breakdown of internal security in the cities might have most serious consequences for Egyptians and others, for which we would bear a heavy responsibility. There was the political aspect. The British and French could not continue their occupation indefinitely. They would have to leave again. If so, the Egyptians would create the myth that they had expelled the foreign Forces and liberated themselves. The British would again figure in the Egyptian school-books, this time not only as the aggressors, but as the aggressors defeated by the Egyptian heroes. When we looked back after the event, we could not think of anything more we could usefully have said. Nor am I now inclined to think that this assessment was wrong.

One is extremely reluctant to question the considered judgement of so experienced a diplomatist as Lord Trevelyan, who was, after all, the man on the spot in Cairo in October 1956, but surely his assessment, so far as it concerned the danger to British subjects, was wrong? There was no breakdown of security when the Anglo-French attack began, no massacre of British subjects or even personal injury to them. There was, of course, sequestration of property and expulsion, but these might well have taken place in time without the pretext of military action. Indeed, they have become the commonplaces of the age in Asia and Africa. As for the second part of Lord Trevelyan's assessment, one can only, with the greatest diffidence, beg to differ about the wisdom and practicability of basing a foreign policy upon calculations regarding the future contents of school-books in other lands.

When actual hostilities commenced, Lord Trevelyan was cast into gloom. 'Why did our action coincide with the Israeli attack? Why had we so suddenly abandoned our adherence to the tripartite declaration and declared that it did not apply to the Israeli attack on Egypt?' (Understandably enough in these distressing circumstances, Lord Trevelyan has forgotten that earlier in his book he had described the tripartite declaration as 'a toothless instrument by 1955'.) The Anglo-French invasion of Egypt was for him 'a miserable business'.

> In three days, the impossible had happened. It did not seem to make sense... I was greatly affected and it was borne in on me that all that I had been trying to build was in ruins and the life that I had led no longer existed. I was not making, I wrote, a political judgement. It was a statement of fact. It was, I confess, difficult at that time not to come near to tears, not of self-pity, but of vexation and despair.

Lord Trevelyan, of course, is not the only senior British diplomatist in recent years to have revealed his shock, horror and dismay over the Suez affair. Sir William Hayter, the ambassador at Moscow in 1956, has since made public his personal feelings on receiving the text of the Anglo-French ultimatum.[2]

> As I read it I could not believe my eyes; I even began to wonder if I had drunk too much at the Kremlin. I felt quite bewildered. The action we were taking seemed to me flatly contrary to all that I knew, or thought I knew, about British policy. . . I believed that we were strongly opposed to the use of force to ob-

2 See *The Kremlin and the Embassy*, London, 1966.

tain national ends, and here we were condoning such use (even though by a friend against an enemy) and apparently preparing to use it ourselves. . . We were, too, it seemed to me, about to use it for a futile purpose. . . I lay awake most of the night wondering, not for the last time during this crisis, whether I ought not send in my resignation.

Sir William 'detested' his government's action in Egypt and he felt ashamed in the company of the other NATO ambassadors in Moscow, 'all anti-Suez to a man' - all, that is, except the French ambassador. 'I drafted several letters of resignation from the Service,' Sir William recalls of those critical days, when his country was being pilloried before the world, 'but in the end sent none of them off.'

The opposition of many permanent officials of the Foreign Office to the Suez venture has, over the years, acquired almost the stature of legend, and for long now it has been the mark of all right-thinking men on the subject of Britain's role in the Middle East that they should condemn, with appropriate expressions of grief and outrage, the Anglo-French intervention in collaboration with Israel. What strikes a mere observer on the sidelines as a little puzzling is why this particular episode should have provoked, and why it continues to provoke, such passionate remorse, such anguished protestations of guilt, and such vehement keening from those who regard the intervention as foolish or perverse. It cannot simply be, as is often contended, that the attack on Egypt was an aberration, an act at variance with the British national character, or, as has been even more vigorously asserted, that it was cynically and conspiratorially conceived, inept and fumbling in its execution, and calamitous in its results. The British are a warlike people and they can also be unscrupulous. In the course of the past two hundred years they have fought Afghans, Indians (both American and Asian), Chinese, Japanese, Americans, Africans (black and white), Sudanese, Burmese, Persians, Turks, Abyssinians, French, Germans, Italians, Spaniards and Russians—and this by no means exhausts the list. Nor have these wars invariably been noble in concept, impeccable in origin, unerring in political calculation, swift and decisive in execution, and beneficial in their consequences. From the political and military points of view, therefore, the British attack upon Egypt in 1956 cannot be said to have been in any way singular. Why, then, should it be regarded in some quarters with such abhorrence, indeed, as representing the very extreme of perfidy? The only answer which suggests itself from a reading of the many anti-Suez tracts which have flowed from British pens over the years is that the abhorrence arises from the single consideration that the campaign was fought against Egyptians and in alliance with Israelis. The inevitable implication residing in this conclusion is that the opponents of the Suez operation subscribe to a notion that some kind of intimate though indefinable bond exists between Englishmen and Egyptians, which does not exist between Englishmen and Israelis; and that for an Englishman to assault an Egyptian, therefore, somehow constitutes an unnatural offence. Unfortunately for the proponents of this belief, and despite all their assiduous efforts to implant it in the national consciousness, there remain among their fellow-countrymen, and even more so among Australians and New Zealanders, whose governments cheerfully supported the Suez expedition, a large number of unregenerate souls who regard the notion of any such bond as derisory, and who, furthermore, consider the very proposition of it to be a consummate nonsense.

*   *   *

One quality of which Lord Trevelyan is wary in the conduct of international relations—indeed, he seems almost to regard it as suspect—is courage. The section of his book devoted to his time in Cairo is prefaced with a quotation from Hilaire Belloc,

> Decisive action in the hour of need
> Denotes the hero but does not succeed;

while that on his years in Baghdad begins with a remark by Andre Malraux to the effect that courage seems nothing more than a curious and banal consequence of a feeling of invulnerability. What we are meant to infer from this is not clear, and we are no wiser by the time that we reach the third and final section of Lord Trevelyan's book, which deals with the British withdrawal from Aden in 1967. Here Lord Trevelyan seems as oppressed by the spectre of anarchy as he was earlier by the futility of courage, and he conveys the foreboding he felt on taking up his appointment as high commissioner to the Federation of South Arabia in May 1967 by quoting not only Yeats's well-known lines

> Things fall apart; the centre cannot hold;
> Mere anarchy is loosed upon the world ...

but also a remark made to him at the time by a more recent sage, Mr Har-

old Macmillan. '"Poor man," he said. "Poor man."'
'My task', Lord Trevelyan writes,

> was to evacuate the British Forces and their stores in peace, including the large Middle East Headquarters, and, if possible, to leave behind an independent Government which could assure peace and stability in the tiny country of South Arabia, so poor and so ravaged by age-long tribal warfare and revolution.

Before he is half-a-dozen pages into his narrative Lord Trevelyan has narrowed his goal still further. 'Our job was somehow to untie the knot and release ourselves without disaster.' It was, then, it seems, to be a rescue operation, along the lines of Roberts's march from Kabul to Kandahar or the retreat from Burma in 1942.

> The situation was bleak enough. We had declared that we would leave by 1968. Revolution was in full swing ... The population was intimidated; the administration was rapidly running down, in spite of heroic efforts by British and Arab civil servants against the odds; the streets were unsafe even in the daytime.

What confronted him, Lord Trevelyan explains, was 'not a strong and coherent nationalist movement but a prospect of anarchy'. 'The only question of importance was whether the country would hold together or be submerged in anarchy.' The Federation of South Arabia had been a failure. Aden colony had been brought into the federation 'by methods which were dubious and widely criticised', and he cites in support of this judgement a book, *South Arabia*, by a journalist, Tom Little. It is a pity that Lord Trevelyan has overlooked the more authoritative account of the merger given by the man responsible for it, Sir Kennedy Trevaskis, a former high commissioner, in his book, *Shades of Amber*. His overriding concern, Lord Trevelyan tells us again and again, was to get the British troops out safely. 'We could not leave British troops to face the alternative of either being drawn into a civil war with an uncertain outcome or of sitting helplessly and dangerously while the place crumbled round them.' When trouble broke out in the Crater district of Aden in June 1967 he feared for the effect it might have upon the evacuation plans. 'We had to keep control of Crater to protect the evacuation.' Yet if British troops had entered Crater and fought and defeated the mutinous South Arabian army and armed police, he tells us, 'this would have meant our early withdrawal, the victory of the dissidents, the abandonment of most of our stores and, most important, a civil war and the probable massacre of many British still in an exposed position up-country or in the Federal capital'. There is an echo here of Lord Trevelyan's argument against the use of force in Egypt in 1956, and it is, perhaps, open to the same objections. Lieutenant-Colonel Colin Mitchell, who commanded the battalion of Argyll and Sutherland Highlanders which subsequently occupied Crater without precipitating the expected bloodbath, dismisses the fear of an up-country massacre of Britons as 'a bogey' in his autobiography, *Having Been a Soldier*. Lord Trevelyan, who obviously does not share this opinion, does not refer to Colonel Mitchell's account of the Aden operations in his book. Yet one might be forgiven for wondering whether his understandable anxiety for the safety of British soldiers and officials in the protectorates did not tend to obscure what one might have expected to be the foremost concern of the governor of a British colony, *viz.*, the protection of the local inhabitants and their liberation from the reign of terror which had been imposed upon the population of Crater after the mutiny of the South Arabian army and police. One is further inclined to ask what function soldiers are meant to serve, and what their role should be in a condition of insurrection, if it is not to uphold the civil power and support it in its endeavours to restore and maintain peace and security. From the way in which Lord Trevelyan writes about the events of 1967 in Aden colony and protectorates, he would appear to be advancing a new interpretation of the respective roles of soldier and diplomatist in situations of limited warfare, the diplomatist's task apparently being to rescue the soldier from the very trouble he is sent to quell. It is not an interpretation, one would think, which would commend itself to the British army, nor can one imagine its proving acceptable to the British troops in Aden in 1967.

After the conclusion of the Crater operation Lord Trevelyan urged the ministers of the federal government to grasp the reins of government more firmly, to initiate reforms, and to enter into negotiations with the two principal terrorist organizations, the NLF and FLOSY. The ministers, *i.e.* the rulers of the states making up the federation, were reluctant to accept the advice, which was hardly unnatural seeing that the NLF and FLOSY were both dedicated to their overthrow. For Lord Trevelyn, however, it was the last straw. 'Our attempt to strengthen the Federal Government had failed. We could do no more for them.' The rulers were left to fend for themselves. All British forces were withdrawn from the protectorate states at the end of June. 'We had no responsibility under the Treaties which we were unilaterally abrogating on independence,' Lord Trevelyan explains, 'except to support the Rulers against attack from outside the country. .. We had to stick to the decision to withdraw.' When, a short time later, an RAF helicopter flew the young ruler of the Wahidi state back to his capital, and the pilot and a British army officer accompanying him were killed by insurgents and the young ruler abducted, Lord Trevelyan did nothing. 'There was nothing we could do. We had left all that country and could not go back.'

> The outlook grew more and more sombre as the days passed. There was no Government, only an army and civil servants with no authority over them. There was serious danger of anarchy. The British and Arab Civil servants from the Federal capital urged an immediate British move. Everyone was looking to us. The NLF were not far from Aden and might at any moment take over the Federal capital.

Naturally, there could be no question of the British high commissioner asserting authority and taking charge of the government himself. On the contrary, Lord Trevelyan made a public statement on September 5 that the federal government had ceased to function, and that he was prepared to negotiate the transfer of sovereignty with the NLF and FLOSY. They, however, spurned the invitation. Though several of the protectorate rulers had by now been deposed or fled the country, others were still ready to fight. Word was received in early September that the Sharif of Baihan, with Yemeni royalist and Saudi support, was preparing to re-enter his principality from across the Yemen frontier. Lord Trevelyan immediately sent him a warning that if he made the attempt he would be attacked by the RAF, acting in support of the South Arabian army. It seems slightly incongruous but Lord Trevelyan makes it all comprehensible.

> We had come to threaten the use of British aircraft against the attempt by a man who was still nominally under British protection, to recover his State by attacking across the frontier the rebels who had usurped his power with the aid of a battalion which we were helping to pay and arm and which was still nominally under British command. We were right to do so. We could not compromise our main objective to leave in peace and leave the country at peace.

Some weeks later, in early November, by which time the bulk of the South Arabian army had declared for the NLF and begun a purge of FLOSY supporters in its ranks, its leaders asked for RAF support against a FLOSY force raiding across the Yemen frontier. The RAF obliged by striking at it.[3] There is no mention of this dubious episode in Lord Trevelyan's book.

The final withdrawal from Aden took place at the end of November. Lord Trevelyan's comments on the sequence of events during that month make a doleful litany.

It was high time we left, whatever we left behind ...

It was by this time obvious that we only had the choice to hand over to the NLF or to nobody. We were lucky in at last finding someone to whom we might be able to hand over in peace ...

It was now November 11. Negotiations were to be held in Geneva, Lord Shackleton leading for the British. Their prospects were highly uncertain.

Our stores were all away. There was nothing to keep us. It was better for us to go as soon as possible.

On November 29 the last British troops left. It all happened in perfect peace ... On the next day, President Qahtan as Sha'abi and his delegation returned to Aden in a chartered aircraft ... The local boys had made good . . .

Looking back, Lord Trevelyan feels that the way in which British rule in Aden ended was not too bad.

We left without glory but without disaster. Nor was it humiliation. For our withdrawal was the result not of military or political pressure but of our decision, right or wrong, to leave. . . It might have been much worse. And, in the end, another little independent Arab country came into being, desperately poor and probably destined to go through periods of violence and revolt ... Our period of occupation did the country little

---

3 *The Times* and the *Daily Express*, November 10, and *The Guardian*, November 11, 1967 quoted in *Middle East Record* 1967, p. 483.

permanent good, for all the selfless work of many devoted Englishmen and so many good intentions. Whatever the rights or wrongs of the way we left, whatever was to come after us, the time for us to be there was over. And if we were to go, it was better not to linger on.

Sic transit imperium ...

7
Nationalism in Asia and Africa[1]

Nationalism in Asia and Africa edited with an introduction by
Elie Kedourie. London: Weidenfeld and Nicolson, 1971, pp.
575.

I t has been the conventional wisdom, for as long as one cares to
remember, that nationalism in Asia and Africa developed as a
response to European imperialism, and it has also been maintained, at
least in those schools where the spirit of J. A. Hobson still presides, that
imperialism itself was the product of Europe's desire to exploit Asians and
Africans for commercial gain. The two phenomena, nationalism and imperialism, are held to be inextricably linked, nationalism being seen as the
natural and inevitable outcome of European economic exploitation. The
syllogism has a certain attraction, which has been felt most strongly in the
West by those intellectuals who are racked by feelings of guilt towards the
deprived and suffering masses of Asia and Africa, feelings which, as often
as not, have their source in the particularities of their own personae but
which, for one reason or another, they prefer to relate to the sins committed by the West in its dealings with the non-Western world.

It is a hypothesis which Professor Elie Kedourie in his latest book
finds eminently resistible, both for its dubious historical foundation and
for its misreading of the nature of Asian and African nationalism. A little
more than a dozen years ago he published a study of nationalism which

1 From *The Journal of Imperial and Commonwealth History*, 2:3, 1974, pp. 364-367.
Published by Routledge. Reproduced by permission.

was a model of scholarly enquiry and elucidation, and which stands today as the best and most thoughtful statement on the subject that we have. Two outstanding characteristics of that work, and of Professor Kedourie's subsequent writings on aspects and manifestations of nationalism in the Middle East, are his strong distrust of the generality of orthodox assumptions concerning the nature and processes of nationalism, and his insistence that the historical evidence relating to it should be read with eyes unclouded by extraneous considerations. These qualities of scepticism and detachment, which are chief among those which set the scholar apart from the publicist, have been conspicuously absent from the body of literature which has gathered about the subject of Asian and African nationalism in recent years. Too much of it is emotional and *parti pris*, while the rest is often bland and evasive, as if its authors were afraid of offending susceptibilities or violating the accepted canons. Under such restraints scholarship is bound to languish.

Professor Kedourie is not afraid to say what he thinks, nor is he daunted by the size and scope of his subject. What he has undertaken here is nothing less than the first full-scale enquiry into the origins and character of nationalism in Asia and Africa that has been attempted. He has read his way through the major and many of the minor works of nationalist literature available in European languages and in Arabic, and from them he has selected and published twenty-five excerpts which he considers representative or important. They range in place and time from India in the 1880s and 1890s to China in the 1850s and 1920s, the Congo in the 1930s, and Kenya and Algeria in the 1960s; and in authorship from the Turkish Ziya Gokalp to the Indian Bipin Chandra Pal, the Arab Nicholas Ziadeh, the Mau Mau Josiah Kariuki, the Tatar Sultan Galiev, and the West-Indian Frantz Fanon. The ideas and arguments embodied in these excerpts are dissected and discussed by Professor Kedourie in a long historical introduction which traces the stages by which the idea of nationalism, essentially a European concept, found its way to Asia in the later nineteenth century and to Africa in the twentieth, to become a vehicle—and in some instances a Juggernaut—for the expression of anti-Western feeling.

It requires little effort on Professor Kedourie's part to dispose of the theory of economic exploitation as the sole or even prime motive for European imperialism. Imperial expansion by the European powers in the nineteenth century had as many varied causes as there were resultant territorial acquisitions, and in many cases economic interest was unimportant or irrelevant to the extension of imperial control, and, indeed, may even have run counter to it. In like manner, Professor Kedourie gives short shrift to the facile reproach with which our latterday Hobsonians are accustomed to mortify themselves and others, that nationalism is the revolt of the poor and oppressed of Asia and Africa, *les damnes de la terre,* against European economic oppression. Poverty may breed discontent but it can also induce passivity and resignation; and even where it breeds discontent such discontent does not necessarily express itself in nationalist upheavals. Nationalist movements, after all, have occurred among peoples not at all inferior, and often superior, in material wealth to their overlords (e.g. the Armenians in the Ottoman empire), or among those who had never been subject to alien rule (e.g. the Japanese).

How, then, did nationalism come to take hold of the Asian and African imagination? It did so, Professor Kedourie believes, because of the intrinsic nature of European rule and the particular circumstances of the age:

> Government by aliens has been the rule rather than the exception in world history, and European domination over Asia and Africa in being alien is far from constituting an exception and a novelty which calls for complicated doctrines to account for it; it falls, on the contrary, into a very old and very familiar pattern. If European rule is exceptional, this is because of its remarkable brevity, and we may suspect that the Asian and African nationalism it has undoubtedly conjured up is a reaction to European domination, not because this domination was alien but because it was European.

The administrative systems by which the European powers governed their empires were, in their complexity and efficiency, far more disruptive of the established ways of Asian and African societies than the rule of previous conquerors, especially in their impact upon the structure of dependent relationships and hierarchies within those societies. To deprive men of their traditional place in their society—and to destroy their belief in that place—produces deep psychological disturbances. These disturbances, coming at a time when the economies of Asia and Africa were being distorted by their increasing involvement in world trade cycles, loosened the bonds of society and set many people adrift. The introduction of Western education, Western ideas, fashions, artefacts, tastes and attitudes helped widen the gap, creating, both in countries under direct European rule and in others exposed to European political, economic and intellectual influences, a class of cultural *mestizos,* disorientated and disaffected, removed from their own societies yet refused entry to those of their imperial masters or exemplars. It was among these men, seduced, in Professor Kedourie's felicitous phrase, 'by the sweet and heady poison of Western enlightenment', that the ideas of nationalism took root.

He is in no doubt that the spread of nationalism to Asia and Africa has been as tragic in its consequences as its growth has proved in Europe, and he argues his case with great eloquence and learning. His book is a sheer delight to read, as much for the elegance of his language as for the clarity of his exposition. Nationalism in Europe, he says, however one judges it, at least has the merit of being a native product, of emerging from the soil of Europe, from the European experience, and from European modes of thinking. In contrast, he contends,

> almost any Asian or African nationalism, considered as scheme of thought or a programme of action, suffers from artificiality, from seeming a laborious attempt to introduce outlandish standards and out-of-place categories, and nowhere do they seem more out-of-place than in trying to adopt the European category of the nation-state.

To create the idea of the nation among the peoples and societies of Asia and Africa requires the subversion of existing traditions, institutions and beliefs. It requires a recourse to history to justify nationalist dogma, to demonstrate—however numerous the shifts, distortions and fabrications employed—the existence of a people bound by ties of race, language, culture and a shared past, to whom a distinctive identity can be accorded and a definite homeland assigned. Nothing is sacred to the nationalist, whether customs, traditions, religion or institutions, and the early stages of nationalism are marked by attacks upon them all in the name of enlightenment. Yet simultaneously and subsequently the nationalist does not scruple to use them to create a mythology with which to beguile the masses. All things, tangible and intangible, are grist to the nationalist mill, and if there is a contradiction between the exploitation of traditions, religion and institutions for nationalist ends and attacks upon them in the name of progress, it is no more than a reflection of the confusion which lies at the heart of all nationalist thinking, a confusion which, Professor Kedourie reminds us, is highly dangerous, both in itself and in its consequences.

The invocation of the past and the excitation of religious feeling can all too easily recapture for a people the memory of a distant and savage past of dark gods and bloody rituals. Thus, the early Indian nationalists who turned to terrorism as both a weapon and a release, associating it with the cult of the goddess Kali; and the Mau Mau of Kenya who invoked the tribal deities of the Kikuyu as witnesses and vindicators of their brutal excesses. The urge towards violence and destruction manifested by so many nationalist movements, Asian, African and European, is reinforced, Professor Kedourie points out, by another common element in nationalist doctrine, the belief in the millennium and the elect. Christianity, Judaism and Islam, he recalls, have long regarded widespread millennial speculation as posing a fundamental threat to law and order in society. 'If some distress or discontent rendered a mass of men susceptible to the lure of an imminent, miraculous, collective, and terrestrial redemption, then destructive passions could be unleashed, and the customary checks on which life in society depended would be utterly destroyed.' The enlightenment of the eighteenth century secularised millennial beliefs, transforming the vision of the kingdom of God upon earth into a dream of endless material progress; while the French Revolution set the political style for the pursuit of the new millennium—terrorism. 'It created', says Professor Kedourie in a memorable quotation from De Toqueville, 'the politics of the impossible, the theory of madness, the worship of blind audacity.'

Meliorism, the belief that the world may be improved by human effort, and millennial hope, its progenitor, give nationalism its dynamism, and meliorism and terrorism go hand in hand. The violent manifestations of nationalism which we have seen in Asia and Africa are not so much a revulsion against European civilisation as the adoption and adaptation of certain of its features at a time when these features, *e.g.* political extremism, were becoming prominent. Every one of the twentieth-century nationalists who appear in Professor Kedourie's book has espoused or promoted, surreptitiously or openly, the cult of violence, whether concealed within a cloak of piety or rationality, as with Gandhi's supple and ingratiating dialectics, or bluntly proclaimed, as with the glittering and venomous polemic of Frantz Fanon. 'Resentment and impatience, the depravity of the rich and the virtue of the poor, the guilt of Europe and the innocence of Asia and Africa, salvation through violence, the coming reign of universal love'—these, Professor Kedourie sadly concludes, are now the dominant elements of nationalist and progressive thought, 'Europe's latest gift to the world'. Who is to say, when all has been considered, that empire is not better than the nation-state?

8
Political Dynamics in the Middle East[1]

Political Dynamics in the Middle East. Ed. by Paul Y. Hammond
and Sidney S. Alexander. New York: Elsevier, 1972. 666 pp.

There are some books, as Dr Johnson is reputed to have said of
the novels of Congreve, that one would sooner praise than read,
and 650-page volumes commissioned by research corporations which aim
to lay bare the heart and soul of Middle Eastern politics fall very much
within this category. The present volume, edited by Paul Y. Hammond of
the RAND Corporation and Sidney S. Alexander of the Massachusetts Institute of Technology, is the fourth to emerge from an ambitious research
programme entitled 'The Middle East: Economic and Political Problems
and Prospects', sponsored by the RAND Corporation and Resources for
the Future Inc., and directed by Professor Alexander. The object of the
programme, so Mr Hammond informs us in his preface, 'has been to contribute to the formation of sound policy judgments about the Middle East
on the part of all concerned through improved understanding about the
economic, demographic, and related political facts of life there'. Plainly we
are in for some rigorous thinking and stiff reading.

Sixteen scholars, many of them well known, have contributed individual chapters on their particular areas of study. Malcolm Kerr writes on
the United Arab Republic and regional Arab politics, P. J. Vatikiotis on the
countries of the Fertile Crescent, Leonard Binder on Iran, J. C. Hurewitz

1 From *Survival: Global Politics and Strategy*, 16:5, 1974, pp. 254-256. Published by
Routledge. Reproduced by permission.

on military affairs, Nadav Safran on the domestic and foreign politics of Israel, and so on. What they all have to say is, as one would expect, informative and judicious, yet, as the contributors themselves would doubtless be the first to admit, it hardly amounts to a striking departure from what they have said in the past on the same subjects. Repetition, in fact, along with a certain blandness, is a key attribute of the whole volume; repetition not only in the sense that most of the contributors have already said elsewhere what they have to say here, but also in the sense that, because they have largely chosen a chronological approach to their subjects, chapter after chapter goes over much the same ground as its predecessor. After being taken several times, in one form or another, through, say, the development of the Arab-Israeli conflict or the decline of European influence in the Middle East, the edges of one's mind begin to curl and a profound sense of lassitude descends. Too much of the writing is dull and insipid, too much of the thinking uninspired. Pierre Rondot's chapter on Western Europe and the Middle East reads almost like a summary prepared by the Quai d'Orsay to demonstrate the consistency and logicality of French policy towards the Arab states since the accession of President de Gaulle. He notes with satisfaction, and even relish, that Western Europe now has no political commitments or interests in the Middle East, 'no worldwide responsibilities having repercussions or requiring a special attitude in the Middle East'. 'It is possible,' he concludes, 'for the nations of the Middle East to enjoy free and profitable relationships with the European peninsula; Europe is, as it were, at the Middle East's disposal.' Indeed it is, and the profits to be made from constant increases in the price of Middle Eastern oil are extremely handsome, as Europe is now ruefully aware. As for the absence of political commitments, M. Rondot seems to ignore the fact that Turkey is a Middle Eastern country and a member of NATO, and is thus linked militarily and politically with Western Europe. But then Turkey, along with the Arabian peninsula, has been excluded from the Middle East for the purposes of this volume.

Even greater satisfaction with the demise of European power and influence in the Middle East is expressed by Peter Calvocoressi, in a contribution on Britain and the Middle East. The entire chapter is a celebration—to the accompaniment of some ritual breast-beating over past sins and a goodly quota of misconceptions and factual errors—of Britain's withdrawal from the Middle East: a withdrawal which Mr Calvocoressi plainly believes was not only ineluctable but also sublimely meet and good. For Britain, he says, is now just another European state, and, like the rest of Europe, has no real interests to safeguard in the Middle East—except, perhaps, oil supplies, and these, he reflects comfortably, will doubtless be secured by the exertions of the United States. Those Britons—and Europeans—who feel that their countries should bear some responsibility for the defence of Western interests outside Europe (as much for the sake of their own self-respect as to assist the ally upon whose support their own survival may ultimately depend) Mr Calvocoressi contemptuously dismisses as 'romantic reactionaries', living in a past when Britain's principal concern in the Middle East was to keep the Russians out. 'Keeping the Russians out of the Middle East,' he declares, 'is a lost cause', and so the *raison d'etre* of British involvement has vanished. Perhaps so, but surely the real questions are, what the Russians propose to do, now that they are in the Middle East, and how will their actions affect the West? To these Arnold L. Horelick of the RAND Corporation returns some chilling answers in a chapter on Soviet policy which is the best contribution in the volume. Possibly because Mr Horelick is a specialist in Soviet affairs, he takes a much less sanguine view than Mr Calvocoressi of what the Soviet presence in the Middle East portends, and in describing how over the years, in one furtive transaction after another, Russian and Arab ambitions and appetites fed each other in an atmosphere of gullibility, conspiracy, spite and greed, he comes closer to exposing the reality of Middle Eastern politics than any of his fellow contributors.

For nearly a generation now, social scientists (especially in the United States) have endeavoured to analyse and explain Middle Eastern politics in accordance with the techniques and terminology of their own disciplines. Laudable though their efforts have been, it is doubtful whether they have brought us any nearer than the musings of more casual observers to understanding Middle Eastern society—the blight of corruption, the canker of superstition, the burden of lethargy, the want of public spirit, and the thraldom of illusion. In short, is there anything to be learned about 'the political facts of life in the Middle East' from passages like the following —only one among dozens in a chapter on United States policy by William B. Quandt of the RAND Corporation?

> Policies designed to resolve or settle problems in the Middle East have included various mixtures of diplomatic, military, and economic efforts. Where the attempt was activist, the goal was comprehensive package settlements. More passive strategies have sought partial solutions to problems. The United States has frequently followed incrementalist strategies dealing with issues one at a time. Behind such efforts lay the hope

that an outside stimulus could start a snowballing process that would reduce tensions. A second American approach has been to try for full settlement of the major causes of instability in the Middle East. This orientation represents a more global attack on problems, on the theory that the United States should do more than resolve issues piecemeal. The interrelatedness of Middle East problems has made this approach seem necessary, but also vastly increases its chance of failure.

The last word, like the first, might well be left to Dr Johnson: 'Sir, a man might write such stuff for ever, if he would abandon his mind to it.'

9

Towards Fanatic Rule[1]

Arabia without Sultans by Fred Halliday, Penguin, 1975.

There are some fairly odd books coming out these days under the Penguin imprint in what one can only conclude is intended to be the Che Guevara Memorial Series, or something of the sort. Mr Halliday's diffuse work is perhaps the oddest of all, a determined analysis of the recent history of the Arabian peninsula in Marxist-Leninist terms; an exercise which succeeds only in demonstrating that the study of Arabia and an infatuation with Marxist politics simply do not blend.

Mr Halliday takes us on a lengthy journey around Arabia, beginning with Saudi Arabia and ending with a glance across the Gulf at Iran. Everywhere, except in parts of southern Arabia, he finds the prospect displeasing; with the traditional rulers and conservative classes hard at work oppressing the masses, conspiring with Western imperialists and oil companies to preserve the present, corrupt, capitalist order, and imprisoning, torturing and executing decent revolutionaries and well-meaning dissidents.

Beyond the peninsula, in the progressive Arab states, things are not much better: despite their show of opposition to capitalism and imperialism, the so-called Arab socialist regimes are hopelessly bourgeois at heart and counter-revolutionary in practice. Only the Tweedledum and Tweedledee of the Palestine Liberation Movement, the Popular Front and the Popular Democratic Front, have shown themselves to be ideologically sound by choosing the path of mass revolutionary violence.

---

1 From *The Times Higher Educational Supplement*, 3 January 1975. Reproduced by permission.

As for Islam, Mr Halliday declared despondently that it provides "no basis for liberation of the Arab peoples", that "it [has] acted as a form of enslavement", that "there is need for both a theoretical break with religion and for a political handling of its role", and that "it is all the more essential to supersede Islam with materialist thought".

Why Mr Halliday should be so distressed by the repressive behaviour of present and past rulers in Arabia is something of a puzzle. Surely this has been the normal order of things in the peninsula all along, as anyone acquainted with its history would recognize? And, surely, too, repression is pretty commonplace everywhere these days, even in the most enlightened Marxist-Leninist states?

But Mr Halliday is not really concerned with history or with the mere observation of society and government in Arabia. His book is a tract, designed to preach the doctrine of redemption through revolution, to publicize the little-known revolutionary groups in the peninsula, and to flay the reactionary shaikhs, imams and sultans who rule its different parts for their sins and extravagances. Much of what he has to say, especially about Yemen, Saudi Arabia and Oman, is quite true, even though it is a rehash of some very stale meats. It would have been far more informative, and effective, if he had displayed something more than a superficial understanding and knowledge of the history of these countries, and their peoples, and if he had not chosen to express himself in the strangulated prose of the approved dialectic.

But perhaps this is to take Mr Halliday more seriously than he intended to be taken, even though, it must be admitted, there are precious few oases of jocularity in the stony desert of his jeremiad. Only someone with a mordant sense of humour could hold up the dour Marxist-Leninist regime in South Yemen and the pathetic fanatics and dupes of the Dhufar Liberation front as the only rays of hope on the Arabian horizon.

Twice, it would appear, in 1970 and 1973, he visited the People's Democratic Republic of Yemen, as the former Aden colony and protectorates are now called, and crossed the border into Dhufar to talk to some of the rebels who were waging a guerrilla campaign against the Sultan of Oman. He reports most affectingly on a conversation he had in one camp with a young recruit, a 12-year old girl named Amina.

Q. What have you learnt from the Front since you fled, Amina?
Amina: I've learnt literacy, politics and revolution.

Q. Do you ever miss your parents?

145

Amina: I don't think about my parents, I think about the revolution.

If Mr Halliday can report this with an air of gravity, it is of little wonder that he feels able to lavish praise upon the politburo at Aden for its splendid achievement in bringing the revolution to south Arabia, complete with show trials, detention camps, the liquidation of opponents, racial and religious persecution, mass expulsions, and other benefits of the modern Marxist-Leninist state. Compared with these excesses, here concealed behind the thickets of Mr Halliday's mawkish pieties, the transgressions of Arabia's rulers seem peccadilloes indeed. If the alternative is some of his heroes, then Arabia would be better off with its sultans for some years to come.

10
Arabic Political Memoirs[1]

Arabic Political Memoirs and Other Studies by Elie Kedourie
London: Cass. 1974. 327 pp. Bibliog. Index.

It is a sobering experience to look about one today and reflect that, for all the long British connection with the Middle East, for all the decades spent in cossetting and cajoling one Arab regime after another, for all the years of earnest debate about Arab affairs, not least within the walls of Chatham House, this country's influence in the Middle East now amounts to naught. What is more, and worse, its very financial survival depends in grotesquely disproportionate degree upon the condescending indulgence of a handful of desert Sheikhs. How, one may well ask, did such a monumental failure of foreign policy occur? A thousand reasons can probably be adduced to explain it, but one that surely merits particular consideration is the utterly illusory conception of the Middle East, and especially of Arab society and politics, which has been fostered in this country over the years by a legion of Arabists and Arabophiles, most notably in official and intellectual circles. To construct a foreign policy on the basis of a phantasm, to wit, a Middle East peopled not by flesh-and-blood Arabs, Persians, Turks, Jews, Armenians or Kurds but by *doppelgängers* bearing these labels, is to invite disaster, and we have been issuing invitations of this kind at regular intervals for sixty years now, ever since the day we encouraged the Sharif Husain ibn Ali of Mecca to rebel against

---

1 From *International Affairs*, Vol. 51, No. 2, April 1975, pp. 278-279. Reproduced by permission.

his lawful suzerain.

Professor Kedourie is not only a rare mind in a field of studies which abounds, today more than ever, with apologists and propagandists of one kind or another, but it is perhaps his supreme virtue as a scholar that he has never confused the real Middle East with the factitious one, or treated with other than profound scepticism the facile orthodoxies of the day and the cant in which they are usually expressed. A number of these orthodoxies, particularly as they concern British policy and policy-making in the Middle East since the First World War, were demolished by him in a memorable collection of essays published some four years ago under the title of *The Chatham House Version and other Middle-Eastern Studies*. He has now, in his latest collection, widened his purview to take in the fate of constitutional government in the Arab states, the intellectual origins and composition of Arab political parties and movements, the emergence of the new and radical style of politics which is now so prevalent, and the vicissitudes of minorities caught up in the turmoil of the past half-century. Within these general categories his choice of topics is as diverse – for example, the Muslim Brotherhood, the Young Turk revolution, the Alliance Israélite Universelle, the Rashid Ali coup—as what he has to say about them is fresh of illuminating. As always, he displays great learning and independence of judgment, and he writes with a lucidity and elegance which few, if any, contemporary authors in this field can match.

One of the most valuable and instructive essays in his collection is the title essay, 'Arabic Political Memoirs,' in which Professor Kedourie takes to task, and rightly so, those western Arabophiles who, he says, 'have managed to give currency to a picture of the Arab as a humourless, solemn, sententious, tediously strident creature' (p.178). Just how distorted a picture this is he goes on to demonstrate by quoting at length from a selection of recently published memoirs by both prominent and obscure figures in Arab political life. All manner of human qualities and emotions is revealed in these extracts—humour, pathos, fanaticism, self-deception, compassion, regret—and no one reading them could fail to realise that they represent the actuality as opposed to the illusion of Arab politics in all its abundant variety and its sometimes bizarre manifestations.

Only a few of the essays are concerned with aspects of British policy in the Middle East, but two in particular give rise to disturbing reflections, one a long examination of the memoirs of Sir Hugh Foot (Lord Caradon), the other, an account, based on Foreign Office sources, of the sack of Basra and the massacre of part of the Jewish community in Baghdad in 1941. To be reminded again of the delusions and feelings of guilt about the Arabs which filled the minds of Foot and other influential British officials in the Middle East in years gone by, or to learn of the ineptitude and pusillanimity of the British ambassador in Iraq in 1941, Sir Kinahan Cornwallis, in allowing British troops to stand by while the Jews of Baghdad, whose sentiments had been pro-British for generations, were butchered by a mob, is to understand why we have lost all reputation and standing in the Middle East, and are today the sport of petty despots in one dusty capital after another.

11
Tales of Arabian Knights[1]

Revolutionary Transformation in the Arab World: Habash and his Comrades from Nationalism to Marxism by Walid W. Kazziba. Charles Knight & Co., 1975.

F or all the publicity that has surrounded the activities of revolutionary groups in the Arab world of late years, especially the Palestinian extremists, surprisingly little information is available in the West about their origins and their relationship to one another. That there was a loose-knit underground organisation called the "Movement of Arab Nationalists", with branches in several Arab countries, has been known for some years, but its exact connexion with groups like the Popular Front for the Liberation of Palestine and the Democratic Popular Front was clouded, and the place in it of such well-known figures as George Habash and Wadi Haddad of the PLFP and Nayif Hawatima of the DPLFP was equally obscure. Now Dr Walid Kazziba has opened the shutters on the Arab Nationalists' Movement, not to their fullest extent perhaps but enough to allow some light in and to enable us to see the outlines, at least, of this shadowy organisation and its even more shadowy principals.

It is a brave action on his part, for he was himself an active member of the Arab Nationalists' Movement for eight years (from 1957 to 1965), and secret societies as a rule do not look kindly upon the publication of revelations about them by former votaries.

---

1 From *The Times Higher Educational Supplement*, 9 May 1975. Reproduced by permission.

The first of Dr Kazziba's revelations, that the ANM had its beginnings in the years 1950-52 as a "literary" society at the American University of Beirut, occasions little surprise. That institution has come a long way from what its founders, a century ago, conceived to be its purpose and function. The second revelation, that it was a group of Palestinian students, led by George Habash and Wadi Haddad, and inspired by the preachings of those notable nationalist divines, Qustantin Zurayk and Fayiz Sayigh, who founded the movement, was equally predictable. What was less apparent before, and even here emerges only from the interstices of Dr Kazziha's account, is how slight was the numerical strength of the ANM, especially in view of the mystique which it gathered about it in later years. Most of its members were recruited from students at the AUB, who in turn came mostly from the middle ranks of Palestinian and Lebanese society. A few more converts were made among students who came to the AUB from other Arab countries.

On their return home, some of them in company with Palestinian émigrés who went to work in Syria, Egypt, Iraq or Kuwait, established new cells of the movement in these countries. But their numbers were not great (Dr Kazziha says that only 15 Syrians had been recruited by 1960), for the ANM did not regard itself initially as a mass movement but rather as an elite "ginger group" of young intellectuals who, by argument and exhortation, would rouse the governments of Arab states to the performance of their duty to avenge the shameful defeat in Palestine in 1948 and to eradicate all traces of Western imperialism and Zionism in the Middle East.

The ANM, as its name indicates, was intensely nationalist, and its predominantly Palestinian leadership made the defeat of Israel the overriding goal of the movement. For the Jews of Israel there was to be only one grim choice—expulsion or extermination. Moreover, as Dr Kazziha makes clear, the ANM refused to distinguish between Zionism and Judaism: Jewry everywhere was the enemy and must be crushed. The Arabs could only triumph if they were united, and the ANM pinned their hopes for the Arab states upon Nasser. He was there hero and paladin until the second disastrous defeat in 1967.

The amalgamation of several Palestinian factions to form the Palestine Liberation Organisation in 1964 stole some of the ANM's thunder, and it also marked, although it did not initiate, a shift in both the strategy and the organization of the movement. Up to 1960, Dr Kazziha recounts, the ANM had adhered to its "theory of the separation of stages", that is to say the political integration of the Arab states and the defeat of Zionism and Western imperialism had to be achieved before the Arabs could turn their attention to social and economic reform. Now some of the ANM's central committee began to argue (and more particularly after the break-up of the union between Egypt and Syria in 1961, when the headquarters of the ANM was moved from Damascus to Beirut), that the struggle was as much against feudalists and capitalists as it was against Zionists and imperialists, and that the movement should widen its appeal so as to encompass the Arab masses.

By 1964 the radicals, led by the Lebanese Muhsin Ibrahim and the Palestinian Nayif Hawatima, were at odds with the "old guard", led by Habash and his fellow Palestinian, Wadi Haddad. Habash now organized the National Front for the Liberation of Palestine from the Palestinian members of the ANM, partly in response to the formation of the PLO but also to offset the growing influence of the radical "theoreticians" of the movement.

The two wings remained in uneasy harness until the aftermath of the overwhelming defeat of the Arab armies by Israel in 1967. That defeat destroyed the ANM's faith in Nasser and led it to condemn his regime and those of the other "progressive" Arab states as "petty bourgeois". Habash was at one with the rest of the ANM leadership in declaring that henceforth the only road for the movement to take was that of the armed struggle of the masses against Zionism, imperialism and the Arab "reactionary classes", and he altered the name of the NLFP accordingly to the Popular Front for the Liberation of Palestine. But Habash had not travelled as far along this road as had Ibrahim, Hawatima and their followers, so that the gap between them still existed. It widened rapidly in the next two years, splitting the ANM wide open, not just the Palestinian-Lebanese leadership in Beirut but every branch of the movement elsewhere, destroying whatever coherence it might have had as a pan-Arab organization. Hawatima established the Democratic Popular Front as a challenge to Habash's PFLP, and before 1969 was out the two groups were fighting openly in the streets of Beirut. The descent from there to today's senseless terrorism has been a steep and ugly one.

Dr Kazziha modestly disclaims any intention of attempting a thoroughgoing assessment of the role of the ANM in Arab political life in the past 20 years, but even so he has given us a most valuable outline of the movement's origins and evolution, and for this we are much indebted to him. He makes the point towards the close of his book that, for all its claims of late years to be a revolutionary movement, the ANM never made any headway among the Arab masses. The only country in which it has achieved any practical success is south Yemen, where the Marxist-Leninist

National Liberation Front has set up its own version of the dictatorship of the proletariat. Otherwise the ANM remains what it has always been, a small and disputatious band of rootless intellectuals, measuring out their lives with coffee spoons in the clubs and cafes of Beirut.

12
Middle East Survey[1]

The Middle East: a Political and Economic Survey edited by Peter Mansfield. London: Oxford University Press, 1973. Fourth edition, Pp. xi + 591, 3 maps, statistical appendices, reading list, index.

I n the days before it became so absorbed by issues relating to the E.E.C., Chatham House used to take a considerable interest in the Middle East, commissioning and publishing books, pamphlets and articles in a seemingly endless stream on subjects ranging from the ephemeral to the enduring, most of them touched with that lustre of authority which the imprint of the Royal Institute of International Affairs and the reputations of its members bestowed upon its publications. One of the best of these from those days was *The Middle East: a Political and Economic Survey*, which appeared in three editions between 1950 and 1958. The third edition was the work of many distinguished hands, and although much of it is now obviously dated it is still deserving of a place on one's bookshelves, not only for itself but as a reminder of better times. There has been no attempt on the part of Chatham House—at least none that has come to the ears of the world outside—in the years since 1958 to bring out a fourth edition, and the one which is now presented to the public is not issued under its auspices although it is published by the same learned press.

The editor of the third edition was Sir Reader Bullard, who began

1 From *Middle Eastern Studies*, Vol. 11, No. 2 (May, 1975), pp. 199-205. Published by Taylor & Francis, Ltd. Reproduced by permission.

his diplomatic career at the British embassy in Constantinople in 1908 and ended it as British ambassador to Iran in 1946, after which he was for several years director of the Institute of Commonwealth Studies, Oxford, and vice-chairman of the board of governors of the School of Oriental and African Studies, London. The editor of the new edition is Peter Mansfield whose diplomatic career ended early, when he resigned from the Foreign Office over the Suez affair, and who has since then been active mainly as a publicist. Sir Reader had at his disposal for the compilation of his survey the resources of Chatham House, and he also enlisted the aid, as the preface to his volume bears impressive witness, of a formidable array of Middle-Eastern specialists and scholars. The contributors to the new edition are drawn, with two or three exceptions, from a much narrower band in the spectrum of Middle-Eastern expertise, even though Mr Mansfield has had the assistance, so he informs us in his preface, of the Middle East Centre at St. Anthony's College, Oxford. In arrangement and appearance his volume is much like that of his predecessor: it opens with a general introduction to the history, society, economy and religions of the Middle East, then proceeds chapter by chapter through the countries of the region, ending with a selection of statistical tables and a list of recommended reading. Where it differs from the earlier editions is in the added novelty of seven 'thematic studies', inserted between the general introduction and the detailed surveys of individual countries.

Clearly, the value of this innovation depends upon the topics selected and even more upon the choice of contributors. Two of these pieces are excellent—'The Oil Industry in the Middle East' by Professor Edith Penrose, and 'Soviet Policy in the Middle East' by Geoffrey Wheeler. Accurate, informative, sensible and well-written, they are everything that contributions to a volume of this kind should be. The same might have been said of Mr Mansfield's own contribution, 'Arab Political Movements', had it not been marred by a degree of involvement and by a failure to address itself to what must surely be the most prominent Arab political movement of recent years, the Palestinian *fronde*. It is a failure which appears all the more surprising when it is set against the attention paid throughout the volume to the Arab-Israeli conflict. Three of the other 'thematic studies', two on cultural trends in the more advanced Arab states and another on the Palestine mandate, have, at most, a curiosity value, but even this slight recommendation could not be accorded the seventh and last study, 'The United States in the Middle East'.

The most that one can charitably say about it is that the author, Robert Hunter, has mistaken his brief, or else that he was given a most peculiar one. From both the title of his essay and that of the volume in which it appears, one would expect to encounter a factual survey of the historical, political and economic connexions of the United States with the Middle East. Instead, we are faced with a disquisition of the type known in journalistic circles as a 'think piece' on the subject of Soviet-American relations in the Middle East and American policy towards Israel, a 'think piece', furthermore, directed towards the situation prevailing in 1971 or 1972 when Mr Hunter wrote, and to what was then the immediate future. We who have seen something of that future may find less satisfaction in his observations and prognostications than he evidently does, and we may further be inclined to question very seriously some of his assertions regarding the nature and limits of American policy in the Middle East. *E.g.*:

> For more than fifty years, American policy in the Middle East has been dominated by the problem of Palestine (p. 90);

> It is not easy to define America's interest in the Middle East, especially since its concern with Israel is not based on traditional political or economic factors (p. 93);

> It is essential, however, that the United States should not see the Middle East as more important than it really is, simply because the Russians happen to be there. The Soviet Union may still be acting on the basis of a nineteenth-century concept of the worth of this nexus of continents and oceans; but this is no reason for the United States to mimic such an outdated view through a failure of imagination (p. 95);

> The one great resource in the Middle East that has any value for the West [is] oil. For the United States, this is a commercial interest, not a strategic one.... Any American strategic interest is indirect.... In this sphere, too, fears expressed about Soviet designs seem to be exaggerated (p. 97).

The burden of Mr Hunter's argument, with its apologetic and accusatory undertones, directed respectively to the Arabs and to the Americans, is that the United States has no vital interest at stake in the Middle East, that Soviet activities there are not inimical to Western interests, that there is consequently no real point of conflict between the United States and the Soviet Union in the region, and that the United States should abate its support for Israel and devote itself instead to assisting the economic development of the Arab states.

What, one may well ask, is such a piece of obvious special pleading-a kind of Pauline epistle addressed to latter-day, transatlantic Romans-doing in a political and economic handbook of the Middle East? Even more, what is it doing in the company of such authoritative contributions as Geoffrey Wheeler's sober and learned analysis of Soviet policy in the region, an analysis every line of which shows up Mr Hunter's submissions for the feverish speculations they are? The question is well worth asking, and asking more than once, for there is a curious bent to sections of this fourth edition of *The Middle East: a Political and Economic Survey* which seems at odds with its avowed character as a work of reference. One fact to emerge with striking clarity from even the most cursory comparison of the third and fourth editions of the survey is the extent and depth of the inroads made by the Soviet Union in the Middle East since 1958. Yet whereas Sir Reader Bullard and his contributors, writing in that year, expressed themselves as greatly disturbed by the very much smaller degree of penetration which the Soviet Union had achieved up to that time, and also as highly apprehensive of what it portended for the Middle East and the West alike, Mr Mansfield and several of his contributors appear to regard the far greater Soviet advances made since 1958 with equanimity, even tending, as in the case of Mr Hunter just noticed, to play down their significance. Their disapprobation, in fact, is only called forth by the consideration that, as Mr Mansfield puts it in his preface, 'Great Power involvement in the Middle East . .. conflicts with the desire of the states of the area to assert their full independence'. For this stifling of regional aspirations', it seems, the United States bears as much responsibility as the Soviet Union.

Objectivity is difficult to sustain in the study of history or politics or even economics, and no one would wish to fetter the editor of *The Middle East: Political and Economic Survey* or his contributors in the expression of their opinions or in delivering judgements. All that can reasonably be required of them is that the opinions should be informed and the judgements considered. The historical and political sections of the third edition were notable for their forthright comments upon the conduct of certain Middle Eastern political figures, and upon the Soviet Union's aims and methods and those of its satraps and protégés in the the Middle East. Mr Mansfield tells us in his preface that these 'valuable historical sections' from the previous edition have been retained in the new edition, 'wherever appropriate'. They have not, however, been retained intact for the years after the Second World War, and as one marks the changes and deletions which have been made one begins to wonder what exactly is meant by 'appropriate' in this context. Take, for example, the relative treatment accorded the Baghdad Pact in the third and fourth editions. The third edition began its account (pp. 28-29) as follows:

> A period of tranquillity might have been expected to follow in Egypt the conclusion of the 1954 [Anglo-Egyptian] agreement, but more than one circumstance may have encouraged in Colonel Nasser an extreme attitude on foreign affairs. Over-population tended to place strict limits on internal social reform; a policy of Arab 'liberation' and unity, respectable enough in itself, might bring within the Egyptian orbit oil-bearing territories whose surplus revenue might help to support Egypt's surplus population. Then the necessity under which a dictator lives, to go on being successful, was always present, and there was the disturbing prospect that Iraq, already a serious rival, might join the agreement for friendly co-operation which Turkey and Pakistan had signed on 2 April 1954, thereby enhancing her importance.

This passage does not appear in the fourth edition. Nor does the explanation put forward in the third edition (p. 30) for the accession of Iran and Turkey to the Baghdad Pact: 'The proximity of Turkey and Persia to the Soviet Union explained their wish for mutual support.' This statement has been transformed in the fourth edition (p. 26) into: 'In the early 1950s the Western countries had not abandoned hope of including the Middle East in an anti-Soviet defence system.'

Nasser's reaction to the Pact was described in the third edition (p. 29) thus:

> What looked like an attempt to divide, or at least to distract, Arab loyalties worried Nasser. His military weakness had been brought home to him, on 28 February 1955, by a sudden and heavy bout of fighting with Israel at Gaza. He therefore tried to rouse the Arab world to its dangers by upbraiding Iraq. He was not entirely successful in enlisting support against the Pact, but he did succeed, in October 1955, in concluding with Syria and Saudi Arabia a military alliance, joined by Jordan a year later, providing for a joint command which was to be headed by an Egyptian.

In the fourth edition this is replaced by the pious observation (p. 26) that 'Nasser, the new leader of republican Egypt, was strongly opposed to any Arab country joining such a pact because he believed that a Western alliance meant the perpetuation of Western influence'. Doubtless it was with the object of evading such a dreadful fate that Nasser concluded his arms agreement with the Soviet Union in September 1955. 'This action', so we are informed in the fourth edition (p. 228), 'was denounced by the British and U.S. governments but applauded by the Arab masses.' The third edition had a sharper comment to make (p. 30) but it is not reprinted here: 'It has been suggested that but for the Baghdad Pact the Soviet Union would not have arranged the sale of arms to Egypt and Syria, but no provocation preceded the Greek Communist invasion of Greece in 1947-9 or the North Korean attack on South Korea.' Similarly, when it comes to the question of the Soviet Union's exploitation of the Arab-Israeli conflict to consolidate its position in the Arab world, the editor of the new edition shies away from the robust comment and plain speaking which were a feature of the third edition, *e.g.* (p. 35):

The Soviet Government finds it convenient and easy to play on the feeling of nationalism among a people who know little about Crimean Tartars and Hungarians but are conscious all the time of the Israelis....

To harp on local grievances has always been the policy of the Soviet Union, even before she abandoned the line that her instruments must be pure-bred Communists and decided to use nationalists as her spearhead, whether in European colonies or in the Middle East....

Even if the Arabs remembered that the Soviet Union was almost as prompt as the United States to recognize the new State of Israel, and that not long before she had been perhaps the main supporter of the United Nations partition scheme and had been prepared to help to put it into force, they would point to Soviet sales of arms to Arab States and to the Soviet Union's attitude during the Suez crisis as recommendation enough. The Middle East expects colonialism and imperialism to come from overseas ...; it is not realised that imperialism may creep up upon you from behind by land.

It is just as well that the United States has a broad back, for it is made to carry a heavy burden of sin in this latest edition of *The Middle East: a Political and Economic Survey*. The third edition explained the American interventions in Jordan and Lebanon in 1957-58 under the Eisenhower Doctrine in these terms (pp. 36-37):

> Within a few weeks a concrete example was furnished by Jordan, where the country was in a state of disorder, and Iraq and Saudi Arabia had sent troops to forestall, it appeared, a possible attack by Israel or an attempt by Syria to annex Jordan....

> Egyptian (and Syrian) interference, by bribery and intimidation, in the Lebanese elections was widely suspected, and interference in Jordan was alleged to include a plot to assassinate the King.

In the fourth edition this becomes (p. 28):

> In 1957 it [the United States] gave assistance to King Hussein of Jordan in his struggle with his own left-wing opposition, under the terms of the Eisenhower Doctrine, and in July 1958 landed troops in Lebanon during this country's muted civil war when the Iraqi Revolution raised fears that all remaining pro-Western elements in the Middle East might be swept away.

Nothing is offered by way of evidence or argument to support this new interpretation of events in Jordan and Lebanon in 1957-58, and the omission becomes even more noticeable when it is set beside a statement made later in the volume (p. 143), in the revised and largely rewritten section on Saudi Arabia, to the effect that 'in April [1957], during the disturbances in Jordan, he [King Saud] sent troops there, as much to forestall any Syrian attempt to take over the country as to guard against an attack by Israel'—which is almost word for word what was said on the subject in the Saudi Arabian section of the third edition.

Editorial carelessness? A case of the left hand not knowing what the right was doing? Perhaps. But whatever the reason it still leaves unanswered the question why the editor saw fit to alter the original explanation. It can hardly be that he did so in the light of new evidence or after profound reconsideration of the old, for nowhere in his volume does he show the slightest disposition to take note of the considerable body of research and writing on the modern history of the Middle East which has appeared in the fifteen years which separate.the third and fourth editions of the survey, still less to incorporate the findings of this research in the narrative of political events up to and after the Second World War which he has taken largely unchanged from the third edition. Yet at the same time he has made some changes in the narrative, especially for the period after 1945, changes which do not appear to proceed, as just remarked, from the consideration of new evidence or the re-examination of old.

What, then, do they proceed from? A clue is to be found in the opening sentence of the preface to the new edition which proclaims the necessity, in view of the changes which have taken place in the Middle East since the publication of the third edition, for the survey 'to be written from a different angle of vision'. What this means becomes clear as one reads through the volume, especially the later sections of the general introduction, the new chapters on Arab political movements and United States interests, and the revised chapters on Egypt, Syria, Jordan and Iraq. It can be illustrated by quoting the categorical statement which appears on page 24 of the general introduction: 'The failure to resolve this [Arab-Israeli] conflict has been the root cause of the chronic violence and instability which are regarded as characteristic of the Middle East. It is the principal reason for the growth of anti-Western feeling in the Arab countries as two Western powers—Britain and the United States—were held to be chiefly responsible for the creation of Israel.' (The third edition simply, and more accurately, stated: (p. 27): 'The Palestine War left the Arabs with a standing grievance against Israel, and against the two Western states held to be responsible for its creation: Britain and the United States.') Where the 'angle of vision' is not so obtuse, as it is here, as to produce astigmatism, it is often so acute as to exclude some objects completely from sight, *e.g.* Egypt's closure of the Suez Canal, and attempted closure of the Gulf of Aqaba, to Israeli shipping after 1950. On this the third edition commented in 1958 (p. 27): 'The most potent weapon in the blockade has been Egypt's assumption of a right to exercise it in regard to the Canal and the Gulf of Aqaba'; and (p. 31): 'The Egyptian blockade of the Canal (and the Gulf of Aqaba) was maintained, in spite of the resolution of the Security Council on 1 September 1951, calling on Egypt to abandon the Canal restrictions. Both comments have been deleted from the text of the new edition, along with any and all mention of the blockade and the closure.

It is much the same story with several of those changes in the Middle East since 1958, the occurrence of which, so we were informed, has necessitated the adoption of 'a different angle of vision'. There is not a word in the entire volume about the Soviet-Iraqi defence treaty of April 1972, and only a fleeting reference in the chapter on Egypt to the Soviet-Egyptian defence agreement of 1971. The Black September organization apparently does not exist, nor have atrocities been perpetrated by terrorists at Lod airport or Munich or anywhere else. The Palestinian guerrillas must have their own pagoda-tree, for they do not appear to obtain their funds from anywhere in particular. Iraq, it would seem, dropped its claim to Kuwait after 1961 without anything so sordid taking place as the passing of money. Egypt had no hand in the revolution in Yemen in September 1962, still less did it undertake two months later to withdraw its forces from that country in return for recognition by the United States of the new republican regime. Even the lot of women in Arabia, we are cheered to learn, has been radically improved. The third edition, in a 'Note on the Position of Women in the Middle East'. remarked (p. 71) that in Saudi Arabia 'the seclusion of women is complete, and polygamy and legal concubinage exist unchanged. Slavery and concubinage favour each other, and easy money from the exploitation of oil resources favours both'. There is no place for such unhelpful comments in the fourth edition, which prefers to report more constructively (p. 47): 'In Saudi Arabia most girls of the settled population go to school and a substantial number to university either at home or abroad, but a Saudi woman is still not permitted to drive a car.' Gorged on such morsels as these, what need have we of the bloodier meat of Middle Eastern politics?

The chapters on individual countries, which, after all, are the main concern of the survey, are a mixed bag. Those on Turkey, Iran, Lebanon and the Sudan are, generally speaking, very good, and the account of political events since 1958 in the chapter on Iran is much superior to anything else of the kind in the volume. The chapters on Iraq, Syria, Jordan and Israel are also competent, although in all of them there is a tendency to ignore the unpalatable and to smooth the rough edges of internal politics. (Why the silence, for example, over the tragic fate of Abdur Rahman al-Bazzaz, who illuminated for a brief moment the rank darkness of post-revolutionary Iraqi politics?) The chapter on Egypt suffers from an obsession with the shade of Nasser, as though its authors were arguing the case for his canonization, and from too sanguine and committed an appraisal of Egypt's economic achievements. But whatever the flaws, serious or trivial, that mar these chapters, they are as bagatelles compared with the blunders which disfigure the chapter on the Arabian peninsula. Here all is bewilderment and confusion, as the editor and his contributors grapple with the exotic or the perplexing in a Laocöon-like struggle. Sects and schisms, tribes and factions, traditional affinities and ancient enmities are blurred or overlooked, mistaken or misplaced. Yemen since 1958 is depicted in the arid phraseology of press clippings with barely a glance at the complexities of tribal and religious differentiation in the country. More of an effort is made in this regard with Oman but it proves misguided; for what is of consequence in that country is as often as not ignored, and when it is not, what is said is liable to be erroneous or even ludicrous. Indeed, the sections on the history of the Gulf states, Saudi Arabia and South Yemen are so inadequate or so packed with absurdities that it would have been a kindness to have suppressed them. In part, the fault resides in the authors' naivety about the realities of Arabian politics, a naivety touchingly displayed in the section on South Yemen (The People's Democratic Republic of Yemen), which is referred to throughout, without any conscious appreciation of the ironic or the absurd, as 'Democratic Yemen'. Of a country which since 1967 has been continually sliding backwards into its historical condition of anarchy and barbarity, they solemnly write (p. 176): 'The draft constitution approved by the ruling National Liberation Front and published on 2 August 1970 . . . provides for free and direct elections to a 101-member People's Supreme Council, to be held before November 1971.' What have written constitutions, with all their panoply of executive, judicial and legislative functions, checks, balances, procedures, amendments, and the elaboration of rights and duties, to do with a backward tribal society insecurely ruled by a semi-military *cheka*? And, why, incidentally, since this fourth edition of *The Middle East: a Political and Economic Survey* did not go to press before the latter half of 1972, did its editor not ascertain whether or not 'free and direct elections' had been held in South Yemen by November 1971?

To continue any further along these lines would be tantamount to paving the way for a revision of the fourth edition of the survey, which would be to no one's interest. A word, however, has to be said about the reading list, which has been taken from the third edition and amended on principles which are neither immediately ascertainable nor demonstrably logical. Why, for instance, has Majid Khadduri's *War and Peace in the Law of Islam* been dropped and M. A. Shaban's *Islamic History, A.D. 600-750* been added? Why has Edward Atiyah's autobiography been kept and Sir Olaf Caroe's *Wells of Power* been dropped? Why have Hans Kohn's *Nationalism and Imperialism in the Hither East* and Lawrence's *Seven Pillars* been retained and Wilfred Thesiger's *Arabian Sands* ignored? Why has the British official history of the Second World War in the Middle East been abandoned in favour of Manfred Halpern's *Politics of Social Change*? Why not include L. Hirszowicz's *The Third Reich and the Arab East?* Why remove Philip Graves's *Life of Sir Percy Cox* and Sir Arnold Wilson's *Persian Gulf* and replace them with John Marlowe's *Persian Gulf in the Twentieth Century?* (If the changes are to be justified on the grounds of contemporary relevance, then why has Doughty's *Travels in Arabia Deserta* been kept and H. M. Albaharna's *Legal Status of the Arabian Gulf States* ignored?) Why Tom Little on South Arabia and not Sir Charles Johnston? The questions are almost endless: if we had answers, they might enable us to conclude even more definitely why it is that this latest version of *The Middle East: a Political and Economic Survey* compares so dismally with its predecessors.

13
The Shah and the Gulf[1]

Although the figure of Muhammad Reza Shah arouses mixed
emotions in the West, there is a general tendency to accept him
at his own valuation as a progressive ruler (or enlightened despot) who is
determined in his lifetime to make Persia a modern industrial state and a
military power without peer in the Middle East.

Few Western governments are disposed to question publicly the desirability or feasibility of these aims. Instead, they are content to humour
his pretensions, sell him large quantities of arms and industrial goods, and
pay him inflated prices for his oil. Any doubts which may intrude about
the wisdom of this policy are usually stilled by reference to the Shah's role
in preserving the peace of the Gulf and the security of oil supplies from
the region.

How justified is this complacency, especially in the light of Persia's
past record in the Gulf and the Shah's own activities? Vanity and *folie des
grandeurs* have long been recognised as prominent attributes of the Persian
character.

Sir John Malcolm, who led a succession of British missions to Teheran from 1800 onwards, recorded in his *History of Persia* that he found the
Persians 'the vainest people on earth', and James Morier, who followed him
to Teheran some years later, delivered a similar verdict in his tales of the
estimable Hajji Baba of Ispahan. Successive rulers of Persia since then have
cherished the illusion that they are destined to sway the destinies of Asia,
to extend their dominion from the Tigris to the Indus, and to annex every
inch of territory where a Persian foot has trod.

---

1 Written for *The Daily Telegraph*, June 1975. Unclear whether it was published.

Their achievements hardly matched their aspirations, and the resultant sense of frustration expressed itself, so far as the Gulf was concerned, in the petulant obstruction of Britain's efforts in the 19th century to suppress piracy, the slave trade and the arms traffic, on the grounds that Persia's sacred and immutable sovereign rights were being ignored or trampled upon.

The fall of the Qajar dynasty and the accession of Reza Shah Pahlevi, the present Shah's father, in 1925 brought no change in the temper of the court at Teheran. Reza Shah was afflicted by the same *folie des grandeurs* as his predecessors, not least with respect to Persia's manifest destiny in the Gulf. Realising that the key to political influence in that sea lay in naval power, he set out to equip himself with a navy; but the attempt foundered upon the resolute incapacity of his subjects to master the arts of seamanship and fighting at sea. His son has now followed in his footsteps, with what success has yet to be seen, although to anyone acquainted with Persian history it would come as a considerable surprise if the fledgling Persian navy turned out to be anything more than a costly folly.

Nevertheless the Shah regards it as a glittering instrument of his will, destined to dominate the Gulf's narrow waters and command its approaches. Similarly, his greatly expanded and expensively accoutred Army and Air Force are clearly designed to overawe his Arab neighbours, Iraq in particular.

The Shah has never troubled to conceal his detestation of the military junta in Baghdad, which he once described as a group of 'crazy, bloodthirsty savages'. The focus of his quarrel with the Iraqi regime was the Shatt al-Arab, over which he claimed equal rights of sovereignty, though his claim had an exceedingly narrow legal and historical basis. In April 1969 he tore up the Perso-Iraqi treaty of 1937, which defined the frontier along the Shatt al-Arab, and began a war of nerves against the Iraqi government, extending it in due course to the arming and support of the Kurds in their revolt against Baghdad.

On their side the Iraqis turned to the Soviet Union for help, and in April 1972, they concluded a treaty with that power which, among other things, granted it naval facilities at the Iraqi port of Umm Qasr. A few weeks ago the Shah reportedly reached an accommodation with the Baghdad junta, which entailed his abandonment of the Kurds in exchange for the acquisition of equal rights in the Shatt al-Arab. It is a shabby compact and one, moreover, which will not endure. The consequences of the Shah's ambitions, however, endure, most conspicuously in the tragic fate which has befallen the Kurds and the establishment by Russia of a position at the head of the Gulf.

Towards the minor states of the Gulf the Shah has so far acted with outward civility, though there is little doubt that he regards them as potential Persian satrapies. Much has been made of his renunciation in 1970 of the longstanding Persian claim to Bahrain as demonstrating his pacific intentions in the Gulf, but as the claim had no foundation in law or in fact its abandonment was a worthless gesture, however politically rewarding for the Shah.

A more accurate pointer to his real intentions was his seizure at the close of 1971 of the islands of Abu Musa and the Tunbs in the lower Gulf. These islands, situated near the Straits of Hormuz, were dependencies of the Trucial sheikhdoms of Sharjah and Ras-al-Khaima. The Shah's justification for occupying them was that he was anxious to prevent them from falling into the hands of extremists who might use them as bases from which to threaten shipping, and particularly oil tankers, passing through the straits. His action caused a certain amount of hubbub in the Arab world, but the only party to suffer from it was British Petroleum, whose holdings in Libya were sequestrated by Col. Gaddafi in revenge for what he considered, not without reason, to be the British government's complicity in the affair.

Western reaction in general to the Shah's move was indulgent. It was rapidly becoming part of the accepted wisdom that the guardianship of the Gulf formerly exercised by Britain had now passed jointly to Persia and Saudi Arabia. It is an impression that the Shah has been happy to confirm by declaring at frequent intervals that the affairs of the Gulf are solely the concern of the states around its shores, and the Soviet Union has been equally happy to support him in his stand.

This circumstance alone should make the West wary of accepting his contention. There are, however, other grounds for disputing it. It is difficult, for instance, to see any advantage in allowing him to exert control over the Straits of Hormuz and to gain a foothold on the Arabian shore.

Those who regard such a prospect with equanimity ignore the record of Persian intransigence and mischief-making in the Gulf in the past two centuries. They also overlook the fact that Persia has never subscribed to any conventions on the law of the sea drawn up in 1958. The straits are an international waterway, a status which has been established, as the whole *status corpus* of international law has been established, by Western nations, almost invariably against the opposition of Oriental powers.

Already there have been dangerous indications from some Middle Eastern states of a desire to exert the kind of control over the narrow seas adjacent to their coasts which is incompatible with international rights of free passage. It is not in the interest of the principal maritime powers of the world—or in anyone's interests, not even the shah's in the last analysis—to permit the international status of the Straits of Hormuz to be eroded.

Although Persia and Saudi Arabia are supposed to share a mutual interest in the maintenance of peace in the Gulf and the suppression of political elements hostile to the existing conservative order, they are in reality deeply divided by racial, religious and cultural antipathies. The Shah regards the Saudis as savage Bedouin, parvenus and religious fanatics. The Saudis in turn consider the Shah a profligate, intoxicated with a sense of his own importance, and the Persian Shia as little better than *kafirs*, infidels.

The two monarchies are expansionist by tradition and inclination, and their ambitions could well overlap and conflict in the south-eastern corner of Arabia, in Oman and the United Arab Emirates. The Shah has already, by the aid he has afforded the Sultan of Oman in his campaign in Dhufar, signified his willingness to intervene militarily in the Arabian peninsula. An uprising anywhere in the sultanate, and more particularly in the Musandam peninsula jutting into the Straits of Hormuz, or an outbreak in one of the United Arab Emirates, directed against the ruling family, or involving Persian immigrants, would give him the excuse to intervene with force for the ostensible purpose of restoring the *status quo ante*.

Saudi Arabia, with its pretensions to paramountcy in Arabia, could not allow such an intervention to go unchallenged, and the result could well be to embroil it with Persia, with incalculable consequences for them both and for the Gulf as a whole. The damage which Western interests would suffer, and the pickings which Russia would enjoy from playing the jackal in a Perso-Arab conflict, require no elaboration.

14
Oil & the West[1]

T o someone removed from the American scene, perhaps the most disquieting feature of Robert W. Tucker's articles ["Oil: The Issue of American Intervention," January, and "Further Reflections on Oil and Force," March] is the insight they offer into the attitude prevailing in what, for the want of a more elegant term, might be called "opinion-making circles" in the United States toward the defense of Western interests in the Middle East. The burden of Mr. Tucker's argument in his January article, that a situation could well arise which would necessitate a resort to force to insure the security of oil supplies from the Persian Gulf to the Western world and Japan, is so eminently reasonable as to preclude the need for comment. Yet it is evident in every line that he wrote that he felt compelled to put his case with the utmost circumspection, a compulsion he would surely not have felt if the critical air had not been rank with the smell of appeasement. As it is, the reaction to his article proves his caution to have been amply justified, even though unavailing: the familiar voices have been raised in the usual quarters in outraged denunciation of anything so reckless and so wicked as to suggest that the West might take up arms in defense of an interest vital to its survival.

What Mr. Tucker's critics seem to overlook in their indignation is that the Persian Gulf is a highly unstable area, subject to frequent and often violent shifts of political fortune. It would be a gross dereliction of duty on the part of any major Western government, not least the government of

---

1 From *Commentary*; Aug 1, 1975; 60, 2. Reproduced by permission.

the United States, if it were not to keep this fact constantly in mind and to shape its policy toward the countries of the region accordingly, even to the extent, if need be, of preparing to intervene militarily to keep oil supplies flowing freely. Yet all the evidence so far indicates that the major Western powers have chosen to ignore the reality of the Gulf's condition, that they are fecklessly hoping that nothing will upset the status quo there, or that Iran and Saudi Arabia between them will somehow maintain the peace and security of the area. It is a forlorn hope: the Shah of Iran himself represents perhaps the greatest single threat to the tranquillity of the Gulf, while the record of Saudi Arabia's relations with the minor states of the peninsula is one of friction and antipathy. Despite the efforts of the United States over a quarter of a century to promote the paramount position of Saudi Arabia in the peninsula, the Saudi government has shown itself to be incapable of exerting a hegemony over its neighbours. Its attempts to do so, however, have been, and will continue to be, a major source of disturbance in the Gulf.

Like Chamberlain facing the dictators, the governments of the major Western powers have failed to take the measure of the regimes with which they are dealing. As a consequence, they have not yet fully comprehended the nature of the menace which now hangs over the West. For all the brou-haha raised about it, the Arab-Israeli conflict is not the reason the Arabs and the Shah are now wielding the oil weapon against the West, however much the conflict might have been the excuse for the imposition of the embargo in October 1973. The Shah, after all, has been in the forefront of those demanding ever higher prices for oil, and he has been neither at war with Israel nor reluctant to sell her oil. It is the price rises, not the threats of an embargo, which are the essential element in the strategy which he and the Arabs are now pursuing toward the West, a strategy which began to take shape early in 1971, long before the Arab-Israeli war in the fall of 1973. What they are endeavouring to do in concert is to hold the Western world for ransom, to place it in thrall, and so to effect a massive transfer of resources from the Christian West to the Muslim East, thereby redressing the balance of power between Western Christendom and Islam which has been tilted in favour of the former for the past three centuries or more.

There is no mistaking the mood of exultation which now grips Sunni Islam, and, to only a lesser degree, Shii Islam. Having suffered for genera-tions from a powerful sense of grievance at the manifest political and eco-nomic superiority of the West, the Arabs and the Iranians now believe that in their control of the greater part of the world's proven reserves of crude oil they possess the means of bringing the West to heel and of reasserting the primacy of Islam. Far-fetched though these ambitions may appear to Western eyes, they nevertheless are real to those who cherish them, and infinitely more seductive than the cooler intimations of reason.

The reaction of most of the Western powers to the economic blackmail being practised against them by the Shah and the governments of the Arab oil-producing states has been supine and pusillanimous acquiescence, deriving apparently from the belief that such an attitude will guarantee them continued access to the oil reserves of the Middle East. It will, of course, do nothing of the kind: appeasement will only increase the truculence which the Arabs and the Shah are at present displaying, and confirm them in their conviction that they have the West at their mercy. The Middle Eastern members of OPEC, it should be recalled, have broken every agreement they have made since 1970 concerning prices, levels of production, and the rate at which they were to acquire a majority holding in the oil companies' equity. Every promise they have made to lower oil prices has been unfulfilled, every threat to restrict production carried into effect. Yet the governments of the West still affect to believe that the various economic nostrums now being peddled around—long-term barter deals, "recycling" of surplus oil funds, "partnership" arrangements, and so forth—will somehow extricate them from the financial difficulties into which they have been plunged by the inordinate increases in the price of oil, and at the same time safeguard the supply of oil in the future. They will not, for the basic reason that none of the Middle Eastern oil-producing states can be relied upon, on the evidence of its past conduct, to honour its undertakings.

Oil is a strategic commodity of prime importance, and it is folly of an almost suicidal order for the West to have allowed itself to drift into a situation where it is incapable of controlling its major source of supply. With the decline of Western influence in the Middle East, and more particularly after the British withdrawal from Aden in 1967 and from the Gulf in 1971, the West lost the control it had previously exercised over the Gulf's oil. It will somehow have to recover that control, not necessarily directly or by a physical presence, but at least to a degree that affords greater security than the present state of near anarchy. The advocates of appeasement in the West maintain that the acquisition of oil is a purely commercial transaction, and they buttress this contention with glib arguments about a sense of self-interest on the part of the Middle Eastern oil-producing states and a further sense of mutual interest between them and the Western oil-consuming countries in keeping oil flowing, arguments whose purpose is to demonstrate that all is really for the best in the best of all possible worlds and that there is no cause for the West to fret. But these arguments not only ignore or distort the record of the past few years, they also depend upon assumptions about good sense, reasonableness, moderation, and the sanctity of agreements which are native to the West but which are not subscribed to by the Middle Eastern governments in question. The issue, contrary to all that OPEC's Western apologists may say, is by no means a purely commercial one but, as the motives which impelled the Arabs and the Shah to raise oil prices to exorbitant levels clearly reveal, it is almost exclusively a political one and should be treated primarily as such. We have got ourselves into the predicament in which we find ourselves today by ignoring this fact—a melancholy consequence of following Keynes instead of Clausewitz.

The vast surplus funds now at the disposal of the Middle Eastern oil-producing states pose a further, and potentially more sinister, threat to the West than mere financial embarrassment. Given the nature of the regimes in power in these states, it is inevitable that they should employ these funds for political purposes, as likely as not of a *louche* variety, beyond their own borders. What signs there may be in the United States of the deployment of these funds for such purposes I have no way of knowing; but here in Britain evidence grows with the passing of each week of the creeping corruption of our political, economic, and social institutions by both the overt and the covert use of oil money, predominantly Arab. Since Britain is now on the verge of economic collapse, mainly as a result of its own profligacy, there is an understandable, if far from commendable, reluctance to resist the inflow of this money, and a corresponding readiness to truckle to the Arab oil magnates and the Shah, especially since the depositing here of the Danegeld they have extracted helps to keep up the spurious appearance of financial solvency which the British government is desperately anxious to maintain. But the canker is by no means confined to political and financial circles in Britain: it has spread far and wide, into commerce and industry, into publishing and journalism, even into the universities and learned societies, to the extent that London is beginning to wear the aspect of being, after Mecca and Medinah, the third holy city of Islam.

To a considerable extent the West has got itself into the precarious situation in which it now stands with respect to the security of oil supplies from the Gulf and the crippling prices it is paying for them by treating the petty states which control the Gulf's oil reserves with far more deference than their standing in the world warrants. None of the oil-producing states of the Middle East is the peer of any of the major powers of Europe, and it is simply ridiculous as well as profoundly humiliating to see the foreign and finance ministers of Europe scurrying from one dusty Middle Eastern capital to another, to wait patiently upon the pleasure of some disdainful potentate, to attend gravely to his plaints, and to plead humbly for his favors. Here, in truth, increase of appetite grows from what it feeds upon: all that Western cajolery serves to achieve is to make these petty despots more intransigent and arrogant than ever and to heighten their contempt for Western power. It is high time that the West began to disabuse them of their illusions by employing the array of political and economic weapons it has at its disposal to end the extortion currently being practiced by Iran and the Arab oil-producing states. It can be done, if the will is there. Cracks have already appeared in the façade of OPEC unity under the pressure of the present glut of crude oil in the world's markets. Further pressure will split the cartel wide open, especially since none of its members, not even the Middle Eastern ones, is the natural partner of the others.

Even if the price-fixing ring is broken, however, the problem of the security of oil supplies remains, which brings us back to the point with which this letter opened. Western Europe and Japan are dependent for their principal supplies of oil upon the good will of regimes notorious for their fickle and perverse behaviour. The political situation in the Gulf is highly volatile and dangerous, and it has been made even more so by the thoroughly shameful and senseless conduct of Britain, France, and the United States in flooding the region with arms for the ignoble purpose of soaking up excess oil revenues. Every state in the Gulf nurses a grievance of one kind or another against its neighbour, and recent events have only sharpened their mutual suspicions and antagonisms. The assassination of Faisal ibn Abdul Aziz has given encouragement to the subversive elements in the Arabian peninsula, while the accord between Iraq and Iran, at least for as long as it lasts, has freed their hands for adventures in the Gulf. No doubt it suits the Shah and others to proclaim that the affairs of the Gulf are solely the concern of the States around its shores, and to weary the world with a lot of *gasconade* about the terrible things that will happen if the Western powers so much as dare to show their faces in the region. The Shah, however, is a paper tiger, and the West should not allow itself to be duped by his growls, or those of his Arabian counterparts, into resigning its economic destiny into his or their hands.

Mr Tucker has courageously grasped the nettle by facing up to the basic question of whether, in the end, the West might have to resort to force to insure control over its major source of oil. His critics have evaded this painful duty by conjuring up instead all manner of dreadful apparitions which, they say, will become reality if the West takes military action in the Gulf – the gigantic figure of the Russian bear, lurching down the valleys of Mesopotamia, snow still clinging to is paws; the sky over Arabia rent with flames from a thousand exploding oil wells; the ferocious hordes of Araby sweeping out of the sands to strike like lightening at the invading infidel, and then vanish, as swiftly as they came, into the desert wastes, there to prepare to strike again before the sun is up (or down). How the Russians would react to armed Western intervention is unknown, probably even to themselves and most certainly to the Western oracles now vociferously prophesying calamity. As for the prospects of a determined and effective Arab guerrilla campaign, they cannot be judged very formidable if the history of warfare in eastern Arabia in the past century or so is a reliable guide. Yet by arguing in the way they do, Mr. Tucker's critics have in a sense, and despite themselves, answered the question to which he addressed himself and which they have refused to face up to squarely. The answer they have given is a depressing one, for it is characteristic of the want of spirit and resolution which today dominates much of the Western world. Instead of congratulating themselves for having so faithfully manifested this malaise, they would do well to reflect that if the West persists in its present abject policy of appeasement toward the Arabs and the Shah, it will render inevitable an eventual recourse to the kind of measures the very thought of which now makes them pale.

Stanley Hoffmann's letter, which appears in the correspondence on Mr. Tucker's articles [Letters from Readers, April], might have been written to illustrate what I have said about the nervelessness and make-believe which characterize fashionable thinking these days about Western relations with Asia and Africa. His arguments are all depressingly familiar: they are those used by a collection of sophists and cut-rate sages in Britain in the 1960's to justify the abandonment of its responsibilities in Africa and the Middle East. Every confident calculation made by these *fossoyeurs* about the beneficial consequences of such an abandonment has been disproved by subsequent events, yet they are still rhapsodizing about the ineffable joys of retreat and appeasement. One of their more sublime moments of triumph came at the end of 1967, when Britain slunk out of Aden, surrendering the British colony and protectorate to a gang of terrorists. Would Mr. Hoffmann care to assert that this retreat and the British withdrawal from the Gulf four years later had no bearing whatever upon the increasing use of intimidation by the Middle Eastern members of OPEC from 1971 onward in order to raise the price of crude oil, expropriate the oil-companies' holdings, and constrict the supply of oil to the West?

I don't know what Mr. Hoffmann's qualifications may be to pronounce upon the affairs of Arabia and the Gulf, but from the remarks he makes about the Anglo-French intervention at Suez in 1956 he would seem to understand little of the political tradition of the East. He might try impressing his theories about the pacific settlement of disputes and the voluntary renunciation of force as a means of achieving political ends upon the Marxist-Leninist junta in Aden, whose bloody deeds of repression provoke such delighted squeals in the cafes of the *rive gauche* and other fashionable intellectual watering-places, where the politics of Asia is excitedly discussed in an ideologically hygienic atmosphere into which the rude breath of reality is forbidden to intrude. Or he could equally well explain his convictions to the rulers of Saudi Arabia and the Gulf states, who know a thing or two about how to settle sectarian quarrels or territorial disputes, or to the Marxist Fedayeen who plot to overthrow them and who also know a thing or two about the power that resides in the barrel of a gun. Mr. Hoffmann is welcome to his breast-beating: for my part, I would prefer to go tiger-shooting in the company of Mr. Tucker.

J.B. Kelly
London, England

15
Britain, India and the Turkish Empire[1]

Ram Lakhan Shukla: *Britain, India and the Turkish Empire,
1853-1882.* xv, 262 pp., 5 maps. New Delhi, etc.: People's
Publishing House, 1973.

What Dr. Shukla has set out to accomplish in his book is a redressing of the balance in studies of Britain's involvement in
the Eastern Question in the nineteenth century, which, he believes, has
hitherto been too heavily tilted on the European side of the question and
insufficiently weighted on the Indian side, which he considers to be of
equal if not greater consequence. Moreover, he maintains that the relationship between British activities in Central Asia and British policy towards
the Ottoman empire has been virtually ignored by historians, who have
also, in his view, 'altogether overlooked' the operation of what he calls
'Anglo-Indian policy' in the Near and Middle East. Perhaps the picture is
not quite so black as Shukla paints it, but then neither is it exactly radiant,
and his book will certainly go an appreciable way towards improving it.

Although Shukla begins his study with a survey of the evolution of
British and British-Indian policy towards the Ottoman empire up to and
including the Crimean war, the bulk of his book is concerned with the
repercussions of the Russo-Turkish war of 1877-8 upon that policy and
upon the position of Indian Muslims *vis-a-vis* both the government of In-

1 From *Bulletin of the School of Oriental and African Studies*, University of London,
Vol. 38, No. 3 (1975), pp. 646-648. Published by Cambridge University Press. Reproduced by permission

dia and the Ottoman sultan, 'Abdülhamïd. Shukla gives a lengthy and absorbing account of the discussions and arguments which went on in British political and official circles, and between the home government and the government of India, over how best to implement the policy of continuing to uphold the integrity of the Ottoman empire, now essentially reduced to its dominions in Asia. The question revolved to a considerable extent around the merits of Cyprus versus Muhammara (or some other spot at the head of the Persian Gulf) as *a place d'armes* from which to sustain the Sublime Porte in the defence of its possessions, and Shukla makes out a strong case for the choice of the latter site over the former, upon which the choice was ultimately to fall.

The commitment to Turkey not unnaturally disposed the British government to look with a certain degree of equanimity upon the pan-Islamic aspirations of the sultan, 'Abdülhamïd, and for a while the British beguiled themselves with a vision of a grand, pan-Islamic front, embracing the Ottoman empire, Afghanistan, and the Central Asian khanates, underpinned by British India, which would effectively block the further advance of Russia in Asia. Shukla is, with good reason, scornful of the whole notion, especially as it depended for its inspiration largely upon the conceit with which British statesmen of the time were wont to deceive themselves that Britain, as mistress of India, was a great Muslim power. This same conceit, along with some rather more realistic calculations, led the British-Indian authorities not only to tolerate the growth of pan-Islamic feeling among Indian Muslims but even to encourage them to revere 'Abdülhamïd as caliph of Islam.

There is a great deal of fresh information in Shukla's chapters on the expression of pan-Islamic and caliphal sentiment in India in the 1870's and early 1880's, especially the portions he has unearthed from the vernacular and Anglo-Indian press, and it goes a long way to support his contention that it was in these years, rather than in the last decade of the century, that the true beginnings of the later *khilafat* movement are to be found. What is disappointing in his otherwise thorough investigation of the British attempts to utilize the caliphate—or, rather, to manipulate the reverence of Indian Muslims for the institution—for their own particular political purposes is his failure to discuss what the British actually understood of the nature of the caliphate, and whether they realized the significance of what they were doing in impressing it upon the attention of their Muslim subjects. He notes, for instance, that after the Russo-Turkish war the *khutba* was read in the principal mosques every Friday in the name of 'Abdülhamïd, but he does not say how the government of India interpreted this recognition of the sultan as caliph. The omission is of particular significance in view of the way in which, as Shukla notes in passing, the attempted exploitation of pan-Islamic and caliphal sentiment by the British-Indian authorities was to backfire upon them some years later. The first faint intimations of such a reaction were received as early as the time of the British occupation of Egypt in 1882, although very few British officials recognized them, let alone paid them heed.

When Shukla comes in the closing stages of his book to analyse what he chooses to call 'anti-Turkish intrigues' by the British among Arab notables and religious dignitaries in the late 1870's and early 1880's, he moves on to insecure ground. Although he quotes at length from the correspondence of British diplomatic and consular officials, in particular Sir Henry Layard, the ambassador at Constantinople, to show how the British became increasingly concerned at the antipathy which 'Abdülhamïd began to exhibit towards them after the Russo-Turkish war, he does not seem himself to have grasped the reason why suspicion of the sultan's designs should have taken root in the first place. In large measure this is due to his having ignored the sequence and character of Turkish activities in the Arabian peninsula, and more especially in Yemen and along the Arabian coast of the Persian Gulf, in the early 1870's, which in sum seemed to point to an intention on the part of the Porte to acquire an ascendancy over the peninsula as a whole, to the ultimate detriment of the British position in Aden and the maritime protectorate which had been built up over the years in the Gulf. Shukla goes even further astray in his account of British contacts with the *sharif* of Mecca in 1879-80, which he says (pp. 186-7) were meant 'to bring the grand sharif under their influence for realising the ambitious scheme of a British protectorate over Arabia and for detaching the Arabs in Baghdad and Syria from Turkish rule'. No such scheme was ever contemplated, as Shukla would have discovered if he had looked more closely at the Foreign Office correspondence on Turkey for these years. He has read too much into the reports of the consular agent at Jidda, James Zohrab, who was given to concocting fanciful proposals involving, among other things, a British protectorate over the Hijaz and Sharifian support for British rule in India, none of which received serious consideration from his superiors. Shukla even goes so far as to allege (p. 218) that the British plotted to set up an Arabian caliphate under their own aegis, and that this 'long-term, sustained policy' had its culmination in the Arab revolt of 1916. Would that British policy towards the Arabs in this century had been so long maturing, so deeply bedded, so consistent, and so calculating! Instead, it was, sad to say, even more haphazard and ill thought out than British policy towards the Turks in the period covered by Shukla's useful study.

16
In the Middle East Labyrinth[1]

Imperialism and Nationalism in the Fertile Crescent. Sources and Prospects of the Arab-Israeli Conflict, by Richard Allen. 686 pp. Oxford University Press.
Peace in the Middle East? Reflections on Justice and Nationhood, by Noam Chomsky. 187 pp. Collins, Fontana.

S ir Richard Allen is a former member of the diplomatic service whose career abroad was mostly spent in Latin America and South-East Asia. His time in the Middle East was limited to two years as an official in the Palestine Government in the 1920s before he joined the Foreign Office. Since his retirement in 1963 he has taught at a succession of colleges and universities in the United States and has published three books, one on Malaysia, another on the history and politics of South-East Asia, and now Imperialism and Nationalism in the Fertile Crescent, which is intended, he says, to provide undergraduates and the general reader, with 'a reasonable clear, simple, and dispassionate account of the deep historical origins of the complex (Arab-Israeli) conflict in its wider Middle Eastern setting'.

Evidently, Sir Richard believes these origins to lie very deep indeed, for he begins his narrative with Abraham and brings it to a close four millennia and 600 pages later in the aftermath of the Yom Kippur War of October 1973. En route, he takes in, among other large subjects, the Jewish diaspora, the rise of Christianity and Islam, the Arab empires, the

---

1 From *The Times Literary Supplement*, 12 December 1975. Reproduced by permission.

Crusades, European imperialism in the Middle East, Zionism and Arab nationalism, the two world wars, the emergence of Israel, and the post-war history of the Arab world. His style, in keeping with his stated aim, is unquestionably clear and simple, and his sentiments are unimpeachedly liberal, understanding and sympathy being accorded to Arab and Jew in equal measure.

Why, then, does the book seem so flat and spiritless, so as to make the reading of it an exercise in tedium? The reason is not just that the author has nothing to say about the Palestine question that has not been said before. After all, it would be a rare feat to produce a fresh thought on a topic about which so much has been written in so short a time. No, the fault lies rather in that very quality of simplicity which Sir Richard has striven to achieve. For the issues involved in the Palestine question have become much too indurative in their nature and labyrinthine in their ramifications to be susceptible of description and analysis at the level attempted here, a level exemplified by the author's solemn explanations of who the Vichy French were and what the Battle of Britain was about.

The same criticism applies to the judgements Sir Richard delivers upon the subjects which occupy the bulk of his book – Western intervention in the Middle East in the nineteenth and twentieth centuries, the growth of Arab nationalism, the advent and progress of Zionism, and the untoward consequences which have flowed from all three. Nationalism in his view is both natural and admirable (at least in its Asian manifestations), Zionism is understandable if regrettable, and Western imperialism, especially in the injustices it has inflicted upon the Arabs, is deplorable.

Since Sir Richard, on the evidence of his book, has only a superficial acquaintance with the modern history of the Middle East, these opinions can hardly be taken as informed judgements but rather as the unthinking reflection of approved attitudes. Nor, considering the sources upon which he so heavily relies, could they be anything else; for these sources are, in the main, limited to general histories, of college-textbook standard, and to popular works by publicists and others with a vested interest in espousing Arab grievances. From the approving comments which he makes about these works, Sir Richard would appear to be oblivious of their true quality.

Much of his distress at the disgraceful way in which Western countries, and more particularly, Britain and France, have supposedly behaved towards the Arabs derives from his conviction that the British defaulted on the promises that Sir Henry McMahon, the British high commissioner in Egypt, made to Sharif Husain of Mecca in the First World War to persuade him to lead a revolt against the Turks. Worse still, even as they negotiated with Husain, the British were cynically engaging with the French in the notorious Sykes-Picot agreement of 1916 to carve up the Arab lands between them. Sir Richard gets himself into a fine lather of condemnation and disgust over these scoundrelly goings-on, mostly as a consequence of having trusted to unreliable or polemical sources like George Antonius's *The Arab Awakening*. If he had read a little more widely and carefully—better still if he had taken the time to read the actual records of the Foreign Office on the subject—he would have learnt that if the British are to be reproached for betraying anyone, it is not their Arab clients and mercenaries who have serious cause for complaint but their wartime allies, the French.

Guilt over Britain's past role in the Middle East would seem to have been all the rage in the Foreign Office of late years, if the memoirs of retired diplomatists are anything to go by. The so-called 'betrayal' of the Arabs after the First World War, especially as regards the Balfour Declaration and the mandate for Palestine, has established itself over the past half-century as an immutable truth, and the conviction that it is at the root of all Britain's subsequent troubles in the Middle East has likewise acquired the quality of holy writ. Why this should be so is beyond the understanding of an outside observer, especially as a careful reading of the Foreign Office's own records of its transactions with the Arabs during and after the First World War yields precious little evidence to support the 'betrayal' theory.

As for Britain's tribulations in the Middle East in the past few decades, they owe as much to her own actions as they do to Arab intransigence or an urge to vengeance. If guilt and shame are victuals on which the Foreign Office like to sup, then it might consume some guilt for the way in which Britain has abandoned her responsibilities in the Middle East in the past thirty years—as well as in much of Asia and Africa—and some shame for the abject posture adopted before the rest of the world by so many of its own officials, past and present. To find a former diplomatist like Sir Richard Allen carrying this abjectness to the point of obscuring or apologizing for Britain's past military and political achievements in the Middle East in a work written for the American college market is a profoundly depressing experience. It was not by the vociferations of Arab nationalists or the dreams of British Arabophiles that the Ottoman Empire was defeated and the Arabs freed from Turkish rule, but by British arms; and Sir Richard would have done well, in the interests of historical accuracy, to have impressed this upon his readers.

Certitude, not contrition, is the keynote of Noam Chomsky's tract on the Arab-Israeli conflict, *Peace in the Middle East?* It consists of an introduction and five essays written between 1969 and 1974. Four of the five have been published previously, and two are based upon talks given to Arab students in the United States. Professor Chomsky's prescriptions for ending the conflict are awesome in their simplicity. Dismissing as misguided all the attempts that have been made to date to resolve it within the existing system of nation-states, he advocates the dismantling of the State of Israel and the erection in its place of a 'socialist binational state' of Palestine which 'will not be a Jewish state or an Arab state but rather a democratic multinational society' permitting 'all Palestinians the right of return, along with Jews, who wish to find their place in this national homeland'.

How is this sublime consummation to be attained? By the replacement, Professor Chomsky explains, of national strife with the class struggle, by the Jewish masses linking up with the Arab masses, and supported by 'the peace movement' and 'the international left', overcoming their oppressors. The Israeli left should reach out to the Palestinian-Arab left, to Al-Fatah which has proclaimed its goal to be 'a non-racist, secular, democratic state of Palestine', and to Marxist groups like the Popular Front for the Liberation of Palestine whose very existence presages a hopeful future. Ultimately, this 'democratic, socialist Palestine' would be merged in a broader federation of the neighbouring Arab states.

Presumably Professor Chomsky intends his ideas to be taken seriously. He has, after all, enjoyed much vogue among campus revolutionaries of recent years as the scourge of the American bourgeoisie. The difficulty is, however, that the stale slogans and mindless abuse of the New Left dialectic of the 1960s have even less application to the hard and bitter realities of the Arab-Israeli conflict than have the pieties of Sir Richard Allen. It is not enough to see the conflict, as Professor Chomsky sees it, predominantly in terms of Israelis domestic politics and American attitudes towards Israel, and to interpret it in narrowly Marxist terms. Although he professes to be mindful of its Middle Eastern context, it is the measure of his almost ignoring of this context that in the entire book there is not a single reference to Islam. Does Professor Chomsky really believe, when the constitution of every Arab country except Lebanon proclaims it to be an Islamic state, that Al Fatah or the Palestine Liberation Organisation as a whole seriously intends to establish a secular Palestinian state in place of Israel.

Considering the nature of traditional Muslim attitudes to Jews and their place in the Islamic order of things, what does he think the position of the Jews would be as a minority in the larger federation of Arab countries that he envisage? Surely he is aware, and if he isn't he should be, that in the eyes of Muslim Arabs, Israel has usurped part of the *dar al-Islam* (Muslim territory) which it is their sacred duty to recover. Once it is recovered they may be prepared to extend to its Jewish inhabitants the tolerance which they accorded to Jewish communities within the *dar al-Islam* in past centuries. But to the fanatics of the PFLP and like groups it is Judaism itself which is the enemy, and they would offer the Jews of Israel only the choice between expulsion and extermination. One would dearly like to see Professor Chomsky expounding his theories about an Arab-Jewish Marxist consensus to George Habash and Nayif Hawatima of the PFLP, or Salah Khalaf of Black September. He might then learn, contrary to what he seems at present to believe, that Palestinian Septembrists are nothing like Russian Octobrists.

Professor Chomsky's attitude to terrorism as a weapon in the conflict is ambiguous. He mentions, and then in passing, only one act of terrorism, the massacre at Lod airport, which was committed by Japanese terrorists against Christian pilgrims. Of Arab terrorism he says nothing, reserving his indignation for the activities of the Israeli security forces. The omission is hardly surprising, given the political faith to which Professor Chomsky adheres. His indifference on this score stands in marked contrast, however, to his sensitivity to criticism of himself or his doctrines. Here he is a veritable tiger, and it is in the many passages of his book where he avenges himself upon his critics for their impieties that the true reason for its publication can be decried.

For *Peace in the Middle East?* is really nothing more than another round in the epic contest of Chomsky versus the rest, on this occasion represented by George Kennan, Walter Laqueur, Seymour Martin Lipset, Irving Kristol and Joseph Alsop *inter alios*. To them, and others like them, it seems, 'the problems of Israel and the Middle East are incidental to [American] domestic political issues and are cynically exploited as a device for undermining the peace movement and the New Left'. There is not a trick of rhetoric or slanderous innuendo which they will not employ in an effort to confound his message or misrepresent it to others. Rancour has made them hysterical, and prejudice blinds them to the true character of the Arab-Israeli conflict, which is part of the continuing worldwide, revolutionary struggle against the forces of capitalism, militarism and imperialism. If they would only attend to the relevant factors, as closely as he has, they would be forced to admit this. Of course; he is absolutely right and we are purblind fools not to heed him. *Domine, non sumus digni.*

17
Farce in the Bazaar[1]

In the Anglo-Arab Labyrinth: the McMahon-Husayn Correspondence and its Interpretations, 1914-1939, by Elie Kedourie. Cambridge University Press, 1976.

On the outbreak of war with Turkey in 1914 the British Residency in Cairo sent a communication to the Sharif of Mecca, Husayn ibn Ali, suggesting that he might care to assist Great Britain in the war in return for the recognition of his independence from Turkish rule.

The suggestion had not originated with the British Government but in approaches made some time earlier by the Sharif's eldest son, Abdullah (later King Abdullah of Jordan), to the Oriental Secretary of the Residency, Ronald Storrs.

Storrs, a man of lively if sometimes wayward imagination, was much taken with the idea of an Arab revolt. So, too, was his late superior in Egypt, Lord Kitchener, now Secretary of State for War, and it was at Kitchener's urging that the first, and as it was to prove, fateful communication was sent to Mecca.

Further exchanges, enlarging and embroidering the theme of an Arab revolt, passed between Cairo and Mecca in 1915 and the early part of 1916, and the various missives eventually passed into history as the 'McMahon-Husayn Correspondence', after its principals, Sir Henry McMahon, the British High Commissioner in Egypt, and Sharif Husayn of the Hijaz.

---

1 From *The Sunday Telegraph*, 22 February 1976. Reproduced by permission.

Many legends, masquerading as facts, have grown up about the correspondence, the most enduring of which is that it committed the British Government to the recognition of the independence of all the Arab provinces of the Turkish empire, and that Britain broke this undertaking when the First World War ended.

How much substance is there to this charge, a charge which depends for much of its force upon the contention that the promises made by McMahon were clear-cut and unambiguous and that his correspondence with Husayn constituted a formal, biding engagement?

Elie Kedourie, who has already earned himself a formidable reputation as a scrupulous and penetrating scholar of British relations with the Arab world, has done what no one else has troubled to do, least of all those who have been most shrill in their denunciations of British perfidy, which is to read carefully the correspondence preserved in the Foreign Office files, to examine the circumstances of its composition and transmission closely, and, in the light of his findings, to test the validity of the interpretation which has held sway these past 50 years.

What a tale *In the Anglo-Arab Labyrinth* has to unfold! It should harrow up the souls and freeze the blood of the Foreign Office clerks for many a long day to come. For as Professor Kedourie guides us with unfailing sureness through the labyrinthine intricacies of negotiation and elucidation, we find ourselves in the middle of a bizarre farce (or perhaps more aptly, a farcical bazaar) of oriental haggling, British ineptitude, Arab importunity and individual delusion, self-serving and deceit.

Sir Edward Grey, the Foreign Secretary, allowed himself to be hustled by Kitchener into encouraging Husayn to revolt, against the advice of the India Office. The Foreign Office tried to frame its proposals to Husayn with some care, only to have its precise formulations and reservations obscured or negated by the extravagant embellishments added by McMahon, Storrs and Gilbert Clayton, the director of intelligence in Cairo.

The effect of 'these rhetorical flourishes', as Professsor Kedourie drily describes them, taken with the inadequacy and dubious accuracy of their translations into Arabic, was to enlarge Husayn's ambitions beyond all reasonable measure. No longer did he merely desire independence as ruler of the Hijaz: he wanted an Arab kingdom stretching from the Yemen to Anatolia, from the Mediterranean to the Gulf, in contrast to the British Government's intention that Syria, Iraq and Palestine should come under French or British tutelage.

Who was betrayed after 1918? Certainly not the Arabs. The British undertakings to Husayn were conditional upon the fulfilment of his commitment, among other things to attack the Turks in Sinai, capture Medina, and raise up the rebellion in Syria and Iraq. He accomplished none of these objects, and the activities of the Sharifian forces under his son Faysal, for all the frantic to-ings and fro-ings of T.E. Lawrence, contributed little to the Turkish defeat.

How then did the legend of the "great betrayal" of the Arabs take root and spread like a mighty banyan tree, under whose shade British Arabophiles still sit today and keen and smite their breasts and chant their sonorous *mea culpas*? Here we come to the second part of Professor Kedourie's masterful feat of detection.

When, at the end of the war, the Foreign Office wanted a summary of the principal undertakings entered into in the Husayn-McMahon correspondence, the task was entrusted initially to Harold Nicolson and Arnold Toynbee, and after them to Hubert Young.

Each produced his own reading of the documents and each made fundamental errors of interpretation. Further distortions occurred in the 1930s when the correspondence came to be interpreted almost exclusively in the context of the Palestine problem, with which, of course, it had never been concerned.

Yet Arab delegates to the conference on Palestine convened in London in 1939, succeeded in convincing the Foreign Office that Palestine had been included in the independent Arab state promised to Husayn by McMahon. The Foreign Office officials responsible for Arab affairs were not by this time even bothering to consult their own files to discover the truth of the matter.

The nadir of Foreign Office incompetence and dereliction of duty came when the Lord Chancellor, Lord Maugham, was induced by the brief prepared for him by the Foreign Office to concede humbly to the Arab delegates that the British Government's undertakings in the war had been misleading.

The extent of the damage done by the perpetuation of the myth of British "betrayal" of the Arabs can never be estimated. For half a century the propagators of this myth have had their way, because no one rebutted their claims or exposed them as fraudulent. Professor Kedourie has now done so: he has shown us the way out of the Anglo-Arab labyrinth, and in doing so has placed us for ever in his debt.

18

The Experience of Revolution in South Arabia[1]

W hen the ill-fated Federation of South Arabia came into being on January 1, 1963, it did not include among its member
states the Hadramaut and the Mahra country to the east. It was not difficult to see the reasons for their exclusion. The Mahra territory, nominally
under the rule of the sultan of Qishn and Socotra, was the wildest and
most inaccessible corner of the eastern Aden Protectorate. Any effective
display of authority there by the sultan or the protecting power was confined to the few villages along the coast. Inland a kind of formalized anarchy reigned among the tribal nomads and cultivators. The Hadramaut was
a rather different case. Although the land was itself forbidding—its very
name means 'death is present'—the energies and enterprise of its inhabitants had made it relatively prosperous, at least by the standards of southern
Arabia. The coastal towns, the chief of which were Mukalla and Shihr, had
been the centres of a wideranging maritime commerce, while in the interior, beyond the *jol*, the broken and desolate plateau which rose abruptly
behind the coastal plain and stretched inland for a hundred miles, the fertile regions of the Wadi Hadramaut supported a thriving agriculture and a
number of imposing towns, of which Shibam, Saiyun and Tarim were the
best known. The comparative prosperity of the Hadramaut, however, did
not derive primarily from its native economy but from the wealth accumulated overseas by the large colonies of émigré Hadramis, especially in India,
the Philippines, Malaya and the East Indies. The constant intercourse they

1 From *Middle Eastern Studies*, Vol. 12, No. 2 (May, 1976), pp. 213-230. Published by
Taylor & Francis, Ltd. Reproduced by permission.

kept up with their homeland, no less than the steady flow of remittances they sent to it, was in large measure responsible for the country's progress before the Second World War; for this intercourse was the means by which innovations and improvements in agriculture, commerce and transport were introduced into the Hadramaut. What the Hadramis, resident and émigré alike, could not do, however, was to put an end to the constant feuding among the tribes, which all too often impeded or stultified the country's development.

Sovereignty over the Hadramaut was exercised by the Qu'aiti sultan of Shihr and Mukalla, whose territory extended for some 200 miles along the coast and another 150 miles inland, to Shibam and its related towns and settlements in the Wadi Hadramaut; and by the Kathiri sultan of Saiyun and Tarim, whose lands formed an enclave athwart the Wadi Hadramaut with no access to the sea. Neither sultan's writ, however, ran much beyond the environs of the coastal and inland towns. Elsewhere the tribesmen, and especially those across whose *diyar* (ranges) the routes to the coast ran, acknowledged no authority but that of their own shaikhs and the more influential *saiyids* (or *sada*), the putative descendants of the Prophet, who were the wealthiest and most prominent class in Hadrami society. It was the great achievement of Harold Ingrams, who first visited the Hadramaut as a political officer in 1934 and three years later was appointed resident adviser at Mukalla, to bring the contentious tribes to conclude a truce among themselves in 1937, and by so doing to reinforce the authority of the Qu'aiti and Kathiri sultans. Ingrams's own account of his time in the Hadramaut is contained in his well-known *Arabia and the Isles*, one of the finest books on Arabia ever written. His widow, Doreen Ingrams, added her account of their days in the Hadramaut in *A Time in Arabia*, published half-a-dozen years ago.[2]

Much of her book is taken up with the lives of the women of the Hadramaut, which Mrs Ingrams was in a unique position to observe, and she brings out very clearly how strongly social customs and domestic conduct were influenced by the Hadrami connection with Hyderabad and the East Indies. She and her husband had much to do with the al-Kaff family, one of the richest and most powerful of the *saiyid* class. Saiyid Bu Bakr al-Kaff, the most prominent member of the family, was a man of considerable enlightenment and foresight. He spent much of his fortune in bettering the lot of his people with schools, dispensaries and agricultural innovations, and he built the first motor road across the *jol* from the coast to the Wadi Hadramaut. He was instrumental, too, through the influence

---

2 London, John Murray. Pp. xi + 160, illustrations, maps, index. £2.25

he wielded with many of the tribal shaikhs, and by his judicious distribution of subsidies to them, in helping Ingrams to conclude the hundreds of trucial agreements which went to make up 'Ingrams's Peace'.

Just what 'Ingrams's Peace' meant to the people of the Hadramaut is brought out in a simple anecdote related by Doreen Ingrams.

> The Ja'ada tribe were not only notorious as fighters but also as kidnappers and slave traders, illegally selling men and women at the annual fairs held in honour of local saints...One of this tribe married a Hindu girl [in Hyderabad] and brought her and her son to Wadi Amd where he promptly sold them to his brother in payment of a debt, and the brother then sold them to another tribesman. The poor woman, who spoke little Arabic, was in despair until one day she saw an aeroplane and felt sure that it came from somewhere where there must be a proper government. She made enquiries, heard about Harold and took her son and fled to him. Harold, who was then in Seiyun, brought them to Mukalla where she stayed with us until her family in India had been contacted when we put her on a ship, together with her son and another Indian boy who had also been enslaved.

'Ingrams's Peace' was renewed in 1940—the original truces had been designed to run for three years- but only with some difficulty, as the old anarchical spirit in the tribes had begun to reassert itself. The outbreak of war with Japan in 1941, however, raised even greater difficulties for the Hadramis. It disrupted the customary intercourse with the East Indies and curtailed the payment of remittances from Malaya, the Philippines and the East Indies. Famine followed in 1943-44, after the failure of the annual rains. Hundreds of people died, and the survival of the remainder was due in large measure to British assistance. The aftermath of the war did little to restore the Hadramaut's depleted fortunes. Dutch rule ended in the East Indies, and the new state of Indonesia, by confiscating estates and businesses and restricting the export of capital, reduced the flow of funds from the Hadrami Indonesian community to its homeland to a trickle. The other Hadrami colonies in Malaya and the Philippines suffered extensive losses in the war, and they were never to regain their previous affluence. A similar fate overtook the Hadramis of Hyderabad, who had for generations taken service in the army of the *nizam*. Their traditional occupation was closed to them when Hyderabad's independence was extinguished by the government of India after the end of the British raj.

For a time, the inhabitants of the Hadramaut pinned their hopes for a revival of their former prosperity on the discovery of oil in their territory, but their hopes were not realized. Meanwhile, with British assistance and guidance, they made the best of their indigenous resources. Economic recovery was gradual but steady, and the standard of living measurably improved as irrigation schemes were put into operation, more schools and dispensaries were opened, and imports of food and manufactured goods grew in volume. More rapid progress was impeded as much by the Hadramis' own outlook and traits of character, their inveterate suspiciousness and proneness to superstition, their rancour and contumacy towards one another, as it was by the drying up of their external sources of wealth. Brigandage and tribal affrays were still far from uncommon, despite the trucial system; and the Hadrami Beduin Legion, a British-officered force raised by Ingrams in 1939, had to maintain a constant vigilance to prevent or suppress outbreaks of tribal disorder.

A good deal of the work of pacification and development in the Hadramaut was accomplished in the years between 1949 and 1958, when Colonel Hugh Boustead was resident at Mukalla. Sir Hugh (he was knighted at the end of his career, in 1965, when he retired as political agent at Abu Dhabi) has had a life so varied, so crammed with high adventure and achievement, that it seems to come straight from the pages of P. C. Wren or Captain Marryat. A midshipman in the Royal Navy at the outset of the First World War, he deserted at Capetown in 1915 in order to see more fighting. Joining the South African Scottish under an assumed name, he fought in the Senussi campaign in 1915-16 and then in France for the rest of the war, being wounded twice, commissioned in the field and awarded the Military Cross. After the war he went to Russia with the British military mission which fought with General Denikin's army in the Don campaign. He captained the British pentathlon team at the 1920 Olympics, and after a year spent at Oxford and eighteen months with the British army of occupation in Turkey, he was posted to the Sudanese Camel Corps, eventually rising to command of the force. His passion for mountaineering led him to the Himalaya, and in 1933 he took part in the expedition to climb Everest. Transferring to the Sudan political service, he served as resident in Darfur in the western Sudan until 1949, although he returned to the army during the war years to fight in the Ethiopian and Eritrean campaigns, winning himself a D.S.O.

Such, in cursory outline which does it no justice, had been Boustead's life before he came to Mukalla. He tells his story himself, with great spirit, humour and charm, in his autobiography, *The Wind of Morning*, published a few years ago.[3] A splendid man, and an admirable representative of the type of British soldier and colonial administrator that has now, sadly, all but passed into history, Boustead gives the lie, in every facet of his personality and at every stage in his life, to all the easy and ill-formed assertions, so fashionable and so unthinkingly accepted today, about the overweening nature of British imperial rule and the resentment it provoked among Asians and Africans. Without the respect and confidence and, indeed, affection, he inspired among the bellicose and fanatically independent tribesmen he had to deal with, Boustead could never have kept them under control, least of all in the Hadramaut. But tribal razzias and bloodletting were not the only sources of violence in the Protectorate during the 1950's. Boustead had also to contend with the beginnings of nationalist agitation, aroused principally from Cairo, and he has no hesitation in condemning the influence of Gamal Abdul Nasser as wholly malign.

> Throughout these years Cairo Radio remained responsible for a very large percentage of the troubles, disorders, deaths and discontent in the Middle East generally and in the two Aden Protectorates in particular. The greatest harm was done to the younger generation, the schoolboys, the students and the schoolmasters, a number of whom (but not the Sudanese in the Hadramaut) seemed to delight in Nasser's mischief, which had been responsible for the destruction of many years of solid achievement by the British, Sudanese, Pakistanis, Indians and educated Arabs in the two Protectorates.

With their traditional avenues of emigration to India and the East Indies now closed to them, many Hadramis began in the 1950's to search elsewhere for work and mercantile opportunity. They journeyed in their hundreds to Aden colony, to the oil states of the upper Gulf, and even further afield. Inevitably, they were influenced by the heady notions they encountered, of Arab nationalism, socialism, revolution and the like, so that it was hardly surprising that when they returned to the Hadramaut they were impatient to overturn the traditional order of things and to put an end to British tutelage. There was a certain irony in what followed. Harold Ingrams and the Dutch explorer, van der Meulen, both believed that the Hadramaut could survive, indeed would be better off, independent of the rest of South Arabia. It was, as we have seen, excluded from both

3 London, Chatto and Windus, 1971. Pp. 240, illustrations, maps, index. £2.80.

the Federation of Arab Amirates of the South in 1959 and the successor Federation of South Arabia in 1963, for reasons closely connected with oil exploration in the Qu'aiti and Kathiri states. Yet in the next five years the National Liberation Front, the revolutionary organization which was to succeed to power in South Arabia when the British left, established a network of cells in the Hadramaut, primarily through the agency of Hadramis in Aden, and it was these cells which in the latter months of 1967 helped ensure not only the triumph of the N.L.F. over the federal rulers- the sultans, shaikhs and amirs of the old Protectorate states—but also the incorporation of the Hadramaut itself in the new unitary People's Republic of South Yemen.

When Hugh Boustead completed his tour of duty at Mukalla in 1958, he was appointed to the post of Secretary for Development in the sultanate of Oman. An agreement had been concluded between the British government and the sultan, Saiyid Said ibn Taimur, in July 1958, for the provision of military, financial and technical assistance to reorganize the sultan's armed forces after the imamate rebellion of 1957, to improve the country's communications and agriculture, and to lay the foundations of medical and educational services. Boustead describes his subsequent three years in Oman as 'intensely frustrating', and with good reason, as will be seen shortly. His military counterpart in these years, Colonel David Smiley, who had been charged with the task of improving the sultan's armed forces and restoring security to the country, was to encounter comparable difficulties, but he was more fortunate than Boustead in the degree of backing he received from his superiors. Although Smiley had originally been a cavalry officer (in the Blues) he had had considerable experience of irregular warfare, mostly in Ethiopia, Greece and Albania in the Second World War, and it was this experience which led Julian Amery, who was then Under-Secretary of State for War and had soldiered with Smiley in Albania, to send him to Oman.

Smiley's first problem, as he explains in his recently published memoir of his years in Arabia,[4] was to force the surrender of the fugitive leaders of the Ibadi imamate revolt who, together with a hard core of 200 or 300 dissidents, had gone to ground high up in the Jabal Akhdar, the central massif of the Hajar mountain range, from which they had been carrying

---

4 David Smiley with Peter Kemp, *Arabian Assignment* (London, Leo Cooper, 1975). Pp. viii + 248, illustrations, maps, index. £6.75. The second part of the book recounts Smiley's adventures in the Yemen between 1963 and 1967, when he fought with the royalist forces in the civil war. It is a story of endurance, fortitude and disappointment, told with an honesty and a generosity which reflect great credit upon the author.

out a series of raids and ambushes since the autumn of 1957. The nominal leader of the rebels was the erstwhile imam, Ghalib ibn Ali, but the driving spirits behind the revolt were his brother, Talib, the former *wali* of Rastaq, and Sulaiman ibn Himyar, *tamimah* or paramount chieftain of the Bani Riyam, and once the most powerful man in inner Oman. At first Smiley could do no more than try to contain the rebels, to prevent them from mining the roads, and to press on with the job of getting the sultan's askaris into shape to assault the Jabal Akhdar. Some help was given by the R.A.F. at Aden and Sharjah, who flew a number of sorties over the plateaux and valleys of the massif, interspersing their attacks with propaganda broadcasts from a slow-flying aircraft fitted with a loudspeaker. They made little impression with their rockets and bombs upon the rebel strongholds, which were located in deep caves in the hillsides, and the only response they received to their propaganda efforts was a request from the rebels for a more efficient loudspeaker so that its calls to them to surrender could be heard more clearly.

The insurgents were kept supplied with arms throughout 1958, as they had been supplied for their original uprising, by Saudi Arabia, the arms being smuggled into the Oman by various routes—overland via the Buraimi oasis, through the port of Dubai on the Trucial coast, and by clandestine landings on the Batinah coast. Most of the weapons originated in the United States and had been supplied to Saudi Arabia under military aid agreements. British representations in Washington for some control to be exerted over the use of these weapons, especially the mines, which were killing British soldiers as well as Omanis, met with the reply that it was no concern of the United States government how the Saudis chose to dispose of their arms shipments. No other answer could have been expected at this time, for, as Julian Amery later revealed in reviewing Smiley's book, the rebels were in regular wireless communication with both the Saudis and the C.I.A.[5] Little wonder that Smiley, in recounting his difficulties, quotes with wry approval the view later expressed by the Swedish general, Carl von Horn, the commander of the U.N. peace-keepng force in the Middle East, of American policy in Arabia in the 1950's and 1960's: 'Basically I had the impression that, under the cloak of a benefactor and supporter of national aspirations in the Middle East, there was a desire to cut the throat of British influence in the Persian Gulf'.

By the late summer of 1958 Smiley had been forced to the conclusion that the assault on the Jabal Akhdar could not be carried out by the sultan's troops alone. Despite the misgivings of the Foreign Office about

5 *The Daily Telegraph*, May 22, 1975.

the adverse reactions that might be aroused at the United Nations by the use of British troops in the Middle East only two years after the Suez expedition, Smiley's request for troops was granted. Two squadrons of the 22nd Special Air Services Regiment and a squadron of the Life Guards reached Oman in the next few months, and in the last week of January 1959, supported by a squadron of the Trucial Oman Scouts and the Omani Northern Frontier Regiment, they scaled the grim heights of the Jabal Akhdar and overcame the rebels in a brief but hard-fought action. The wily trinity of Ghalib, Talib and Sulaiman ibn Himyar, however, evaded capture. They made their way through the Sharqiyah country to the east coast, and from there slipped away by dhow to Saudi Arabia. Although they continued for the next two or three years to smuggle arms and mines to their supporters scattered throughout central Oman, the heart had gone out of the insurgency with the storming of the Jabal Akhdar. The subsequent programme of development carried out under Hugh Boustead's direction in the valleys and plateaux of the *jabal* soon banished whatever traces of nostalgia may have lingered among its inhabitants for their brave days as carefree badmashes.

Boustead and Smiley are both highly critical of the way the sultan, Said ibn Taimur, treated his people, neglecting their welfare to the point of abandonment, and entrusting the responsibility for ordering their affairs entirely to others, while denying them the authority necessary for them to function effectively. Saiyid Said's outlook was governed by mistrust— of his people, of his neighbours, of his servants, of his family. Considering the history of his dynasty, the Al Bu Said, and the vicissitudes it had experienced in the course of its existence, the mistrust was perhaps not ill-founded. To warnings that he was courting danger by failing to exert himself, at a time of nationalist and revolutionary ferment in the Arab world, to lift his country out of the slough of medieval backwardness in which it lay, he invariably pleaded poverty as his excuse for inaction. Yet, as Boustead points out with some severity, his customs revenues alone were double those of the Qu'aiti sultanate of Mukalla, where so much more had been achieved. He had also come into three million pounds in 1958 when he sold the enclave of Gwadur, on the Makran coast, to Pakistan, and he was receiving, in addition, payments both for oil exploration rights and from the British government for social and economic development.

The real reason for Saiyid Said's attitude lay in his fear of what the improvements he was being forced to make under pressure from the British - rather gentle pressure and consequently rather trifling social and economic improvements—would bring in their train. 'We do not need hospitals here', he told Smiley on one occasion. 'This is a very poor country which can only support a small population. At present many children die in infancy and so the population does not increase. If we build clinics many more will survive—but for what? To starve?' When Boustead tried to persuade him to set up primary schools to educate the sons of tribal shaikhs and other dignitaries, he snorted in reply, 'That is why you lost India, because you educated the people'. He expressed a similar opinion to Smiley:

> Where would the teachers come from? ...They would come from Cairo and spread Nasser's seditious ideas among their pupils. And what is there here for a young man with education? He would go to the university in Cairo or to the London School of Economics, finish in Moscow and come back here to foment trouble.

There was no denying the strength of the last argument, especially when one glanced northwards at Kuwait and Bahrain, and even Saiyid Said's harshest critics were forced to admit that as often as not he had logic on his side.

Ian Skeet, who spent two years in Oman with Petroleum Development Limited in the 1960's, frequently, if regretfully, acknowledges the sultan's perspicacity in his recent book, *Muscat and Oman: the End of an Era*.[6] As its title suggests, it is largely a work of valediction, a fond leavetaking of the old Oman in the days before the oil revenues began to flow and to work their inexorable change in the life of the country. The book is a mixture of historical anecdote, personal reminiscence and geographical description, good-natured and unpretentious in tone, and shot through with a genuine warmth of feeling for the Omanis. The only times that Skeet allows himself to be slightly acerbic are when he discusses the faults of Saiyid Said; and even here he confesses to mixed feelings towards the late ruler—indignation at his refusal to spend his revenues on bettering the lot of his people, bafflement at his disdain of his neighbours in Arabia and his remoteness from the world beyond, and rueful admiration for his adroitness, especially in enlisting the support of the British government for his rule, while fending off its suggestions that he move with the times.

British support was certainly needed in the 1960's, as much as it had been in the preceding decade, for Saiyid Said was confronted in his

---

6 London, Faber and Faber, 1974. Pp. 224, illustrations, maps, appendixes, bibliography, index. £3.95.

southern province of Dhufar with a growing insurrection, more insidious and more pernicious than the imamate revolt had been, and considerably more difficult to cope with, for reasons that will be referred to shortly. The world, however, had changed since the mid-1950's, and British patience with Said ibn Taimur had worn wafer thin. When, in the summer of 1970, the repercussions of the Dhufar rebellion showed signs of spreading to Oman proper, they decided that the time had come for him to go. He was deposed in July 1970 and his son, Qabus, was installed in his place. Saiyid Said disappeared into exile in England, where he died in October 1972 in surroundings both fitting and reminiscent of happier days—the Dorchester Hotel in London.

It may be, as most contend, that his deposition was unavoidable, and that it was justified by the circumstances of the time. But it should be borne in mind, in passing judgement upon Said ibn Taimur, that his troubles were not wholly of his own making. Those which he faced in Oman originated in some measure in the equivocations of the British Foreign Office over the responsibilities it inherited for the Gulf region from the former government of India. Those which arose in Dhufar were greatly exacerbated by the British government's total abdication of responsibility in South Arabia in the closing months of 1967.

The British abandonment of Aden Colony and Protectorates in November 1967 left them in the hands of the National Liberation Front, the revolutionary organization that had set out in October 1963, with the uprising in the Radfan mountains, to destroy the Federation of South Arabia. In the intervening four years it succeeded not only in forcing the British to withdraw but also in destroying the power both of its rivals among the Aden nationalists and of the traditional rulers of the Protectorates. Its victory over 'British imperialism' and 'Arab reaction' was naturally hailed with delight by the radical Arab governments and by similar regimes elsewhere in Asia and Africa. It was a cause of especial celebration, however, in certain revolutionary Palestinian circles in Beirut and Damascus, which formed the core of the secret society known as the 'Arab Nationalists' Movement' (*harakat al-qawmiyyin al-arab*) with cells in most of the Arab states. Many of the leading spirits in the National Liberation Front were members of the Arab Nationalists' Movement, which had been founded in the early 1950's by George Habash and Wadi' Haddad when they were students at the American University of Beirut. Its numerical strength was never very great, its members regarding themselves rather as an intellectual elite working for the unification of the Arab lands and goading the Arab governments into encompassing both the destruction of Israel and the eradication of Western influence from the Middle East.[7]

In the early 1960's the A.N.M. became more leftist in its orientation, a development accelerated by the formation in 1964 of the Palestine Liberation Organization, which stole some of the A.N.M.'s thunder. Some of the movement's radical theoreticians, notably the Lebanese Muhsin Ibrahim and the Jordanian Nayif Hawatima, argued that it should widen its aims so as to take in the overthrow of capitalism and feudalism as well as the elimination of imperialism and Zionism, and thereby enlist the support of the Arab masses. Habash was not yet persuaded of the desirability or the need for a mass movement, and to counter the influence of the radical theoreticians, as well as to cock a snook at the P.L.O., he organized the National Front for the Liberation of Palestine from the Palestinian members of the A.N.M. The two wings of the movement remained in uneasy harness until the June 1967 war and its aftermath. That war shattered the A.N.M.'s faith in Nasser as the paladin of their cause, and led them to condemn his regime and that of the other 'progressive' Arab states as 'petty bourgeois'. Habash now joined with the others in declaring that the only policy henceforth for the movement to embrace was that of the armed struggle of the masses against Zionism, imperialism and 'Arab reaction'. Accordingly he changed the name of the N.F.L.P. in December 1967 to the 'Popular Front for the Liberation of Palestine'. The gap between the two wings, however, still remained, and it widened still further in the next two years as Nayif Hawatima broke away to form the rival Popular Democratic Front for the Liberation of Palestine, and other splinter groups followed him. The A.N.M. was split wide open, not only in its Palestinian-Lebanese leadership but also in every branch of the movement elsewhere, robbing it of any cohesion it might have possessed as a pan-Arab organization.

The schism that developed in the leadership of the N.L.F. in Aden after independence arose from the same cause and followed much the same chronology. From its beginnings, the National Liberation Front for Occupied South Yemen (to give it its full title) had been a coalition of nationalist groups, of which the Aden branch of the A.N.M., led by Qahtan al-Shaabi and his cousin Faisal al-Shaabi, was the most influential. Its ascendancy within the N.L.F. continued after the Front's accession to power, with Qahtan al-Shaabi becoming the first President of the People's Republic of South Yemen on December 1, 1967. Within weeks, however, his position and his policies were being challenged by the radical faction

---

7 The best account of the ANM is in Walid Kazziha, *Revolutionary Transformation in the Arab World: Habash and his Comrades from Nationalism to Marxism* (London, 1975).

of the N.L.F., led by those members of the A.N.M. who sided with Muhsin Ibrahim and Nayif Hawatima in the ideological battle being waged within the movement at large. The dispute was brought into the open at the first post-independence congress of the N.L.F. at Zinjibar in March 1968, when the Left, led by Abdul Fatah Ismail, condemned the republic that had been established so far as 'petty bourgeois'. Ismail demanded its destruction and its replacement by a revolutionary state based upon a system of village soviets, a 'supreme council of the people', and a people's militia which would defend the revolution at home and abroad.

The struggle for power thus initiated within the N.L.F. was decided in favour of the left wing, or as it might now properly be called, the Marxist-Leninist faction, in June 1969, when Qahtan al-Shaabi was forced to resign. Throughout the contest the Left had drawn much of its strength from the Hadramaut, where its adherents had been in control since August 1967. They had broken the power of the *saiyids* and the other privileged classes—the merchants, the tribal shaikhs and the former sultanate officials—in the way that power has always been broken in Southern Arabia- by the sword. Landholdings were expropriated, commercial property confiscated, and the late owners reduced to penury, imprisoned, executed or forced into exile. The Hadrami Beduin Legion was turned into a political instrument, and a people's militia was raised and organized into brigades with the mellifluous titles of the 'First of May Brigade' and the 'Che Guevara Brigade'. What had happened in the Hadramaut was to be repeated throughout the republic after the deposition of al-Shaabi. 'Scientific socialism' was declared to be the basis of the new state, which naturally led to a campaign of wholesale expropriation and the persecution of dissidents. A hundred thousand people gave their verdict on the new regime by fleeing the country. All power was concentrated in a politburo at Aden composed of men like the N.L.F.'s new Secretary-General, Abdul Fatah Ismail, all young, all dedicated Marxist-Leninists and all utterly ruthless. Although a new President, Salim Rubayyi Ali, was appointed to succeed al-Shaabi, he counted for nothing; and the solemn promulgation of a constitution in November 1970 (at which time the country's name was changed, after the fashion of Hawatima's P.D.F.L.P., to the 'People's Democratic Republic of Yemen'), vesting sovereign authority in a 'Supreme Council of the People', elected by local soviets throughout the country, was nothing more than cynical window-dressing. Elections were never held, and when the Supreme Council, made up of the Politburo's nominees, finally met, its sole accomplishment was to transfer all power, legislative, executive and judicial, to the Politburo.

In foreign affairs the regime followed a predictable course. It declared itself to be at one with 'liberation movements' around the world, and established diplomatic relations with, among others, North Vietnam, North Korea and Cuba. At the same time it courted the Soviet Union and the Chinese People's Republic for the economic and military aid they could furnish, and both powers were not slow to recognize the strategic advantages of obtaining a foothold in Southern Arabia. The Russians provided arms and technical assistance, the Chinese built a road to the Hadramaut and supplied medical aid, the Cubans assisted with agriculture and the training of the air force, and the East Germans organized the internal security system. Towards the other Arab states the P.D.R.Y. government behaved with equal predictability. It condemned the conservative regimes outright, criticized the 'progressive' states as 'petty bourgeois', and lined itself up with the so-called 'rejection front' in the Palestinian movement. It was, in short, a maverick in the Arab world, almost as isolated from its fellows as was the sultanate of Oman, away on the other side of Arabia and at the opposite end of the political spectrum. Even its closest neighbour, the Yemen Arab Republic to the north, with which it had ties of blood and history, and union with which had been one of the ostensible aims of the campaign to end British overlordship, regarded it with horror.

Outside the Arab world, however, the P.D.R.Y. had its champions. The appearance of such an exotic phenomenon as a full-fledged Marxist-Leninist state in the Arabian peninsula caused a palpable fluttering in Marxist dovecotes in the West, and it occasioned an especial *frisson* of delight among the French theoreticians of Marxism-Leninism in Asia and Africa. Tracts and exegetical disquisitions began to flow from their pens, earnestly detailing every step in the N.L.F.'s career from the rising in the Radfan onwards, and dissecting and explaining with Gallic precision every pronouncement of policy and ideological declaration made by the regime since its inception. That both the pronunciamentos and their laboriously contrived interpretations bore little relationship to the actualities of South Arabia, or to historical accuracy, or even to the character of South-Arabian society, did not apparently trouble the French dialecticians in the least. They had a ready outlet for their expositions in *Le Monde*, whose own principal correspondent in the Middle East, Eric Rouleau, took a decidedly indulgent view of the N.L.F. regime and all its works, and reported upon them with what can only be described as rapturous bemusement.[8]

8 See, e.g., his four-part report, '*L'étoile rouge sur le Yémen du Sud*', in successive issues of *Le Monde* in the last week of May 1973. Some examples of the Marxist or quasi-Marxist interpretations referred to above, and of related reports on the insur-

Nothing comparable was put out in English until the appearance in 1975 of Fred Halliday's *Arabia without Sultans*, an extensive survey of society and politics in the Arabian peninsula presented in uncompromisingly Marxist-Leninist terms. The book seems to have been written largely for the purpose of extolling the South-Yemen revolution and the insurrection in the neighbouring territory of Dhufar, the direction of which had, for all practical purposes, been taken over since early 1968 by the N.L.F. in Aden.

Dhufar is somewhat remote from the rest of the sultanate of Oman, both in distance and in character. It is also quite distinct, despite its physical proximity, from the Hadramaut and the Mahra country to the westward. Geographically it consists of a coastal plain and a mountain range, both of which are watered by the south-west monsoon. Beyond the mountains the *najd*, a barren, stony plateau broken by ravines, stretches northwards to the southern rim of the Rub al-Khali. The people of Dhufar are of South-Arabian stock, with admixtures of eastern-Arabian tribes, Africans, Ethiopians and Indians. They speak a language derived from ancient Himyarite. It has no written form, although it is akin in many respects to Arabic from which it has also borrowed. The Dhufaris are Sunni Muslims (mostly Shafi), although their religious beliefs and practices are riddled with animistic superstitions, fetishes and tabus. Most of the population earns its livelihood from pastoralism, agriculture, trade, fishing and seafaring. Like Hadramis, Dhufaris also have a tradition of migrating in search of work and fortune. There are two major tribal confederations: the dominant Qara, who live in the mountains and raise cattle, and who once cultivated frankincense on a large scale; and the Al Kathir, who dwell in the coastal plain and who are mainly cultivators and fishermen. They are distinct from the Bait Kathir, who roam the *najd* and the sands north of the Jabal Qara. Mahra, originating further westwards, also inhabit the eastern and western reaches of the *jabal*. Two smaller but important tribes are the Bait Qatan of the western region, and the 'Awamir of the western *jabal* and the western *najd*. Another, rather amorphous, tribal group is the Shahara, descendants of the original inhabitants of Dhufar before the Kathiri and

---

rection in Dhufar, are: Rene Lefort, '*Révolution au Sud-Yémen: la nouvelle gauche arabe il'epreuved u pouvoir*', Le Monde Diplomatique, February 1971; Gordian Troeller and Claude Deffarge, '*Sud-Yemen: une révolution menacée?*', Le Monde Diplomatique, April 1972; Jean-PierreViennot, '*La guérilla du Dhofar entre dans une nouvelle phase*', Le Monde Diplomatique, August 1972. Viennot is the most prolific of the Marxist commentators. See, e.g., his '*Aden: de la lutte pour la libération à l'indépendance*', Orient, nos. 43/44, 1967; '*Communiqué du front de la libération du Dhofar*' Orient, 3/4 quarters, 1967; and '*L'expérience révolutionnaire du Sud-Yémen*', Maghreb-Machrek, September/October 1973.

Qara migrations, who exist today in a condition of virtual servitude to the Qara. Dhufari society is divided by other than tribal affiliation. There is a caste system, derived from centuries of intercourse with India, where the Dhufaris went to trade or, like the Hadramis, to enlist as soldiers in the service of Indian princes. Again, as in the Hadramaut, there is also a class of *saiyids,* or Hashimis, who constitute an aristocratic class among the Qara and are revered by most of the population.

Dhufar came under the nominal sway of the Al Bu Said rulers of Muscat in the second quarter of the nineteenth century, but it was not until the last quarter of the century that the Al Bu Said made any effective display of authority there. Even then successive sultans ruled Dhufar in perfunctory fashion until the middle of this century through a series of *walis,* who administered the province by the time-honoured method of setting tribe against tribe. From the early 1950's onwards, Saiyid Said ibn Taimur took up more-or-less permanent residence at Salalah, the principal town, which he found a more agreeable abode than Muscat. He tended to treat Dhufar as his personal domain and its people very much as serfs. Tribal factionalism was encouraged, to make the tribesmen more tractable, and their shaikhs were reduced to mere ciphers. Heavy imposts were laid upon the products of the region and upon imports, and trade in items of any consequence became a monopoly of the sultan. The economy stagnated, driving more and more Dhufaris to seek work in the Gulf, either as labourers or as armed retainers in the service of the Gulf rulers. There was as yet little or no political content in their dissatisfaction: this was to come later, after they had been exposed to nationalist, Ba'thist and Nasserist propaganda in the states of the upper Gulf.

How and when some of these émigré Dhufaris began to contemplate rebellion against the sultan, and to prepare actively for it, is not wholly clear. It would seem, however, from the available evidence,[9] that by 1960-61 there were at least three, loosely organized, clandestine, organizations in being—a league of Dhufari soldiers, a Dhufari branch of the Arab Nationalists' Movement, and an oddly named 'Dhufari Benevolent Society'. The first, which was largely apolitical, was made up of Dhufaris serving, or who had served, in the armies or police forces of the various Gulf states, including Oman itself. The second consisted mostly of Dhufaris who had been sent to Syria—mainly from Kuwait—for guerrilla training in 1959,

---

9 See the books and articles already mentioned by Kazziha, Halliday, Viennot, Troeller and Deffarge. There is also a lengthy account by Gerard Laliberte (pseud. ?), 'La Guerilla du Dhofar', in *Etudes Internationales,* vol. iv, nos. 1-2, March-June 1973. Information collected in Dhufar has also been used.

and who, while there, had been recruited into the A.N.M. The third was an offshoot of this group, which broke away in 1961 to lay the ground for armed revolt in Dhufar under the guise of charitable activities, aiding the poor and raising funds for mosques.

Under pressure from the Kuwait branch of the A.N.M., and also with encouragement from Cairo, the three groups coalesced in 1964 to create the 'Dhufar Liberation Front'. They were joined by a group of disaffected Dhufari tribesmen under the leadership of a shaikh of the Bait Kathir, Musallim ibn Nufl, who had not only grown tired of the sultan's coercive ways but was also resolved that any oil that might be discovered by the American company then prospecting in Kathiri territory should be used for his benefit and that of his tribe. He made contact with the exiled Ibadi imam, Ghalib ibn Ali, who had some acquaintance with such matters, and through him with the Saudis and Iraqis, who were each at this time, for their own separate purposes, supporting the remnants of the imam's following in Oman. After attacking some oil company vehicles late in 1963, Musallim ibn Nufl fled to Iraq. There, in company with several dozen Dhufaris, he underwent military training at an army camp near Basra. The following winter, Musallim and his band returned to Dhufar by way of Saudi Arabia, being provided with arms, money and transport across the desert by the Saudi government, with the promise of more aid to come if they were successful in raising a rebellion against the sultan.

The rebellion was proclaimed at a 'congress' of the Dhufar Liberation Front in the Wadi al-Kabir in central Dhufar on June 1-9, 1965. For the next two years or more it made little progress. There was only a trickle of support from outside, mainly from Egypt and Kuwait, the Saudis having grown suspicious of the Front's political orientation. The insurgents could do little more than carry out haphazard raids, although in April 1966 some askaris in the sultan's service, who had been recruited by the Front, came near to success in an attempt to assassinate him. The number of insurgents was small, no more than fifty at the start of the rebellion, but it began to grow after the sultan, in reprisal for the uprising and the attempt on his life, forbade all Dhufaris to go abroad to work. Deprived of one of their chief means of supporting their families, many tribesmen took to the *jabal* to join the rebels.

As time went by, differences began to make themselves felt within the Dhufar Liberation Front. Most of the tribesmen regarded the rebellion as being directed primarily against the repressive rule of the sultan and the Omani ascendancy in Dhufar in general. They were concerned to preserve Dhufar's individuality—its linguistic singularity, its religious particularism, its caste system—and, consequently, they viewed the revolt as fundamentally a domestic affair, possibly, but not inevitably, terminating in the secession and independence of Dhufar from Oman. The A.N.M. faction, on the other hand, wanted to make the revolt part of the wider campaign in which the A.N.M. as a whole was engaged throughout the Arab world. Hence they kept insisting upon the 'Arabness' of Dhufar, upon its identity as part of the 'Arab nation', and upon the role it should play in the great Arab struggle against the forces of reaction, capitalism, imperialism and Zionism. Rhetoric of this kind was unintelligible to most of the rebel tribesmen, and it did not make any discernible impression upon them until events outside Dhufar from the latter half of 1967 onwards tipped the scales in favour of the A.N.M. minority.

The principal event, of course, was the accession of the National Liberation Front to power in Aden, which put it in a position to supply the Dhufar Liberation Front with arms by way of the Hadramaut and the Mahra country. There were other far-reaching results of the N.L.F.'s assumption of defacto control of the Dhufar rebellion. This was a time, it may be recalled, when the Arab Nationalists' Movement as a whole was breaking in two, with the Marxist-Leninist wing making the running. At a conference in Beirut at the turn of 1968, the Kuwait branch of the movement was deprived of the control it had hitherto exercised over subversive activities in the Gulf region, on the grounds that it had exhibited 'bourgeois tendencies'. A strategy of 'revolutionary violence' for the movement was adopted by the Marxist-Leninist majority, and at a further conference in July 1968 the membership of the Kuwait branch was suspended. A new Politburo and Regional Command for the Gulf were set up, and within a brief space of time the intestine quarrels in Beirut were finding an echo in the leadership of the Dhufar Liberation Front. In the contest for power that ensued, the Marxist-Leninist faction in the A.N.M. component of the leadership, backed by the N.L.F. in Aden, carried the day. At the 'Second Congress' of the D.L.F. at Himrin in central Dhufar on September 1-25, 1968, a Marxist-Leninist revolutionary programme was adopted for the rebellion.

Dhufar was to be transformed according to the principles of 'scientific socialism', whatever these may have been thought to be. (At the A.N.M. conference on the Gulf in July the Kuwaiti delegate had, with eminent reasonableness but to no avail, protested,' The Movement has adopted scientific socialism, but we do not yet know exactly what it means . . . '.) The insurrection in Dhufar was declared to be not only part of a wider revolution by the masses of Arabia against 'imperialism, colonialism, Arab reaction and the rotten bourgeoisie', but also part of the national liberation movement throughout the Arab world, and, indeed, of the armed struggle of the peasantry and the proletariat in Vietnam, Cuba and elsewhere. To succeed in Dhufar, so the D.L.F. programme went on, the revolution had to be spread to all parts of Arabia, it had to be unified under the leadership of 'the proletarian left', to be inspired by 'correct ideology', and to follow a strategy of 'constant struggle, multiplying its revolutionary efforts against colonialism and the bourgeoisie, overturning the old social order, and creating a state of poor workers in place of the bourgeois reactionary state'.[10]

Such was the language of the communique issued at the end of the Congress, a document stuffed with the dreary vulgarities and stale tautologies of standard Marxist-Leninist literature, yet which nevertheless purported to speak in the name of the simple and untutored tribesmen of Dhufar. To celebrate the transmogrification of a local tribal revolt into an ideological struggle of heroic proportions, the D.L.F. was solemnly renamed the 'Popular Front for the Liberation of the Occupied Arab Gulf'. The old leadership of the movement was dismissed, and several members, including Musallim ibn Nufl, were expelled altogether as 'bourgeois deviationists'. Control of P.F.L.O.A.G. was henceforth exercised by a small Marxist-Leninist Politburo headed by a Qara, Muhammad Ahmad al-Ghassani, in the post of 'Secretary-General'[11].

What happened in the next half-a-dozen years in those areas of Dhufar which were liberated by P.F.L.O.A.G. will be only too familiar to students of the process of 'liberation' by Marxist-Leninist revolutionaries in other parts of Asia and in Africa. How one interprets the process, naturally, depends as much upon one's personal and political outlook as it does upon the availability of pertinent information. We are fortunate in the case of Dhufar to have two recently published accounts of the guerrilla campaign there, written, in both the literal and the ideological senses, from opposing sides. One, Fred Halliday's *Arabia without Sultans*, has already been mentioned. The other is *Where Soldiers Fear to Tread*, by Sir Ranulph Fiennes, a regular army officer who served for two years in Oman and Dhufar from the summer of 1968.[12] There is also a highly informative short study of the

---

10 *'Communique du front de la liberation du Dhofar'*, Orient, 3/4 quarters, 1967.
11 Others who subsequently achieved prominence in PFLOAG's 'general command', included Salim Ahmad Said al-Ghassani ('Talal Saad'), Ahmad Abdul Samaid Daib, Ali Muhsin, Salim Huf, Salim Mustahail Ahmad Sarhan and Bakhait Ali Suhail Majawda. The last two were Bait Qatan.
12 London, Hodder and Stoughton, 1975. Pp. 256, illustrations, maps, index. £3.50.

campaign by D. L. Price, who travelled in Dhufar late in 1974.[13]

The Chinese were the first to begin aiding P.F.L.O.A.G., although the Russians, who could not afford to be left behind in the competition, followed hard on their heels. Chinese officers based at Mukalla oversaw the transport of arms to the rebels and occasionally visited their camps. How far they were involved in the tactical direction of guerrilla operations is uncertain. P.F.L.O.A.G. recruits were taken off to China for guerrilla training and political indoctrination for periods of up to nine months. They travelled mostly by way of Kuwait, which was the clearing house for much of the clandestine movement of revolutionaries and arms in the Gulf area. Recruits sent to Russia for training likewise passed through Kuwait. Several of these Chinese-and-Russian-trained guerrillas later deserted from P.F.L.O.A.G., particularly after the accession of the young sultan, Qabus ibn Said, in July 1970. One of Saiyid Qabus's first acts was to declare an amnesty for all rebels who surrendered with their arms, and one of the first rebels to come down from the hills was Musallim ibn Nufl. A great deal of information about recruitment, training and organization, political proselytizing, and Russian and Chinese involvement in the rebellion was obtained from these defectors (or in some cases, captives), and Captain Fiennes has drawn upon this information for much of his book.

The main rebel base was at Hauf, just across the border in South Yemen. Here P.F.L.O.A.G. set up a 'Lenin School' for military training and political education. Halliday visited Hauf and parts of western Dhufar in February 1970, and again in April 1973. He was vastly impressed with what he saw.

> For the first time young children received primary education. In addition to learning history, mathematics, politics and languages, the children shared the tasks of the camp cooking, cleaning and guard-duty—and had group discussions on the tasks they had to perform...Such was the demand for education that in April 1972 P.F.L.O.A.G. also set up the June 9 School, to which the older children were sent. By early 1973 850 children attended the two schools . . . At this stage 25 per cent of the students were women. The schools aimed to fulfil two functions: to educate the children to understand the revolution, and to teach them basic technical skills. Military training formed an integral part of the curriculum.

13 'Oman: Insurgency and Development', *Conflict Studies*, no. 53, London, Institute for the Study of Conflict, 1975. Pp. 19, map, bibliography. £1.50.

There was also a so-called 'Revolution Camp' for young men and women, where the inmates spent a sixteen-hour day in military training, political instruction and domestic chores. Halliday was greatly moved by what he saw as the devotion and eagerness of all these young volunteers, many of whom, and especially the young women, had made strenuous efforts to reach Hauf and, enlist in P.F.L.O.A.G.'s ranks. Fiennes, however, has a somewhat different version of what went on at Hauf, obtained from defectors from P.F.L.O.A.G., especially about the way in which women and children were recruited for the cause.

> In the spring of 1969, when child recruits were first sought, it had been with parental consent, but when this brought little response, groups of guerrillas were sent out to bring back a set number of children regardless of the parents' feelings...

> Salim Amr remembered the morning in April when a weeping girl accompanied the latest batch of children into the camp. She could have been no more than twenty: he liked the look of her. One of the little boys was her son and that evening an Idaara [punishment unit] member had caught her attempting to take the lad away from the camp.

> First they stripped and flogged her. Then, since she still screamed for the release of her child, the Idaara leader had caught her up by the ankles and swung her round and round. The uproarious mirth of the onlookers had affected the man's judgement—he later received a reprimand—for he swung ever faster, moving towards a rocky hummock, until with a final swing, he split the girl's head open like an overripe pomegranate.

Of course, the difference in perspective in the two accounts may simply be due to the fact that Halliday was in South Yemen and Dhufar as a visitor anxious to ascertain how the revolution was faring, whereas Fiennes was in Dhufar as a fighting soldier, stalking and being stalked by P.F.L.O.A.G. guerrillas through the ravines and along the ridges of the Jabal Qara. It might also account for the contrast between Halliday's rhapsodizing about P.F.L.O.A.G.'s recruitment of women and children and Fiennes's laconic comment on the subject: 'Following the example of the Fedayeen and many Asian guerrillas the *adoo* [enemy] had begun to recruit women and children to fight alongside them: the war was getting dirtier'.

Halliday was also delighted with what he found on his visit to western Dhufar in the spring of 1970.

> Wherever we went we saw people wearing Mao and Lenin badges, reading socialist works and discussing ... For the militants in the camp [at Hauf] and for people in the liberated areas a basic text was Mao Tse-tung's selected quotations. The reason for this was not China's training of guerrillas or support for the revolution ... The popularity of Mao's works is due to the fact that they were written for a situation similar to that of Dhufar—for a newly literate peasantry suddenly wrenched into a guerrilla war, having to administer a liberated area and fight a protracted war against an imperialist enemy.

Two Chinese visitors to Dhufar a short time earlier, he informs us, had been similarly inspired by what they saw there. On their return to China they wrote an account of their visit for the *Peking Review* under the heading, 'Dhufar Liberation Army Fighters and People Warmly Love Mao-Tse-tung Thought'. It had all been made possible, so Halliday assures us, by P.F.L.O.A.G.'s decision to institute

> a campaign of mass education throughout Dhofar, in which the teaching of literacy and of the Arabic language went together with political education. The Front distributed as widely as it could Arabic translations of revolutionary classics—Lenin's *State and Revolution and Imperialism*, Marx's and Engels's *The Communist Manifesto* and writings of Mao, Stalin, Ho Chi Minh and Che Guevara. These, with texts from the Palestinian P.D.F.L.P., formed part of the political education programme taught to all cadres and provided the basis of discussion and lectures.

There was only one slight blemish, as Halliday notes *en passant*, in the portrait he has painted of a pastoral-intellectual idyll up on the *jabal*—the Dhufaris were illiterate. However, he assures us, P.F.L.O.A.G. overcame this drawback by 'an introductory course in political education designed to make the basic revolutionary concepts accessible to the people as a whole'.

Some idea of the nature of this course may be gained from Fiennes's account, which he himself obtained from a shaikh of the Bait Qatan, of the way in which it was taught to two elderly shaikhs of the eastern Mahra. They had been somewhat outspoken, it appeared, in their rejection of the new enlightenment, so a P.F.L.O.A.G. *idaara* was sent to show them the error of their ways. Before their assembled tribesmen the two old shaikhs had their eyes burned out with a redhot knife, which was wielded by one of their nephews.

> After the operation on his uncle and the other patriarch, neither of whom died for several days, he had made the words of Karl Marx heard above their screams. And the gathered *jebalis* listened without understanding the new phrases of politics and the ranting of the khaki-clad youngster whom everyone remembered as an idle child, good only at shirking his duties with the cattle. They failed to see why they should stop praying, why Islam should be discredited, nor why such happenings as they had just witnessed should lead the way to a new and glorious way of life. But they understood the meaning of the young men's gleaming weapons and bandoliers. So they began to concur.

Islam, and its relationship to Marxism-Leninism, provided P.F.L.O.A.G. with something of a problem, though Halliday makes light of it and dismisses charges of irreligion against the Front as mere propaganda. 'Its own teachings are secular, but people in the liberated areas are free to engage in religious practices and visibly do so; and religious believers are encouraged to see that there is no contradiction between anti-imperialism and a belief in Islam.' Not to put too fine a gloss upon it, this is absolutely untrue. P.F.L.O.A.G. pursued a systematic policy of decrying Islamic belief and practice, and of intimidating anyone within the movement's orbit who openly professed his faith. Fiennes publishes a photograph of an old *jabali* showing the wounds he suffered as a result of being tortured over hot coals for performing his devotions, and he also has a horrifying account of the kind of punishment inflicted by the more fanatical P.F.L.O.A.G. adherents.

> Five old folk from a mountain village close by Shahayt had been caught praying in the open, contrary to the new unwritten law that religion was reactionary. The local *Idaara* had summoned a number of villagers from the locality and held a public trial to show that they were just. All five old men were found guilty

and held down over red hot coals until their backs were raw and blistered. Then they were beaten and taken to the Dahaq cliff at Darbat, wreathed as it was in mist.

One by one they were thrown over the edge, at hourly intervals, a refinement which Salim [a P.F.L.O.A.G. informer]could not help admiring.

P.F.L.O.A.G. more or less carried all before it up to the summer of 1970 and the deposition of the sultan, Said ibn Taimur. The success of the amnesty declared by his son and successor, Saiyid Qabus, whose mother came from the Qara tribe, disconcerted the P.F.L.O.A.G. Politburo and led it to take drastic measures to halt the stream of defections from the movement. Over 300 executions of political recalcitrants were carried out in Dhufar and across the South-Yemen border in the prison camp at Hauf. The children of the executed tribesmen were sent to the Lenin School for 're-education'. There is no mention of these happenings in Halliday's book. A good deal of space, however, is given over to the dissection and elucidation of P.F.L.O.A.G.'s manifestoes and proclamations, to praise of its ideological purity ('the Front's analysis is in conformity with Engels in *The Origin of the Family, Private Property and the State,* Marx and Engels, *Selected Works,* Vol. 2, Moscow, 1958'), and to the reasons for its successive changes of identity and the doctrinal shifts which accompanied them.

It is all of little consequence now. The revolt is virtually over, the insurgent leaders have all fled or surrendered, or been captured or killed. How this has been accomplished is now fairly well-known, but what is not so well-known is what the campaign in Dhufar was like at close quarters. The great merit of Captain Fiennes's book is that it gives such a picture by recounting the experiences of his platoon of Omani soldiers as they patrolled and fought for eighteen months, in conditions that tried men's souls, and over a brutal terrain where death often lay in wait at the next water-hole or the next bend in the trail. Reading of the dangers they shared, the hardships they endured together, and the bonds of trust, affection and loyalty which developed between Scot and Omani, one cannot help feeling regret for the passing of the imperial age, when there will be no more books by British officers of the like of Boustead, Smiley and Fiennes. The loss will be a severe one in a particular respect, for almost without exception they can be relied upon to relate their adventures with candour, modesty and good sense, qualities which are themselves a reflection of the character of the authors - open, decent, unassuming and generous. The dry treatises of dons and dialecticians will be a poor substitute.

Hadramaut, Oman and Dhufar have all now had their experience of revolution in the past fifteen to twenty years, and so, too, has the rest of South Arabia and Yemen to the north. Oman's experience was unlike that of the others, in that the imamate revolt was in large measure a reaction to the present, a harking back to the theocratic Ibadi past, rather than a leap into the future. It was also unsullied by atrocities of the kind that accompanied the ideologically motivated campaigns in the south. What will probably prove more revolutionary in its impact upon Omani society than the *ci-devant* imam's bid for power in the 1950's is the gradual transformation now taking place as a result of the onset of oil wealth and the accession of a modernizing sultan. Arab nationalism and socialist dogma have so far played no part in Omani politics, although their influence will doubtless make itself felt in time—with what consequences it is impossible to predict, even with the examples of South Yemen and Dhufar before us.

One of the ironies, as indicated earlier, of the triumph of Marxism-Leninism throughout south Yemen, is that it would probably never have occurred without the initial creation of the Federation of South Arabia, which was so vociferously opposed at the time by left-wing circles in Britain and elsewhere on the grounds that the uniting of Aden with the Protectorates would both retard the Colony's political development, especially in a socialist direction, by tying it to the backward shaikhdoms and sultanates of the hinterland, and impede the eventual unification of South Yemen with, as it was then thought to be, the socialist, revolutionary republic of North Yemen. *Tempus edax rerum.* Marxist-Leninist Aden has now devoured the hinterland, though it has not quite yet digested it. Three obstacles stand in its way, and in the way of the N.L.F. Politburo's ambition to create a full-blown socialist state out of an untamed and semi-medieval land. The first is a shortage of money and resources, which forces the Aden government, since the Soviet Union is always reluctant to part with cash to underwrite its clients, to give some heed to its relations with its potential and actual benefactors among the wealthier Arab states, Kuwait and Libya in particular.

The second obstacle is tribalism, which still exerts a stronger claim upon the loyalties of the people of South Arabia than the nebulous concept of the P.D.R.Y. It is one thing to declare tribalism outmoded, as the Aden Politburo and its apologists abroad have done, and to condemn it as a relic of the feudal past whose survival is incompatible with the Marxist-Leninist vision of society. It is another thing for the Politburo to compel obedience to its ukases from men who neither know nor understand any other arrangement of human society, whose very sense of personal identity is inextricably bound up with their tribal affiliations, and who are all too ready to impress this fact upon others. Detribalization may occur with comparative rapidity and facility in the heterogeneous setting of the towns and seaports of the Arabian littoral, but in the interior of the peninsula the tribe is still the dominant social phenomenon. The final obstacle is Islam, which has been an inseparable component of men's lives in Arabia for thirteen centuries. However much the N.L.F. regime may believe, as the author of *Arabia without Sultans* expresses it, that 'there is need for both a theoretical break with religion and for a political handling of its role', that Islam 'has been used by the ruling classes to confuse the population and to block socialist or communist thinking', and that consequently 'it is all the more essential to supersede Islam with materialist thought and . . . for religious conceptions to be purged from revolutionary thought', Islam will not be easily displaced in men's minds by Marxist-Leninist abstractions, even when these are backed up by the apparatus of a cheka. The assertion applies with equal force to Dhufar, where P.F.L.O.A.G. tried to impose Marxism-Leninism by methods akin to those employed by its South-Yemeni patrons. (The same might equally be said of P.F.L.O.A.G.'s boasts that it had eradicated tribalism. Many of the atrocities perpetrated by the guerrillas were committed in pursuit of tribal vendettas, while others had the predictable effect of laying the foundations of fresh tribal feuds.) Islam constitutes the only spiritual and temporal order that the people of South Arabia and Dhufar know; it is the only social and political system that they comprehend. Against this rock the windy pronouncements from Aden beat in vain. Who knows but that the N.L.F. commissars themselves may even sense the futility of their exertions? For they, too, for all their unrelenting Marxist-Leninist blague, are still inveterately Muslim in their hearts.

19
Such Decent Chaps, the Arabs[1]

The Arabs by Peter Mansfield. Allen Lane, 1976, 572 pp.

I t seems from all that Peter Mansfield has to say about them (and this is a very great deal indeed) that the Arabs are really a very decent bunch of chaps. Back in the days before Islam they spent their time in the desert making up *qasidahs*, or odes, about how wonderful they were, and Mr Mansfield evidently feels it is high time this noble tradition was revived.

According to his *qasidah*, the Arabs have been having a rotten time of it since the decline of the great Arab empires of the Middle Ages, and the blame for their misfortune lies squarely at the door of the West. Fired by avarice and religious prejudice, the West has been exploiting the Arabs for the past two centuries, and the worse exploiters of all have been Britain and France—although the United States is fast overtaking them.

Since the Arabs have invariably been in the right in their quarrels with the West, the only proper thing for the scoundrelly British, French, Americans and other Western reprobates to do is to atone for their sins by doing whatever the Arabs want them to do—which includes paying them the earth for their oil.

It is simply disgraceful, fumes Mr. Mansfield, that the Western oil companies should ever have had the power to control the oil market and to fix prices. Such power is solely the prerogative of the members of OPEC, and now that it is in their hands ineffable blessings will flow for all of us.

---

1 From *The Sunday Telegraph*, 21 November 1976. Reproduced by permission.

As a sensitive Englishman, Mr. Mansfield positively seethes with embarrassment over his country's record of 'imperialism' in the Middle East, over her 'squalid betrayal' of the Arabs after the First World War, over her shocking error in issuing the Balfour Declaration (and even more shocking presumption in implementing it) and most of all over her utterly unwarranted hostility towards that great and good man, Gamal Abdul Nassser.

Yes, indeed, these were monstrous crimes, and it is perfectly understandable that Mr. Mansfield should be so incensed by them, so engrossed in cataloguing and delineating them (that is, when he is not lyrically extolling the qualities and achievements of the Arabs) that he should overlook or pass impatiently over some of the more awkward footnotes of modern history, such as the Arab slave trade (and its suppression by the British).

Nor do we hear much in *The Arabs* of Palestinian terrorism or its innocent victims—though we are indignantly told that King Hussein's hammering of the Palestinian guerrillas in September, 1970, was 'atrocious'. Mr. Mansfield is a great man for the Palestinians, and their rights, and the wrongs done them, but he is very muted on what they have done to the Lebanon in recent times.

He is also very free with his censures upon Westerners for their ignorance and prejudice regarding Islam and the Arabs, but it is doubtful whether he has done much himself to help their understanding with this emotional, error-strewn and awesomely partial effusion.

20
Philby of Arabia[1]

Philby of Arabia by Elizabeth Monroe. London: Faber and Faber, 1973. Pp. 332, illustrations, maps, bibliography, index.

Just how unpleasant a man Harry St. John Bridger Philby was never became known to the world at large during his lifetime. Most of us might still be in ignorance of his true character if Miss Elizabeth Monroe had not come forth with this admirable biography, at once forthright, judicious, understanding, inquiring, detached. When it comes to cataloguing Philby's unattractive qualities Miss Monroe is unsparing. He was a prig at school, a Fabian afterwards, and in later life an avowed if muddled communist. He was an admirer of Hitler and at the same time a vociferous pacifist—although, as Miss Monroe cuttingly observes, his pacifism did not extend to Ibn Saud's wars nor did it inhibit him from trafficking in arms himself. He stood as a 'peace' candidate in a by-election in July 1939, and when war came he returned to Saudi Arabia (the offer of his services having been rejected, hardly surprisingly, by the War Office) to preach defeatism and anti-British sentiment. He, who had been an agnostic—if not an atheist—since his schooldays, and in old age was to profess materialist beliefs, became a Muslim in the early nineteen-thirties in order to further his commercial speculations, to improve his standing with Ibn Saud, and, with perhaps better justification, to facilitate his journeys of exploration in Arabia.

1 From *Middle Eastern Studies*, Vol. 13, No. 1 (Jan., 1977), pp. 144-146. Published by: Taylor & Francis, Ltd. Reproduced by permission.

Towards his family he was negligent, capricious, moody, often miserly, occasionally generous. He was a bigamist (at least under English law), an undiscriminating philanderer, yet (or perhaps because of it, for who can say in such arcane matters?) he was admired and respected by women of character. His wife endured so much from him, stoically and loyally, for so long that she richly deserves a medal to be struck in her honour, something along the lines of the Royal Asiatic Society's Burton Memorial Medal, to be awarded to the ill-used spouses of Englishmen 'crazed with the spell of far Arabia'. As a champion of Arab unity—a concept about which his formulations were vague in the extreme—Philby never ceased to revile Britain for the wrongs, real or supposed, she had done the Arabs since the first world war. His rancour over 'Western imperialism' was so consuming that it led him into intemperate, almost hysterical, acclamations of the Soviet Union and its benign influence in the world, especially the Arab quarter of it.

How far Philby's political attitudes can be attributed to genuine ethical convictions or a selfless indignation at the woes and tribulations of mankind, how far to his own temperament, to ambition frustrated, vanity offended or acquisitiveness thwarted, it is difficult to decide. He was arrogant in demeanour, dogmatic in opinion, irascible in disputation. Two obsessions dominated his life—the making of money and the winning of fame. From the time that he joined the Indian Civil Service in 1908 he showed himself to be tenacious in his pursuit of money, shameless even in his determination to extract every penny to which he considered himself entitled. He was less punctilious, however, in accounting for other people's money entrusted to his care, as he demonstrated on his two missions to Najd in 1917 and 1918 as the representative of Sir Percy Cox, the chief commissioner in Iraq. Miss Monroe, who gives an entertaining account of Philby's travels and his negotiations with Ibn Saud, does not go into the subsequent controversy over Philby's handling of the large sums of money put at his disposal by Cox. Nor can she be reproached in the slightest for by-passing it, for it was a complicated affair, ultimately involving the political and constitutional propriety of using Indian revenues as well as those from enemy-occupied territories for purposes of British imperial policy.

Philby's part in the affair, however, was confined within much narrower limits. He did not submit a full report on his mission until the end of 1918, and then much of it was taken up with his observations on the geography, tribes and politics of central Arabia. The financial aspects of the mission, which were, after all, its *raison d'etre*, were relegated to an appendix, where they were accorded rather sparse treatment. When Philby was in London on leave after the close of the war he was requested to call at the India Office to explain the various discrepancies and omissions in his book-keeping which were causing his superiors a certain amount of puzzlement. Philby refused the request, saying that he had no intention of interrupting his leave. A copy of the financial appendix to his report, therefore, was sent to him, along with a list of queries to which his answers were invited. His reply was characteristically impertinent, consisting of a series of flippant or ill-tempered remarks scrawled in pencil alongside the queries. The India Office was not prepared to let him slide out of his responsibility so easily, and it kept after him for a proper accounting throughout the time (1921-24) that he served, on secondment to the Colonial Office, as British representative in Transjordan. It was a hopeless pursuit: Philby, who in Transjordan also had trouble with his superiors over money, evaded the reckoning that the India Office wanted to force upon him, and he was still successfully eluding his pursuers when he resigned from the Indian Civil Service in 1925.

The next half a dozen years were probably the most unhappy of Philby's life, as he strove to establish himself as a merchant at Jiddah and to use his acquaintance with Ibn Saud to prosper his commercial ventures and to open the way for him to explore the interior of Arabia. Exploration, he believed, would be the means by which he would win the public adulation that he craved, and, as fate decided, his faith was rewarded. His passion for exploration was not assumed: on the contrary, it was genuine and abiding, and he fully deserved the accolades he received for his great feats of travel. Philby would not have been Philby, however, if he did not contrive somehow to sour his own accomplishments. He did so early on, in 1931, when Bertram Thomas stole his coming thunder by making the first crossing of the Empty Quarter, from Dhufar in the south to Qatar in the north. Philby's fury was unrestrained (there is a wickedly accurate fictional portrayal of him in Josephine Tey's novel of a few years later, *The Singing Sands*) and he sulked for years afterwards, denigrating Thomas's crossing as being inferior to his own longer journey in 1932. Philby, however, travelled for much of his journey under the protection of Ibn Saud, whereas Thomas travelled most of the time under no one's protection. The point is not altogether insignificant, which is why it is a pity that Miss Monroe does not make it. Possibly she was slightly unsure of her ground, for she seems to be under a misapprehension when she observes of Thomas's crossing that it was made 'without so much as a by-your-leave to Ibn Saud', and that, since it was 'performed without permission, it was a slight'. But there was no reason in the world why Thomas should have sought permission from Ibn

Saud to cross the Rub' al-Khali, or even informed him of his intention to do so. Ibn Saud's effective jurisdiction in 1931 barely extended eastwards as far as the Jafurah and not much farther south than Jabrin. It certainly did not reach the central and eastern stretches of the Rub' al-Khali, nor did the principal tribes that roamed the sands—Murrah, Rashid, Awamir, Manahil—acknowledge his authority. Why, then, should he have taken it as a slight that Thomas crossed the eastern sands without his prior knowledge or consent?

All this, however, is incidental to the central purpose of Miss Monroe's book, which is to tell the story of Philby's life, something she does remarkably well, rather than to discourse upon the history and politics of Arabia in this century. (Any reservations one might be inclined to make about some of her historical or political interpretations can mainly be ascribed to the impression she gives of having allowed herself to be influenced by the Aramco school of history, which has taken on the mantle of the Arabian court chroniclers in assiduously hymning the 'right praise and true perfection' of the Saudi dynasty.) One feature of her book stands out particularly, and this is her unerring eye for the exact quotation to illustrate one aspect or another of Philby's character. Thus, on his immense vanity (possibly the most marked of his qualities) she quotes from a letter he wrote in 1930 putting himself forward as the most suitable candidate for the post of British minister to Jiddah. 'If I had the job I should of course run the show and expect the Foreign Office to leave me to do so without questioning my discretion as they must surely realise that in my judgment of the Arab situation I have never made a mistake.'

There is, perhaps, another, darker, life of Philby to be written, less generous and forbearing than Miss Monroe's. For all her skill in assembling the pieces, for all her care and fairness in interpretation, she still leaves essentially unanswered the question why Philby should have hated Britain so much. Was it because of his love affair with the Arabs? Was this for him a passion so intense, so destructive of other affections and loyalties, that its consummation could only be satisfactorily attained through the renunciation and vilification of the land that nurtured him? (That his renunciation did not extend to the spurning of the comforts, rewards and plaudits Britain offered him is wholly consonant with the kind of man he was.) Was the foundation of his creed what Sir Reader Bullard early detected it to be, 'a simple dualism in which the powers of darkness are represented by His Majesty's Government'? If so, his infatuation with the Arabs was not reciprocated, within Arabia or without. Only one of his books, *Arabian Jubilee*, his devotional work on the life of Ibn Saud, was translated into Arabic. (The literate Levant Arab is not really interested in Arabia per se, only in what comes out of it.) It is, in a melancholy way, the supreme irony of Philby's life and of his fierce quest for fame that his name should be perpetuated in the public memory largely through the treason of his eldest son. Their lives, Kim Philby's much more than his father's, are a terrible vindication of the grim truth residing in T. E. Lawrence's judgment upon men who, 'for love of the glamour of strangeness, go out to prostitute themselves and their talents in serving another race. A man who gives himself to be a possession of aliens leads a Yahoo life, having bartered his soul to a brute-master.'

21
OPEC Should Be Put In Its Place[1]

E ver since the Middle Eastern members of OPEC (the Organisation of Petroleum Exporting Countries) took advantage of the
Arab-Israel war of October, 1973, to double and re-double the export
price of crude oil, the Western world has been frantically trying to cope
with the resultant dislocation of its economy, and almost as frantically
trying to devise excuses for acquiescing in the oil producers' *coup de main*.
Not a month goes by without some new rationalisation being added to
the formidable body of received opinion which has grown up around the
subject, much of it questionable and some of it dangerously misleading.

Among those notions which belong in the latter category the following have pride of place: that an amelioration of the Arab-Israel conflict
(more specifically, a withdrawal by Israel from the territories occupied in
the 1967 war) will bring about an abatement of oil prices; that another
element working towards a lowering of prices is the Arabs' and the Shah's
sense of self-interest, which will operate to restrain them from seriously
injuring the West by damaging its economy and therefore by impairing its
ability to prevent the Soviet Union from dominating the Middle East; that
there is nothing much the West can do in any case to induce the Shah and
the Arabs to being the price of oil down to more realistic levels; and that
the huge surplus revenues the oil producers are now receiving can somehow be absorbed by the rest of the world, either by investment in the West
or by "recycling" through the international monetary system.

None of these propositions, or any of the other incantations which

---

1 From the *Daily Telegraph*, 1977 or 78 (exact date uncertain). Reproduced by permission.

the Western world keeps murmuring to itself for comfort, will stand close examination. They are based on assumptions—about a community of interests between the Arabs and the West, about common modes of thought, identical standards and values, and qualities of reasonableness and moderation—which have no foundation in fact.

The exorbitant prices which the Arab oil producers and the Shah are now exacting from the West, to the accompaniment of threats of embargoes and cut-backs, have little to do with the world of commerce or the laws of supply and demand. They are simply tribute, exacted from a supine West by a resurgent Islam.

To argue, as do so many Western apologists of the Arab cause, that the Arabs would never have employed the oil weapon against the West had it not been for their quarrel with Israel, is to ignore the nature of relations between the Western and Moslem worlds.

Moslem jurisprudence views the world in the uncompromising terms of the *dar al-islam*, Moslem territory, and the *dar al-harb*, enemy territory, of which the most prominent segment is Western Christendom. Between the two there can exist only a condition of latent or active hostility.

Now that the Arabs have the weapon against the West for which they have long been searching, they are unlikely to discard it even if the Arab-Israeli dispute were to be resolved overnight and to their complete satisfaction.

It was also Arab hostility towards the West which brought the Russians into the Middle East—which makes nonsense of those comfortable assumptions current in the West about an identity of interest in keeping the Russians out. Nor are they there simply because of the conflict with Israel, but rather because the well-worn Arab adage of 'the enemy of my enemy is my friend' was bound to operate sooner or later to encompass the West's most powerful and baleful enemy.

Paying Danegeld, or reparations, to the Arabs and the Shah in the form of excessive oil prices, far from securing supplies of oil, will only heighten their contempt and increase their intransigence. The notion of reparations—for alleged previous exploitation—may arouse a flutter in the breasts of those prone to feelings of guilt over Europe's relations with Asia and Africa, but reparations are no more justified by the record of the past than are the present exorbitant prices by the oil supply situation in the world.

Oil is not a precious or even a scarce commodity. Its price has only been pushed to ludicrous heights in the past 12 months by the activities of the OPEC cartel, whipped on by the ambitions and resentments of the

Shah and the Arab oil potentates. It will not be brought down to a realistic level —however many times Sheikh Ahmad Zaki Yamani, King Faisal's messenger, may girdle the earth like a fretful Puck, scattering promises of price reductions like so much fairy dust—while Western Europe continues to adopt towards OPEC the posture of the rabbit confronted by the stoat.

We would do better to heed the advice of Edmund Burke in his 'Thoughts on the Cause of the Present Discontent': 'When bad men combine, the good must associate: else they will fall, one by one, an unpitied sacrifice in a contemptible struggle.' There is no basis unity in OPEC, not even among its Arab members.

If Western Europe were to combine with the United States and Japan in a consumers' cartel, and at the same time drastically reduce its consumption of oil, intensify the search for oil in politically stable parts of the world, and resort to alternative sources of energy for its industry, the façade of OPEC unity would crumble.

The fearful and the *fainéant* will immediately cry that to embark on such a course is to court disaster in the shape of retaliatory acts by the Arabs and the Shah—embargoes, cut-offs, expropriations. True; but surely the risk is preferable to the certainty of economic ruin if we go on as we are going? And, surely, also, the West possesses more effective weapons in its economic armoury than do the Arabs and the Shah?

As yet, the Government of this country has made no attempt to prepare the British people for the dangerous times ahead, as the French Government, despite is many delusions concerning its relations with the Arabs, is now preparing the French people. Indeed, we are being dosed with placebos about long-term agreements and barter arrangements, which are supposed to guarantee us secure supplies of oil, while the incubus of financial disaster which looms over us is being conjured away by the ritual chanting of the magic word 'recycling'.

What is being ignored, or suppressed, is the fact that Arab oil producers and the Shah cannot be trusted to keep their word. OPEC has broken nearly every agreement it has concluded since 1970, the Shah has torn up the oil consortium agreement of 1954, and King Faisal has kept neither his reiterated pledge never to use oil as a political weapon nor his promises to lower its price.

As for 'recycling', neither the Arabs nor the Shah have shown much real inclination—as opposed to public relations exercises—to set up funds to assist even their fellow Moslems in Asia and Africa who have been hard hit by the inflated oil prices. How much less will they feel inclined to assist Western Christendom in its present predicament! (Putting money on loan would, in any case, set King Faisal a pretty problem, since the charging of interest is prohibited by Islamic law according to the Hanbali rite, which is followed in Saudi Arabia, and also by the civic Ordinance on Commerce introduced in that country in 1931—a small point, doubtless overlooked by our Chancellor of the Exchequer when he made his proposals to the International Monetary Fund).

The surplus revenues from oil in the hands of the Arabs and the Shah will amount this year to some $70 billion. By 1980, if they continue to accumulate as at present, they will amount to between $500 and $700 billion. To pay such huge sums will bring about the ruination of the West's economy. The vast, unearned riches from oil have already corrupted the societies of the oil-producing states. The even vaster riches which the Arabs and the Shah will dispose of in the near future will, no doubt, be used for political ends outside the Middle East, to the corruption ultimately of Western society and its institutions.

The evidence is already with us not least in the abject way in which successive British Governments have conducted themselves in recent years towards the Moslem world.

22
Diplomacy Among the Derricks[1]

Oil and Empire. British Policy and Mesopotamian Oil, 1900-1920, by Marian Kent. Macmillan/London School of Economics. 273 pp.

P erhaps the most striking feature of all the brouhaha occasioned by the activities of the Organization of Petroleum Exporting Countries over the past three or four years has been the almost total absence of any serious public discussion in the West about the strategic aspects of crude oil production and supply. Instead, actors and audience alike, in what has by now become a recurring sacred drama, have confined themselves strictly to the ritual petitions and responses embodied in a threadbare litany of 'recycled financial surpluses', 'long-term contracts', 'barter deals', 'economic interdependence', and the like. When and how in the past decade or so this indifference to strategic control over the principal sources of Western Europe's oil supply took root is not readily determinable, although there is little doubt that it is the consequence, as Corelli Barnett perceptively remarked some four years ago, 'of following Keynes rather than Clausewitz' in the conduct of Western relations with the oil-producing countries of the Middle East.

Until the middle years of the century access to Middle-Eastern oil was conceived of by the two European powers most involved in its discovery and exploitation, Britain and France, primarily in strategic terms. The British attitude originated in the years immediately preceding the First

1 From *The Times Literary Supplement*, 4 March 1977. Reproduced by permission.

World War, and it is the genesis of that attitude and the development of British governmental oil policy down to 1920 that is the subject of Marian Kent's highly competent and illuminating study, *Oil and Empire*. In these years, as she points out, almost every barrel of oil that Britain imported came from sources outside her control—80 per cent of it from the United States alone. It was a situation which the Admiralty, in particular, thought intolerable, and so a determined effort was made from 1912 onwards to acquire an independent, British-controlled source of oil supply for the Royal Navy.

The effort culminated in the acquisition by the British government of a majority interest in the Anglo-Persian Oil Company (of late years, British Petroleum) in 1914. Dr Kent does not spend much time upon this familiar episode, except to correct some long-held misconceptions about it, her main purpose being to trace the stages by which the British government, and the Foreign Office in particular, sought to secure a British monopoly, or near monopoly, of oil exploration and exploitation in Turkish Iraq (or Mesopotamia) comparable to the one Anglo-Persian had established in Persia.

The chosen instrument of penetration was the D'Arcy group, the alter ego of the Anglo-Persian Oil Company, headed by William Knox D'Arcy who had obtained the original concession. There was too much competition at Constantinople, however, for the bid to succeed, no matter how strongly the Foreign Office might support it. Three powerful financial and commercial interests, the British-controlled National Bank of Turkey, the Deutsche Bank and Royal Dutch-Shell (through its subsidiary, the Anglo-Saxon Petroleum Company) had created in 1912 the Turkish Petroleum company to bid for an exploratory concession for the vilayets of Mosul, Baghdad and Basra.

Fifty per cent of the shares in the company were held by the National Bank, and 25 per cent each by the Deutsche Bank and Anglo-Saxon. When it became clear, as it did very quickly, that there was no hope whatever of the D'Arcy group's supplanting the Turkish Petroleum Company in the lead that it had established at Constantinople, the British government switched its efforts to securing a dominant position within the company for the D'Arcy group. It succeeded in its object in March, 1914, when the National Bank agreed to transfer its shareholding to the D'Arcy group, *i.e.*, to Anglo-Persian.

One of the more surprising revelations to emerge from Dr Kent's careful and lucid exposition of the convoluted negotiations that secured the majority shareholding in Turkish Petroleum for Anglo-Persian is the suspicion and antagonism with which the British government viewed Royal Dutch-Shell and all its works. Dr Kent, who has consulted not only the Foreign Office archives and those of other interested government departments but the records of Royal Dutch-Shell as well, says that the reasons for this hostility 'cannot be clearly deduced from the documentary record of these negotiations'.

There were, as she observes, certain obvious considerations which influenced the British government's thinking. The desire for the Mesopotamian concession arose from strategic calculations, the principal of which was the necessity to secure for Britain and her armed forces, through the medium of British companies, direct and exclusive control over adequate reserves of crude oil. Royal Dutch-Shell had been created in 1907 by the amalgamation of the Dutch company with the British Shell Transport and Trading Company, the former holding 60 per cent of the shares of the merged company and the latter 40 per cent. One objection raised in Whitehall to Royal Dutch-Shell's participation in the Mesopotamian concession was the uncertainty created by the vulnerability of the Dutch—indeed, it was alleged their subservience—to German influence. Yet the Foreign Office happily accepted the participation of the Deutsche Bank in the Turkish Petroleum Company, and it showed no compunction at all in negotiating directly with the German government as a means of pursuing its objective of 'dishing' Royal Dutch-Shell in Mesopotamia. Little wonder that Dr Kent, normally so restrained in her comments, refers sharply to 'the somewhat cynical approach of the Foreign Office to the whole Mesopotamian oil affair'.

The Foreign Office was not merely cynical, it was also inept, notably in its handling of the central issues of Anglo-Persian's acquisition of the majority shareholding in Turkish Petroleum and the assertion of British control over the company as a whole. Moreover, in its treatment of the British directors of the National Bank of Turkey, without whose willingness to surrender their shareholding in the Turkish Petroleum Company in the interests of British policy the transfer to Anglo-Persian could not have been effected, the Foreign Office was both cavalier and lacking in decent appreciation; while in contrast it was at once feeble and dilatory in countering the German ascendancy at Constantinople. It is difficult to avoid the conclusion that the Foreign Office took its tone in this affair from the Foreign Secretary himself, Sir Edward Grey, who constantly bent over backwards to conciliate the Germans—as he was doing for much of the time to nearly everyone he had to deal with thereby setting a style in anxious pliancy which was to be aped by too many British Foreign Secretaries in the sixty years since.

Here, too, in the disdain and distrust which the Foreign Office customarily exhibited towards Royal Dutch-Shell, regardless of the patent loyalty of its directors to British interests, can be detected the lineaments of those prim convictions which were to make the Foreign Office in years to come such an ineffective guardian of British oil interests in the Middle East.

War came in 1914 before the Turkish Petroleum Company had succeeded in negotiating an oil concession with the imperial Turkish government. The war also invalidated the agreement reached in March, 1914, regarding the shareholding of the company. By the time the war ended the situation had altered radically. The Ottoman Empire was no more, Iraq was under British military occupation, the Germans were out of the running for an oil concession, and the Americans were jostling to take their place.

What was more, the war had revealed more sharply than before the extent of Britain's dependence upon non-British sources of oil, reinforcing the British government's determination to bring substantial reserves of foreign oil under British control. These reserves, it was decided, lay in Persia and Iraq—in spite of the fact that Persian oil production in the war had been minimal to Britain's needs and the existence of oilfields in Iraq was only conjectured. (Oil in commercial quantities was not to be discovered there until 1927).

To exploit the potential reserves of Iraq on the scale required was beyond the resources of the Anglo-Persian Oil Company. Like it or not, the British government could not come anywhere near to achieving its aim without the assistance of Royal Dutch-Shell, whose commercial strength far exceeded that of Anglo-Persian and Burmah Oil, the other British company.

So discussions were set in train immediately after the war, both to decide the terms of Royal Dutch-Shell's participation in the exploitation of Iraqi oil and to alter the basis of its shareholding so as to establish British control over the company. The history of these negotiations, never before made public, makes sobering reading. So confused and serpentine were the tactics of the British ministers and officials involved that it is scarcely surprising that neither of the British government's desiderata had been gained by 1920, when Dr Kent's narrative comes to a close.

More success attended the negotiations which had been going on simultaneously with the French Government for the inclusion of the Mosul vilayet in the projected kingdom of Iraq, the mandate for which was to be acquired by Britain. A series of Anglo-French exchanges culminated in the San Remo understanding of April, 1920, which settled the mandates for Iraq and Syria and provided for French participation, as partial compensation for France's renunciation of her claim to Mosul, in the eventual exploitation of Iraqi oil. It also opened the way for the reconstitution of the Turkish Petroleum Company as the Iraq Petroleum Company, and for the grant to it in due course of a concession for Iraq.

An account of these developments, and of the further evolution of official British oil policy between the wars, is promised by Dr Kent in a subsequent volume. If one might venture to offer a suggestion, unappreciative of the value of her present work, it is that she might consider allowing herself a little more rein in the future. Her style is very tight and disciplined, too much so in places, where it tends to be the dry prose of the official and semi-official documents which are her raw material. So scrupulous is she in her attribution of sources that she has given her book a lop-sided appearance: 88 pages of notes and appendixes are far too heavy an anchor for 155 pages of text. She has no need to be so meticulous or restrained: her scholarship is faultless, her approach cool and incisive. We should all be the richer and wiser if she were more expansive, especially in her own opinions, suspicions and judgements.

23

Lament for the Lebanon[1]

Death of a Country: The Civil War in the Lebanon, by John Bull-och. Weidenfeld, 1977, 202 pp.

The civil war that ravaged the Lebanon from the spring of 1975 to the close of 1976 killed 44,000 people, injured 180,000 and destroyed property to a value of hundreds, if not thousands, of millions of pounds. It was a brutal and horrifying struggle, as civil wars are apt to be, especially when they are exacerbated, if not actually initiated, by religious animosity between the contestants.

John Bulloch saw the war at first hand, as *The Daily Telegraph* correspondent in Beirut, and it is clear from his poignant, indeed harrowing, account of it that it affected him deeply. For all the vividness and felicity of his descriptions of people and events, a sense of sadness lingers over his pages, turning his book, *Death of a Country*, in effect, into a lament for the Lebanon that was and may never be again. It is a sentiment that those who know the country well fully share.

Would the war have been so savage—would it have broken out at all?—if it had not been for the presence in the Lebanon of 300,000 Palestinians, many of them armed to teeth and backed to the hilt from outside?

Mr Bulloch believes that an insurrection was almost inevitable, since large numbers of the Moslem majority population of the Lebanon were poor and depressed, and bitterly resented the political and economic ascendancy enjoyed by the Christian minority. It was only after the militant,

---

1 From *The Sunday Telegraph*, 1 May 1977. Reproduced by permission.

Left-wing factions among the Moslems raised a revolt, he says, that the Palestinians were "sadly and reluctantly" drawn in on their side.

It is an honest opinion, honestly given, yet it begs the question: would the Left among the Moslems have resorted to arms if they had not been certain that the Palestinians would be with them? To support his interpretation, Mr Bulloch tends to portray the Christian community, and especially the Phalange, or Kataeb, organisation, in blacker colours than it merits.

The Phalange is more than just a "Right-wing" group—if, indeed, it deserves that pejorative at all. Its *raison d'etre* was much more complex than a bigoted defence of entrenched Christian and capitalist privilege. Its members saw themselves primarily as Lebanese patriots, fighting for the sovereignty and independence of the Lebanon, and to preserve its singularity as the only parliamentary democracy in the Arab world, a stand in which they were at one with the conservative Lebanese Moslems.

Set against the background of the Arab Middle East, against the revival of Moslem intransigence and the prevalence of despotic governments, the Lebanese Christians' view of themselves as a beleaguered minority is readily understandable.

If there is a flaw in Mr Bulloch's book, which is otherwise thoughtful and well-informed, it is his failure to take more account of this wider dimension of the conflict. What also remains unresolved is the basic argument about whether or not the alleviation of the grievances of the poorer Lebanese Moslems really required the agony of a civil war and the humiliation of a Syrian occupation for its accomplishment.

Not, of course, that the Lebanese poor are anything but worse off today. But, then, were they not really the cause of the conflict? Or was its ultimate purpose to replace the Moslem-Christian partnership in the Lebanon with a Palestinian supremacy?

24
Time To Fold Those Tents[1]

T.E. Lawrence, by Desmond Stewart. Hamish Hamilton.,1979, 332 pp.

With rare exceptions (the most notable being Richard Aldington's 'biographical enquiry' in 1955), biographies of T.E. Lawrence give the impression of being devotional exercises, a retelling, in language of cloying piety, of a sacred legend of a blonde demi-god and his swarthy minions who set the sands of Arabia singing with their mighty exploits. They are also, taking colour perhaps from their subject, equivocal, tendentious and misleading.

There is nothing in Desmond Stewart's book to set it apart from this tradition. We are taken on yet another weary pilgrimage through Lawrence's youth, surely one of the dullest on record, passing at the customary wayside shrines (his bastardy, his domineering mother, his bicycle rides) to ponder devoutly upon the 'Significance of it All'.

For sustenance, we are offered a *réchauffé* of the tainted meats of his Arabian adventures, mixed with some very stale chestnuts indeed ('intelligence agent' in pre-war Syria, the Arab capture of Damascus), and tricked out with bits and pieces of para-scholarship (a thousand footnotes and acknowledgements to a hundred individuals and institutions) to beguile the unwary and impress the gullible.

Large and absurd claims for the book are advanced by Mr Stewart's publishers: 'Many surprising discoveries await the reader. The truth behind

---

1 From *The Sunday Telegraph*, 3 July 1977. Reproduced by permission.

the myths of which Lawrence was the source...Stewart has been the first... who has had direct access to contemporary Arab sources.' All of this is patently untrue. There are no discoveries of any consequence here. Unaware, it would seem, of the research of the past 20 years and more, Mr Stewart clings to an out-of-date and discredited interpretation of the Arab Revolt, attributing for instance, the capture of Damascus in 1918 to the Sherifian forces, when it has been known for years now, that the city fell to the Third Australian Light Horse Brigade.

As for the myths about the Arab Revolt, poor Lawrence had less to do with their manufacture than did the galere of vociferous Arabophiles who emerged in political and literary circles in England after the First World War, and whose influence has persisted to this day. Mr Stewart is evidently of their persuasion, plaintively rambling on about Britain's 'betrayal' of her pledges to the Arabs and simultaneously obscuring, like others before him (not least his hero, who started the miserable practice), the historical truth that the Arabs were liberated from Turkish rule, not by the posturing of Lawrence and his Bedouin mercenaries far from the battlefront, but by the exertions and sacrifices of the armies of the British Empire.

But perhaps he can be forgiven his omissions and misrepresentations on this score since he is clearly out of his depth in dealing with politics and war in the Middle East in this century. Errors and misconceptions of the most fundamental kind litter his pages (apparently, for example, Curzon was Foreign Secretary in 1909), and he manages, like Lawrence himself, whom he is inclined to patronise for his poor Arabic, to confound his own pretensions to linguistic erudition or familiarity with Islamic beliefs and institutions. One almost begins to feel sorry for Lawrence in the hands of such an inept hagiographer.

Speculations about Lawrence's submerged sexuality, the dark recesses of his spirit, and the secret springs of his more bizarre actions, are obviously more Stewart's *metier*. Plunging eagerly into these murky depths he dwells at boring length on Lawrence's gropings, or supposed gropings, with one or another, real or imagined, Arabian and Syrian catamites.

Sodomy, of course, has always figured prominently in the necromantic rituals of the Lawrence cult, no less than in the heated and feverish milieu of Arabophilia in which they are celebrated still. It takes second place, however, in Mr Stewart's learned discourse, to psycho-pathological ruminations on the sexual gratification Lawrence may have achieved from being whipped by husky males. So carried away does Mr Stewart become with his abstruse theorising about this tantalising topic that he is moved to quote from a current and obscure American publication catering to exotic sexual tastes, thoughtfully adding in a footnote the address in California from which it issues. *Chacun a son gout.* For my part I prefer the cooler insights of Aldington.

25
Kuwait Oil[1]

The First Kuwait Oil Concession Agreement: A Record of the Negotiations 1911-1934, by Archibald H. T. Chisholm. London: Cass. 1975, 254 pp.

I t is hard to believe today that only fifty years ago the consensus of opinion among oil geologists was that there was no oil to be found on the Arabian side of the Persian Gulf. One man who refused to subscribe to this opinion was Major Frank Holmes, a New Zealand mining engineer who had worked in a number of countries around the world before landing up in Bahrain in 1922 as a trader and an undisguised concession hunter. Holmes has been rather roughly treated in most published accounts of the beginnings of the Gulf's oil industry, mostly because at different times he trod on the toes of the British government and the major oil companies; and it is one of the many virtues of A.H.T. Chisholm's absorbing and splendidly documented narrative of the conclusion of the Kuwait oil concession of 1934 that he treats these occasions as the peccadilloes they were, and generously accords Holmes his proper place in the modern history of the Gulf.

Holmes was pretty successful in his concession hunting. From Ibn Saud in 1923 he obtained for the company of which he was a partner, the Eastern and General Syndicate, an oil concession for Hasa. A year later he secured a similar concession for the Saudi-Kuwaiti neutral zone, and

1 From *International Affairs*, Oct., 1977, Vol. 53, No. 4, pp. 703-705. Reproduced by permission.

the following year he acquired another concession for Bahrain. All three concessions were sold by the Eastern and General Syndicate to the Gulf Oil Corporation of Pittsburgh in 1927, after they had first been offered to, and refused by, the Anglo-Persian Oil Company (now British Petroleum). Holmes then turned his attention to Kuwait, whose ruler, Shaikh Ahmad al-Jabir al-Sabah, he had known since his early days in the Gulf and with whom he enjoyed a friendly, even close, relationship. Anglo-Persian had made a half-hearted approach to Shaikh Ahmad for a concession in 1923, only to draw back after a hurried, preliminary, geological survey in 1924 had indicated the unlikelihood of oil being present in the sheikhdom in any quantities. For his part, Shaikh Ahmad was in no hurry to award a concession to anyone, especially to APOC in which the British government had a majority shareholding. He greatly resented the British government's action in handing over Kuwait territory to Ibn Saud when the neutral zone between Kuwait and Hasa was established in the frontier negotiations at Uqair in 1922, and he suspected that APOC, if it held the concession in Kuwait and found oil there, would gear its producing operations in the sheikhdom to the requirements of its production levels in Persia, not to Kuwait's financial needs or ambitions. When Holmes reappeared, therefore, in 1928, to seek a concession on behalf of Gulf Oil, Shaikh Ahmad gave him a warm welcome.

Although the terms that Holmes offered were rejected by the shaikh as inadequate, the fact that Gulf Oil was bidding for the concession caused flutterings in Whitehall. By treaty the shaikh was required to have any concession granted by him approved in advance by the British government. A further requirement was now imposed in the shape of a 'British nationality' clause, which was to be inserted in any concession and which stipulated that the company to which a concession was awarded had to be British and have a majority of British directors on its governing board. Although this attempt to block Holmes's negotiations failed (it had to be abandoned after a similar requirement respecting the Bahrain concession, which Gulf Oil had sold to Standard Oil of California in 1928, was withdrawn under pressure from the United States government in 1932), other obstructions were thrown up by the British government in the next few years to make sure that APOC would not be shut out of Kuwait—even if it was not exactly itching to get in. It was the removal of the British nationality requirement in April 1932, accompanied by some prodding from Whitehall, that aroused APOC from its torpor. Confronted with the possibility that Gulf Oil might obtain the Kuwait concession, yet reluctant still to compete for it lest the sheikhdom should prove dry of oil, APOC compromised by asking Shaikh Ahmad in June 1932 for a three-year prospecting licence. The shaikh refused the request. Oil had been struck in Bahrain at the end of May, and he, like Holmes, was convinced that Kuwait, too, had oil. Only a concession of sixty or seventy years' duration, he told APOC, was of interest to him.

It was at this stage that Chisholm, then serving with APOC in Persia, became involved in the story. Sent to Kuwait in August 1932 with APOC's draft concession, he found himself up against Holmes in soliciting Shaikh Ahmad's consent to a concession. His subsequent rivalry with Holmes was, for the most part, a friendly one, the two men, although differing widely in temperament and outlook, as well as background, sharing a mutual liking and respect. The contest went on for more than a year, the two competing negotiations being subject to frequent and prolonged interruptions. Perhaps inevitably, APOC and Gulf Oil at the close of 1933 decided to merge their interests in Kuwait and to make a joint approach to the ruler for a concession. The Kuwait Oil Company, owned fifty per cent by APOC and fifty per cent by Gulf Oil, was incorporated in December 1933, and in February 1934 Chisholm and Holmes returned to Kuwait as joint negotiators. Months of hard bargaining lay ahead of them, made perhaps harder by some of Holme's idiosyncrasies and intrigues, before the concession was finally secured in December 1934.

For Shaikh Ahmad the concessionary agreement represented possibly an even greater triumph than it did for the two negotiators, for he had got what he had wanted from the start—the participation of American oil interests in the exploitation of Kuwait's oil without alienating the goodwill of the British government upon whom he depended for the security of his sheikhdom against his larger neighbours. He was helped by events, notably by the discovery of oil in Bahrain in May 1932 and the grant of a concession by Ibn Saud to Standard Oil of California in May 1933; but he also owed a good deal to the men with whom he treated and to the decent respect they showed for Kuwait's integrity and well-being.

The Kuwait concession was to run for seventy-five years. It ran, in fact, for not much more than half the time. Whether or not its premature termination should be regretted remains to be seen. Times have changed, and the days of the old Arabian oil concessionaires have passed. Yet their achievements were of an order greater than the contemporary mood, perhaps, will allow; which is one reason why the narrative and documentary record set out here in Chisholm's book is so valuable, recalling, as it does, the true spirit in which those early oil ventures into Arabia were undertaken.

26
Seeking Refuge in the RAF[1]

Solitary in the Ranks: Lawrence of Arabia as Airman and Private Soldier, by H. Montgomery Hyde. Constable, 288 pp.

When T.E. Lawrence decided in 1922 to turn his back on public life and the fame he had acquired by his exploits in Arabia during the 1914-18 war, he sought refuge and anonymity in the ranks of the R.A.F. by enlisting as an aircraftsman under an assumed name.

The Chief of Air Staff, Sir Hugh (later Lord) Trenchard, assisted him in this deception, and he again came to his rescue, after the discovery and publication of Lawrence's identity had forced him to leave the R.A.F and spend two unhappy years as a ranker in the Tank Corps, by allowing him to re-enlist in the R.A.F. in 1925 under the name of 'T.E. Shaw'. During these years and up until Trenchard's retirement at the close of 1929, the two men kept up a personal correspondence and it is this correspondence that forms the basis, if not the substance, of *Solitary in the Ranks*.

What is one to say about it? H. Montgomery Hyde evidently believes the correspondence is of value, both for the fresh information it provides and for its revelation of the high regard in which Trenchard held Lawrence and his opinions. Read with a less engaged eye, however, the correspondence yields a good deal less. It is pedestrian, trifling, mundane – in sum, distinctly boring.

Lawrence whines and snuffles about his discomforts and inconveniences, interspersing his dreary litany with slick, off-hand pronounce-

1 From *The Sunday Telegraph*, 15 January 1978. Reproduced by permission.

ments on international politics—all couched in a stylistic short-hand meant to convey the impression of diffidence, modesty and reticence, but which was really a form of inverted boasting.

As to Trenchard's attitude to him, it emerges as a mixture of compassion and forebearance. Whatever the causes of Lawrence's particular distemper, men like Trenchard and Churchill and Bernard Shaw who cared about his welfare plainly thought he would be best off in some kind of semi-monastic institution; and the institution chosen for him was the R.A.F. Trenchard's own interest in him lapsed after his own retirement from the R.A.F; he corresponded with him rarely and never once sought his company.

However, hard Mr Montgomery Hyde tries to invest his hero with a concern for other people and other causes, Lawrence appears in his pages as a man concerned exclusively with himself and his own affairs. Though he spent two years in India with the R.A.F., there is nothing in his letters to show that he took any real interest in India or that he learned anything about it. Again, though he is portrayed as being devoted to the R.A.F. and its future, there is little hard evidence in Mr Montgomery Hyde's account of anything approaching the selfless devotion to the service displayed by men like Trenchard. Instead the R.A.F. seems merely to have served Lawrence as a vehicle, a stage, a context for his endless and incurable posturing.

27
Trying, Egypt, Trying[1]

In Search of Identity, by Anwar el-Sadat. Collins, 1978, 360 pp.

Though the President of Egypt, Anwar el-Sadat, has shown signs before now of being something of a wag, it is only with the publication of his autobiography, *In Search of Identity*, that he reveals himself to have more than a dash of James Thurber in his make-up, not to say a capacity of sustained farce worthy of S.J. Perelman.

The Thurber touch is very much to the fore in Sadat's account of his trials, as a young officer, on charges of spying for the Germans during the war and of complicity in political assassination afterwards. As he tells it, it is Walter Mitty in the dock, confounding his inquisitors with his moral indignation, quiet dignity and patriotic fervour.

Later in the book he has another sly Thurberesque tale about Nasser in 1967 being treated for a skin complaint with injections of female hormones, a treatment which, Sadat adds innocently, 'gave rise to severe fits of nervous tension'—as well it might, considering the virile image that Nasser liked to project to the Arab world. What gives added piquancy to the story is that the treatment was recommended by a British doctor, which only confirms what Sadat complains of throughout this book—that the British, who didn't even help him re-open the Canal in 1975, were a rotten bunch.

His portrayal of the deliberations of the Egyptian junta under Nasser reads like a script for the Marx Brothers. When war with Israel loomed at the end of May 1967, Nasser asked his commander-in-chief, Abdul

---

1 From *The Sunday Telegraph*, 4 June 1978. Reproduced by permission.

Hakim Amer, whether the forces were ready. According to Sadat, 'Amer pointed to his neck and said: "On my own head be it, boss! Everything's in tip-top shape".'

On another occasion in 1970, when Nasser returned from rejuvenation treatment in the Soviet Union, Sadat welcomed him at the airport with the words, 'I say, I say, boss! What youthful looks!' Nasser's response to this was impenetrably Delphic. 'He gave me a long look and said, "Anwar! The Soviet Union is a hopeless case".'

Presumably this music-hall phraseology is the consequence of the book's literal translation from the Arabic ('boss' here being an infelicitous rendering of *rais*). No indication is given by the publisher, however, of the fact that it is a translation, though its literary origins are apparent in the high rhetoric and verbal histrionics it sustains throughout, and especially in the chapter on the October, 1973, war.

Here, surely, Sadat must be engaging in an extended leg-pull, with all his taradiddle and braggadocio about how the Israelis were hammered into the ground ('The Egyptian Air Force achieved an epic feat – heroic and glorious'; 'Dayan collapsed and wept...the road to Tel Aviv was now open'). He strains our credibility just a tiny bit, however, when he claims that only his 'ethical code' preventing him from emulating Israel's 'unmanly violation' of the ceasefire and unleashing the Egyptian Third Army— then trapped on the east bank of the Canal—on the Israeli salient west of the Canal and wiping it out.

Beside the Canal he has at last found his Innisfree. 'Nowadays I am never happier than when I am on the banks of the Suez Canal. I sit there for hours on end in a small log cabin...' Smiling a little, perhaps, over the way in which he has managed to tell the story of all the tribulations visited upon Egypt during Nasser's reign without accepting a scintilla of personal responsibility for them?

28
Suez: A Story of Sabotage[1]

Suez 1956: A Personal Account, by Selwyn Lloyd. Cape, 1978, 282 pp.

I t is surprising that no enterprising manufacturer has yet marketed a game called 'Suez'. As the many tracts that have appeared in the past 20 years on the subject of Britain's attack on Egypt in 1956 have convincingly demonstrated, it is a game that anyone can play. No particular knowledge of Middle Eastern politics and history, or even of British foreign policy, is required.

Indeed, all a participant needs is a basic set of preconceived attitudes and political prejudices, along with a goodly store of moral scruples, *mea culpas* and rent garments. The player collecting the greatest number of prize chips marked 'I told you so' would be declared the winner – or, rather, the loser, since losing is much more acceptable to enlightened opinion these days.

For those caught up in the toils of the Suez affair, who had to endure the heat of the battle and shoulder the responsibility for its conduct, it was not so amusing; which is one reason why Selwyn Lloyd, the Foreign Secretary of the day, allowed 20 years to pass before setting down his account of Suez 1956. Sadly he did not live to see his book published; all the more sad because it is a reflection of the man himself – decent, straightforward, unassuming and restrained.

Two features stand out in his retelling of the Suez story. One is the

---

1 From *The Sunday Telegraph*, 9 July 1978. Reproduced by permission.

assiduous sabotage by the United States of every successive British and French endeavour to settle the crisis in a way beneficial to Western interests. The other is the cobbled-up nature of the collaboration with the French and the Israelis in launching hostilities against Egypt.

American animosity and disingenuousness should not have come as such a surprise to Selwyn Lloyd as they apparently did. Among officials in the State Department concerned with the Middle East there had long existed a determination to destroy British and French influence in the region and replace it with American power.

It was a determination which had its beginning in the inter-war years, grew in strength during the Second World War and reached its efflorescence in the decade and a half after 1945. Much of the animosity was occasioned by the ambitions of the major American oil companies (whose principal advocate in the State Department in the 1950s was the Under-Secretary of State, Herbert Hoover Jr), but it also arose from American inexperience of alliances and from a consequent narrow assumption that they could, and should, be run on the lines of one chief and several Indians. In Nasser these officials found a useful instrument for their purposes, and it pursuit of their vendetta against the British they engaged in some fairly *louche* transactions with him in the early 1950s.

None of this would have mattered greatly if Dulles, the Secretary of State, and Eisenhower, the President, had not themselves shown so much ambivalence in their attitude to Britain and France. Selwyn Lloyd, believing that the old wartime spirit of comradeship still animated Anglo-American relations, was greatly taken aback by the duplicity of Dulles and by Eisenhower's petulance and shilly-shallying. For Eisenhower, the only thing that counted in the summer and autumn of 1956 was the impending presidential election. Hag-ridden by fears that he might not be re-elected, he sought to bolster his chances by playing the pacifist in public, while off-stage he pretended, by means of veiled hints and obscure promises, to support Britain and France, a deception which, as Selwyn Lloyd notes, he endeavoured to conceal years later in his memoirs, mawkishly entitled 'Waging Peace'. Dulles, meanwhile, shamefully deceived the British and French over American intentions. He hardly made amends for his duplicity by his subsequent confession to Selwyn Lloyd and Pineau, the French Foreign Minister, that they had been right about both Nasser and Suez, addressing to Selwyn Lloyd the plaintive reproach: 'Selwyn, why did you stop? Why didn't you go through with it and get Nasser down?'

On the other major issue, the collaboration with Israel, Selwyn Lloyd perhaps does less than he might have done to stress its ineluctable quality.

From the moment the Anglo-Egyptian agreement for the withdrawal of British troops from the Suez Canal base was signed in October 1954, hostilities between Egypt and Israel became a certainty. So, too, did Nasser's nationalisation of the Suez Canal. For the withdrawal of British troops from the Canal removed the buffer between Egypt and Israel, allowing Nasser to move his forces into Sinai hard up against the Israeli frontier. By June 1956, when the last British troops left the Canal Zone, two-thirds of the Egyptian Army were deployed in Sinai.

To the Israelis the signs were transparently clear, and when they saw that the Americans were undermining every step that Britain and France were taking, they decided to strike. The French read the same signs, and they approached the Israelis with a suggestion of joint action. By early October the Israelis were engaged in feverish preparations for an offensive in Sinai, probably at the end of the month.

It was not until October 16, Selwyn Lloyd writes, when he and Eden met Pineau and Mollet, the French Prime Minister, in Paris, that he learned of the Franco-Israeli plans. On October 22 he and Pineau conferred at Sèvres with Ben-Gurion and Moshe Dayan and reached agreement on a contingency plan. It was not a particularly cordial meeting, much less a marriage of true minds. Anglo-Israeli military co-operation, the subject of much speculation and recrimination since, never saw the light of day.

Far from the charge of 'collusion' being a damning one, let alone the heart of the matter, as some have claimed, it is almost irrelevant to the circumstances of the time. While it might have been preferable, in the context of British relations with the Arab States, to insulate the Anglo-French quarrel with Egypt from the politics of the Arab-Israeli question, it could not be done.

Israel intruded herself into the quarrel with Egypt for her own purposes, and in view of the singular tenacity with which the Israelis are accustomed to pursue their own interests, it would have been impossible to exclude her. The real issue is whether the intentions behind the plans were fraudulent or disreputable. That they were neither is self-evident.

Britain and France sought the internationalisation of the Suez Canal and the downfall of Nasser. To judge from all that has occurred in the years since 1956 it would have been better for all concerned—British, French, Arabs and Israelis—if they had succeeded. To Selwyn Lloyd's credit, it was no fault of his that they didn't.

29
A Damning Indictment of a Repressive
Ruler[1]

Nasser and his Generation, by P.J. Vatikiotis. Croom Helm,
1978, 375 pp.

Twenty years ago one of the best-known catch-phrases in the handbook of contemporary political enlightenment was 'Coming to
terms with Nasser'. Its postulates were that Egypt had been rescued from
corruption, misery and degradation by the military *coup d'etat* of 1952;
that Gamal Abdul Nasser, the leader of the coup and subsequently president of Egypt, was idolized by the Egyptian people and the Arab world at
large; that the strength of Arab nationalism as personified by the Egyptian
president was irresistible; and that the days of Western dominance in the
Middle East were numbered. *Ergo*, so the thesis concluded, the West must
bow to the forces of destiny and reach a *modus vivendi* with the Colossus
of the Nile.

Some of the more sceptical and unregenerate of us at the time doubt-
ed the truth of these propositions, without, however, being able to offer
much in the way of hard evidence to refute them. Little information was
available about the condition of Egypt under the military regime—in itself
a fair pointer to the regime's character—other than what was purveyed by
Western correspondents in Cairo.

Most of these, with certain honourable exceptions, had constituted

1 From *The Times Higher Education Supplement*, 17 November 1978. Reproduced by
permission.

themselves a voluntary claque for Nasser and his works, and when they were not celebrating his triumphs or agonizing over his troubles they were apt to fall to wailing and blubbering about the brutality and perfidy of the British and French governments in launching a wholly unprovoked and unjustified attack upon this great and good man in 1956. The same crowd, or their counterparts, are with us still, diligently selecting what they think fit to report about Sadat's Egypt and between times tortuously elucidating the past anew, with all the zeal of Soviet encyclopaedists, in an effort to preserve something of Nasser's faded glory.

They will have a much harder job of it now, following the publication of P.J Vatikiotis's *Nasser and his Generation*, which is the most thorough and able dissection of the late ruler of Egypt and his entourage ever to be undertaken by a Western scholar. Professor Vatikiotis, of the School of Oriental and African Studies in the University of London, is a leading authority on modern Egypt, and, what is equally important, he is a man of independent mind. His study of Nasser's regime, its origins, character and conduct, is based almost entirely on Arabic sources, and in particular on the reminiscences and revelations of former adherents or critics of the regime who have, since Nasser's death in 1970, been able to express themselves freely.

His book is a most careful and thoughtful analysis of the source of Nasser's political ideas, his relations with his brother officers in the junta, his methods of government and, most pertinent of all, the nature of the man himself. Backed every step of the way by solid and incontrovertible evidence, it adds up to a damning indictment of a corrupt and repressive ruler and his *camarilla*, an indictment which is a powerful antidote to the sickly hagiography which for two decades and more has comprised the bulk of Western and Arab writing on the subject of Nasser and his times.

As Professor Vatikiotis emphasizes from the start, the focus of his study is as much Nasser's generation as it is the *rayyes* (chief) himself. The Free Officers' Movement, the name given to the group of conspirators within the Egyptian officer corps who engineered the coup of July 1952, was composed almost exclusively of officers of lower middle class background who had entered the military academy in the late 1930s after its doors had been opened to entrants other than those from the ruling and upper classes.

For these young *baladi* (native as opposed to Turkified or Westernized, Egyptians) an army career represented a means of improving their social and economic fortunes, even though the senior appointments remained effectively closed to them on account of their origins.

What put fire in their bellies was not a passion for soldiering or a genuine dedication to the profession of arms but personal resentments and jealousies. They were half-educated, and their political ideas, in keeping, were half-baked, a compound of raw populism, crude patriotism and Islamic fundamentalism. Even these they had not thought out for themselves but had taken ready-made from the Young Egypt Society or the Muslim Brethren (*al-ikhwan al-muslimin*).

The young Egypt Society, the 'Green Shirts', was founded in 1930 and took as its inspiration German Nazism and Italian Fascism. It changed its name in 1940 to the 'National Islamic Party' and again in 1948 to the 'Socialist Party', changes which precisely reflected and delineated the movement's character—nationalist, socialist, religious and xenophobic, all in extreme degree. (Ahmad Hussein, its youthful founder, delivered himself of the opinion while on a visit to Italy in 1938 that the only true democracies in Europe were Germany and Italy).

The assumption of power by the junta in 1952 was in effect the triumph of Young Egypt. It also represented the defeat of those Western ideas of liberal democracy, of constitutionalism, parliamentary government and organized parties, which, however imperfectly applied, had nevertheless animated Egyptian politics since the early years of the century.

For, as Professor Vatikiotis makes clear beyond any doubt, Nasser and his co-conspirators intended from the very start to wield absolute power, tolerating no political rivals or alternative sources of authority and requiring from all classes of Egyptian society unquestioning and undeviating obedience. Because they were youthful, active and decisive, because they *looked* so stern, dedicated, clean-cut and incorruptible in their crisply pressed uniforms, the liberal maidens of the West fell madly in love with them, as they have been wont to do with every nationalist revolutionary who bounds upon the Afro-Asian political stage vowing to erase the last pathetic traces of the European liberal legacy from the Asian and African continents.

For this is exactly what the Nile-green incorruptibles of the Revolutionary Command Council were bent upon accomplishing. Egypt, which since the time of the last Pharoahs had been essentially a Mediterranean land, was henceforth to be enclosed within the narrow perimeters of Nasser's three circles—the Arab, the Islamic and the African. Nasser set out deliberately to sever Egypt's links with Europe, cutting her off from the intercourse and influences which since the days of Muhammad Ali Pasha had made her the most advanced of all the Arab countries. It was a return to the Pharaonic tradition, with the structure of government, as befitted the regression, a pyramid, with Nasser himself, *Pharoah redivivus*, at its apex. Whatever the style he affected—'prime minister' in 1954, 'president' from 1956—he was in actuality a despot.

To the members of his cabinet, most of them fellow officers of pre-revolutionary days, he was never *primus inter pares* but always the *rayyes*. They were there to execute his commands, not to share power or decide policy. Yet the impression gained from what Professor Vatikiotis has to say about the relationship between Nasser and his associates—and even more from the account given by Anwar el-Sadat in his recently published memoirs (*In Search of Identity*)—is less that of the court of an oriental despot, of Abdul Hamid and the Yildiz Kiosk, than that of the 'godfather' and the *famiglia*, the Mafia capo with his toadies, 'soldiers' and 'hit men'.

Under Nasser Egypt was ruled by a combination of methods derived directly from the underworld and from twentieth-century totalitarianism. A vast apparatus of security services, *mukhabarat*, controlled the populace, detecting and silencing dissenters by the liberal use of torture, imprisonment and exile. The reverse side of the coin of Nasserist autocracy was the corruption rampant in the Egyptian officer corps. The military establishment had brought Nasser to power and its prime function thereafter was to serve as the main prop of the regime, its loyalty bought with money, preferment and perquisites. As Professor Vatikiotis points out, 'Nasser did not perceive the role of the army in society strictly as a military institution, but as a bureaucratic system that could administer sanctions, and as an old boys' network that could dispense patronage. He denied it the chance of developing a corporate military professional ethos.'

The grim consequences of this denial were to manifest themselves in the futile and bloody campaign in the Yemen between 1962 and 1967, which claimed the lives of tens of thousands of Egyptian soldiers, and in the disastrous defeat at the hands of Israel in June 1967. Professor Vatikiotis is hard put to conceal his contempt for the instrument of Nasser's debasement of the Egyptian army, Abdul Hakin Amer, the commander-in-chief, a man whose unfitness for military command was almost as great as his capacity for deception and blague. He displayed both qualities to the full, according to the account given by Anwar el-Sadat in his memoirs, at a cabinet meeting called at the end of May 1967, to discuss the possibility of war breaking out with Israel in the immediate future. Asked by Nasser whether the Egyptian armed forces were ready for battle, Amer, so Sadat relates, 'pointed to his neck and said: "On my own head be it, boss! Everything's in tip-top shape".'

The debacle of June 1967—for which Amer paid with his life while

Nasser deftly dodged all responsibility—was the outcome of Nasser's unnecessary involvement of Egypt in the Arab-Israeli dispute a decade earlier. Before 1956, neither in his speeches nor in his actions had Nasser shown any real interest in the Palestine question. His victory over Britain and France in November of that year, however, made him a hero in Arab eyes everywhere, opening up glittering new horizons to him.

By posing as the champion of the Arab cause against Israel he believed that he could harness the forces of Arabism to Egypt's chariot and his own extensive ambitions. Instead, he found himself a captive of his own rhetoric and intrigues, and he dragged Egypt down with him, into a series of sordid entanglements in Syria, Iraq, Jordan and Arabia, sapping her strength, dissipating her treasure and leaving her a down-at-heel client of the Soviet Union.

When Nasser died in October 1970, he bequeathed Egypt, after 18 years in power, no abiding legacy, temporal or spiritual, only bankruptcy and the bleached bones of her sons scattered across the sands of Sinai or lying in deserted sangars on the hillsides of Yemen. He built no political institutions to replace those he had destroyed, least of all any that were expressive of popular sovereignty. He had ruled by the *mukhabarat* and by direct demagogic appeal to the Egyptian masses – 'the 18-year-long monologue', as one Egyptian writer, quoted by Professor Vatikiotis, calls it, or, in another's laconic judgement, 'the larynx became the mind'.

Here, in Nasser's singular rapport with the masses, in his ability to fuse his own sense of inferiority and obsession with dignity with their feelings of resentment and humiliation at the domination of Egypt by the West, lay the source of Nasser's strength and success. He was, as Professor Vatikiotis emphasizes again and again, a true native Egyptian, a *baladi*, not an alien aristocrat of the kind that that ruled Egypt for numberless generations.

As such he could articulate with passionate conviction all the fears, longings, woes and discontents of the Egyptian people. He did so over and over again, month after month, year after year, until his speeches came to seem like one enormous, unrelenting bill of complaint against history, fate and the rest of mankind. His rhetoric tapped all the baser instincts in his audience—envy, greed, religious fanaticism, hatred of foreigners, delight in the fall of the great—and personalized every issue, domestic or international, so that it was reduced in the end to the petty proportions of a squabble between Nasser and someone else, the latest in a long succession of pugilistic bouts pitting the Muhammad Ali of modern Egypt against all comers. The Egyptians, mesmerized by the insistent rhetoric, by the *rodomontade* and tantrums about 'dignity', by the ceaseless cataloguing of Egypt's ills and the attribution of them to 'Western imperialism' and other dark forces, scarcely had opportunity to reflect that it was not in the gift of other nations to grant Egypt the dignity Nasser was demanding. On the contrary, with peoples as with individuals, dignity emanates from within, and Nasser, with his ceaseless vapouring and ranting, was hardly the embodiment of this particular virtue. Nor, for all his vociferous reiteration of the afflictions endured by the Egyptian masses—poverty, disease, malnutrition, illiteracy, ignorance and squalor—did he institute any radical and consistent campaign to cure them, knowing full well in his heart they were incurable.

Looking back over all that Egypt has seen and suffered in the past 25 years one has the feeling that it has been a grotesque Jacobean melodrama, or an *opera bouffe* staged by a troupe of incompetent *gulli-gulli* men or conjurers. Nor is the feeling entirely unwarranted, for the political and intellectual progenitor of Nasser's dictatorship, Ahmad Hussein, the founder of the Young Egypt movement, was himself a frustrated actor, who, when he failed to make a theatrical career for himself, turned to political demagogy as an outlet for his histrionic urges. So, too, in the final analysis, may Nasser and his entourage be looked upon as mere mummers, posturing and play-acting rather than actually governing Egypt—Nasser (the *rayyes*), Hakim Amer (the commander-in-chief), Anwar Sadat (the speaker of the assembly), Ali Sabri (the prime minister), Salah Salim (the factotum), to name only some of the preposterous cast. The essential hollowness of their performance, as well as its uglier aspects, has been concealed for years by their ideological *claquers* in Egypt and abroad. It is both illuminating and significant that Professor Vatikiotis passes over, in his search for the truth about Nasser and his regime, not only every biography of the *rayyes* that has appeared in English but also the multiple contributions to the public record of Muhammad Hasanein Heikal, the former editor-in-chief of *Al Ahram*, whose smooth and supple rationalizations of Nasser's deeds, both during his lifetime and since, so captivated his fellow newspaper editors in England and France that they were forever handing on the enlightenment shed by his discourse to the readers of their own journals.

It is impossible to imagine Heikal or his European *confreres* delivering the kind of judgement upon Nasser that Professor Vatikiotis quotes from one of the most thoughtful and perceptive of contemporary Egyptian scholars, and in which he fully concurs himself, to the effect that Nasser's entire career was essentially spent in destruction. He destroyed the monarchy, parliament, the rule of law, political opposition, freedom of speech, landed estates, the foreign communities, private enterprise, the connexions with Britain and France—the list is endless. He put nothing in place of what he had obliterated except a monstrous and all-pervading security system and a new privileged class of bureaucrats, technocrats, planners and propaganda experts, a host of apparatchiks and parasites drawn from the same stratum of society as Nasser himself and wholly dependent upon the state's control of the economy for their continued prosperity.

Professor Vatikiotis's own verdict upon the man, delivered at the close of this masterly study, is that he was:

a soldier by chance, a politician by instinct and a conspirator by ability and inclination. He contributed little to soldiering or politics. But he elevated the more native art of conspiracy to new technical heights. At the end of the day, however, he was by formation, tradition and force of circumstances an Egyptian despot.

30
What the Editor Saw[1]

Sphinx and Commissar: The Rise and Fall of Soviet Influence in the Middle East, by Mohammed Heikal. Collins, 303 pp.

For more than 20 years, from the mid-1950s onwards, Mohamed Hasanein Heikal was in a position, as editor-in-chief of Egypt's leading newspaper and as a confidant of the late President Nasser, to observe from close quarters the progress of Soviet relations with the Arab world and with Egypt in particular. The account of these relations which he gives in *Sphinx and Commissar* is a highly personal one, more along the lines of "What the butler saw" than a study of history and politics, full of entertaining anecdotes and shrewd pen-portraits.

Towards the general phenomenon of Soviet penetration of the Middle East Mr Heikal himself displays a certain ambivalence of feeling. While he argues quite justifiably that the Soviet Union cannot be excluded from the region, and also, perhaps more questionably, that the Arabs have benefitted from the Soviet presence, at the same time he has ruefully to concede that a veritable chasm of misunderstanding and incomprehension separates the two.

It is hardly surprising that this is so, since, on the evidence of his book, even a man as intelligent, knowledgeable and worldly-wise as Mr Heikal seems unable to appreciate the true nature of the Soviet leadership and the Soviet system of government.

Throughout his book he gives the impression of equating the Soviet

1 From *The Sunday Telegraph*, 21 January 1979. Reproduced by permission.

Union, the world's greatest despotism, with the United States, the world's greatest democracy, and of finding little to distinguish their policies, one from another, in the Middle East. He wonders at Western antipathy towards Soviet activities in the area, yet he ignores the long-standing Soviet strategy (it was one of Lenin's theses) of striking at Western capitalism through its dependence on overseas sources of materials. One of the more remarkable omissions of his book is the absence of any consideration of the Marxist regime in Aden, its subservience to the Soviet Union and the threat it poses to continued Western access to the Gulf's oil.

Yet there is much also in the book that can be read with profit and amusement, not least his descriptions of the plebeian entertainments the Soviet and Egyptian hierarchies afforded each other during their numerous negotiating sessions. He reminds us, too, of the mischief-making propensities of Tito, of the boorishness of Khrushchev, of the *folie de grandeur* of Nasser—indeed, of the whole grim gallery of vulgarians, coxcombs and buffoons in whose hands the fate of the world now rests.

31
Militant Islam[1]

Militant Islam, by G.H. Jansen. Harper & Row, 1979.

I slam has been getting a bad press in the West of late, a circumstance which distresses Mr Jansen, who attributes it primarily to
Western misunderstanding and to a lingering hostility between the Christian and Moslem worlds which can be traced back to the Crusades. He has
set out, therefore, to enlighten us about the true nature of Islam and in so
doing to demonstrate that the hostility between the Christian West and
the Moslem East emanates almost entirely from the Western side. Barely is
he out of the starting gate, however, and almost before he can utter his first
cry of "Allahu Akbar!", than he is off and running around the old, familiar,
anti-imperialist track, already churned up by the hooves of a thousand
polemical hacks before him.

The West, so Mr Jansen fervently informs us, has held the Moslem
East in fear and contempt for centuries. It has oppressed and exploited the
Moslem peoples, occupying their lands, depleting their natural resources,
denigrating their religion, and generally debasing their lives. Most pernicious of all has been the West's cultural imperialism, which has among
other things destroyed the structure of traditional Moslem education and
put nothing of comparable value in its place. (According to Mr Jansen,
the European imperial powers founded no universities in the territories
they ruled, an accusation that will raise a few eyebrows in India, Pakistan,
Malaysia and Africa.) The *ghazis*, or shock troops, of this cultural offensive,

---

1 From *The New Republic*, 26 January 1979. Reproduced by permission.

it seems, have been the Western scholars of Islam, whose attitude toward their subject is one of dislike, if not downright antipathy.

All this, it need hardly be said, is a travesty of the history of Western relations with the Moslem world. Mr Jansen, who has an engaging line in half-truths, evasions and distortions, shows about as much respect for historical accuracy as the student mobs of Tehran show for the principles of international law. Take, for instance, the glowing account he gives of the Islamic penetration of Africa ("a story of epic proportions...the finest, truest expression of militant Islam"), spearheaded by Moslem traders, "who, as a class, seem to have been men of extraordinary spiritual power." What Mr Jansen somehow fails to indicate, by even so much as a whisper, is that one of the staples of their trade was slaves, and that this traffic in Africans by Moslem Arabs was only brought to an end by the efforts of Western Christians. It is difficult to understand how such a devout anti-imperialist as Mr Jansen could have overlooked such a splendid example of imperialism in action as the destruction of the East African slave trade—a trade in Africans, conducted by Arabs, financed by Indians, and suppressed by the British. It is equally puzzling why he fails to address himself, for all his tedious sermonizing about the superior morality of Islam, to the question why no movement for the abolition of slavery, comparable to that which developed in the Western world, ever arose of its own volition in the Moslem world. Why, in fact, it required the forcible intervention of the Christian powers of Europe, with Britain in the van, before the Moslem East could be brought, slowly and sullenly, to cease its trafficking in human beings.

The explanation for Mr Jansen's avoidance of these and other potentially embarrassing topics would appear to lie in his own animosity against Western Christendom, an animosity which informs nearly every page of his book and which expresses itself, among other ways, in his categorization of Christianity as a religion unsuited to black Africans, in his ridiculing and vilification of the labours of Christian missionaries, in the silence he observes about the slave hunts conducted in the Sudan by successive rulers of Egypt, in his traducing of the aims and methods of the former British administration in the Sudan which wiped out slave-trading, and in his perverse allocation of blame for the massacre a decade ago of black Christians in the southern Sudan not to the Moslem government in Khartoum but to the Christian missions in the south. His lengthy section on Islam in Africa ends with a disingenuous boast. "Islam's frontier is still moving forward in Black Africa, a fact of which the rest of Islam knows, of which it is very proud, and which adds to its militancy." How many Moslems, one wonders, are proud of such converts as Idi Amin, or of the fact that during his reign of terror in Uganda he was protected by a praetorian guard of Palestinian mercenaries and propped up by arms and money supplied by Colonel Qaddafi of Libya?

Mr Jansen, as we shall have occasion to note more fully later, is very free with his sneers at and aspersions upon Western scholars of Islam, whom he accuses of displaying bias and ignorance in their writings. On the evidence he affords here of his own defective knowledge of Islam and Islamic history, he would do well to hold his tongue. He equates the division between Sunni and Shi'i Islam with that between Protestantism and Roman Catholicism, a misconception that qualifies—to employ a phrase of Mahatma Gandhi—as a Himalayan blunder. He alleges that because of the Sunni ascendancy, Islam, unlike Christianity, "escaped the destruction of wars made in the name of religion and it escaped the erosion of spiritual values that is bound to result from such wars...In fact, inter-Muslim wars have been surprisingly few." In fact, as a closer acquaintance with Islamic history would confirm, sectarian conflict has marked the course of inter-Moslem relations since the early wars of Islam: three out of the first four caliphs, after all, met their deaths by an assassin's hand. And if no erosion of spiritual values has taken place in Islam, why, may one ask, have there been so many movements of revival and reform?

The other elementary errors and omissions in Mr Jansen's book, which there is no space here to list, are of a similar kind. The Moslem state, he says, has to be a republic: it cannot be a monarchy nor can it countenance hereditary succession. What, then, of the Umayyad, Abbasid, and other caliphates? Were they illegitimate? What of the scores of Moslem dynasties that have reigned at one time or another in the lands between Morocco and India? Were they too illegitimate? What of the descendants of the Prophet? What of the Hashemite dynasty in Jordan? Or the Saudi dynasty in Arabia? Mr Jansen is silent on these questions. He does not even consider the nature and function of the caliphate, an institution central to the history of Islam. Likewise he slides rapidly over the position of women in Moslem countries and in Moslem law, and over the fate of minorities under the Moslem dispensation that he favors—heedless, apparently, of the fact that the Middle East is a mosaic of minorities. He dismisses the imposition of the *jizyah*, or poll tax, upon Christians, Jews, and other "people of scripture" (*ahd al-kitab*) in a Moslem state as one of the "crudities" dredged up by the Ayatollah Khomeini. It has a much longer pedigree and active application than that.

Never once in his protracted diatribe against the West for its antagonism to Islam does Mr Jansen allude to those provisions of the *shari'a*, the law of Islam, which divided the world into the *dar al-Islam*, "Moslem territory," and the *dar al-harb*, "hostile territory," (of which Christendom is the principal constituent); and which go on to declare that between the two entities there can exist only a condition of continuous warfare, which, while it may be interrupted by truces, can never be terminated. Again, in taking the Western world to task for becoming exercised over so-called "canonical punishments," *i.e.* beheadings, floggings, stoning to death for adultery, and so forth, he indignantly asserts that these penalties are only inflicted by "the political exploiters of Islam," those professional politicians and generals in Moslem countries who, "not knowing the deeper truths of their religion," resort for motives of expediency to the Islamic system of punishment. In so doing, he argues, "these secular Islamic leaders...give Islam a bad name and give militant Islam an even worse name." Whether Mr Jansen likes it or not, these punishments are those prescribed by the *shari'a*, and they will be implemented by a Moslem government that is true to the letter of the law of Islam. As for those "secular Islamic leaders" who do not know "the deeper truths of their religion," would he number among them the Ayatollah Khomeini and his fellow divines? Or the late King Faisal of Saudi Arabia and his successor, King Khalid, neither of whom has hesitated to enforce the Koranic penalties whenever the occasion required? Far from being mere secular rulers, successive Saudi monarchs have borne the title of *imam* of the Wahhabi sect of Islam. But Mr Jansen tells us nothing of these matters: they tend rather to spoil his case.

In the light of his own less than convincing mastery of the essentials of Islamic law and history, Mr Jansen's strictures upon Western Islamicists for misinterpreting and misrepresenting Islam strike one as little short of impertinent. Two particular targets of his anathema are the great Dutch orientalist, C. Snouck Hurgronje, and the eminent British Islamicist, Sir Hamilton Gibb. Hurgronje is accused of manifesting "prejudice and fear" toward Islam, and of being "ignorant about some of the most important and elementary facts about Islam." Leaving to one side the sheer falsity of these charges and Mr Jansen's unfitness to prefer them, what are we to make of his own attempt to denigrate Hurgronje further by a sneering reference to the fact that he wrote "in the unimportant Western European patois that is Dutch"? The disparagement of Gibb's scholarship is of a similar kind ("strangely inept," "solemn nonsense," "dismissive and patronizing") and is equally unjustified. Moreover, it is the rankest ingratitude, for Gibb, whatever Mr Jansen might say to the contrary, toiled long and hard in the vineyard of Anglo-Arab amity and to foster respect for Islam among

Western students. One begins to wonder just what will satisfy Mr Jansen when he is so ready to bite the hand of someone so sympathetic to Arab and Moslem aspirations.

His attack on Western Orientalists of the past is succeeded by a demand that contemporary scholars of Islam and the Middle East should declare their individual interests, "and to say whether they are Arab or pro-Arab, Israeli, pro-Israeli or pro-Zionist." "A very large number of present-day writers on Islam and the Middle East," Mr Jansen writes,

> patently belong to one of the last three groups mentioned. The Arab writers, of course, stand out because of their names, and their works tend to be taken automatically as being partisan and propagandist. Such is not the case with the Israeli or pro-Israeli writer: their works are accepted as the product of objective scholarship, which in very many cases they are not.

It would seem, when taken in conjunction with Mr Jansen's remark elsewhere, that the work of western Orientalists "is in need of revision, if not rewriting," that what he is advocating is the establishment of some kind of Moslem Holy Office, which would examine what is written on the Middle East and then, depending upon whether or not the work in question conformed to the doctrinal requirements of the Islamic lobby, either grant or withhold its imprimatur. Substance is lent to this conjecture by Mr Jansen's outburst later in the book against an English journalist for making

> a remark of such arrogant silliness as to convince a militant Muslim that the spirit of the arrogant missionary and the silly Crusader is still alive in England today, and that only a greater degree of punitive militancy will bring the West to understanding or at least politeness.

While Mr Jansen's call for scholars to be branded according to his narrow categories can be dismissed for the insolent nonsense that it is, it might nevertheless be instructive to apply his injunction about a declaration of interest to his own book. What does Mr Jansen offer us by way of a prefatory warning about his own political, national and religious loyalties? Not a word. Instead we are left to deduce what we can from the few clues he scatters about, inadvertently or otherwise, and from the scraps of information afforded by his publisher. We are told by the latter that he is "the Levant correspondent of the *Economist*," that he now "lives in Cyprus (where he enjoys gourmet picnics)" and that he "worked in the Indian diplomatic service." Now who would have guessed from his name that Godfrey Jansen was an Indian? Next we find Mr Jansen, in the dedication to his book, according to his wife the prefix "Hajja," *i.e.*, one who has made the pilgrimage to Mecca. Could it be that Mr Jansen's wife is a Moslem?

Further evidence of a special interest is provided by the fact that when his book appeared in Britain it was reviewed in the *Economist* by Barbara Smith, who is the Middle East correspondent of that journal. And what did Smith have to say of her colleague's work? Not only that it was "a splendidly timely book" which "demolishes a wall of Christian myths about an Islam red in tooth and claw," but also that it was "gently erudite, felicitously phrased," and "full of glancing enlightenment." Among the shafts of enlightenment that it dispensed, according to Smith, was the revelation that the character and role of the imamate in Shi'i Islam approximated that of the papacy in Roman Catholicism—another blunder that qualifies for the Gandhi award. (It would be interesting to see how the Ayatollah Khomeini, who has been accorded the title of "imam" by the Iranian Shi'a would react to being told that he was something like a pope.)

With advocates like Mr Jansen, Islam has little need of detractors. His pious avowals that Islam is a religion of compassion ring rather hollow when set against the economic distress caused to the poorer countries of Asia and Africa by the huge increases in the price of oil imposed by the Moslem oil-producing states in recent years—a subject on which Mr Jansen maintains a discreet silence. There is a hollow ring also to his reiterated claim, the central thesis of his book, that the militancy now being exhibited by Islam is in reality nothing more than a "sincere" and "laudable" attempt "to square the conduct of public life with the principles of religion." "The one encouraging factor for Muslim reformers today," he asserts, "is that the attempt is now being made more seriously and intelligently than ever before and in more than one country at the same time." Where exactly is this "sincere," "laudable," and "intelligent" Moslem reformation taking place? In Libya, where a sinister buffoon holds his people in thrall while acting as the paymaster and instigator of terrorism in a dozen countries? In Iraq, where the Sunni Ba'athist junta, allied to the Soviet Union keeps the Shi'i majority of the population in subjection? In South Yemen, where a Marxist dictatorship itself securely under the Soviet thumb, has turned the country into a large concentration camp? In Iran? In Afghanistan? To ask such questions is not to be anti-Moslem, as Mr Jansen would doubtless have it, but to act in the spirit of free enquiry which is at the heart of modern Western civilization. If independence of thought and an aversion to cant are held to be synonymous with inveterate hostility, then there is little hope of understanding between Christendom and Islam.

32
Acute Triangle[1]

The Palestine Triangle: The Struggle between the British, the Jews and the Arabs, 1939-1948, by Nicholas Bethell. Deutsch, 1979, 384 pp.

P alestine, it might be said, is a state of mind. How one views the transformation of the British Mandate into the State of Israel depends in large measure on whether one was a participant in that transformation, a legatee of it or a mere observer, distanced from the tumult and the strife by time and space.

Anyone in this last category who ventures to pronounce on the people and the issues involved in the struggle for Palestine is under a particular obligation to be both objective and compassionate in his approach to one of the great tragedies and triumphs of modern times. Nicholas Bethell acquits himself most honourably of this obligation in *The Palestine Triangle*, which is fair, reasonable and balanced.

Lord Bethell has made use of official British, American and other archives for the years up to 1948, he has interviewed many of the participants in the events of the period, and he has consulted a substantial portion of the extensive literature on his subject. Yet there is about his book a curious remoteness, a want of vitality and sense of engagement, which proceeds one suspects, from his anxiety to be impartial.

One reason for the impression of remoteness he conveys is the method he has adopted of constantly juxtaposing the attitudes of the prime

1 From *The Sunday Telegraph*, 27 May 1979. Reproduced by permission.

adversaries in the conflict—the Jews, the Arabs and the British. The effect of this technique is to endow the book with a pronounced rhythmic quality, as predictable (and ultimately as benumbing) as the tolling of the mourning bell.

It is not enough for an historian merely to state the case for each and every side (especially in its own terms); he has a duty to examine the worth of each separate case and to arrive at an independent judgement. Lord Bethell does not judge: he contents himself with recording.

Although his publishers claim that he has 'unearthed startling new evidence about many of the most controversial new issues', there is not a great deal—apart from quotations from Cabinet and Foreign Office papers—that is new or particularly startling here. He proves, for instance, from contemporary Palestine police reports, that the excuse used for the past 30 years in extenuation of the Irgun Zvai Leumi's crime in blowing up the King David Hotel in 1946 (*viz*, that ample warning was given to the British authorities of the impending explosion) was false. But the excuse, when all is said and done, was always a pretty miserable one.

A more fundamental question to which Lord Bethell might profitably have addressed himself is whether there could ever have been any compatibility between the political traditions of Eastern Europe, where Zionism had its genesis, and those of the late British Empire.

33
Of Valuable Oil and Worthless Policies[1]

There has been a great squawking and flapping of wings of late in the capitals of the West as the chickens from the Middle East have come home to roost. Not only has the noise been heard in the halls of the Pentagon and the State Department and along the halls of impotence in Whitehall but it has also disturbed the tranquillity of the academies and the think-tanks and other *ateliers* of informed opinion. For the convulsion which swept away Muhammad Reza Shah and the apparatus of orderly government in Iran in the winter of 1978-9 also exposed the rickety foundations upon which Western policy in the Gulf region had rested throughout the present decade, a policy which was initially fashioned from illusion and has been sustained ever since by deceit.

When the government of Harold Wilson announced in January 1968, two months after abandoning Aden and South Arabia to the crypto-Marxist National Liberation Front, that it intended also to withdraw from the Gulf by the end of 1971, the shadow foreign secretary, Sir Alec Douglas-Home, condemned the decision in the House of Commons as "a dereliction of stewardship, the like of which this country has not seen in the conduct of foreign policy before." Three years later, as foreign secretary in Edward Heath's administration, he implemented the decision. No provision was made at the time for the future protection of Western interests in the region beyond the grant of limited assistance to the Sultan of Oman in defeating the guerrilla insurgency in his southern province of Dhufar, an insurgency which had only assumed dangerous proportions after the British abandonment of Aden at the end of 1967.

---

1 From *Encounter Magazine*, June 1979. Reproduced by permission.

262

After 150 years of keeping the peace of the Gulf Britain had walked (or rather sidled) out. Her departure represented a triumph for that school of thought which, ever since the defeat at Suez fifteen years earlier, held that there was no call any longer for a "British presence" anywhere in the Middle East. For the United States, which had tried—rather late in the day—to prevail upon Britain to reconsider the decision to leave the Gulf, the British withdrawal posed a twofold problem. There could be no question of the United States actively assuming the role that Britain had relinquished; for the national neurosis induced by the war in Viet Nam had already begun the slow paralysis of American foreign policy which has today almost reached a terminal stage. On the other hand, an area as intrinsically unstable as the Gulf, containing half the known oil reserves in the world, could not simply be left without any form of regional security, especially as there were other outside powers inimical to the West, the Soviet Union in particular, who would welcome the opportunity now granted to them to intervene, in one guise or another, in the Gulf's affairs. Confronted with this dilemma, the United States sought an easy solution—and found it in the expedient of building up Saudi Arabia and Iran, the twin pillars, as guardians of the Gulf.

The basic flaw in this arrangement was that these two states had been the principal troublemakers in the Gulf for a good century-and-a-half, and they showed no signs of changing their spots. Ever since the close of the 19th century the House of Saud had been trying to extend its sway over the entire Arabian peninsula, desisting only when internecine quarrels or the intrusive activities of its neighbours periodically distracted it. By the early 1930s King Abdul Aziz ibn Saud (the father of the present ruler) had conquered the bulk of the peninsula, the further extension of his power being blocked by Britain's treaty relationship with the petty states of the Arabian littoral of the Gulf, as well as her protectorate over South Arabia and her longstanding friendship with Oman. The discovery of oil in Hasa, the eastern province of Saudi Arabia, did not abate Ibn Saud's appetite for fresh territory. On the contrary, beginning in 1934, he advanced large claims to the Rub al-Khali, the "Empty Quarter" and parts of Oman and Abu Dhabi, on the assumption (which time was to prove correct) that they might also contain oil deposits. His sons and successors persisted with the claims after his death in 1953, resorting to a fair number of dubious tactics in an effort to enforce them – including gun-running, bribery, attempted assassination, subversion in Oman and encouragement for a tribal rebellion in Dhufar. An eventual accommodation was reached in 1974-75—in so far as anything can be said to be settled in the flux and reflux of Arabian politics—when some substantial pieces of Oman and Abu Dhabi, one of them containing a large oilfield, were made over to Faisal ibn Abdul Aziz as the price of his recognition of the newly-formed "United Arab Emirates."

Iran, like the Saudi amirate of Najd, had resisted every effort by Britain in the 19th and 20th centuries to civilize the Gulf and bring it under the rule of law, whether by the suppression of piracy and maritime warfare, the outlawing of the slave trade, the curbing of arms traffic, the charting of the Gulf's waters, the laying of the telegraph or the establishment of quarantine stations and regulations. This policy of obstruction was accompanied by, indeed, largely arose from, an almost pathological addiction on the part of Persian governments to the assertion of large and insubstantial claims to dominion over much of the Gulf region—to the Shatt al-Arab and parts of Kuwait, to Bahrain and other islands in the Gulf, to tracts of Seistan, Makran and Baluchistan, and to western areas of Afghanistan. In part these claims were occasioned by a desire to compensate for territory lost to Russia in the Caucasus, and as such they were often encouraged by the Russians. They also sprang, however, from a conviction (similar to that held by the Al-Saud of Najd) that wherever in the world an Iranian foot had once trod that spot remained thereafter irrevocably and eternally Iranian.

Illusions of grandeur and an obsessive preoccupation with what were held to be Iran's sovereign rights in the Gulf region also dominated the thinking of Muhammad Reza Shah. His modest ambition was to bestride Western Asia like a Colussus, to recreate the empire of Darius and to make Iran, within the space of one or two decades, into the second industrial nation in Asia after Japan.

Casting around for ways in which to impress his neighbours and the world outside with his puissance and majesty, he tore up in 1969 the treaty with Iraq governing the maritime regime in the Shatt al-Arab, gave conspicuous aid to the Kurds in their revolt against the government of Baghdad, seized the islands of Abu Musa and the Tunbs on the eve of Britain's withdrawal from the Gulf, with the intention of controlling the Straits of Hormuz, and a couple of years later sent troops to Dhufar to help suppress the insurgency there.

The benefit to the West of these various actions was highly questionable. His quarrel with Iraq and the seizure of Abu Musa and the Tunbs led to the Soviet-Iraqi treaty of April 1972 and to Colonel Qaddafi's expropriation of British Petroleum's assets in Libya. The contribution of Iranian arms to the defeat of the insurgency in Dhufar was hardly decisive, while at the same time it caused ripples of apprehension along the Arabian shore of the Gulf. As for the Kurds, the Shah unceremoniously abandoned them in the spring of 1975 in order to improve his relations with the Baathist junta in Baghdad.

While all this was going on, the United States, having promulgated the theory of the "twin pillars," had been trying to invest the conceit with substance.

In May 1972 President Nixon and his secretary of state, Henry Kissinger, stopped in Tehran on their way back from disarmament talks in Moscow. They gave the Shah assurances of virtually unhampered access to America's arsenal, without having to run the gauntlet of the normal scrutiny accorded arms requests by the Departments of State and Defense. It was an unprecedented act of policy by a US administration towards a non-Western power, for it allowed the Shah to purchase advanced weapons of a kind whose export had hitherto been restricted to NATO countries. What Nixon and Kissinger did not foresee was the huge increase in Iran's oil revenues following the quadrupling of oil prices by OPEC late in 1973, an increase which enabled the Shah to indulge to the point of satiety his passion for the deadly trinkets of war.

Much the same kind of *carte blanche* was subsequently given to Saudi Arabia, and for the same inadequately considered strategic reasons. The policy was given an added impetus, as well as a meretricious economic justification, by the oil price rises of 1973-74, the accepted wisdom of the day being that the money paid out for oil could be "recouped" by selling the Arabs and the Iranians vast quantities of arms and other expensive gewgaws. Much rubbing of hands and greasing of palms ensued on both sides of the Atlantic as Britain, France, and the United States set out to array the Saudi and Iranian armies like Caesar's legions. In so doing, as the United States Senate Committee discovered in 1976 in its investigations into the Lockheed and Grumman scandals, they managed to plumb some exceedingly murky depths.

To sell the "twin-pillar" policy to Congress, some members of which in both the House and the Senate were inclined to question its practicability, the State Department conducted a tireless campaign to depict Saudi Arabia and Iran as dependable allies of the United States: dynamic, stable, forward-looking, economically progressive, and militarily strong, or at least potentially so. It was an undertaking which called for a fair degree of ingenuity and considerable powers of imagination; but the State Department, with some assistance from the Pentagon, was equal to the task. From 1971 onwards, in appearances before Congressional committees concerned with foreign affairs, witnesses from the State Department built up a picture of the Shah as an enlightened despot (the particular phrase was not actually used, being perhaps a little inapt to the purpose at hand), anxious to regenerate his country, to modernise its economy, educate its people, and defend them against their enemies. More than this, however, it was earnestly asserted, the Shah was capable of being entrusted with the care of Western interests in the Gulf and its surrounding seas, since there was a close and even irresistible identity of interests between Iran and the United States.

Thus, Philip C. Habib (under-secretary for political affairs at the State Department) told a sub-committee of the Senate Foreign Relations Committee in September 1976 that the United States and Iran "have generally seen our respective interests as parallel, at times congruent, and we share many objectives." He was, he explained, only reflecting the views of his chief, Kissinger, who more than once had stated that the policies of the United States and Iranian governments "have been parallel and therefore mutually reinforcing," and that cooperation between the two "grew out of a leadership that is clearly independent, that pursues its conception of its own national interest based on a history of 2,500 years of Iranian policy…" (The most charitable comment that one can make upon this syntactic bizarrerie is that Kissinger was not a close student of Iranian history). Habib's statements were made in the context of the proposed sale of yet more advanced aircraft to Iran—160 F-16s at a cost of $3,800 million—a subject which was at that moment engaging the attention of Senator Frank Church's sub-committee on multi-national corporations. Though the Church sub-committee hearings were uncovering some fairly *louche* transactions between American aircraft and armaments manufacturers, the State Department did not appear in the least disconcerted by them. Nor did it—nor did anyone else for that matter—profess the slightest unease at the possibility that the Shah's profligate expenditure upon arms might be bankrupting Iran, to the eventual detriment of his own position and his function as America's northern sentinel of the Gulf.

Much the same kind of creative license, with appropriate adjustments, was used in depicting the strength and importance of Saudi Arabia. Here, instead of a contemporary Xerxes and the burgeoning "second industrial power in Asia," we had the Badu kingdom, ruled over by the stern and benevolent House of Saud, supported by and themselves upholding the austere verities of the Wahhabi practice of Islam. Borrowing heavily from the propaganda circulated in the United States for many years by the Arabian-American Oil Company, the State Department in successive hearings before the congressional committees spun a tale about the Saudi ruling house, its rise to power, its mode of government, and its conduct towards its neighbours that the ghost of Scheherazade could not have bettered. At the heart of the State Department's presentation lay the argument—first propounded and assiduously propagated for many years afterwards by ARAMCO for its own obvious purposes—that a natural affinity existed between Americans and Saudi Arabs, a sense of immediate camaraderie that made them logical allies. To give this notion of a mutuality of interests and outlook between the citizens of the world's most advanced democracy and the inhabitants of one of the world's most unenlightened states a little more credibility, ARAMCO in its publications had employed a terminology deliberately evocative of the American west in pioneer days, of Badu homesteaders, of grazing ranges (*diyar* in Arabic), of the Saudis as Unitarians (*muwahiddun*, "believers in the unity of God"), of manifest destiny—in short, of Arabia as America's last frontier. The State Department adopted the same practice, while updating the imagery to that of Pittsburgh and Houston arising by the Red Sea, of a grand economic Saudi-American partnership, with the Saudis supplying the oil and finance and the Americans technology, arms and political guarantees.

To some extent the State Department was aided in its endeavours to portray Saudi Arabia as a rapidly evolving, modern kingdom by the gullibility of some Senators and Congressmen.

"The notion that we are dealing in Saudi Arabia with primitive Bedouins is not only patronizing but obviously mistaken," George McGovern informed his colleagues in the Senate in May 1975 after a lightening visit to that country. As one American Embassy official had put it to him, "What you are dealing with here is a government run by 3,000 American university graduates…" Further testimony to the efficiency of the Saudi government—its constructive use of its oil revenues, its benign outlook upon its smaller neighbours in the Gulf, its reliability as an ally of the United States, and its solicitude for the economic health of the West, as evidenced by its moderating influence in the counsels of OPEC—was liberally provided by the parade of witnesses from the universities, the oil companies and other outside bodies who appeared before the Congressional committees from 1971 onwards.

It was a rare display of an even rarer unanimity of views, made all the more interesting by the fact that no Western scholar or casual inquirer was allowed to travel to Saudi Arabia to see conditions there for himself and form an independent judgement about the country.

Where does the West stand today with respect to the security of its oil supplies from the Gulf—now that the great over-arching edifice of

Saudi-Iranian cooperation, which the United States, Ozymandias-like, had decreed should dominate the Gulf, has turned out to be a sham? ..."Two vast and trunkless legs of stone/Stand in the desert..."

Strategic control over Middle-Eastern sources of oil was deemed essential by the major Western powers until recent years. Britain had exercised such control through the British government's shareholding in British Petroleum, through British management of the Iraq Petroleum Company, and through her political and military presence in the Gulf. France, which had a minority shareholding in the Iranian consortium, in IPC and in operations in the lower Gulf shaikhdoms, tried in the 1960s to ensure security of supply by means of her "special relationship" with Algeria, an attempt which ended in failure in 1971. The United States after the Second World War entrusted the protection of her strategic interest in Middle-Eastern oil to the major American oil companies operating in the Middle East, which meant, in effect, turning the responsibility over to ARAMCO and its parent companies.

During the 1960s the argument developed and took hold that physical control of Middle-Eastern oil, as exercised by the oil companies' concessionary rights and the British presence in the Gulf, was no longer necessary, indeed, was positively detrimental in its effects. The irresistible strength of Afro-Asian Nationalism, the shifting balance of power in the world, the passing of the imperial age and all the other familiar excuses with which the West has cloaked its descent into lethargy were invoked in support of the argument. The supply of oil, like its price—so it was contended—was purely a commercial question, a matter of supply-and-demand, and to be treated as such. The reigning consensus of opinion was summed up by the fashionable adage, "The Arabs can't drink their oil." As we have come to learn, however, they, and the Iranians, are not averse to attempting the feat.

Neither the creeping nationalisation of the oil companies (under the disingenuous label of "participation") nor the oil embargo and the huge price increases of the autumn of 1973 had much effect in casting doubt upon the validity of the dogma. A few cosmetic adjustments were made and the dogma re-emerged in the guise of "re-cycling," a magical process by which the vast sums paid out for oil would be recovered both by the sale of an equally vast quantity of industrial goods and arms and by luring the Arabs into investing their financial surpluses in the West. What few paused to consider, or if they did, resignedly rejected as impracticable, was whether it would not be wiser to press for a reduction of oil prices. After all, if for any reason the contracts for arms and other Western manufacturers were to be cancelled, the West would still be compelled to pay excessive prices for oil without being able to offset them by the sale of Chieftain Tanks and F-16s.

The battle against higher oil prices, however, was lost almost as soon as it began in the early summer of 1970, when Colonel Muammar Qaddafi unilaterally raised the price of Libyan oil under the threat of shutting down production by the western oil companies operating in Libya. Despite efforts made by the major American and British oil companies to impress upon the US government the consequences of allowing Qaddafi to succeed with his extortion, the State Department refused to stand up to him. When the rest of OPEC emulated the Libyan leader's tactics and threatened the oil companies with an embargo unless their demands for increased prices were also met, the State Department, after initially assisting to make a combined negotiation by the companies legally permissible under US anti-trust legislation, then proceeded to sabotage the subsequent negotiations with OPEC at Tehran in January 1971 by withdrawing its support when the going got rough.

From that moment onward the struggle with OPEC was lost. Henceforth oil prices were progressively to be fixed, not be negotiated as in normal mercantile transactions (*pace* the exponents of treating oil like any other commercial commodity) but by OPEC fiat. The unedifying display of pusillanimity and *sauve qui peut* which constituted Western Europe's reaction, and in particular that of Britain and France, to the Arab oil embargo of 1973 only confirmed the Middle-Eastern members of OPEC in their contempt for the Western powers. It is little wonder that, with allies like these, the Americans turned in the summer of 1974 to making their own arrangements to safeguard their oil interests in the Arabian peninsula by entering into a comprehensive agreement with Saudi Arabia for the provision of arms, military training, and assistance with economic development in return for guaranteed oil supplies and promises of Saudi financial investment in the USA. The agreement amounted, in sum, to an American undertaking to preserve the integrity of Saudi Arabia and the primacy of the Al Saud within it.

However advantageous or disadvantageous this arrangement may prove for the United States, it does little to safeguard the vital interests of Western Europe and Japan in the Gulf. In the final analysis, the United States can do without Middle-Eastern oil. Western Europe and Japan cannot. Moreover, it would be unwise as well as politically undesirable for them to place the entire responsibility for the defence of Western interests in the Gulf upon American shoulders alone. That the Americans are at present alone in bearing this responsibility is largely a consequence of their own actions and policy since the Second World War in striving to eradicate British and French influence from the Middle East. The attitude adopted by the State Department towards the nationalisation of the Anglo-Iranian Oil Company (BP) in 1951—which in many ways can be regarded as the starting point of the eventual loss of Western strategic control over Middle Eastern oil was equivocal, to say the least. Subsequently the State Department pushed the major American oil companies into participating in the Iranian consortium as a means of underwriting Iran. By failing to curb the Shah in the early 1970s, when he was leading the OPEC pack in its hunt for higher oil prices, the State Department simply fed his megalomania and paved the way not only for his downfall but also for the eventual extinction of the Western oil companies' rights in Iran.

Across the Gulf in Saudi Arabia, where the State Department had effectively resigned the making and conduct of American policy into the hands of ARAMCO, it had watched with placid indulgence the efforts of the Al Saud from the late 1940s onwards to subvert the authority of the legitimate rulers of Oman and Abu Dhabi within their own borders with the object of annexing their ancestral territories along with any oil deposits that might lie beneath them. The British persisted in their determination to uphold the independence of Oman and Abu Dhabi against Ibn Saud and his successors. So ARAMCO set itself the task, which it accomplished without undue effort, of persuading the State Department that the ending of the British connexion with the Gulf would not only benefit American oil interests in Arabia but was also a desirable end in itself, as eliminating an anachronistic remnant of Imperialism and thereby improving American relations with Saudi Arabia and the Arab world at large. *Tempax edax rerum.* When the implications of the Harold Wilson government's decision of January 1968 finally sank in, the State Department began to experience some slight misgivings. By then it was too late. The British had lost their spirit and were packing their bags. The State Department had to make the best of a situation it had had more than a hand in creating.

It did so by conjuring up the "twin-pillar" conceit and by pretending that the Gulf, with each passing year, was becoming more and more like Chesapeake Bay.

It is almost redundant to say that it is not. Beneath the veneer of modernity it is as turbulent and unpredictable as ever, and the same tinder that started the conflagration in Iran is present in some measure in all the principalities along the Arabian shore.

The vast riches which have flowed into the Gulf in this decade have generated prodigality and corruption on a comparable scale. The native tribesman, now that the age of abundance has arrived, will no longer soil his hands with toil; so the heavy manual work of building the contemporary Xanadus arising along the Gulf coast is done by Iranian, Baluchi and Pakistani labourers in their thousands (and in Saudi Arabia by hundreds of thousands of Yemenis, while the skilled tasks are performed by Europeans ("white coolies") and Arab emigres (most of whom are Palestinians).

Well over half the population of Kuwait is made up of immigrants. It is the same in Qatar. In the United Arab Emirates immigrants outnumber the indigenous inhabitants two or perhaps three times over.

Yet the bulk of the oil wealth is reserved for the native Arab population, distributed to them in the form of public services, housing, welfare benefits and cash allowances, all of which are designed to ensure their continuing allegiance to their rulers. For the mass of the immigrant population there are no such benefits. The resultant discontent, aggravated by the mindless extravagance all about them, affords a potentially fertile breeding ground for political agitation.

Radical political notions, of Marxist, Baathist or other provenance, have been circulating in the Gulf states for some years now. This had been particularly so among sections of the Palestine community and among the *jeunesse doree* of Kuwait and Bahrain. They have dabbled in the shallows of revolutionary politics in much the same way as their counterparts in the West have done, and for similar reasons of satiety and boredom. Whether they will ever translate the hotchpotch of ideas which excite them into political action is a moot question. They are also influenced by the current mood of Muslim revivalism which is so pronounced around the shores of the Gulf and which has expressed itself in Iran in a virulent outbreak of anti-Western sentiment.

Over and above the problems of internal security which exist in the Gulf states, the states themselves are divided by long-standing and vexatious antagonisms arising from dynastic rivalries, tribal vendettas, sectarian antipathies, territorial disputes and other historical causes. They have rarely, if ever, been able to sink their differences for any length of time in order to confront a common danger; and there is no sign of their successfully doing so today. On the contrary, they are as ready as ever to settle their differences by the sword.

Should any of the numerous irritations which bedevil relations among Iran, Iraq, Saudi Arabia and the minor Gulf states erupt into open conflict, the entire oil industry of the Gulf, thanks to the indiscriminate arming of most of these states by the West with the fearsome weapons of modern war, could be at deadly risk.

Why the State Department has persisted in playing Pollyanna over the Gulf defies understanding. It may simply be incomprehension on its part, or conscious self-deception, or it may also be deliberate misrepresentation for some obscure purpose. Henry Kissinger, in an interview published in *The Economist* (10 February), excused the failure of American policy in Iran, a policy of which he had himself been author, by saying that

> all of us paid insufficient attention in Iran to the proposition that political construction should go side by side with economic construction. The failure was less of intelligence agencies than of a conceptual apparatus.

But could it not also have been due to a lack of understanding of Iranian society and history, an insufficient appreciation of the force of Shi'i Islam in Persian life, and a refusal to see where the Shah's profligate expenditure upon arms was leading?

A staff report to the Senate Foreign Relations Committee in the summer of 1976, for instance, described the arms programme as running out of control, the Iranian armed forces (the Air Force in particular) as being incapable of absorbing the complicated weaponry with which they were being inundated, and the State Department as being uninformed as well as unconcerned about the whole affair. Yet when questioned about the report in September 1976, the State Department's spokesman assured the committee that the arms programme, around which American-Iranian relations revolved, was going swimmingly.

The same heedless and badly thought-out policy has been pursued, and is still being pursued, with respect to the arming of Saudi Arabia. Here, again, huge quantities of advanced weapons are being poured into a country whose armed forces are even more ill-equipped to handle them than were the Iranians. Nor is it entirely clear that the Saudi budget, despite all the common assumptions to the contrary, is capable of sustaining the expense involved in their purchase. The United States is even more deeply committed to Saudi Arabia than she was to Iran. If the need for American intervention should arise—to safeguard American oil interests or to defend the ruling house against its enemies from within and without, the United States will be faced with a series of acute dilemmas. Intervention will have been made domestically difficult because of conflicting statements on the subject made by members of President Carter's administration and the hostility to the idea expressed at various times by leading Democratic senators. Intervention would be hazardous in the Middle-Eastern context because of the religious as well as political antipathy it would arouse. Nor, in the form one would expect it to take in military terms, would it necessarily prove effective, as least so far as the preservation of the integrity of Saudi Arabia and the rule of the Al Saud were concerned. A military occupation of the Hasa oilfields might well send reverberations across the peninsula which would surface in insurrection in the Hijaz—and no Western troops could be despatched to the holy Places of Islam to suppress it.

What has to be weighed, in the final assessment, is the importance of the Gulf's oil to the West and the dangers which would attend any positive move to assure strategic control over it.

Every passing year since the start of this decade has revealed more clearly the folly of depending for continued access to the region's oil reserves upon the goodwill, capacity and sense of responsibility of the wilful and capricious regimes that rule the Gulf. Every year, too, has seen the dangers to the region's security multiply, whether from the rarely glimpsed but nevertheless active seditious elements within the Gulf states or from the steady encirclement of the area by the Soviet Union and its clients.

The Russians are now established in Afghanistan, Iraq, and Ethiopia. Down in the south-western corner of Arabia they sit entrenched in the former British base at Aden, along with their Cuban and East German auxiliaries, ready to direct them and their South Yemeni vassals eastwards into Dhufar or northwards into the Yemen. Their need for oil, for themselves and their East European satellites, is growing: and they cannot afford to pay for it in hard currency or acceptable manufactures. The temptation to take by subversion what they cannot afford to purchase will surely grow at a commensurate pace. They have learned the lessons of sea-power, which the West is in danger of forgetting, and they recognise the truth (which the Western powers flinch from acknowledging) of Macaulay's dictum—"that the essence of war is violence, and that moderation in war is imbecility." Those flapping wings and harsh cries we hear around us may not be chickens, after all, but birds of a more sinister and predatory aspect.

34
A Time for Toughness in the Gulf[1]

A t the height of the oil crisis in 1973, when the Arabs had placed an embargo on the sale of oil to the United States and other Western countries, and, in company with the Shah of Iran, quadrupled the price of oil, an official from one of the Gulf oil states exclaimed in the midst of the excitement, 'This is our revenge for Poitiers!'

In thus harking back to the defeat of the Arab armies by Charles Martel of France in 732 AD, he was demonstrating not only the endurance of the Arab memory but also the depth of the animosity borne by the Moslem East against the Christian West. For Moslems, convinced of the superiority of Islam as the only true revealed religion, the primacy of the West in terms of wealth and industrial power is a source of galling resentment. At the same time, however, they are themselves enamoured of the West's material products—even while they reject the philosophy and culture that permitted their creation. The resultant emotional and intellectual confusion to which this attitude gives rise in the Moslem world is prone to express itself in periodic outbursts of fanaticism such as we are now witnessing in Iran and Pakistan.

The danger in which the West finds itself today, especially with regard to the security of oil supplies, is not wholly the consequence of Moslem intransigence or malevolence. Through their assiduous propitiation of the Arab oil states and Iran over the past half-a-dozen years, in a vain attempt to ensure both continuity of oil supplies and stability of prices, the western Powers have only confirmed these states in their *hauteur* and conviction of their own intrinsic importance. Through electing to attempt to soak up

1 From *The Sunday Telegraph*, 2 December 1979. Reproduced by permission.

the excessive oil revenues accumulated by the Gulf states by encouraging them to prodigal expenditures on Western manufactures, instead of striving in concert to force oil prices down, the West has helped to create the unrest that now infects the whole Gulf and that, in Iran, has vented itself in a violent upsurge of Islamic and anti-Western sentiment.

Nowhere has the bankruptcy of Western policy been more evident than in the sale of vast quantities of expensive armaments to Iran, Saudi Arabia and the minor Gulf states. They were heavily importuned to make such acquisitions by the United States, Britain and France. Not only was the policy short-sighted for many reasons—not least because it will make any possible Western military operations more hazardous than need be—but, in the case of Britain, it was positively foolish. Having been the peace-keeper of the region herself—suppressing arms traffic, piracy and slave trade—she then pulled out and armed the Shah to the teeth in the mistaken belief that he could act on the West's behalf as the 'policeman of the Gulf'.

It was the Shah's inordinate expenditure on arms, together with his grandiose projects for the industrialisation of Iran overnight, that generated much of the discontent with his rule which articulated itself eventually in the form of Shi'ite zealotry. Somewhat the same phenomenon could well occur in Saudi Arabia, where the profligacy of the ruling house and its innumerable hangers-on has been of a comparable order. There have been occasional reports of disaffection in the Saudi armed forces, erupting in mutinies both in 1977 and earlier this year, the source of which appears to have been offended Moslem sensibilities, particularly in the ranks of the National Guard. Many of the tribesmen in the National Guard are descendants of the old Wahhabi *ikhwan*, the religio-military brotherhood organised by Ibn Saud earlier this century to serve him as an instrument of conquest. He later suppressed the movement with severity, for which some tribes have never forgiven him. The tribesmen implicated in the recent seizure of the Great Mosque at Mecca are said to have come from Ataiba and Harb, two of the most prominent of the old *ikhwan* tribes. If so, they were presumably motivated by anger at the Saudi ruling family for its luxurious style, its intimacy with infidels and its neglect of its religious duties.

The mood of exultation now sweeping both Sunni and Shi'ite Islam bodes little good for the West's interests in the Gulf. Over the past decade we have lost control not only over oil production and prices as a result of the neutralisation of the oil companies, but strategic control over the region as well. For this loss Britain bears a heavy responsibility through her abandonment of Aden and her withdrawal from the Gulf in 1971. Had we only tried harder and waited longer, it should have been possible at the time to have converted Britain's political and military position into a defensive alliance between the resolute Sultanate of Oman and the United Arab Emirates, an alliance that would have afforded some protection today to Western nations in the region, as well as to Western oil interests. The opportunity was not taken, with the melancholy consequences that we now see around us.

If the West is to recover strategic control over the Gulf, it will have to steel itself to take some hard decisions. The threats now posed to our interests there by Islamic militancy can be overcome by resolution, steadfastness and the skilful use of the numerous political, economic and military resources at our disposal. They will not be averted by a humiliating display of pusillanimity such as that with which Western Europe reacted to the Arab oil offensive in 1973. Rather than attempting to placate a resurgent Islam that is utterly implacable, the West should reassert the naval supremacy in Arabian and Persian waters it held for four-and-a-half centuries after Vasco de Gama first rounded the Cape. Command of the sea is the prerequisite of power in the Gulf, and the West should make it plain to the littoral states, and to the Soviet Union, that it is prepared to exert that command to protect its very interests in the region and the lives of its nationals.

Such a declaration of intent, backed by a demonstration of naval strength and air power, would go a good way towards calming the feverish speculation about Western resolve now agitating the Gulf states, and restore a measure of stability to the region as a whole.

35
The Kremlin and the Gulf[1]

The gains made by the Soviet Union in the Middle East in the 20 years or so after 1955 had been achieved by the policy of supporting Arab nationalist governments against the Western powers. At the 20th Congress of the Soviet Communist Party in 1956 the doctrine of "the class struggle" as the fundamental and indispensable element in the progression to communism in the countries of Asia was played down. Cautious approval was given instead to the possibility of different and even non-violent paths to socialism, as well as to the notion of "the national bourgeoisie" as an ally in both the struggle against Western imperialism and the victory of the national liberation movement.

Traditionally, Soviet ideology regarded "the national bourgeoisie" in the states of Asia under European dominion as necessary only at the stage of winning their independence from the powers of Europe. Thereafter, so the dogma had it, the national bourgeoisie was bound to become unstable, would lose its "progressive" character and would compromise with its late imperial masters. It would therefore become the task of the proletariat, after initially supporting the national bourgeoisie in the struggle for independence, to turn upon it in due course, and, under the leadership of the local Communist parties and with the backing of the Soviet Union and other socialist states, overthrow the national bourgeois governments as a preliminary to building the socialist state.

So much for Soviet theory. By 1960 the national bourgeois regimes which had emerged as the successors to European imperial rule in Asia had consolidated their positions and were, most of them, beginning to

1 From *Encounter*, April 1980. Reproduced by permission.

develop their own kind of socialist state. More often than not this process involved the intimidation or suppression of the local Communist parties, a consequence which implicitly challenged (even if unwittingly) Soviet dogma that the transition from the national-bourgeois to the socialist state should be directed by the Communist party. For sound practical reasons—among them the weakness of the local Communist parties and the lack of "working-class cadres" in most Asian countries—the Soviet government suppressed its ideological reservations and continued to support the national-bourgeois regimes. They were, after all, accomplishing the Russians' objectives for them, by their unceasing display of hostility to the West and by their constant extension of state control over their own economies. Thus, in the Middle East, the Soviet Union followed the wholly pragmatic policy of supplying military, economic, and technical assistance to the military dictatorships which ruled over Egypt, Syria, Iraq, and later Algeria, without allowing herself to be distracted by the deviations from the doctrinally legitimate path to socialism which they represented.

The subordination of dogma to expediency in the conduct of Soviet foreign policy was all too apparent in the Russians' exploitation of the Kurdish separatist movement in Iraq from the mid-1950s to the mid-1970s. Soviet policy in Arabia in the same period likewise demonstrated the secondary role assigned by the Russians to ideology in the pursuit of their strategic objective in the Middle East.

A new Treaty was concluded with the Yemen in October 1955 in which the Soviet Union recognised "the full and absolute independence of Yemen and also the full independence and absolute legal sovereignty of the King." It seemed to matter little that the King in question, the Imam Ahmad ibn Yahya, was an absolutist and theocratic sovereign, utterly aloof from, indeed immovably opposed to, everything the Soviet Union stood for. What mattered (as in the case of his father, the Imam Yahya, with whom a similar treaty had been concluded in 1928) was that he was actively hostile to the British in Aden. Further agreements covering the supply of arms and economic aid followed in 1956 and 1957, their latent purpose being to underwrite the campaign of harassment which the Yemenis were conducting against the British along the borders of the Aden Protectorate. As late as 1961, a year before Imam Ahmad's death and the revolution which overthrew his successor, the Soviet propaganda machine was still grinding out encomiums to the aged monarch, particular stress being laid upon his unrelenting struggle against the "imperialists" to the south.

In contrast, the Soviet attitude towards Saudi Arabia in these years became increasingly churlish. Although no serious attempt had been made after the Second World War to renew the earlier diplomatic ties which had been abandoned in 1938, the Soviet government had observed a considerable degree of caution in its approach to the Saudi regime, exempting it from the kind of criticism to which governments of a monarchical or theocratic character were normally subject. When it seemed, however, in the late 1950s that Saudi Arabia was aligning herself with the "imperialist" camp in the Middle East, the tolerance formerly accorded the Al Saud and Wahhabism in general vanished. Modern Wahhabism was accused of having discarded its "positive" (*i.e.* egalitarian) attributes, and of having forsaken its original mission to restore the pristine simplicity of Islam. Instead, it had become a mere tool of the "feudalists" for the exploitation of the Saudi people, part of the wider conspiracy to substitute religion for the growth of class feelings among the Arab masses. The criticism intensified when the revolution in the Yemen in 1962 brought a republican regime to power in Sana and the Saudis gave aid to the royalist forces in the ensuring civil war.

The anti-Saudi propaganda did not diminish when Faisal succeeded his brother as ruler and instituted a programme of reform in Saudi Arabia. On the contrary, it reached new heights when Faisal organised the Islamic Pact in December 1965 as a counter to Nasser's influence in the Arab world. Pravda proceeded to denounce the Islamic Pact as

> an imperialist creation similar to the notorious Baghdad Pact, an instrument for combating the Arab national liberation movement…a means of bolstering the reactionary forces…a spearhead against the spreading of socialist ideas in the Middle East.

Much the same kind of hostility was evinced towards Kuwait in these years, partly for ideological reasons but mainly out of political calculation. The desire to preserve the influence it had acquired in Baghdad led the Kremlin both to adopt a more or less neutral stand over the merits of the Iraqi claim to Kuwait in 1961 and to curry favour with Qasim by vetoing Kuwait's application to join the United Nations. After Qassim's fall in 1963, however, the Russians responded favourably to an approach from Kuwait for the establishment of diplomatic relations, consented to Kuwait's admission to the UN, and appointed an ambassador to the sheikhdom in June 1963. Pragmatism had smothered ideological misgivings. There was clearly more to be gained from acquiring a diplomatic foothold in Kuwait (the only such foothold the Soviet Union had in the Arabian

peninsula other than that in the Yemen) than from indulging in denunciations of the Al Sabah's "feudal" and "reactionary" rule on the lines of that
uttered by Khrushchev in 1964.

There was more to the Soviet Union's veering and tacking over policy
in Arabia in the 1960s, however, than simply the growing ascendancy of
pragmatism.

The Kremlin's own ideological conceptions were in flux, largely as a
consequence of the challenge that had been thrown down by the Chinese
Communists. Whereas the Soviet Union was prepared, in the interests
of securing her own objectives as a great power, to accept the notion of
"gradualism"—of separate and peaceful paths to socialism, of the role of
the national bourgeoisie in effecting the transition to the socialist state
and in fomenting and sustaining anti-Western sentiments in the Middle
East as well as in Asia as large—the Chinese were not. They rejected all
such compromises, declaring that the triumph of socialism in the world
could only be achieved through the national liberation movement, a violent uprising of the urban and rural proletariat led by the Communists and
directed against the "colonialists" and "feudalists." No trust or hope was to
be reposed in "the national bourgeoisie," however one defined, or failed to
define, this anomalous body: its members were bound in the long run to
throw in their lot with "the imperialists" against the "progressive" forces.

Under the impact of the Maoist assault the Russians were forced to
revise some of their ideological formulations concerning the progression
to socialism in the backward countries of the world. By the mid-1960s less
emphasis was being placed upon the role of the national bourgeoisie as an
instrument of political transformation, especially in countries where more
than one political movement was active. More confidence was reposed instead in those one-party states where the governments, although not Communist in complexion, were nevertheless strongly anti-Western, as well as
interventionist in their national economic policies.

In truth, however, the ideological arguments were becoming increasingly diffuse, contradictory, and irrelevant as opportunism gained the upper hand in Soviet foreign policy. This became particularly evident in the
Middle East after the disaster which befell Arab arms at the hands of the
Israelis in the war of 1967, a disaster which grieved the Kremlin sorely.
It had tied its fortunes to those of Nasser's "Arab socialist" regime without having sufficient influence over the Egyptian dictator to ensure that
his fortunes prospered. The Russians were not going to make the mistake
again of allowing themselves to be ideologically identified with an Arab
regime which claimed to be "socialist." Thus Soviet commentary on the

Arab world after 1967 made a point of emphasising how far the states of the area were from making the transition to "true socialism."

It was this attitude of caution which regulated Soviet relations with South Yemen in the years immediately following that country's attainment of independence in 1967.

The Russians had been relatively slow to take notice of developments in Aden and the protectorates in the years after the Second World War. It was not until 1958, in fact, that they began to comment upon them, and then largely as a consequence of their own activities in the Yemen. The usual propaganda resulted. Britain was "exploiting" Aden and the protectorates, using them as a base for "aggression against the peace-loving countries and national liberation movements of Asia and Africa." Over the next few years the Russians, in accordance with their theories about the national bourgeoisie, affected to regard first the South Arabian League and then the Aden People's Socialist Party as the leaders of the struggle for independence. They never seemed to grasp the fact that from 1963 onwards the running was being made by the NLF, and to a lesser extent by FLOSY; so that when the NLF emerged at the end of 1967 as the new masters of Aden and South Arabia, the Kremlin was taken by surprise. It was also uncertain of the character of the new regime, even though some of the NLF leadership were quick to show their Marxist-Leninist colours. Another factor inhibiting the Russians' approach to the NLF regime was the prompt appearance on the scene of their ideological rivals, the Chinese, with offers of technical aid for the new republic and support for the insurgency in Dhufar. Though the Russians lost little time in making comparable offers, they still hesitated to clasp the NLF leadership in a fraternal embrace, even after the Marxist-Leninist faction within it had overthrown its opponents and proclaimed its intention to build a society based upon the principles of "scientific socialism" in South Yemen.

Moscow's reluctance to give its ideological imprimatur to the South Yemeni revolution was based primarily upon practical considerations. Ideological approval implied a willingness to provide economic, political and even military assistance, especially if the standing of the Soviet Union as the true and legitimate heir of Marx and Lenin, and the dynamic centre of world communism, was not to be impaired. Yet a commitment to a country such as South Yemen, virtually bankrupt and highly unstable, could well prove very costly financially and extremely embarrassing politically. The uncomfortable lesson of Cuba, and all that it had entailed in the way of incalculable economic and political liabilities incurred in haste, was still very much in the forefront of the Soviet government's mind a decade later.

It was also uncertain of how the Western powers might react if it were to make a client of South Yemen. Moscow was still digesting the implications of Britain's withdrawal from Aden in 1967 and her proclaimed intention to leave the Gulf in 1971. It seemed to the Kremlin inconceivable that the United States would not compel the British to change their minds, still less that the Americans would sit idly by and allow the Soviet Union to occupy Britain's former base at Aden.

Britain's action in quitting the Gulf at the end of 1971 removed most of the Kremlin's doubts and hesitations about the wisdom of becoming involved in South Yemen.

What few misgivings remained were completely dispelled two years later by the panic displayed by the Western powers in the wake of the Arab oil embargo of October 1973. Developments in South Yemen itself also played into the Russians' hands. The Aden regime had by this time managed to alienate not only the Western powers but the conservative Arab regimes as well, thereby cutting itself off from two potential sources of aid to alleviate South Yemen's desperate economic condition. The Chinese could not compete with the Soviet Union in the provision of material goods and arms, which left the radical Arab states, like Libya, and the Soviet Union and her European satellites as the only possible countries to which South Yemen could turn for succour. At the same time the Aden politburo was experiencing growing difficulty in maintaining its hold upon the country, especially as it was frequently distracted by outbreaks of feuding within its own ranks.

As every ruler of South Arabia since time began has learned, the only way in which order and authority can be imposed upon the country is by the ruthless and widespread application of force. The British never attempted, or wished to attempt, to enforce their rule outside Aden colony in this fashion, with the result that they have since been criticised for having left the hinterland, the former Aden Protectorate, in as backward a condition as they found it. Its perversion of the truth apart, the criticism is misconceived; for if Britain had employed the measure of severity necessary to subdue the inhabitants of South Arabia and cause them to abandon their age-old pursuits of rapine, slaughter, and brigandage, not to mention their cherished superstitions, tribal customs and primitive social habits, she would have been execrated by enlightened opinion everywhere. Unlike the British, the NLF politburo had no compunction about endeavouring to crush the resistance of the tribesmen of South Yemen. Moreover, being Marxist-Leninist and therefore counted among the "progressive" regimes of the world, it provoked no outraged protests in enlightened circles about the methods it used in erecting the grotesquerie of a Marxist-Leninist state in southern Arabia. Its only real problems were those created by its own limited economic resources, a lack of arms, and deficiencies in modern techniques of repression.

All of these were supplied in increasing quantities by the Soviet Union and her allies from the mid-1970s onwards. For the Russians it was a small price to pay to secure access to Aden's incomparable strategic location, commanding at one and the same time the passage of the Red Sea, the southern gates of Arabia and the Horn of Africa. The benefits accruing to both partners to the arrangement were complementary. As the National Front regime was enabled to employ more brutal and effective methods for the subjugation of its people, so also the Soviet grip on Aden and South Yemen progressively tightened. The army was placed under the de facto command of Soviet officers, while the popular militia was trained by Cubans. East Germans (eventually to the number of 2,000) were brought in to take charge of the police and security services. They proceeded to introduce their own methods of dealing with political dissidents, including the setting up of concentration camps for the detention of real of suspected opponents of the regime. A South Yemeni air force was created, the aircraft being supplied by the Soviet Union, the air and ground crews by Cuba.

By the outset of 1978 South Yemen had progressed from being a client state of the Soviet Union to the status, for all practical purposes, of a Soviet colony. At the former RAF station at Khormaksar, outside Aden now an operational base for the Soviet air force, were located the Russian military and intelligence headquarters for the Red Sea region. Aden itself furnished the Russians with naval facilities. A second naval station and air base had been established at Mukalla, in the Hadramaut, while on Socotra Island the Russians had installed communications and surveillance equipment. Whatever the Kremlin might privately think of the "Marxist-Leninist" pretensions of the National Front, it had now identified itself with the regime and with its fortunes.

In any case, the ideological veneer on Soviet policy in this corner of the world, never very substantial at any time, had by now almost completely worn away. It mattered not in the least to the Kremlin that South Yemen was a pariah state, with an unsavoury reputation as a haven and training ground for the terrorist riff-raff of the world. On the contrary, its involvement in international terrorism only increased its attraction in Soviet eyes. Opportunism of the most flagrant kind was the governing factor in Soviet policy towards South Yemen, as it was towards its neighbours, Somalia and Ethiopia. Just how subject South Yemen had become to Soviet direction was amply demonstrated during 1977 and 1978 by the use of Aden as a logistics centre for the Ogaden and Eritrean campaigns, and by the employment of South Yemeni troops as Soviet auxiliaries in the latter conflict. It was displayed even more, however, by the Soviet intervention in the crisis which erupted in the leadership of the Aden politburo in the middle of 1978.

How the crisis came about and the course it took are still unclear, and doubtless will remain so for some time yet. Supreme power in South Yemen up to June 1978 had been wielded by a presidential council of three men—Salim Rubayyi Ali (the President), Ali Nasir Muhammad (the Prime Minister), and Abdul Fattah Ismail (the chairman of the central committee of the National Front). The personal and political rivalry which had long existed between Salim Rubayyi Ali and Abdul Fattah Ismail attained violent proportions in late June 1978, when the presidential palace in Aden was assaulted by South Yemeni army units and militia detachments loyal to Abdul Fattah Ismail. They were supported by Cuban troops, five thousand of whom had been flown in from Ethiopia only the previous week. Cuban pilots flying MIG fighters attacked the palace and the defence ministry with cannon fire, while one or more Soviet warships off shore shelled the same targets. The fighting lasted for most of 26 June, ending with the capture and swift execution of Salim Rubayyi Ali and his closest associates. Ali Nasir Muhammad was installed as acting president in his place, but the real victor was the fanatical Marxist ideologue, Abdul Fattah Ismail.

Fighting broke out at various places in South Yemen in the days and weeks that followed. It was probably inspired less by sentiment for the late president than by hatred for the victorious faction in the politburo, who called upon the Russians and the Cubans to help suppress the outbreaks. Russian naval vessels were reported to have shelled districts in the Hadramaut, while Cuban pilots flew sorties against rebel strongholds. Thousands of South Yemenis fled for safety to the Yemen, Saudi Arabia and Dhufar, among them army officers and police officials who feared the consequences of yet another vindictive purge of the army and police force. An entire battalion of the army in Beihan defected to the Yemen, its place being taken by an Ethiopian battalion brought in by the Russians.

Whatever other benefits the Soviet Union may have reaped from the ascendancy she has established at Aden, three at least are plain to see. She has acquired a base for the penetration of Africa; she has placed herself within striking distance of the Gulf oilfields; and she has gained control of one of the most important strategic out-posts in the world, an importance which Aden has possessed ever since the early years of the 16th century when the great Portuguese captain, Afonso d'Albuquerque, sought to capture the trade of the Indies by seizing its traditional outlets, the Red Sea, the Gulf, and the Straits of Malacca. Moreover, the Russians have learned the uses of sea power, which the West is in danger of forgetting, and they are ready to act upon this knowledge in the seas east of Suez.

How far the Soviet Union may desire access to the oil reserves of Arabia and the Gulf for her own sake, how far to deny them to the West, can only be matters for speculation. Much depends upon the Russians' reliance upon outside sources of oil to meet their own needs and those of their Eastern European allies.

Up to about 1966 the Soviet Union produced sufficient oil each year to have a surplus after satisfying these requirements. Normally, the surplus was exported to the West in order to earn the hard currency needed to import industrial goods and machinery. After 1966, however, consumption of oil in the Soviet bloc began to exceed production, despite a rise in the volume of oil produced annually—from 148 million tons in 1960 to 353 million tons in 1970 and perhaps as much as 520 million tons in 1976. Consumption has continued to increase in recent years and will probably go on doing so, though to what extent it will exceed production it is impossible to forecast with any precision.

Western estimates of the probable size of the gap between the two have varied considerably: from 20 million to 100 million tons annually in the mid-1970s, up to as much as 160 million tons annually by the early 1980s. So far the deficiency has been made good by the importation of oil from the Middle East by the European satellite states, the transaction being arranged as a form of barter—oil in exchange for machinery and other industrial equipment. Barter deals of this kind have been concluded, for instance, between Iran on the one side and Romania and Czechoslovakia on the other, and between Iraq on the one side and Hungary, East Germany, and Czechoslovakia on the other. Although these transactions have been conducted with Soviet approval, the Soviet government is still anxious to retain the major part of the Eastern European market for itself, for obvious political purposes. It also wants to remain in a position to export oil to the West and Japan for financial reasons.

There are only two ways open to the Soviet Union of meeting these various requirements: one is by expanding Soviet domestic production of oil; the other is by importing more oil from the Middle East. Most of the oil produced in the Soviet Union at present comes from the Volga-Urals region. It is doubtful, however, whether the deposits there will be sufficient to supply even half the volume of oil needed in the near future. There are large deposits in Siberia, especially around Tyumen in western Siberia, but their exploitation depends upon capital investment and advanced technological resources beyond the present reach of the Soviet government. Hence the Russian efforts in recent years to interest both the United States and Japan in the development of these oilfields. Even if these efforts were to bear fruit, there is little likelihood that oil would begin to flow from the Tyumen fields in any quantity for some time to come. Meanwhile the Soviet Union will become increasingly dependent upon Middle Eastern oil to fill the gap between demand and supply and to provide the surplus needed for sale to Western Europe and Japan.

The Russians, however, are having to pay much higher prices for Middle Eastern oil than they were before October 1973, and the extent to which they can increase their trade with the oil-producing countries to meet the bill is limited. Up to date the Russians have paid for Arab oil mainly with arms, to a value of $500-600 million annually over the past few years. Oil imports have been of comparable value, *viz.* 20 million tons in 1973 at a cost of $800 million at pre-October 1973 prices. The same volume of oil at prices obtaining in 1980 would cost anything between $4,500 million and $5,000 million.

It seems unlikely that the Russians will be able to increase the value of their arms shipments to anything approaching these figures, and ordinary Russian manufactured goods have little appeal in the oil-producing countries, where there is a strong preference for Western and Japanese manufactures. The Soviet government's inability both to supply acceptable manufactures as substitutes for Western and Japanese products and to pay for oil in the requisite amounts of hard currency would appear to limit severely its power to purchase oil from the Middle East in appreciably larger quantities than those it is at present purchasing. Certainly it lacks the financial and economic means needed to induce the governments of the oil-producing states to divert oil exports from the West to the Soviet bloc on a scale sufficient to cause serious damage to the West's economy.

It would seem, therefore, in so far as any judgments are possible in such uncharted terrain, that the Soviet government is faced with an ever widening margin between oil production in the Soviet Union and consumption of oil by the Soviet bloc; that the cost of developing the Soviet Union's own untapped oil reserves—a cost per barrel well above that for Alaskan or North Sea oil—is beyond her financial capacity, even if she had the technological skills and equipment required, which she does not; and that similar financial and economic constraints limit her ability to purchase Middle Eastern oil in excess of what she now obtains through barter agreements and sales of arms.

If this assessment is correct, the temptation for the Russians to acquire by political or military means what they cannot afford to purchase must be a strong one. It can only be made stronger by the consideration that the acquisition of preferential access to the Gulf's oil would enable the Soviet Union to dictate the terms upon which oil would thereafter be supplied to the West.

Soviet Russia is now in a stronger position than ever before in her history to accomplish her ambitions in the Middle East, whether they be to dominate the routes from Europe to the East, to command the landward and maritime approaches to the eastern Mediterranean, the Red Sea and the Gulf, or to lay hands upon the massive oil reserves of the region. She is entrenched in Iraq and Afghanistan by virtue of extensive arrangements for the supply of arms, the equipment and training of their military forces and the provision of economic and technical assistance, as well as by actual treaties of friendship with both countries. In the case of Afghanistan the treaty concluded in December 1978 was the direct outcome of the violent overthrow of the republican government in April 1978 and the subsequent installation, after further bloodshed, of a Marxist regime at Kabul. The opportunities which the Marxist *coup d'état* in Afghanistan and the civil turmoil in Iran in 1978-9 opened up to Russia to advance her strategic interests in the direction of the Gulf and the Indian Ocean were almost infinite.

Leaving to one side the implications of Russian military paramountcy in Afghanistan for the politics and security of the Indian sub-continent, the combination of radical governments in Kabul and Baghdad and domestic chaos in Iran directly threatens the political and territorial integrity of the latter country. For both Iraq and Afghanistan harbour deep animosities of a religious, racial and cultural kind against Iran, which, if they were to find active expression—whether under Russian inspiration or guidance is almost immaterial—at a time when Iran was torn by internal dissension, could lead to the disintegration of the Iranian state as it is now constituted.

While the Soviet Union's favoured position in Iraq and Afghanistan has increased her strategic options, it is Iran which has been the focus of Russian attention since Czarist times and which offers the Russians the richest potential rewards. Iran is by far the most important of the three states. She also possesses the greatest natural advantages, whether these consist in her oil and mineral resources or in her long coastline on the Gulf. The Russians have acknowledged this fact by maintaining at Teheran their largest embassy in the Middle East, twice as large in terms of personnel as the embassies at Ankara and Cairo and with the biggest contingent of KGB and GRU officers. Whatever covert role the latter may or may not have played in precipitating the collapse of governmental authority in Iran in the latter part of 1978, there can be no doubt of the large benefits the Russians may expect to derive from that collapse, and, conversely, of the grim harvest of troubles the Western world may expect to reap in consequence.

The Russians are just as well placed to bring pressure to bear upon the Gulf region from its southern approaches, their obvious base of operations being Aden and the Hadramaut. From there they can proceed, under cover of reactivating the guerrilla war in Dhufar, to sow the seeds of subversion in a wide arc through Oman to the shores of the Gulf. It is a most promising line of advance, especially as the Russians now have the naval and air power to support a campaign of this nature fought by their South Yemeni auxiliaries. They may equally elect to initiate or encourage seditious activities, or *soi-disant* "national liberation movements," within the Gulf states, where radical political elements of all shades, including Marxist-Leninist, are to be found, not least among the extremist factions in the Palestinian émigré communities. The clandestine running of arms to dissidents to raise rebellions has been a commonplace of political life in eastern Arabia since the Second World War, and there is no reason why the Russians should be any less successful at this activity than the Saudis, Iraqis, Egyptians and South Yemenis have been.

Should the Russians decide to intervene more forcefully in any insurrection which may occur in one of the Gulf states, they have at their disposal a highly effective instrument, viz. naval power, the means by which dominion over Arabia's coasts and seas has been asserted and sustained down the centuries.

One could sum up the Soviet Union's position at the outset of the '80s by paraphrasing Palmerston's well known comment of 150 years ago: "Russia pursues the same system of strategy against Arabia and Iran; she creeps down the Red Sea and wants to do the same down the Gulf, and to take both Arabia and Iran on each of their flanks."

Yet to present the situation in such literal terms would be over-simplification. For one thing, the actual intentions of the Soviet Union towards the Gulf are inscrutable, and any attempt to divine them depends upon the interpretation of a host of considerations, the greater part of which have little or no direct connection with Arabia and the Gulf. For another, it would be wrong to view the progress of Russia in the Middle

East over the past 60, or even 30, years as a chronicle of uninterrupted successes, or as the preordained and irresistible fulfilment of some grand design. The necessity to compress historical material here may have produced an impression of the ineluctability of this progress; but such an impression would be a misleading one.

While there is undoubtedly a consistent central theme in Soviet policy towards the region, the Soviet Union is as prone to make *ad hoc* moves and decisions in the face of changing circumstances as are the Western powers. The Kremlin is far from being infallible in its political judgments, as the record of its relations with the Arab world since the Second World War bears witness. It has revealed no signs of possessing any unique insight into the hearts and minds of the Arabs, nor has it exhibited any unusual dexterity in handling them. What it has shown has been an unremarkable ability to exploit for its own purposes the numerous grievances held by many Arabs against the West.

Whatever view one may take of Soviet intentions towards Arabia and the Gulf, and of the Soviet Union's capacity to carry them into effect, it remains that the Russians now possess considerable strategic and tactical advantages in the region which they did not possess a decade ago. These advantages, moreover, have been gained as much through the ineptitude and infirmity of the Western powers as they have by the Soviet Union's own efforts. While the Russians may have miscalculated at times, they have at least attempted to ground their policy upon reality and not upon wishful thinking. Western policy, on the other hand, has been based upon illusions, upon self-deception and upon calculations of short-term advantage.

36
Saudi Censors[1]

An awe-inspiring lack of balance and perspective characterizes the current brouhaha in Britain over the adverse Saudi Arabian reaction to the televising of Anthony Thomas's film, "Death of a Princess." Public figures of high and low estate have been falling over themselves in their eagerness to proffer effusive apologies for the intolerable affront offered to Saudi sensibilities by the film's content, proclaiming at the same time their respect for the beauties of the Saudi penal code and their profound understanding of the sublime verities of Islam. Interspersed with these contrite protestations are plangent appeals to the Saudi government not to retaliate by cancelling the lucrative contracts that British firms have secured in Saudi Arabia. The British fear of offending the Saudis has spread to the US. Public television stations in South Carolina, Houston, and Los Angeles have announced they will not air the film as scheduled on May 12.

What on earth has happened to the fabled British imperturbability? Where is the languid indifference with which Britons were once wont to view the prejudices and susceptibilities of others? And would the Saudis themselves have assumed such a wrathful demeanor if they had not been encouraged to do so by the hubbub raised by their self-appointed champions?

Behind all the fuss and palaver lie two possibilities. Either the leading members of the Saudi royal family were genuinely and grievously offended by "Death of a Princess," or they saw the anxious scrambling by the British Foreign Office and British interests to placate them as a splendid opportunity to turn the screw on the British government and remind it of

---

1 From *The New Republic*, 17 May 1980. Reproduced by permission.

its subservient place in the Saudi view of the world. (The two hypotheses, of course, are by no means mutually exclusive.) But even if the Saudis were deeply offended by the film, they knew full well that in the free societies of the West the power of governments to interfere with what is published or broadcast is severely limited.

It is absurd as well as dishonest for their sycophants in Britain to argue, as they have, that the Saudis simply cannot comprehend that the British government could not have banned the showing of "Death of a Princess." The Saudi royal house is thoroughly cognizant of the ways of Western society: hundreds of its members have visited the West (often for long periods of time), and scores of them, including the present foreign minister, the Amir Saud ibn Faisal, are Western-educated, as are thousands of their fellow-countrymen. It seems fairly certain, therefore, that when the Amir Saud gave the British ambassador to Saudi Arabia his marching orders, he was as much exhibiting the arrogant and overbearing disposition that has long marked the House of Saud as he was expressing displeasure at what was deemed an impertinent intrusion into private Saudi affairs.

Two things have been lost to sight amid the indignant bleating, the plaintive intoning of *mea culpas*, and the ritual prostrations in the direction of Riyadh by the functionaries of the British government and the editorial writers of *The Times*, the *Financial Times*, and other Arabophile organs of the British press. (*The Times* in particular has been enjoying its finest hour since the 1930s, shrilly advocating the appeasement of everyone in sight between Riyadh and Tehran.) One is that a young woman of the royal house was actually put to death for an adulterous liaison with a commoner, while her unfortunate lover was decapitated. (See "Saudi Duty Time," *TNR*, February 11, 1978). The other is that Anglo-Saudi relations, the natural and traditional harmony of which is supposed to have been irrevocably damaged by the filmed reconstruction of the tragedy, were, in the days when Britain was ruled by men with a high sense of national honor, marked more by acrimony than by cordiality.

Death by stoning is the penalty prescribed by *shari'a*, the law of Islam, for a woman taken in adultery. (It may be reduced, in certain circumstances, to 100 lashes). Like the other drastic punishments laid down in the *shari'a* (flogging, mutilation, decapitation), it has been customarily enforced in Saudi Arabia since the beginning of the Wahhabi movement in the 18th century. As the ruler of Saudi Arabia is also imam of the Wahhabiya, a particular duty devolves upon him to see that the provisions of the *shari'a*, in all its aspects, are duly observed by the populace. Recently, however, under the impact of vast oil wealth, the obligation would appear to have been honoured, so far as the Saudi ruling classes are concerned, as much in the breach as in the observance. Why then, the exception in the case of the young princess, with all the gruesome panoply of a public execution?

The princess (named Mish'al or Misha', according to different versions) was the 19-year-old granddaughter of the Amir Muhammad ibn Abdul Aziz, the eldest surviving son of the old King Ibn Saud. Amir Muhammad is, by repute, of somewhat unstable character and irascible disposition, which is presumably why he has been passed over twice in the succession to the throne. It may well be that, on discovering his granddaughter's transgression, he ordered her death in a fit of rage. But under the *shari'a*, a sentence of death can only be handed down by a *qadi*, or judge, in a *shari'a* court. Certain conditions must obtain if the accusation is to be regarded as juridically admissible, and there must be four male witnesses to the act of adultery—though not necessarily at one and the same time, or to a single act. The law also dwells at entertaining length upon the clinical details that the witnesses are required to furnish about the accomplishment of the act of intercourse.

Whether Princess Misha'al was tried and adjudged guilty by a *shari'a* court is unknown. So also are the circumstances surrounding the condemnation of her lover. Was he tried and sentenced to death, and if so under what provisions of the *shari'a*? It has to be remembered that the concept of adultery, in the modern Western sense, is unknown to Islamic law. A wife has no exclusive right on the person of her husband. Extramarital intercourse on her part, however, is regarded as a crime because it offends against religion, and as such it has to be punished. Even so, why did the Saudi royal family make a public spectacle of the execution of Princess Misha'al and her lover? There have been, and still are, discontented murmurings in Saudi Arabia about the al Sauds' excessive indulgence in luxury, their infatuation with ways and things Western, and their consorting with infidels—all of which are said to have led them to neglect their fundamental duty to uphold the primacy of Islam in their private affairs as well as in the affairs of the kingdom. (The most forceful expression of this discontent was the seizure of the Great Mosque at Mecca last November by several hundred Wahhabi fanatics). It may not be too much to suggest, therefore, that Princess Misha'al's execution was intended to serve as a dramatic refutation of accusations that the House of Saud was delinquent in its application of the sterner precepts of the *shari'a* to its own members. As for Misha'al's lover, his beheading may have been simply an act of revenge, an exaction under the ancient *lex talionis*, or punishment of the crime of *lese majeste.* In either case, it was designed to serve as a deterrent to the regime's critics.

The high-handed dismissal of the British ambassador last month and the threats to review Britain's trading connections with Saudi Arabia may also have been prompted by calculations about the effect they might have on two separate constituencies: the Saudi Arabian people, to whom the ruling family's actions would be a demonstration of its contempt for and power over Western infidels; and the governments of those Western countries, the United States in particular, where the film was due to be shown subsequently. If the British government, which the Saudis obviously considered to be a soft touch, could be easily intimidated, then, so they reckoned, other Western governments could be coerced similarly into prohibiting the transmission of the film. Indeed, there are signs that the Saudi calculation is beginning to have the desired effect in the US. The South Carolina Education Network, in an act of disguised loyalty to former governor and current ambassador to Saudi Arabia John C. West, cancelled "Death of a Princess" on its five stations throughout the state. KLCS-TV in Los Angeles followed suit, and the station manager of Houston's KUHT-TV explained his station's decision not to air the film by declaring that "we just don't believe it's in the national interest," according to a recent report in the *New York Times.* The Mobil Corporation, much of whose oil comes from Saudi Arabia, published an advertisement in the *Times* calling on the Public Broadcasting Service not to air the docudrama. Mobil has provided financing for several ambitious projects of PBS. Some of the stations showing the film will follow it up with a program giving opponents an opportunity for rebuttal, not at all a common occurrence. This is a lesser manifestation of the power of oil than outright censorship, but it is striking nonetheless.

Whatever the true explanation of the reason for the tragic deaths of Princess Misha'al and her lover may be, there is no denying that the deaths actually occurred, and that the incident says a lot about the character both of Saudi society and of the ruling house. It has been all the more sickening, therefore, to witness the display of hypocrisy with which some British politicians and businessmen, and certain sections of the British press, have responded to the Saudi government's blustering protests about Anthony Thomas's film. None of the critics remarked upon—if they even noticed—the skill with which Thomas evoked the atmosphere of urban life in modern Arabia, more particularly the oppressive and sinister face of Saudi officialdom—outwardly bland, equivocal, even ingratiating at times, while underneath, never far from the surface, lurks a consuming urge to break the rod across a suppliant's back.

A persistent theme in all the blague that has been uttered on the subject is that relations between Britain have long been amicable, marked by mutual respect and admiration. Nothing could be further from the truth. From the early years of the 19th century up to the eve of Britain's departure from the Gulf in 1971, Anglo-Saudi relations have been consistently cool, distant, and mutually suspicious. While the Saudis strove throughout this period of a century and a half to bring the greater part of Arabia under their domination, the British resisted their attempts whenever these threatened the peace of the Gulf or the security of the small shaikhdoms along the Arabian shore. British resistance began to weaken, however, after World War II, as the permanent officials of the Foreign Office came to exercise more and more influence over the conduct of British policy in Arabia. Their hour of triumph came in 1971 when they procured Britain's withdrawal from the Gulf, leaving the sheikhdoms to fend for themselves against the Saudis. Since then, appeasement has regulated the conduct of British relations with Saudi Arabia, growing in strength with each passing year. It is a policy evidently very much to the taste of the British foreign secretary, Lord Carrington, just as it was to that of his predecessor in office, the Labour party's David Owen.

When news of Princess Misha'al's execution first came to the attention of the outside world some two years ago, Owen delivered himself of a few uncomplimentary remarks about the Saudi judicial system. A mere 48 hours later, when it became clear that the Saudi government had not taken his remarks very kindly, he made a grovelling apology for his temerity in commenting upon matters that were none of his concern. Likewise, as soon as Thomas's film was shown in Britain, Carrington hastened to express his regret to the Saudis for any offense it may have given them. A couple of weeks later he and his deputy, Sir Ian Gilmour, the Lord Privy Seal (who earlier had brought pressure on ATV England to prevent the showing of the film), led a doleful antiphon in Parliament about the damage done to Britain's "close political and economic relationship" with Saudi Arabia and to "the friendship which has characterized Anglo-Saudi relations in the past."

Carrington and Gilmour are both notorious for their pro-Arab sentiments (So is James Craig, the expelled British ambassador to Saudi Arabia, which makes his expulsion from the country one of those enjoyable diplomatic ironies occasionally sent to cheer us up.) Before his appointment to the Foreign Office last year Gilmour had an interest in a company established to channel financial investments from the Gulf states. His son

David is the deputy editor of *Middle East International*, a magazine published in London by the Council for the Advancement of Arab-British Understanding, a body whose *raison d'etre* is indicated by its treacly title and whose activities are marked equally by sycophancy toward the Arabs and antipathy to Israel. Carrington's elder son, Rupert, is employed by Morgan Grenfell, a merchant bank deeply involved in Arab financial transactions. Another employee of Morgan Grenfell is David Douglas-Home, the son of the former prime minister and foreign secretary, Lord Home. Several former members of the British diplomatic service are also to be found immersed in the murky waters of "recycled" Arab oil funds.

To draw attention to these facts is not to imply that the occupations of Carrington's, Gilmour's and Home's sons should be used as a stick with which to belabour their fathers. What is being suggested is that the employment of the sons of ministers of the Crown in so corrupt an environment as that which surrounds the deployment of Arab oil money indicates a lamentable want of judgement and sense of political propriety on the part of their fathers. We have only to look about us today to see the degree of debasement that Arab oil money has caused in Western society and politics over the last ten years. If such degradation can occur in so short a time, what on earth will be our condition 10 years hence? The indignation now being vented in Britain over the offense given the Saudi royal family by a television film would be better directed at those who have brought us to our present ignominious pass *vis-à-vis* the plutocrats of the Arabs.

37
Great Game or Grand Illusion?[1]

In Central Asia the position of affairs changes not
Every hour, but every minute. Therefore I say,
Vigilance, vigilance, vigilance.
—General Mikhail Dmitrievich Skobolev, 1881

I do not exclude the intelligent anticipation of facts
Even before they occur.
—Lord Curzon, 1898

U p until the beginning of the last decade the forward defence of Western interests in the Gulf region rested upon the Central Treaty Organization and the British political and military position in the Gulf itself. CENTO, whose Middle-Eastern members were Turkey, Persia and Pakistan, was the successor alliance to the Baghdad Pact, which had been formally inaugurated in 1955. Like that earlier ill-fated coalition, CENTO was the reconstitution in modern form of the system of "barrier powers" for the defence of the Middle East against Russia, which had had its beginnings in the first half of the nineteenth century. The British position in the Gulf also dated back to the early decades of the nineteenth century, when, to assure the safety of commerce and shipping in the Gulf, and to safeguard both the "direct" route from the Mediterranean and the maritime approaches to India on the north-west, Britain had first subdued and then entered into treaty relations with the maritime shaikhdoms

---

1 From *Survey*, Vol. 25, No. 2 (111), Spring 1980. Reproduced by permission.

along the Arabian shore. Until the end of 1967 the British position in the Gulf was underpinned by the British base at Aden, possession of which also helped to ensure Western command of the Straits of Bab al-Mandab. Taken overall, the British presence in South Arabia and the Gulf was the principal stabilizing force in the Arabian peninsula.

If one were forced to make an arbitrary choice and to say at what particular point this defensive structure began to be undermined, one would probably fix upon the publication of the British White Paper on defence in February 1966. (To say this, of course, is to set to one side all the larger issues which determined or influenced British and Western policy in Arabia and the Gulf at the time—such as Britain's decline as a great power; the general Western retreat from Asia and Africa since 1945; the political, intellectual and moral climate in Britain in the 1960s; the growing ascendancy of that school of thought which believed Britain's post-imperial role outside Europe was drawing to a close, and which, since the *débâcle* at Suez 10 years earlier, also considered it better ended; the growing American involvement in Vietnam—to name but a few.) The defence White Paper of 1966 proposed a drastic reduction in British military commitments east of Suez, withdrawal from Aden colony and protectorate (the Federation of South Arabia), and the repudiation of the previous undertaking to conclude a defensive treaty with the federation on independence. The abandonment of Aden duly took place in November 1967, power being handed over to a quasi-Marxist terrorist organization, the National Liberation Front. A few months earlier the defeat of Egyptian arms by Israel in the six-day war had virtually assured the evacuation of the Egyptian expeditionary force from the Yemen; for one of the conditions laid down by King Faisal of Saudi Arabia, at the Khartum Conference of Arab states in August 1967, for the rescue of Egypt from bankruptcy was that Nasser should remove his troops from the Yemen. With the Egyptians gone, the National Liberation Front would have lost its principal supply base, which would have severely impaired its ability to carry on guerrilla warfare in South Arabia against the British forces. Yet in the face of the Egyptian withdrawal from the Yemen, and despite the clearly expressed desire of King Faisal that Britain should remain in South Arabia, the British government of the day persisted in carrying out its decision to leave Aden before the year was out.

It was clear at the time, and has become even clearer since, that the aversion felt by the more influential sections of the British Labour party for the continuance of defensive commitments and residual treaty obligations outside Europe (or even within Europe, for that matter) was primarily responsible for the decision to quit Aden. The same doctrinaire aversion to any defensive responsibilities east of Suez underlay the subsequent announcement by the Labour government in January 1968 that the British position in the Gulf was to be relinquished by the end of 1971. Although financial stringency was put forward as the reason for the relinquishment, there is little doubt that the prime motive behind it was the appeasement, for domestic political reasons, of the left-wing ideologues of the Labour party. For the sum of money involved in the maintenance of the British position in the Gulf, some £12 million annually, was inconsequential when set against the total savings which had to be effected in the British economy at the time, some £850 million, and infinitesimal when viewed against the profligacy of British governments then and since.

Over the next two years leading figures in the Conservative party several times proclaimed their intention to reverse the decision to leave the Gulf if the Conservatives should be returned to office. (At the time of the announcement of the decision of the former prime minister, Sir Alec Douglas Home, had condemned it as "a dereliction of stewardship, the like of which this country has not seen in the conduct of foreign policy before"—strong words from one who had been Neville Chamberlain's parliamentary private secretary at the time of Munich.) Whether any pressure to reconsider the decision was exerted from Washington upon the government of Harold Wilson after President Nixon assumed office in January 1969 is not readily ascertainable; but as no convincing evidence has yet emerged to substantiate a presumption that such pressure was in fact applied, it is only logical to conclude that it was not—or that it was half-hearted at best. The Conservatives were returned to power in the general election of June 1970. It took the government of Edward Heath little more than three months to decide (although the decision was not to be made public until March 1971) to adhere to the timetable of withdrawal from the Gulf laid down by its predecessor.

While the Heath government was swayed in its decision by a diversity of considerations, the influence of the Foreign Office in the decision-making would appear to have been paramount. The Foreign Office had never felt comfortable in the Gulf. Ever since it inherited charge of the British position there from the government of India in 1947 when the British raj came to an end, it had always felt uneasy about the role it had to play in the area, which was one more of an imperial than a diplomatic nature. Indeed, it would not, perhaps be going too far to say that few officials in the Foreign Office in 1970-71 really understood what constituted the foundations of Britain's historical and legal position in the Gulf. That position was based upon the trucial system, *i.e.* the series of agreements with Bahrain, Qatar and the Trucial Shaikhdoms for the maintenance, under British supervision, of maritime peace; upon the successive treaties with those states for the suppression of the slave trade and the arms traffic; upon the so-called "exclusive" engagements providing for the conduct by Britain of the shaikhdoms' foreign relations and the non-alienation by them of any portion of their territories to foreign powers; and upon a series of subsequent agreements concerning the granting of oil and other mineral concessions, and the exercise by Britain of extra-territorial jurisdiction. It also depended, though buttressed by fewer formal and less restrictive engagements, upon the longstanding British connexion with the sultanate of Oman.

In the Foreign Office's eyes the major Gulf states—Saudi Arabia, Persia and Iraq—bulked larger and more important than did the minor Gulf principalities, with the possible exception of Kuwait. Despite the fact that these three states, and Saudi Arabia and Persia in particular, had been the principal sources of disruption in the Gulf since the early nineteenth century, and that they had throughout this entire period resented the British presence there as an obstacle to the pursuit of their territorial designs upon the littoral shaikhdoms and Oman, the Foreign Office had for many years treated them with considerable deference—far more, in fact, than the British government of India had been inclined to accord them. Thus in the years before the second world war the Foreign Office had exhibited a readiness to accommodate Reza Shah's ambitions to acquire a navy and to extend Persian jurisdiction in the lower Gulf. It was also prepared to gratify, in part at least, Ibu Saud's territorial demands upon the littoral shaikhdoms of eastern Arabia. The same disposition was evinced by the Foreign Office in 1970-71 towards Muhammad Reza Shah and Faisal ibn Abdul Aziz. Having persuaded the Shah in the early months of 1970 to renounce his ill-founded claim to sovereignty over Bahrain, the Foreign Office was not in the least averse to his obtaining as his *quid pro quo* the Arab islands of Abu Musa and the Tunbs, which were situated near the entrance to the Gulf, for the ostensible purpose of safeguarding the passage of shipping through the Straits of Hormuz. Likewise the Foreign Office brought pressure upon the ruler of Abu Dhabi to concede the demands for territory that King Faisal was making upon him, the satisfaction of which, so Faisal insisted, was the price of his recognition of the United Arab Emirates, the federation of the former Trucial Shaikhdoms which was then in the process of being formed.

Though little in the way of a convincing case can be made out in defence of the Foreign Office's and the Heath administration's abdication of responsibility for the security of the Gulf at the end of 1971, the abdication has to be viewed in the light of the prevailing wisdom of the day, which held that the era of European authority and dominion overseas had ended, that the strength, moral as much as physical, of Afro-Asian nationalism could no longer be resisted, and that in the Middle East the Arabs' and the Persians' hour had come. According to this doctrine, the British political and military presence in the Gulf, far from helping to preserve the peace and to protect Western interests there, was a positive irritant to local feelings and consequently a potential source of trouble in the future. The argument was held to apply in particular to the international oil companies operating in the Gulf, whose relations with the concessionary governments were said to be adversely affected by the continuance of Britain's tutelary role. The extraction and sale of oil, so the conventional wisdom had it, was a purely commercial affair, best left to the oil companies, the concessionary governments and the operation of market forces. As the comforting adage of the day expressed it, "The Arabs cannot drink their oil." That oil had a strategic importance virtually unequalled by any other raw material, and that its extraction had invariably been closely bound up with politics—and nowhere more so than in the Middle East—was conveniently ignored by the advocates of disengagement.

Another argument current in leading political and intellectual circles in Britain in 1970-71 concerned the inevitability of internal political upheavals in Saudi Arabia, the minor Gulf states and Oman. Taking their cue from what had happened in Egypt, Iraq, Algeria, Libya and elsewhere in the preceding two decades, the proponents of the theory of imminent revolution contended that the traditional regimes in the Arabian peninsula were bound, sooner or later, either to broaden the basis of their authority by admitting a greater number of their people to a share in political power, or they would be swept away on a wave of popular uprisings. In such an event, Britain might find herself caught up in successive struggles for power in the Gulf shaikhdoms by virtue of her treaty relations with their rulers. Since the leaders of the putative revolts would be drawn from the emergent, educated, younger generation of Gulf Arabs, who would not tolerate for an instant any lingering form of Western tutelage, Britain would find herself faced with the choice of beating an embarrassing retreat from the scene or of becoming embroiled on the side of the established rulers in a bloody and long-drawn-out conflict, with incalculable results for her standing and interests in the Arab world as a whole. Better, therefore, so the argument concluded, that she should withdraw gracefully while she could.

Little point would be served here in commenting upon the numerous flaws in this hypothesis or upon the want of spirit displayed by those who propounded it. Suffice it to say that it was very much the product of its times, proceeding as it did, less from a rigorous examination of the realities of Arabian politics, than from the personal and ideological convictions of its exponents, who themselves retained a touching faith, a legacy from the days of Nasser and his imitators, in the therapeutic and cleansing powers of revolutions conducted by youthful army officers of austere habits and patent rectitude. No matter that each successive *bouleversement* in an Arab capital since 1952 had brought to power a regime more oppressive than its predecessor. The issue was one of faith, not of reason, and both the Foreign Office and the Heath administration subscribed—or affected to subscribe, the distinction is immaterial—to the approved doctrine. Britain's future, they firmly believed, lay in Europe, in membership of the European Community, and in Britain's return to her role as an industrial and trading nation, freed from her tiresome post-imperial responsibilities overseas. So Heath and his Cabinet chose in 1971 to heed the importunities of those local powers which wished, for one reason or another, and none of them particularly creditable, to see Britain withdraw from the Gulf (an assemblage which included Saudi Arabia, Persia, Iraq, Kuwait and South Yemen) rather than to hearken to the entreaties of those who wished her to remain—Bahrain, the United Arab Emirates and the sultanate of Oman. So anxious were the Cabinet and the Foreign Office in 1971 to be quit of any and all future ties to the Gulf that they refused to entertain the idea of concluding a defensive treaty with the UAE, or to explore the possibility of promoting a political and military *entente* between the UAE and Oman, backed by a British defensive undertaking.

With Britain gone from the Gulf, responsibility for its security and for its oil reserves devolved, perforce, upon the major local powers. From the West's point of view, this meant Persia and Saudi Arabia, for Iraq had removed herself from the defensive equation by concluding a treaty of friendship and cooperation with the Soviet Union in April 1972. All the local states, whatever their differences, were as one in professing that the defence of the Gulf and its oilfields was henceforth the sole concern of the states around its shores, and these professions were solemnly echoed by the Western governments most concerned with the Gulf's future.

So far as Muhammad Reza Shah was concerned, he entertained not the slightest doubt of his country's fitness and right to take Britain's place as the guardian of the Gulf's peace. Evidently the United States shared his confidence, for when President Nixon and his secretary of state, Henry Kissinger, visited Tehran in May 1972 they gave the Shah virtually *carte blanche* to purchase from the United States whatever arms he considered he needed to perform his allotted task. Over the next half-a-dozen years, with the eager assistance of the armaments and aircraft manufacturers of Europe and the United States, the Shah was able to indulge to the full his infatuation with the deadly trinkets of war. At the same time, again with the ardent encouragement of Western governments and manufacturers, he pressed ahead with the implementation of his grandiose design to make Persia, within the space of a decade or two, the second industrial power in Asia after Japan. These vast ambitions were to be accomplished by the expenditure of Persia's oil revenues, which grew by leaps and bounds from 1971 onwards, thanks in no small measure to Muhammad Reza Shah's unremitting efforts in the counsels of the Organization of Petroleum Exporting Countries to force the price of oil higher and ever higher.

It does not lie within the purview of this article to examine either the domestic reasons for the Shah's downfall in 1978-79 or the contribution made to that downfall by the Western powers' cynical exploitation of his obsession with military grandeur. What is of proper concern to us here is why the Western powers most involved—the United States, Britain and, to a lesser extent, France—should ever in the first place have considered Persia capable of serving as the northern sentinel of the Gulf. Since the inception of CENTO Persia had been the weakest link in the barrier chain. Unlike Turkey and Pakistan she had no military tradition of any relevance to the modern world. The Persian army, again unlike the armies of Turkey and Pakistan, had had no experience of war on anything approaching a significant scale since the Russo-Persian war of 1826-28 or, at best, the Anglo-Persian war of 1856-57. While some of the peoples who go to make up Persia's population—in particular, the Kurds, Afghans and Turcomans—are warrior races, no Persian government, until the reign of Reza Shah, had been able, despite the efforts of successive European military missions, to weld them into a disciplined national army. Even Reza Shah's exertions in this respect yielded fairly unimpressive results. The fault lay less with the Persian soldiery, ignorant, ill-nurtured and dispirited though they were, than with their officers, who possessed little military competence themselves, were largely indifferent to the well-being of their troops, and lacked any real dedication to the profession of arms.

While improvements in the training and morale of the Persian armed forces, and in the quality of the officer corps, undoubtedly were effected during the reign of Muhammad Reza Shah, their actual fighting calibre never came near to justifying the enormous sums of money he had lavished upon their arms and equipment. The lack of education and technical skills in the ranks of the Persian army and air force meant that they could not operate or service the bulk of the advanced weaponry and aircraft, with which the Shah insisted upon equipping them, without the assistance of thousands of American and British technicians and military advisers. On the only occasions on which the Persian army was tested in battle, *viz.* in the campaign against the guerrillas of Dhufar in the mid-1970s and in the recent conflict with Iraq, it hardly covered itself with glory. As for the Persian navy, it remained, however much the Shah cared to spend upon ships and dockyard facilities, as much a Gilbertian enterprise as it had been since the eighteenth century, when Nadir Shah had tried to create a marine with the aid of Portuguese renegades and Arab pirates.

Military weakness apart, there were psychological factors, arising from the Persian past, which threw doubt upon Persia's ability and willingness to serve as the guardian of Western interests in the Gulf. From the early nineteenth century until the dissolution of the Indian empire in 1947 the continued existence of Persia as an independent state was largely due to the support of the British raj. Thereafter her independence was underwritten by the United States. The knowledge of this dependence did not, and still does not, sit well with the Persians, one of whose more striking national characteristics, remarked by generations of students of Persian society, is excessive vanity. Despite the fact that Britain never annexed a single inch of Persian soil during the entire period of her diplomatic and military intercourse with Persia—in contrast to Russia, who appropriated large tracts of Persian territory in the Caucasus and Transcaspia in the nineteenth century—the Persians retained an almost pathological suspicion of Britain's ulterior designs upon their country. At the root of this suspicion lay a fear that the British were bent upon repeating in Persia the pattern of piecemeal annexation which they had followed in India and which had eventually brought the entire sub-continent under British rule. (It was this fear, for instance, which lay behind the Persian government's adamant rejection of occasional British approaches to secure the cession of a Persian island in the Gulf to serve as a naval base for the policing of its waters).

Apart from their suspicion of Britain's ultimate intentions towards their country, the Persians were also irritated by Britain's refusal, backed where necessary by armed demonstrations, to allow them to compensate themselves for the loss of their Caucasian provinces to Russia by expanding eastwards into Afghanistan. More than once the Persians turned to St Petersburg for encouragement in the prosecution of their schemes of Afghan conquest. As often as not, this encouragement was readily forthcoming, for the Russians were only too pleased to divert the Persians from brooding upon their losses in the Caucasus by directing their gaze eastwards to the Afghan principalities, where any disturbance of the status quo was bound to unsettle the British rulers of India. A further irritant to Persian feelings was the British ascendancy in the Gulf. Conscious of their own lack of sea-power, and therefore of the means to exercise authority in the Gulf, successive Persian governments gave vent to their frustration by obstructing Britain's efforts to suppress maritime warfare, the slave trade and the arms traffic, and by putting forward extravagant claims to dominion over territories and people, some of which have persisted down to the present day. The peculiar mentality induced by the amalgamation of these feelings of resentment, fear, suspicion, frustration and injured vanity was exemplified by the Persian reaction to the Anglo-Russian *détente* of 1907. Obloquy was heaped upon Britain at the time—and has never ceased to be heaped upon her—for what was regarded as the callous partitioning of Persia into spheres of influence, regardless of the affront to Persian national sentiments; while towards Russia, the real oppressor of Persian nationhood over the preceding century, the Persians observed, and still observe, a prudent reticence.

Muhammad Reza Shah harboured in his own person all the constituent elements which went to create this national neurosis. In addition, he nursed a galling resentment of Britain for having deposed his father in 1941 at the time of the Anglo-Russian occupation of Persia. That the circumstances surrounding the deposition of Reza Shah hardly supported this simplistic interpretation of that event was something that Muhammad Reza Shah refused to entertain. He was also convinced that Britain had exploited Persia economically, especially over oil, so that he was inclined to view with marked satisfaction, only partly allayed by apprehensions for his own future, the expropriation of the Anglo-Iranian Oil Company's assets in Persia by the government of Muhammad Musaddiq in 1951. Despite the fact that his throne was saved for him two years later by the intervention of the United States, and that it was also as a result of the United States' initiative that a settlement of the oil crisis, on terms highly favourable to Persia, was achieved in 1954, he never ceased to regard the Western oil companies operating in Persia with anything but hostility. As soon as he felt bold enough to do so, which he did early in 1973, after observing the obsequious respect with which the Western powers were becoming accustomed to treat him, he tore up the oil consortium's concession altogether.

Yet for all that the Shah's extravagant posturing was in large measure responsible for bringing his country to its present parlous condition, the Western powers must also bear a substantial share of blame for the precarious situation in which their own interests in Persia now stand. In the geopolitical scheme of things Persia has long occupied the position of a buffer state, a role which may offend Persian pride but which is nevertheless a fact of life in a harsh world. For Persia to fulfil this function required that the Soviet Union, on the one side, and the Western powers led by the United States, on the other, should refrain from trying to acquire an absolute ascendancy over the country; and conversely, that each side should strive to prevent the other from acquiring such an ascendancy. By thrusting the role of sentinel of the Gulf on the Shah—albeit that he eagerly sought the part—and subsequently arming him to the teeth so that he might play it properly, the Western powers acquired a preponderance in Persia (that it was, perhaps, more apparent than real is beside the point) which could only serve to unsettle the Soviet Union. For the arming of the Shah was on such a massive scale that it could only have aroused misgivings in Moscow about the purpose behind it. That the whole martial extravaganza was simply the product of greed, culpable irresponsibility and addled opportunism on the part of the West would have appeared to the Russians an implausible explanation. Yet it is, by and large, the true one. No real thought seems to have been given in Washington or London to the implications and consequences of indulging Muhammad Reza Shah's insensate passion for military gewgaws. Was it deemed conceivable, for instance, that Persia, regardless of the amount of weaponry she accumulated, could ever withstand, for more than the briefest instant, an assault from the Soviet Union? Was any consideration given to the possibility that the Shah, bewitched by the glittering arsenal he had assembled, might be tempted to provoke the Russians by some truculent gesture or other along their common borders? Or to the likelihood that this extensive array of arms was intended, not to deter the Russians but for use against his neighbours in the Gulf, to the inevitable detriment of stability in the region and the security of Western interests there?

It is difficult to avoid the conclusion that over the past decade, through inattention rather than design, the West has failed to abide by the rules of the Great Game as it is played in Persia, thereby inadvertently paving the way for the Soviet Union, in her turn, to break them in Afghanistan. For all his faults, Muhammad Reza Shah was perhaps more aware of how the game should be played; although it has to be said that he tended to grow reckless as he came more and more to take for granted not only the anxious deference paid him by the West but also the protection afforded him by his connexions with the United States. Much of the peevish sermonizing he was wont to address to the West during the 1970s was intended for the Kremlin's entertainment, to demonstrate his independence of, and even disregard for, Western goodwill. (Needless to say, he would never have dared to bait the Soviet Union in this fashion.) Taking a leaf from the record of the Qajar Shahs, he several times solicited and received Russian backing for one or another of his policy initiatives, and especially for his insistence that the maritime security of the Gulf should be the sole concern of its littoral states—a claim which translated itself in his mind into a determination to make that sea once more the *sinus Persicus* of old. It is worth noting that in all the *gasconade* he was prone to utter on this subject, and especially about the wickedness of the very idea that the Western powers might establish a naval presence in the Gulf, there was not so much as a whisper of protest against the visits of Russian warships to the Gulf or their use of supply facilities at the Iraqi port of Umm Qasr.

For all this, however, it has to be said that the volume of complaint and criticism which the Shah levelled at the West in the last years of his reign was far in excess of what was required to maintain the balance in his country between the Soviet Union and the United States. It was evident that he was labouring under a deeper compulsion than personal arrogance and paranoia, and the roots of this compulsion are to be found in those attributes of the Persian national character adverted to earlier. The grievances he articulated about economic exploitation, the obsessive suspicions he evinced about the West's covetous designs on the soil of Persia, the ambivalence he displayed towards the Russians, his indifference to the need to conciliate those upon whom the security of his country ultimately depended—all were part and parcel of that peculiar distemper which has afflicted the Persian people, or at least their ruling classes, in their dealings with the West over the past two centuries. This distemper is even more evident today, heightened as it is by religious hysteria, in the leadership and following of the new republican regime. Whether it is in the railing of the Ayatollah Khomeini against the West for its debauchery and its evil influence abroad, or in the ranting of his placemen about Western and especially American "imperialism," the echoes of an atavistic fixation are all too clearly audible. Further speculation on the subject would be pointless. To try to determine why the Persian people and their leaders insist upon exhausting their emotional capital in frenzied vilification of the West while the Soviet Union draws the noose tighter around their necks would necessitate venturing into realms of psychopathology as yet uncharted by rational men.

The second bulwark of the Gulf's defence was, and presumably still is, Saudi Arabia. Here again the Western powers have made a number of assumptions about the country's fitness to play the role assigned to it, and about its commitment to Western interests, that may prove to have been ill-founded. Like Persia, Saudi Arabia has in the past been a prime agent of disturbance in the Gulf, and as Persia is now a dangerous source of instability in the region, so also might Saudi Arabia become another.

The motive power behind the progress of the house of Saud over the past two centuries has been a sense of religious mission coupled to a drive for territorial conquest. The one, needless to say, has helped fuel the other. It was the early Saudi forays into south-eastern Arabia, under the impulse of the Wahhabi reformation, that were responsible in large measure for Britain's eventual assumption of the maritime protectorate of the Gulf. For the spread of Wahhabi influence among the maritime tribes of the southern coast of the Gulf sharpened their already well-developed piratical instincts, leading them to embark upon large-scale piratical campaigns in the Gulf and even further afield, eventually bringing retribution upon themselves in the shape of two British punitive expeditions sent from India in 1809 and 1819. Thereafter the British authorities in the Gulf set their faces against the assertion of a Wahhabi or Saudi ascendancy over the littoral shaikhdoms, lest it provoke a renewal of organized piracy. A contest for influence ensued, which was to continue for the greater part of the century, between the Saudis, who strove to impose their will not only upon Bahrain and the Trucial Shaikhdoms but also upon the sultanate of Oman (for the inhabitants of which the Saudis cherished a particular enmity on religious grounds), and the British, who were determined both to keep the maritime shaikhs to the due observance of their treaty obligations and to preserve the independence of Oman. Although the ill-feeling between the Al Saud and the British diminished with the eclipse of Saudi power in Arabia at the close of the century, and diminished further in the circumstances of the first world war, it left a legacy of suspicion on both sides which was to linger for several decades to come.

The renewal of Saudi attempts in this century to dominate the Trucial Shaikhdoms and Oman followed the reconstitution of Saudi authority over the greater part of the peninsula in the 1920s and the proclamation of the kingdom of Saudi Arabia by Abdul Aziz ibn Saud in 1932. A year later he granted an oil concession for the eastern portion of his dominions to Standard Oil of California. It was scarcely coincidental that he should at the same time have seen fit to revive his ancestral claims to dominion over a fair portion of the shaikhdoms of Qatar and Abu Dhabi, and to the desert marches of Oman. Like his ancestors, Ibn Saud found his path blocked by the British authorities in the Gulf, who were further stiffened in their resolve to oppose the extension of Saudi sovereignty over the littoral shaikhdoms by the very consideration which had led Ibn Saud to put forward his claims in the first place, *viz.* the potential existence of oil deposits in the territories in question.

Ibn Saud returned to the attack after the second world war, having in the meantime secured for himself a powerful ally against the British—the United States. Even since the beginnings of American involvement in Saudi Arabia in the early 1930s the United States government had to all intents and purposes resigned the conduct of American relations with the Al Saud into the hands of the Arabian American Oil Company, a consortium made up of Standard Oil of California, Standard of New Jersey, Texas and Socony-Vacuum (afterwards Mobil). ARAMCO, which had from the very first served the house of Saud nobly and was to continue to serve it with spaniel-like devotion in the years to come, threw itself with enthusiasm after 1945 into the Saudi quarrel with the British over the location of Saudi Arabia's eastern frontier. The company also persuaded the United States government, without too much difficulty, that American interests in Arabia and in the Middle East generally would be advanced by siding with the Saudis over the frontier question and working for the elimination of the British presence in Arabia and the Gulf altogether. By the time that the State Department was forced in the mid-1960s, by the Egyptian campaign in the Yemen and the apprehensions which this aroused in Riyad, to assert more direct control over Saudi-American relations and to assess for the first time the consequences of having allowed itself to be led by the nose by ARAMCO, the damage had already been done. The British were abandoning Aden and preparing to retire from the Gulf.

Having no real policy of its own to pursue in Arabia, the State Department simply picked up the one bequeathed to it by ARAMCO—that of acting as servitor to the Saudi royal house. The situation has not really changed up to the present time. After witnessing the contemptible performance of the Western European powers at the time of the Arab oil embargo and the concurrent price offensive in 1973, the United States not unreasonably concluded that with allies like these she had better make her own arrangements to secure her economic and political interests in Arabia. In June 1974, therefore, she entered into an understanding with the Al Saud, whereby she engaged to assist with the development of Saudi Arabia's economy and the expansion and modernization of the Saudi armed forces, in return for an undertaking from the Saudi government to keep up a steady flow of oil to the United States at reasonable prices and to deposit the bulk of Saudi Arabia's surplus oil revenues in the United States. How far this arrangement has committed the United States to the preservation of the independence and integrity of Saudi Arabia under her present rulers is not entirely clear.

It is almost unnecessary to say that Saudi Arabia has failed in more than one respect to keep her side of the bargain. Saudi oil production has never attained the levels agreed upon, while oil prices have risen from $11.65 a barrel in June 1974 to $28 a barrel in May 1980. Moreover, the Saudi government has expressed strong objections to the creation by the United States of a national strategic petroleum reserve, a good part of which was to have come from the surplus which the Saudi fields were supposed to have been producing by 1980. On the other side of the ledger, the United States has all too amply fulfilled her obligations for the supply of arms, military training and economic expertise. She has also in her official conduct towards the Saudi regime continued to exhibit a fulsome regard for Saudi feelings and prejudices which the Saudi royal house has no doubt found highly gratifying, and which it had come to accept as only due and proper as a result of its past experience with ARAMCO.

How beneficial the relationship has been to the United States, and to the Western world in general, is another question. As in the case of Persia up to 1978, the United States, in company with Britain and France, has deluged Saudi Arabia with advanced weaponry and aircraft. While this policy may have been conceived with the cynical object of mopping up some, at least, of Saudi Arabia's excess oil revenues, its consequences may differ somewhat from what its architects had in mind—as they did in Persia. The sheer moral and political bankruptcy of the policy apart, what exactly was the arming of Saudi Arabia supposed to achieve? There were even fewer grounds for believing that Saudi Arabia was capable of protecting the Gulf's oil reserves and maintaining the peace of the Gulf than there were in the case of Persia. Like Persia, Saudi Arabia had long been a source of disturbance, not a force for tranquillity, in the Gulf. Nor was her military tradition such as to render other than ludicrous the notion that she could serve as the West's surrogate in warding off any threat from the Soviet Union. If the object was to enable the house of Saud to maintain order and security within the kingdom, then most of the sophisticated weaponry that the Al Saud have acquired is superfluous to that purpose. It certainly proved irrelevant in coping with the tribal and other fanatics who seized control of the great mosque at Mecca in November 1979, as apparently did most of the military training which the Saudi armed forces had received up to that date. The fact that the rebels could only be subdued after a three weeks' struggle is comment enough on Saudi Arabia's military capacity.

Presumably the possibility that the arms and aircraft with which Saudi Arabia is being equipped are intended for use against Israel can be dismissed. Not only would it be a strange internal contradiction in American policy if they were so intended, but the retaliation which such a step would invite could well prove ruinous to Saudi Arabia and fatal to her ruling house. Besides, it is doubtful, to say the least, whether the Saudis would be able to operate or service their complicated military equipment and aircraft without the aid of American and British technicians. Are the Saudi government's eyes, and those of the administration in Washington, fixed then upon Iraq, whose Baathist rulers seem, for all practical purposes, to be in league with Moscow, and who abominate the house of Saud and the principle of monarchical rule alike? If the build-up of Saudi Arabia's military strength is meant to give the Iraqis cause to reconsider any aggressive designs they may harbour upon the kingdom, or to deter them from an invasion of Kuwait, will it prove sufficient for this purpose? Or is the intention, perhaps, to enable Saudi Arabia to undertake a campaign against South Yemen, to unseat the Marxist regime in Aden and to put an end to the Russian presence in South Arabia? If so, then one can only ask what makes the Saudi government believe that it could carry such an undertaking through to a successful conclusion?

There is no avoiding the suspicion that the macabre carnival of arms sales has no systematic reasoning or calculated purpose behind it—other than the shabby goal already mentioned of soaking up a sizeable portion of Saudi Arabia's financial surpluses. The incalculable dangers implicit in such a disreputable tactic require no lengthy recitation here. The inevitable consequences of indiscriminately arming the Gulf states have been conclusively demonstrated by the Iraqi-Persian conflict and the accompanying destruction of oil installations. One also wonders whether any serious thought has been given to the possibility that the present Saudi government (or, what may be more ominous, a new regime of different complexion in Riyad) may be tempted to use its newly acquired military power to pursue the longstanding ambitions of the house of Saud in eastern and southeastern Arabia—in other words, to subvert the independence of Bahrain, Qatar, the UAE and Oman. Sheer besottedness with the deadly toys they now possess, and frustration at their inability to use them elsewhere, might well induce the Saudis to employ them to such ends. Whatever happens, the Western powers and more specifically the United States, Britain and

France, cannot escape their share of responsibility for it. Through their foolish pretence, to themselves as well as to the world at large, that Saudi Arabia could ever serve as a pillar of the Gulf's security, and through their flaccid accommodation of every one of the Saudi regime's arrogant demands and petulant whims, they have needlessly increased the dangers of instability in the Arabian peninsula.

It is not only our pathetic reliance upon the cardboard pillars of Saudi Arabia and Persia to protect our interests in the Gulf that has exposed the vacuity of Western policy over the past decade. It is also revealed by the way in which we have allowed the Gulf's oil to slip from our grasp and to be used as a weapon against us. In a mere half-a-dozen years or so, beginning in 1970, we lost physical control of the oilfields through the nationalization of the oil companies' concessions and assets; we lost control over the volume and rate of oil production; and we lost control over oil prices, which have come to be fixed by the member states of OPEC without any reference to the state of the market. So abject a state have we sunk to that when, for example, the Arab oil-producing states raised the price of oil by a further $2 a barrel in May 1980, an increase utterly unjustified in terms of current demand, not a cheep of protest was to be heard in the capitals of the West. Nor did anyone see fit to comment publicly that this latest increase, which was by no means the largest to have occurred during the preceding 18 months, was in itself more than the entire cost of a barrel of oil 10 years ago.

The pusillanimity of the West has been excused on the grounds that to offer any resistance to the Arabs and Persians and their partners in OPEC would have brought retaliation in the shape of embargoes, severe cutbacks in production, even more extravagant price rises, and so forth. At the same time we have been told by those in public life to whom we look for the instruction and guidance that the immense sums of money that the Western industrial nations and Japan have paid out for Arab and Persian oil can be recouped by the magical process of "recycling." More than that, exorbitant oil prices are said to be a blessing in disguise, since they act as a stimulant to Western industry. (Some of our mentors even go so far as to exhort us to regard this mulcting of the West as a well-merited punishment for our past crimes against the peoples of Asia and Africa.) The arguments ring rather hollow when one contemplates the economic condition of the industrial world today, where even the economies of West Germany and Japan are beginning to falter under the impact of cumulative and continuing oil price rises. Yet all that our leaders can offer us by the way of advice in coping with our creeping impoverishment is to counsel us to bend the knee even further, and bow even lower in the direction of Riyad, Baghdad or Abu Dhabi, in the hope that the new arbiters of our destiny will abate their demands.

Another pearl of the conventional wisdom which has been proffered for our delectation these past few years is that the Arabs and Persians will be restrained in their use of the power that the oil weapon gives them by the consideration that, if they weaken the West economically, especially by the imposition of high oil prices, they will impair the West's ability to contain the Soviet Union and to prevent Russian domination of the Middle East. It is a pretty tale, its only flaw being that there is not a shred of evidence to support it. On the contrary, by their behaviour over the past 10 years the Middle East members of OPEC have played the Soviet Union's game for her, to such a degree that they could not have improved on their performance if their organization's headquarters had been located in Moscow. To take only one example from among many: the year 1979, as all would agree, was a highly dangerous one in the Middle East. It opened with the fall of the Shah and closed with the Russian invasion of Afghanistan. Yet those 12 months also saw the greatest increases in the price of crude oil that had ever taken place in the entire history of the oil industry in the Middle East. Nor were those increases the full measure of the Middle-Eastern oil states' contempt for the theory of interdependence with which the West is wont to comfort itself. Two days after the Russian invasion of Afghanistan, Kuwait, as always the bell-wether among the Gulf oil states, raised the price of her oil yet again, and in May 1980, with the Soviet Union consolidating its occupation of Afghanistan by killing Muslims by the hundreds, if not thousands, the Muslim oil states imposed further increases in the price of oil.

It may be, of course, that deep in their hearts the Western proponents of the theory of interdependence do not actually believe in it. Their public affirmations of faith in the rationality of the governments of the Middle-Eastern oil states may simply be camouflage for their private convictions of the actual irrationality of these governments, and for their fears that this irrationality may at any time impel these governments to violent and arbitrary action. "They would do almost anything," a former chairman of Standard Oil of California told the Senate Foreign Relations Committee in June 1974. "You are completely at their mercy and that is why I have always felt that it is extremely important to have friendly relationships with those countries." But if the Western governments are convinced of the capriciousness and volatility of the regimes in power in the Middle-Eastern oil states, is a policy of propitiation and subservience the best way of handling them? There is a confusion of thought in the arguments which have led the Western powers, if only by default, to adopt this policy. On the one hand, they project onto Eastern minds Western modes of thought, Western values, and Western ideas of moderation and good sense in the conduct of national and international affairs. On the other hand, they may acknowledge to themselves (for, to judge by their actions, there is no absolute certainty that all of them do in fact make this acknowledgment) that Middle-Eastern governments, as just observed, are influenced by a very different set of beliefs and sentiments. One can only surmise, in an attempt to resolve the paradox, that the governments of the West have found it expedient to will themselves to believe (as a way of stilling their fears) in the ultimate rationality of the regimes now in control of the Middle East's oil. A necessary adjunct to this exercise in self-deception is that a scapegoat should be found to excuse any wilful or erratic behaviour on the part of these regimes; and, by great good fortune, one is conveniently to hand in the shape of Israel.

Finally, it must be said that, by acquiescing so nervelessly over the past decade in the larceny practised by the Middle-Eastern oil states, the Western powers have not only injured their own economics and those of the poorer countries of Asia and Africa, but they have done perhaps irreparable damage to the peoples of the oil states. The revenues from oil of the Middle-Eastern members of OPEC in 1970 were something over $6,000 million. In 1978 they were reckoned to be in excess of $140,000 million, in 1979 they were over $200,000 million, and this year they are estimated to reach $250,000 million. Arabia, Persia and Iraq have been inundated by vast sums of money over the past few years, which, given the nature of their governments and societies, was bound to have the most deleterious and corrupting effects upon them. The derangement that is now evident in every aspect of life in Arabia, Persia and the Gulf poses a serious threat to the safety of Western interests in these countries, a threat which is perhaps even more immediate than that represented by the designs of the Soviet Union. If the West had been more resolute in its resistance to the upward spiral of oil prices, if it had disputed with the utmost vigour the expropriation of the oil companies, and if it had shown its determination to defend, by whatever means were necessary, its right of access to the Gulf's oil, the combined effect may well have been to inject an element of sanity and a measure of calm into the region, even perhaps to have headed off the hysteria which, in the absence of any effective sedative agent, has come to reign there instead. Who knows but that the Shah, his soaring ambitions curbed by Western parsimony over oil revenues and arms supplies, might still be on his throne?

Now that the strategy pursued by the West in the Gulf since 1971 lies about us in ruins, what are we to do next? Are we to continue with the pretence, in the face of all that has happened in these past nine years, that the local powers are either disposed to protect the West's interests or capable of preserving the security of the region, especially against outside powers? And even if we were to persist in this pretence, as the major Western powers seem disposed to, will it suffice in the changed condition of affairs created by the descent of Persia into chaos, the after-effects of the Iraqi-Persian war and the Russian invasion of Afghanistan? Or has the time now come for serious consideration to be given to the projection of Western military power into the area?

Even today, one is inclined to question whether the magnitude of the shift in the balance of power in the Gulf region caused by the Russian occupation of Afghanistan has been fully grasped in the West. Certainly there seems to be little real appreciation, as opposed to ritual huffing and puffing, of the need for the West's response to be on the same scale of magnitude. There is a tendency instead, at least in some quarters, to try to divest the situation of its urgency—even to make out a case for inaction—by advancing various hypotheses designed to demonstrate that the Soviet Union was impelled to act as she did against the Afghans, not out of aggressive intent but for valid reasons of state. If the extension of a Russian ascendancy over Afghanistan is a natural, or at least a logical, development arising from the Soviet Union's position in Asia, and therefore, by implication, one that should not give rise to undue alarm in the West, then why was Britain at such pains up to 1947 to preserve the independence of Afghanistan as a neutral buffer state? Why, after an interval of 30 years in which there has been a great expansion of Russian power around the globe, including the Middle East, should the destruction of Afghanistan's independence now be of less moment to the West? The questions, one trusts, will be taken as rhetorical.

The evidence of the Soviet Union's ultimate intentions towards the Gulf is surely unmistakable. Why otherwise should the Russians be established in South Yemen and Ethiopia, why should they be linked by defensive treaties to Iraq and Syria, why else should they have incurred the odium of being labelled aggressors in Afghanistan? The Gulf's oil is one of the great strategic prizes in the world, possession of which would place the Soviet Union in a position to throttle the economies of Western Europe and Japan, and to tilt the balance of world power decisively and perhaps irrevocably. What other strategic initiatives may be portended by the subjugation of Afghanistan is a matter for wild surmise. Afghanistan is the northern gateway to the Indian sub-continent. It is also the eastern gateway to Persia. Even more resplendent distant prospects, however, may be visible from the battlements of the Kremlin. After his crushing defeat of the Turcomans at Geok Tepe in 1881, the Russian Commander-in-chief in Turkestan, General Mikhail Dmitrievich Skobolev, wrote:

> To my mind the whole Central Asian Question is as clear as the daylight. If it does not enable us in a comparatively short time to take seriously in hand the Eastern Question, in other words, to dominate the Bosporus, the Asiatic hide is not worth the tanning. Sooner or later Russian statesmen will have to rec-ognise the fact that Russia must rule the Bosporus; that on this depends not only her greatness as a Power of the first magni-tude, but also her defensive security, and the corresponding development of her manufactures and trade. Without a serious demonstration in the direction of India, in all probability on the side of Kandahar, a war for the Balkan Peninsula is not to be thought of. It is indispensable to maintain in Central Asia, at the gates of the corresponding theatre of war, a powerful body of troops, fully equipped, and seriously mobilized.

It is perhaps worth recalling in this connexion that in nearly every crisis that arose over the Turkish Straits in the nineteenth century a Rus-sian intrigue was concurrently set on foot in Afghanistan or Persia or both. To take but one example: at the time of the Russo-Turkish war of 1877-78, despite a specific recognition five years earlier by the Russian foreign minister, Prince Gorchakov, "that Afghanistan was completely outside the sphere within which Russia might be called upon to exercise her influ-ence," a plan for the invasion of India was drawn up by Skobolev, and a Russian mission was despatched to Kabul to urge the amir "to treat the English with deceit and fraud, until the present cold season passes away, when the Almightly Will be made manifest to you; that is to say, the Russian Government having repeated the Bismillah, the Bismillah will come to your assistance." The contemporary parallels require no delinea-tion. Who is to say that the Straits of Hormuz are today the only straits that the Russians have in their sights? "The Game," as Mahbub Ali, the Pa-than horse-trader, told Kim, "is so large that one sees but a little at a time."

38
Yamani's Book of Revelations[1]

Another performance of OPEC's long-running sacred drama has come and gone, preceded as always by much twittering in the Western press about the awful solemnity of the familiar rite and followed just as inevitably by the lavishing of flowery tributes upon the assorted mummers who make up the permanent cast. As is only proper, the most fragrant bouquets were accorded to the chief mummer, Sheik Ahmad Zaki Yamani of Saudi Arabia, whose elegant execution of the role of high priest or master of the revels was as flawless and effortless as ever.

Yet for all the impressive staging and the evident histrionic versatility of the players, backstage there was a considerable degree of uneasiness among the managers and promoters. They had for the first time in many years been faced with a glut of oil on the world market of sufficient proportions to undermine the cartel's confidence in its ability to continue dictating the price at which its members would sell their oil. OPEC production, which only a couple of years ago had stood at 31 million barrels a day (b/d), was down to 23 million b/d. and even at this level there was a surplus of two or three million b/d worldwide.

To the interested bystander the situation was not without an engaging symmetry; for OPEC owed its creation 21 years ago to a similar glut, a glut which had led the major oil companies in 1959-60 to cut oil prices by 28 cents a barrel. To try to retrieve the loss in revenue which they suffered as a consequence, Saudi Arabia, Kuwait, Iran, Iraq, and Venezuela banded together in September 1960 to form the Organization of Petroleum Exporting Countries. There was this additional irony: that the glut had been

1 From *National Review*, July 10, 1980. Reproduced by permission.

created in the first place by the greed of the oil-producing states, and of Saudi Arabia in particular, for higher revenues, which had led them to put pressure upon the oil companies in the late 1950s to produce more oil than the market could absorb.

Plus ça change …. Greed still dominates the counsels and actions of OPEC, overriding all other considerations. At the conclave in Geneva in the last week of May, the delegates of Iran and Iraq, the war between their countries conveniently relegated to oblivion, sat amiably side by side, cordially discussing premiums, production levels and price differentials, and tactfully ignoring the fact that the Iranian oil minister, who had been taken prisoner while on an ill-advised visit to the battlefront, still languished in confinement in Baghdad.

The Gullible West

Saudi Arabia's current insistence on producing the lion's share (10.3 million b/d) of OPEC's output is represented by Sheik Yamani - and the explanation has been dutifully swallowed, with appropriate noises of appreciation, by the more gullible Western commentators—as part of a grand design by the Saudi government to bring "unity" into OPEC's price structure, the eventual aim being to reduce the present high level of oil prices as a necessary prelude to their orderly augmentation on a yearly basis. (If this seems contradictory, it is all of a piece, as we shall soon see, with Yamani's customary verbal legerdemain.) Price "unity" in this case means a return to the system which prevailed up to the end of 1978, when the prices charged for their oil by individual members of OPEC were calculated on the basis of the Saudi marker crude (standard Arabian light) with allowances for geographic location, specific gravity, and other differentials. This system was thrown to the winds in January 1979, when the curtailment of Iran's oil production and the overthrow of the Shah panicked many oil-importing countries into a rush to purchase oil on the spot market at grossly inflated prices lest a shortage should develop.

There was, however, no real scarcity of oil at the time (spare producing capacity in the world was then some five million b/d, approximately equal to Iran's normal output), although Saudi Arabia deliberately engineered the appearance of one by suddenly cutting her production, which she had raised some weeks earlier to take advantage of the Iranian shutdown. As soon as the bogus shortage had achieved the intended result of driving up prices in the spot market, the Saudis resumed full production and raised their prices accordingly, along with the rest of OPEC.

Over a period of little more than 12 months the price of Saudi Arabian oil rose from $12 to $32 a barrel—and all in the interest, so we have repeatedly been told by Yamani and his indefatigable apologists in the Western press, of exercising a "moderating" influence upon OPEC. Perish the thought that the Saudi royal family (who were not above dabbling in the spot market themselves) were motivated by avarice! Or that extravagance, fiscal mismanagement, and corruption on a monumental scale had brought about a severe deficit in the country's finances in 1978-79, thereby necessitating a substantial rise in the price of oil if the hectic pace of expenditure was to be maintained.

Now Sheik Yamani has claimed (initially on the NBC program *Meet the Press*, on April 19) that Saudi Arabia "engineered" the present glut of oil in order to stabilize oil prices and to impose both "moderation" and "price unity" upon the rest of OPEC. There is no reason why any more credence should be accorded this claim than any of Yamani's other tall tales.

Only four months earlier, in interviews with both *Time* magazine and the West German newspaper *Die Zeit*, he had complained vehemently about the existence of the oil glut, and more particularly about the size of the stockpiles held by the major oil companies. "If the oil companies and the governments concerned do not start reducing their oil depots," he observed darkly, "a heavy demand pressure will ensue on the speculative spot markets, the spot prices will soar, and the oil producers will not resist the temptation for long to drive the regular contract prices up…. The price will go to at least $60 per barrel…. I promise you that." To say the least, these are hardly the kind of sentiments one would expect to hear from the self-styled architect of the 1981 oil glut. But then consistency has never been the Saudi oil minister's strong suit.

The real reason for his unhappiness, as he revealed in an address at the University of Petroleum and Minerals at Dhahran on January 31, is that the Saudi royal house now realizes that it committed a blunder in engineering the enormous price increases of 1979-80. Having spurred the Western industrial countries to embark seriously upon the development of alternative energy supplies, the Saudis now face the nightmare of a declining demand for their oil and consequently a drastic reduction in their revenues. It is this prospect which haunts Yamani and his masters, and which drives them to try to reassert their ascendancy over the rest of OPEC. If they can bring the other members of the cartel to heel, they will be in a position to exercise some control over production levels, and to implement Yamani's long-term strategy for the annual augmentation of oil revenues by price increases of a size which will not antagonize or frighten off Western consumers.

If Yamani had confined himself in his public utterances, especially to Western audiences, to the exposition of these particular views, he might have made something of a plausible case. But he apparently finds it impossible to repress his fondness for gasconade. Thus, in his interview with the correspondent of *Die Zeit* alluded to earlier, he asserted that Saudi Arabia was producing more oil than was necessary to meet her financial requirements, solely as a "favour" to the West. "We can live quite comfortably with an extraction of five million barrels a day," he claimed blandly.

Not to put too fine a point on it, this is patently untrue. The total revenues of the Arab oil-producing states in 1980 were $209 billion, of which Saudi Arabia's share was about half. If her oil production were to be cut from more than ten million b/d to five million b/d, her revenues would fall to around £50 billion. But the Saudi government has only recently adopted a budget for 1981 of just under $90 billion. Income from investments is estimated at $15 billion per annum, which means that there would be a shortfall of about $25 billion in revenues for the current year. Obviously Saudi Arabia needs to produce a great deal more than five million b/d, and this is the sole reason why her oil production remains at a high level, just as the sole reason for the lower prices she charges is to enable her to sell her oil in greater quantities than her competitors in OPEC can sell theirs. (Saudi Arabia's sales have increased 3.7 per cent so far this year, while those of OPEC as a whole have declined 12.6 per cent.)

Yamani Unmasked

What is so endearing about Yamani is that occasionally he drops the mask of reasonableness and reveals his true feelings, and those of his masters, about the West. At the University of Khartoum this past March he spoke of Saudi Arabia's intention to use her oil to obtain "a massive transfer of technology from the industrial nations to the Third World." "The oil is not only a weapon in the Arab-Israeli conflict, it is also a weapon in the hands of the Third World to impose its will." To the correspondent of *Die Zeit* the previous December he spoke of securing from the Western world "a massive prosperity transfer for the development of the Third World."

"The West," he went on, "will never get a guarantee from us with regard to its oil supply without first handling the central problems of the Third World and leading them to a solution." But there was an even stronger, more deep-seated reason for the irritation he displayed during the interview. "The Moslems, Arabs as well as non-Arabs," he told his interviewer, "have suffered for a long time from the injustice and humiliations of the West. Their reaction led them in the past to the Left, to the Marxist ideology and toward leaning on the Soviets.... The reason for their leftist trend was not love for Marxism-Communism but hatred and rebellion against Western humiliations." Yamani terminated the interview with a final splenetic outburst: "You Western people are so stingy, egotistic, and greedy. You want to rule everything with your power. Oil is our wealth ... We hold the oil cards in our hand, but you put up such a dogged resistance and paint the future in the darkest colors because it does not belong solely to you anymore."

There is good cause for viewing the future darkly. OPEC's record for the past ten years and more has been one of deceit, rapacity, extortion, lies and a profound contempt for the sanctity of freely negotiated agreements. Saudi Arabia's behaviour, notwithstanding her prolonged and expensive propaganda campaign to the contrary, has been little better, if at all, than that of her fellow OPEC members. After an initial show of resistance to higher prices at every OPEC meeting, put on for the entertainment of impressionable Westerners, she has unfailingly raised her own oil prices before very long. However, this time it may be different.

Asked at the close of the OPEC meeting in May—at which the decision was taken to maintain prices at their previous level, despite the downward pressure being exerted by the oil glut—whether Saudi Arabia contemplated raising her oil prices closer to those of her fellow cartel-members. Yamani replied that an increase "is not on the agenda." His assurances were echoed by the Saudi deputy oil minister, Abdul Aziz Ibn Turki, a member of the ruling family, who stated: "In the absence of a unified price, we are going to stay at $32." In the past such assurances could confidently be regarded as a ritual prologue to a subsequent price increase. Now, however, with a surplus of oil on the world market, the Saudis may be forced, for a change, to live up to their promises. It is a prospect which we in the West can contemplate with cheerful fortitude.

39
The Oil Cringe of the West[1]

The nerveless acquiescence of the Western nations in the frequency of oil-price rises since the Tehran confrontation of 1971 has been prompted in the main by the hope that the acquiescence will gain them security of oil supplies. It will, of course, do nothing of the kind. All that continual surrender does is to strengthen the financial weapon in the economic armoury of the Middle-Eastern oil states. But there are even more insidious dangers to the West in the inexorable accumulation of great wealth by these states than the threat to its economic health. Because this wealth has been obtained without effort on the part of the states in question, it has had a profoundly corrupting influence upon their governments and upon numbers of their subjects, a corruption made all the more inevitable by the nature of Arab and Persian society. As greater riches are amassed, the process of corruption will intensify, hastening the spread of instability in Arabia, Persia and the Gulf. It is doubtful whether at any time in the history of mankind a group of intrinsically insignificant polities, at a comparatively primitive stage of economic, political and social development, has possessed such enormous financial power as the handful of Gulf states now dispose of. As the governments of the Gulf states are moved to employ this power for political and other purposes abroad, the corruption will spread beyond the Gulf, influencing and disturbing governments and societies in lands far removed from them in customs, culture and religion.

It is difficult, indeed impossible, to believe that the governments of Britain, France and the United States are not fully aware of the nature of the Middle-Eastern regimes with which they are treating and of the cor-

1 From *Quadrant*, July 1980. Reproduced by permission.

rupting effects which Arab and Persian oil money is having in Western society. This being so, their indifference to what is happening—one might almost say their encouragement of it—is presumably occasioned by fear and greed; fear of offending the Arabs and Persians lest they reduce oil supplies or raise oil prices; greed for the expenditure and investment of their oil revenues in the ailing economies of the West. How else is one to account for the obsequious contortions performed by British, French or American politicians and officials to ingratiate themselves with the rulers of the Gulf states and, until his fall, the shah? How else to interpret the insensibility of the British and French governments to the feelings of the citizens of London and Paris as they watch the more select parts of their cities being turned into Middle-Eastern caravanserais, bazaars and bagnios; or are forced to witness assassinations and gun-battles in their streets between warring Arab factions, whose presence in their capitals, along with arms and money with which they are amply furnished, has largely been made possible by the excessive oil revenues paid to the Arab oil states?

The lure of Arab and Persian oil money has also exerted its attraction outside Western financial and political circles. Its influence is discernible in publishing and journalism, in the professions, in the universities and learned societies, most of it unnoticed and unrealized by the Western public at large. Throughout the past decade, newspapers like *The Times*, *The Financial Times* and *Le Monde* have shown themselves increasingly ready to cater to the desire of Saudi Arabia and the petty states of the Gulf for self-esteem and self-advertisement by publishing a seemingly endless stream of supplements about the vigour, wisdom and capacity of the governments of these countries, the charm and talents of their peoples, the giant strides they are making towards the millennium, and the gratifyingly large sums of money they are spending in the process upon Western goods and services. The content of the articles which appear in these supplements, hemmed in by acres of advertising, is best passed over in silence. A reminder of what it is like, however, is not out of place here.

A special supplement on King Abdul Aziz University, Jiddah, put out by *The Times Higher Educational Supplement* in October, 1977, had this to say about the aims of this new seat of learning.

The main campus of King Abdul Aziz University one day ... will house one of the most prestigious centres of learning in the Middle East—and, it is hoped, the world. Named after the charismatic monarch who earlier this century welded the ancient warring tribes of Arabia into today's modern nation state, its expansion is really taking off.

Airborne himself on a flight of rhetoric, the *Times* correspondent goes on to enthuse over "the Master Plan" to spend £3,000 million on buildings and equipment, the recruitment of a distinguished academic staff ("in large numbers from Europe and North America: salaries are high and this is reflected in the quality of applicants") and the high standards of scholarship students will be expected to attain. The presiding genius over all this, the correspondent informs us, is "Sheikh Ahmad Salah Jamjoom, one of the founding fathers of the university," who is "keenly concerned about the preservation of quality during expansion. He is insistent that the flood of students and staff into the university should not water down the ideals of academic excellence. The university is aiming to ensure undergraduate excellence by laying down tight entry qualifications...." Nor is this the limit of Sheikh Jamjoom's vision. "Knowledge must not only serve society: it must also serve good," he told his interlocutor from *The Times*, who himself goes on to embroider the theme rather richly in the concluding sentences of his article.

> The Muslim would in general and Saudi Arabia in particular sees the wealth generated by the oil bonanza as a chance to reverse the eclipse by the west of learning. They are convinced of the possibility of developing highly sophisticated systems of, for example, "Islamic" social science, "Islamic" economics, "Islamic" medicine and even "Islamic" mathematics. The aim is the creation of a new Islamic Golden Age of culture and learning: Islam with a modern face. The de-westernization of knowledge is the first central task of the enterprise.

It is not only the savants and schoolmen of Saudi Arabia who see "the wealth generated by the oil bonanza as a chance to reverse the eclipse by the west of learning." A number of ambitious academics and administrators in universities and other institutions of learning in Europe and North America have also had their glimpse of El Dorado and made for it hotfoot. Sums of money, some of them of considerable proportions, have been solicited from the oil shaikhs and the court of the "Shadow of God upon earth" for the establishment or expansion of programmes of Arab, Persian and Islamic studies in France, Britain, Canada and the United States. Georgetown University in Washington, a Jesuit foundation, has accepted, without any evident misgivings, several hundred thousand dollars of Arab oil money for the establishment of a chair of Islamic and Arabic studies. The donor is the government of Libya, the head of which, as is well known, is a fanatical Muslim, a supporter of terrorist movements and one of the principal paymasters of the Muslim *fidaiyin* who lately endeavoured to crush the Latin Christian community in the Lebanon. At institutions as different as McGill University in Montreal and the University of Exeter in Devon there are now chairs or lectureships in "Arabian Gulf studies," endowed by one or another of the lesser Gulf governments. Indeed, it would almost seem as if Edward Gibbon's musings two centuries ago upon what might have been, had the Arab armies not been halted at Poitiers a thousand years earlier, were more of a prophetic than a visionary nature. "Perhaps the interpretation of the Koran would now be taught in the schools of Oxford, and her pulpits might demonstrate to a circumcised people the sanctity and truth of the revelation of Mahomet."

One could go on listing the ancient and modern foundations in the Old World and the New, some members of which have been driven by the *auri sacra fames* to curry favour with the oil potentates of the Middle East by paying exaggerated deference to Islamic history and culture (not to mention "Islamic" social sciences and "Islamic" economics); but the exercise would be as depressing as it would be futile. The only point to be made is that the rulers of the Arab oil states are neither simple philanthropists nor disinterested patrons of the humanities. They expect a return upon their donations to institutions of learning and their subsidies to publishing houses; whether it be in the form of subtle propaganda on behalf of Arab or Islamic causes, or the preferential admission of their nationals, however unqualified, to Western universities and colleges, or the publication of the kind of sycophantic flim-flam about themselves and their countries which now clutters sections of the Western press and even respectable periodical literature.

If the peoples of the West do not take heed of what is happening and act to halt it, they will inevitably suffer a debasement of their national lives, standards and institutions from the penetration of their societies by Arab and Persian oil money. It is worth recalling in this connection that Muslim jurisprudence views the world in uncompromising terms, dividing it arbitrarily into the *dar al-Islam* (Muslim territory) and the *dar al-harb* (hostile territory), of which Western Christendom is the principal constituent. Between these two territorial entities there can exist only a state of active warfare or a condition of latent hostility. If the West continues in its present abject and infirm posture towards the Arabs and the Persians, it may well contribute a third category to the Islamic order—the *dar al-abid*, or land of slaves.

How and when in the past two decades the Western world's indifference to the retention of strategic control over its Middle-Eastern sources of oil took root is not readily determinable; although there is little doubt that it was the consequence, as Correlli Barnett has remarked, "of following Keynes instead of Clausewitz" in the formulation of Western policy towards the Middle-Eastern oil states. The erosion of British and French power in the Middle East went hand in hand with—indeed, was in large measure the direct consequence of—the growth of a debilitating conviction that the tides of history were flowing against the exercise by Western Europe of any power beyond its shores; that in the Middle East the Arabs' and Persians' hour had come; and that the whole question of access to oil was a purely commercial matter of supply and demand, an outlook summed up by the fashionable precept of the day, "the Arabs cannot drink their oil."

With the departure of Britain from the Gulf at the close of 1971 the last pretence of maintaining any kind of physical hold over sources of supply was abandoned. Henceforth, Britain, France, Western Europe in general, and Japan would have to rely for the bulk of their oil supplies upon the goodwill of the Gulf oil states and (to whatever extent it might prove effective) upon the influence and authority wielded in the area by the United States. The United States, however, as has already been observed, had entrusted the care of its strategic oil interests to the Arabian-American Oil Company, and ARAMCO had proved unequal to the trust when put to the test in October 1973. So the United States is now in much the same case as Western Europe and Japan, with no security of access to the oil reserves of the Gulf beyond what she can obtain by pursuing the hazardous policy, bequeathed to her by ARAMCO, of identifying herself and her interests with the present Saudi regime.

Now and for some years to come, Western Europe and Japan must draw their major supplies of oil from an area of extreme political instability, relying for the uninterrupted continuance of these supplies upon the good faith and good sense of regimes notorious for their fickle and contentious behaviour. It is not a comforting thought. The Middle-Eastern members of OPEC have broken almost every agreement they have entered into since 1970, whether it was the Libyan settlement in September of that year, or the Tehran agreement in February 1971, or the Geneva formula for the adjustment of prices against the international value of the dollar, or the provisions for the extension of the 1954 Persian consortium agreement, or the timetables for the implementation of participation, or the prices at which the oil companies could buy back participation crude. Nearly every pledge by an Arab oil state not to use oil as a political weapon has been dishonoured, nearly every undertaking to reduce oil prices or moderate price increases has been broken. In contrast, almost every threat to restrict or embargo the shipment of oil, to reduce production or to raise oil prices has been carried out. It is a sorry record.

For Western Europe to have abandoned all vestige of strategic control over its major sources of oil is folly enough; but to compound this folly by offering further hostages to fortune in the shape of earnest predictions about oil shortages, embargoes and price rises to come can only be construed as evidence of a profoundly felt death-wish. Yet this is exactly what Western governments and the garrulous tribe of Western pundits have been doing for some time now, apparently oblivious of the part played by similar predictions in bringing about the OPEC offensive in the autumn of 1973. Whether oil shortages will occur in the years ahead it is beyond the power of anyone to predict with utter certainty. Much will depend upon the discovery and exploitation of new oil reserves, upon the rate of depletion of the known ones, upon the levels of oil consumption in the industrial and non-industrial countries of the world, upon the development of alternative sources of energy and the increased utilization of existing ones—in short, upon a long list of variable and even unforeseeable factors.

What can be said with some assurance is that it is unwise in the extreme for the West to shape its current policy towards OPEC upon the basis of hypothetical oil shortages in the future. To do so is to play straight into the cartel's hands, allowing it to manipulate the West for its own political and financial purposes. Whether OPEC, and its Middle-Eastern members in particular, has the power and the skill to go on accomplishing these purposes is again dependent upon a number of variable circumstances which it would require a book in itself to examine properly. Here we can do no more than glance at a few of them.

Reduced demand for oil after the price rises late in 1973 caused a slight drop in production world-wide in 1974, and a bigger drop of 5.4 per cent in 1975, the first of this magnitude since 1942. The fall in OPEC's production in 1975 was much larger—12 per cent, with Venezuela (21.3 per cent), Nigeria (20.9 per cent) and Kuwait (19.2 per cent) suffering the heaviest losses. Iraq, in contrast, raised her output by 12.8 per cent, mainly through price-cutting. While there has been some recovery in world consumption since 1975, it has not returned to the average annual increase recorded in the years 1955-73, *viz.* 7 per cent, but has persisted at around 1 per cent. With new oil discoveries coming on-stream (North Sea, Alaska,

Mexico), the result has been a net decline in consumption, and therefore production, of OPEC oil. So many fluctuations in the production of Middle-Eastern oil have occurred in the past five years that it is impossible to discern any significant pattern to them. Producers of heavy and high sulphur crudes like Persia, Kuwait and Saudi Arabia seem to have suffered the largest falls, though in the case of Saudi Arabia the fall has been mitigated by other circumstances. Some of the fluctuations were caused by the oil companies stock-piling in advance of expected price increases, as was the case before the OPEC meeting in Dauhah in December 1976 where prices were raised by 10 per cent. Others, however, can only be attributed to falling demand. Thus, Saudi Arabia's production in the first six months of 1978 was down 17.5 per cent on that of the comparable period in 1977. Persia's production was down 7 per cent in the first quarter of 1978 on that of the first quarter of 1977. Kuwait was 36 per cent down in January 1978 on January 1977, and 40 per cent down in February 1978 on the previous February.

It would be unwise to read much into these figures: as just remarked, there is more confusion than clarity in the recent pattern of oil production in the Middle East. What is fairly clear is that the fall in production and the decline in value of the US dollar means that only three states, Saudi Arabia, Kuwait and Abu Dhabi, can count upon a continuing surplus of revenue over expenditure in the immediate future, and even this surplus is diminishing—or it was until the oil-price increases of 1979. What this portends is as unpredictable as most occurrences in the Middle East, although Kuwait, as in other instances, may well prove to be the bellwether.

Up to 1973 Kuwait's oil production ran at roughly 3 million b/d. By the end of 1974 it had dropped to 2.5 million b/d, and Kuwait had become the leading proponent of "conservation" as a means of extending the productive life of its oilfields and of maximizing the financial return on oil exports. The final nationalization of the Kuwait Oil Company (jointly owned by BP and Gulf) took place in December 1975, and even before then the Kuwait government had imposed a ceiling of 2 million b/d on production. It proved to be a flexible ceiling: late in 1976 production was averaging 3.3 million b/d as the companies stockpiled before the Dauhah meeting of OPEC in December. Therefore production dropped to 1.3 million b/d early in 1976, recovering to 2 million b/d by the middle of 1977. A further fall, as we have seen, occurred in the early months of 1978. The effect of this stagnation, which should have gladdened the hearts of the Kuwaiti "conservationists," was to provoke insistent calls from the Kuwait government in the late summer and early autumn of 1978 for an increase in oil prices.

Although it was a call calculated to arouse a natural response in the breasts of the other members of OPEC, things were not quite as they had been five years earlier, nor was "conservation" the tactical weapon it had once promised to be. Demand for oil was still depressed, selling prices were well below posted prices, the depreciation in the value of the dollar had further reduced real income, and most of OPEC's members were having difficulty in covering their expenditures out of current revenue. Several, in fact, had either contracted, or were actively seeking, loans to cover their deficits. On the face of it, a price increase seemed only logical as a means of recovering lost financial ground. Yet there were sufficient imponderables in the situation to induce caution. A price rise could lead to a further drop in consumption, to a reduction of economic activity in the Western industrial countries, to a fresh decline in the value of the dollar and, at the end of the day, to diminished oil revenues. Even the adoption of proposals which had long been floating about to end the system of fixing posted prices in dollars and to peg them instead to a "basket" of strong currencies might not alter the outcome.

"Conservation" was an equally sterile option. In the case of Kuwait, for instance, an absolute minimum of 1.5 million b/d of oil had to be produced to provide sufficient associated gas to run the shaikhdom's utilities, including the electricity needed for the thousands of air-conditioners to which the Kuwaitis had become addicted, OPEC's main problem, in any case, was to sell its oil in quantities and at prices sufficient to meet its members' current financial needs, rather than to conserve it as an asset for the future, an asset which might well turn out to be largely illusory. It was a problem which weighed more heavily upon countries like Persia, Algeria and Iraq, with large populations and ambitious programmes of modernization, than it did upon sparsely populated countries with limited potential for development, like Saudi Arabia, Libya and Abu Dhabi. A glut of oil on the market, as existed at the first half of 1978, could well have led the two groups to compete for buyers, thereby straining the unity of OPEC and perhaps even endangering its whole structure.

From this cheerless prospect the organization was rescued by the revolution in Persia in the autumn of 1978 which eventually unseated the shah and established a republic of sorts. Persian oil production dropped rapidly in the last two months of the year, from 5.2 million b/d to less than 0.5 million b/d and then ceased altogether for a time at the turn of the year. As usual, the industrial nations of the world panicked at the thought of an oil shortage, forgetting overnight that there had been a surplus of oil on the market only a short time previously, and that spare producing capacity had been some 5 million b/d, roughly equivalent to the normal output from Persia. A much relieved OPEC convened at Abu Dhabi in mid-December 1978 where it proceeded to wring what advantage it could from the changed situation. The posted price of the marker crude, standard Arabian light, was raised by 14.5 per cent, the increase to be imposed in four stages, commencing with 5 per cent on 1 January 1979, when the price would rise from $13.66 to $14.34 per barrel.

Western reaction to the increase was generally passive, being conditioned, as OPEC had intended it should, by the fact that the new price was to take effect in stages. The mildness of the reaction, together with the predictable cries of alarm about a looming oil shortage which issued from the usual pack of Western soothsayers, persuaded the magnates of OPEC that they were foolish to content themselves with a finger when an arm was theirs for the taking. One after another they proceeded to add surcharges of a dollar or more a barrel to the price of their oil until eventually, at an extraordinary session of OPEC called in the last week of March 1979, the organization resolved to bring forward the full increase for the year of 14.5 per cent to 1 April. What was perhaps more significant than OPEC's readiness to exploit any opportunity to raise prices was the abandonment of all pretence at regulating the official selling prices (as posted prices were now called) charged by individual members for their oil. All states, as the official communiqué delicately phrased it, were entitled to levy whatever surcharges or premiums "they deem justifiable in the light of their own circumstances." What this meant in practice was that, on top of the usual premiums for specific gravity, geographic location and other differentials, every member country was at liberty to impose whatever additional charge it wished.

A free-for-all followed, which entered its manic phase in May when price leap-frogging took place on almost a daily basis. Some peculiar incidents occurred of which the Western public was mostly unaware. The revolutionary government in Tehran demanded that BP and Shell pay *pishkesh*, in the form of the obligatory purchase of a quantity of Persian oil at spot market prices (up to $35.00 a barrel), if they wanted to qualify for six or twelve months' contracts, and then in late June it tore up the contracts it had signed, even though they were supposed to run to the end of the year. The Algerian government increased the price of its crude to $21.00 a barrel in the third week of May in direct violation of its contracts with the oil companies, which stipulated that prices could only be raised at quarterly intervals unless OPEC had authorized a mid-quarter increase, which it had not. To get around this obstacle the Algerians asked for the voluntary compliance of the companies with the increase, adding pointedly that if it was not forthcoming, oil prices would be revised at the outset of the next quarter in such a way as to compensate Algeria for any loss of potential revenue she might have suffered in the interim. There were also moments of light relief, such as that afforded by the oil minister of Abu Dhabi and the UAE, and current president of OPEC, who solemnly averred on 9 May:

> Although the market can now justify more or less any size of increase in crude oil prices owing to the current imbalance between supply and demand, nevertheless I think we should not go for any further price increases this year…. This is a duty we have to fulfil.

Eight days later Abu Dhabi raised the official selling price of her oil by a further 80 cents a barrel.

At its semi-annual conference in Geneva in the last week of June 1979 OPEC unblushingly ratified the results of the prices free-for-all of the preceding quarter. Saudi Arabia, which had for the most part kept her prices steady since April, agreed to raise the price of the marker crude, standard Arabian light, to $18.00 a barrel. To recover some of the revenue she had lost in the interim, the increase was made retrospective to 1 June and the period allowed for payment of purchases of Saudi crude, hitherto sixty days, was reduced to thirty days. The Persian delegation, perhaps unhinged by revolutionary zeal, promptly raised the price of Persian light crude, customarily pegged at 11 cents above the price of Arabian light, to $21.00 a barrel, thereby creating in effect a second Gulf marker price. All the delegates were agreed that in the prevailing condition of the market their governments were entitled to impose a surcharge of $2.00 a barrel on the Saudi marker price, and to charge whatever they saw fit for quality and geographic location premiums, up to a ceiling price of $23.00 a barrel. With the sole exception of Saudi Arabia every member state imposed the surcharge from 1 July, and, where applicable, the quality and location premiums. The effect was to bring the average price increase for a barrel of OPEC oil for the six months since December 1978 to an aggregate of 65 per cent, with Iraq (71 per cent), Libya (69 per cent) and Algeria (67 per cent) leading the field, and Saudi Arabia (42 per cent) trailing well behind. Such was the volume of Saudi Arabian production, however, that the Saudi government would be the principal financial beneficiary of the price increases. The total revenues of OPEC, which had been in the vicinity of

$140,000 million in 1978, were expected to exceed $200,000 million in 1979.

Although the combined price increases of the first half of 1979 were by far the highest that had occurred since the quadrupling oil prices late in 1973, they failed to elicit from the Western world any response other than a sustained bout of indignant bleating. The finance ministers of the OECD, meeting in Paris in the middle of June 1979, could propose no solution to the severe economic problems which the price increases would create for the industrial nations other than to say that their peoples should resign themselves to a lower standard of living. Just how excessive a price increase is needed to provoke some real resistance from the Western powers and Japan there is no way of knowing: their submissiveness seems boundless. However, should the improbable occur and they should find the modicum of courage required to resist some particularly outrageous demand, what measures could the Middle Eastern members of OPEC adopt to force the West to resume its habitual obedient posture? The obvious ones are a reduction in output and the imposition of an embargo, probably under cover of redress for some political grievance or other to give it a spurious respectability. A reduction in output, needless to say, depends for its effectiveness upon the state of the market and the level of world consumption at the time. It also calls for the exercise by the Arab oil states of a degree of self-restraint and disciplined co-operation which, on the evidence of their past showing, they may not be capable of attaining.

It has been estimated that it would take a cut-back in oil production by the Arab oil states of 60 per cent for a period of six months to exhaust the present IEA stockpiles. The loss of revenues which the Arab governments could expect to suffer as a consequence of such a cut-back would be formidable enough to make some of them, at least, hesitate before committing themselves to this course. On the basis of their output and revenues for 1976, for example, it has been reckoned that a 60 per cent loss of earnings for six months would have amounted in the case of Saudi Arabia to around $10,000 million, in those of Kuwait and Iraq to about $2,600 million each, and that of Abu Dhabi to $2,000 million. The loss to Persia, on the basis of her production and revenues for the same year, would have been about $6,600 million. Obviously, with the higher oil prices obtaining in the summer of 1979, the loss of revenue would be correspondingly greater, perhaps by as much as 50 per cent. While the richer oil states might be able to bear the strain, the less wealthy and more populous could not. Nor would the richer states' clients (notably Syria, Jordan and the various Palestinian organizations) forgo their accustomed subsidies with good grace.

That the Arab members of OPEC would have to resort to such extremes to secure the acquiescence of the West in any price rise is, however, highly unlikely. The inevitability of continual price rises is now accepted by the West with much the same fatalism as that with which an Australian aborigine, at whom the bone has been pointed, accepts the certainty of impending death. Indeed, most public commentators on the subject go further and take a perverse pleasure in enumerating the economic tribulations which are about to be visited upon the sinful and self-indulgent West by the avenging angel of OPEC.

Ahmad Zaki al-Yamani and the country he serves are the principal focus of Western hopes, fears and speculations about oil supplies and prices. The Saudi oil minister's comings and goings about the world are devoutly chronicled by the Western press, his every utterance reverently recorded and sifted for hidden significance as if he were the Pythian oracle. Yamani, in his turn, has played the role assigned him with great verve, ceaselessly girdling the earth like a fretful Puck, scattering golden promises of price reductions and unfettered supplies, intermingled with dark allusions to possible embargoes and restrictions—and simultaneous assurances that they are a thing of the past.

> My conscience hath a thousand several tongues,
> And every tongue brings in a several tale …..

Yamani has been allowed to get away with this mixture of blague and gasconade for so many years that he must long ago have concluded that the West has taken leave of its senses. Not only are none of his protestations and admonitions ever challenged but instead they are accorded the utmost respect and credence. Thus, when he haughtily proclaimed in an interview on French television at the end of May 1979,

> You had a lesson in 1973 and you learned nothing from it. Now there is another lesson, and you are trying to avoid the meaning of this lesson in the West.

His interviewer practically fell off his chair in his eagerness to prostrate himself and to crave the oracle's forgiveness.

It is the same with Yamani's melodramatic performances as the incarnation of sweet reason and gracious moderation at the conferences of OPEC. When, for instance, at the Dauhah meeting in December 1976 he refused, amid scenes of high emotion, to commit Saudi Arabia to the 10 per cent increase in oil prices adopted by the majority of OPEC, the Western world rang with jubilant encomiums to the new Horatius who had defied the fearsome ranks of Tuscany and saved the treasuries of the West from spoliation. When the tumult had subsided it emerged that the 5 per cent increase with which Saudi Arabia and the UAE had declared themselves satisfied worked out in practice at 7½ per cent, while the 10 per cent which the cads in OPEC had insisted upon would be reduced by market conditions to 8½ per cent. What is more, Saudi Arabia and Abu Dhabi greatly increased their oil production in the first six months of 1977, at the expense of their partners in OPEC, so as to offset the slightly lower prices they were receiving for their oil. Then, on 1 July 1977, they quietly raised their prices the full 10 per cent to bring themselves into line with the rest of OPEC.

However captious and overweening Yamani may be—and he is by no means as captious and overweening as some of his ministerial colleagues in OPEC—he is by virtue of what others, and particularly ARAMCO and its parent companies, have made him. In evidence before the sub-committee on multinational corporations of the Senate Foreign Relations Committee in June 1974, a former chairman of Standard Oil of California, Otto Miller, gave this reply when the chairman of the sub-committee asked whether, if the political situation in the Middle East became inflamed, the Arabs might not again cut off oil supplies to the industrial nations, regardless of the consequences to themselves:

> They would do almost anything …. You are completely at their mercy and that is why I have always felt that it is extremely important to have friendly relationships with those countries….

It was a view commonly elicited from representatives of the major American oil companies who testified before the sub-committee. Behind it lay the tacit admission that the companies regarded the governments of the Arab oil states as both wilful and mercurial slaves of suspicion and emotion, whose words and actions alike were unreliable and unpredictable. The only way to handle them, so the companies had long ago concluded, was as one would treat fractious children, by indulging their whims, feeding their vanity and abstaining from provocation. That there are other and more beneficial ways of treating fractious children than by the tactics which the companies have employed (and which have been largely responsible for bringing them to their present unhappy and precarious situation *vis-à-vis* the governments in question) is a possibility which the companies would seem to have contemplated only for as long as it took them to reject it. The record of their negotiations with OPEC since 1970, with a few short-lived exceptions, only reinforces this conclusion.

Saudi Arabia occupies a central place in the counter-strategy which the Western powers, and the United States in particular, have adopted in an endeavour to ensure stability of oil supplies and prices. The key element is the size of the Saudi Arabian oil reserves, and the extent to which production from them can be raised, both to meet the oil requirements of the industrial countries and to frustrate any moves by the rest of OPEC to raise prices. The success of the counter-strategy (the implementation of which is closely bound up with the Saudi-American "special relationship") depends to a considerable extent upon the correct answers—"correct," that is, from the stand-point of the West—being given to a number of questions.

Does Saudi Arabia actually possess, or will she possess in the immediate future, the requisite spare producing capacity? Is she willing to act as "residual supplier" in the Western interest, boosting her production, if required, to prevent the rest of OPEC from threatening a cut-back or even a shut-down as a means of forcing up the price of oil? Conversely, will she act as "residual supplier" in OPEC's interest, lowering her output whenever a glut occurs on the market so as to enable those members of OPEC with the greatest need for revenue (Algeria, Persia, etc) to keep up their oil exports as well as to prevent a fall in oil prices? Or, again, will Saudi Arabia simply consult her own interests, primarily if not exclusively, and adjust her production of oil to her own financial and political desiderata?

Even without the constraints imposed by the Saudi government and the problem of raising the large amounts of capital necessary to finance future development of the oilfields, the fields themselves present formidable technical obstacles, which there is not space to describe here, to the expansion of Saudi Arabian oil production. Accidents like the Abqaiq fire, or unforeseeable Acts of God, moreover, underline the risks of basing Western policy upon predictions of future Saudi production levels. But there are other reasons for casting doubt upon the willingness or ability of Saudi Arabia to act as "residual supplier" in the Western interest, particularly in order to keep oil prices down.

Despite numerous promises of price reductions, usually conveyed through the mouth of Yamani, the price of oil has continued to rise and it has done so, however much the Saudis and their Western apologists may endeavour to camouflage the fact, with Saudi encouragement. William Simon, the United States secretary of the treasury, told the Senate sub-committee on multi-national corporations in July 1974 that Yamani had assured him that an auction of Saudi Arabian oil would be held the following month, the intention of the Saudi government being to demonstrate that the real market price of oil was well below its posted price, and thereby to induce the other OPEC governments to lower it. The auction never took place. Asked by the sub-committee in May 1976 why it had not, James Akins (who had been the American ambassador to Saudi Arabia at the time) explained that there was opposition to the move from within the Saudi government as well as from Persia, Iraq and Algeria. Because the United States government did not pursue the matter, Akins added, Yamani and his masters concluded that it was not really interested in bringing down oil prices. It is a pretty tale, its only flaw being that it omits to mention that a short time later, at an OPEC meeting in Abu Dhabi in November 1974, Yamani took the lead in pushing through a further price increase which was completely unwarranted by prevailing circumstances.

Two months later Saudi Arabia reduced her output of oil from 8.5 million to 7.6 million b/d. A further cut, to 6.5 million b/d was made the following month, February 1975, and for the same reason, *viz.* to prevent a glut in the oil market, which was then in a depressed state as a result of the economic depression in many industrial countries. To what degree the major companies may have co-operated in implementing this policy it is difficult to determine. The companies themselves maintain that monthly production levels are determined by market conditions, and that the market for oil early in 1975 was slack. There was no point, therefore, in producing at a higher level than the market warranted, as excess production entailed additional costs, not least in transport and storage charges. Yet the fact remains that the cuts in Saudi Arabian output in 1975 were ordered by the Saudi government and carried into effect by ARAMCO, even though the Saudis' motives in ordering them were transparently clear, *viz.* to prevent the latest price increase from being undermined by price-cutting in a buyer's market, and to allow the other members of OPEC a sufficient share of the market so as not to tempt them into discounting their oil in order to sell it. All could then expect to benefit from the latest price increase when demand picked up.

At first glance, Saudi Arabia's actions in 1975 would appear to indicate that if she is to play the role of residual supplier at all, she will do so in OPEC's interests, not the West's; and substance is lent to this view by Yamani's frequently repeated claims in the past that Saudi Arabia's financial needs could be met by a daily production of 4.5 million barrels.

Yet the situation is not quite as clear-cut as this. When world demand for oil fell in 1976 and 1977 Saudi Arabia increased her production, from 7.1 million b/d in 1975 to 8.5 million b/d in 1976 and to roughly 9 million b/d for the first six months of 1977. Together, Saudi Arabia and the UAE (*i.e.* principally Abu Dhabi) increased their oil exports in 1976 and 1977 by 120 million tonnes, while all the other Arab oil states combined increased their exports by 30 million tonnes. Saudi Arabia, in other words, at a time when demand was slack, raised her production as she saw fit, kept oil prices steady and increased her share of the market at the expense of her Arab partners in OPEC. Her conduct has been a repetition of what it was in 1971 and 1972, when she raised her output by 26 per cent in both years while that of Iraq, Libya and Algeria declined. That she intends to go on this way was indicated by the loquacious Yamani in September 1977, when he warned that Saudi Arabia would not increase her production above 8.5 million b/d to meet the industrial world's needs unless some progress was made towards a settlement of the Arab-Israeli dispute. As production at that time was 7.65 million b/d the warning did not carry a great deal of weight.

An even stronger pointer to Saudi Arabia's intended policy was the condition laid down by the Saudi government, in its negotiations with ARAMCO for the complete nationalization of the company's concession and assets, that the company should lift a minimum of 7 million b/d of Saudi oil. "Significant" penalties would be imposed if ARAMCO's off-take fell below this figure, which was equivalent to 20-25 per cent of OPEC's total average daily output in 1976 and 1977. Yamani's nonchalant pretence that 4.5 or even 4 million b/d is sufficient to meet Saudi Arabia's financial needs is plainly a thing of the past. The Saudi government's appetite for revenue has grown in direct proportion to its lavish expenditure and the soaring costs of its current five-year development programme. The sum of $28,400 million per annum originally budgeted for the implementation of the programme has proved grossly inadequate. The oil revenues for 1978 were in the vicinity of $34,000 million, which at prices current in that year represented an output of around 8.4 million b/d, (ARAMCO's average production for 1978 is said to have been 8.1 million b/d. Production from Saudi Arabia's share of the former Saudi-Kuwaiti neutral zone averaged 300,000 b/d). Perhaps as much as $20,000 million per annum more is needed to carry out the development programme in its original form. Where is the money to come from? Increased production of any significant dimensions seems out of the question, for the reasons already adverted to, including the fluctuating state of the market. To trim the programme to fit the financial cloth would require sweeping economies of expenditure upon industrial development, the armed services, the bureaucracy, education and other social services, economies which could not fail to produce adverse effects, especially in terms of political unrest. The only alternative, it would seem, is to seek higher oil prices.

All the indications are that the Saudi government intends to continue to impose restraints upon oil production so as to prolong the technical life of the fields—which in turn implies that it will seek to raise prices at intervals in order to maintain revenues at a desired level. The only way to achieve this aim is through the survival of the OPEC cartel, which is why Saudi Arabia, one of the principal founders of the organization, will strive to ensure its survival. How much, if at all, her "special relationship" with the United States may hamper her pursuit of these aims has yet to be seen. Her equally special relationship with ARAMCO is unlikely to act as a brake upon her activities and ambitions, even though the Saudi government sorely needs the company's assistance, not only to operate its oil industry but also as an instrument with which to regulate or manipulate the volume of oil on the market, and its price. Under the terms that have so far been revealed of the arrangements worked out between the Saudis and ARAMCO for the continued operation of the Saudi oil industry, ARAMCO will remain a wholly American-owned services company, responsible for producing operations, exploration and development, as well as for marketing Saudi Arabian oil through its parent companies. Ownership of the oil reserves and the company's physical assets in Saudi Arabia, TAPline excepted, passes to the Saudi government, which will also control output, as it has done for some years past.

Much the same relationship has been established between the governments of the other Arab oil states and the companies operating in their territories. The companies' concessions and assets have been fully nationalized, or, if the companies have been permitted to retain a minority shareholding (as is the case, for instance, in Abu Dhabi), it is because the local government is reluctant to assume responsibility for matters beyond its competence to handle. (Because of the dearth of competent local personnel the Abu Dhabi National Oil Company is in effect run by Algerians, who may be counted upon, whenever the occasion warrants it, to find trumped-up reasons for restricting production). Whatever the case, the companies have placed themselves at the service of the Gulf oil states, regulating oil production on their behalf and raising prices at their behest.

Rivalry between the companies themselves nowadays takes less the form of competition for a larger share of the world market in oil than that

337

of a contest for long-term contracts with the Gulf oil states and preferential terms of access to their reserves of crude. Until very recently the companies were wont to justify their progressive submission to the dictates of the governments of these states by arguing that their concessions, however much they might be modified by each successive participation agreement, still gave them access, albeit in ever diminishing degree, to their own reserves of crude. Now even this flimsy justification is denied them, and all that the companies have to fall back upon by way of excuse for their unfailing deference to the wishes of the governments of the Arab oil states is that it allows them privileged access to government-owned crude. It is a dubious privilege, as the companies know full well. For not only can it be revoked in an instant, at the whim of any one of these governments, but it has also been obtained at very high cost, *viz.* the abdication by the companies of their prime responsibility to their customers, the oil-consuming countries. This abdication, and the drastic diminution of their power over the past decade, has left the companies virtual prisoners of the Arab oil states.

Further tribulations doubtless lie in store for them. They may be forced, after the precedent set by the Saudi government in its negotiations with ARAMCO, to lift a minimum quantity of crude, whatever the state of the market. As the price of their preferential access to crude, they may be required—and some companies already have been—to enter into partnership with the host government (even to put up the major part of the capital needed) in huge and expensive schemes of industrialization, most, though not all, of them related to the oil industry, whose chances of economic success are problematical in the extreme.

The Gulf oil states have made no secret of the fact that they intend to move more and more into the "downstream" operations of the oil industry, to build more refineries, petro-chemical plants and other associated facilities in their own countries, to transport and market abroad crude oil, gas and refined products. In short, they are bent upon extending their control over the world oil market by expansion into the secondary and tertiary sectors. There is little chance that the Gulf oil states could compete on even terms in the market for refined products.

The cost of building and operating refineries, petro-chemical plants and petroleum-related facilities in the Gulf is far higher than it is in the industrial countries. So also is the cost of transporting refined products as compared with that of shipping crude oil in bulk. Unless the governments of the oil states are prepared to sustain large losses on their investments, the prices they will have to charge for their refined products will make them uncompetitive. Faced with this unpalatable conclusion, they may well resort to intimidation to dispose of their unwanted output, by making it a condition of continued access to their reserves of crude that the oil companies accept a certain proportion of their off-take in refined products—and transport them in host-government flag vessels.

How the oil companies view their present situation *vis-à-vis* the Arab oil states it is impossible to deduce from their rare and excessively sibylline utterances on the subject. It is hard to believe that they are content with it or that they are not apprehensive about the future. Perhaps it would be no bad thing, as some qualified observers have suggested, if the companies were to withdraw completely from direct operations in the Arab producing countries. After all, they have lost their *raison d'être* for being in these countries, *viz.* ownership of the oil reserves. If they were to become simply purchases of the crude at the pierhead, they could use their position as world-wide distributors of oil to negotiate sensible prices, instead of merely bowing to the caprices of the governments of the oil states and passing on arbitrary price rises to the consumers. The obvious drawback to this course of action is that the national oil companies which these governments have set up to assume ostensible control over oil production and "downstream" activities in their countries are, most of them, incapable of running the oil industry by themselves. Unless the Western oil companies were to provide the necessary engineers and technical staff, they would quickly run the industry into the sand.

However chimerical the "partnership" between the oil companies and the governments of the Arab oil states has become, the West in general is still relying upon it to ensure security of oil supplies and stability of prices. The IEA apart, the Western governments have made no real effort to co-ordinate their oil policies or to present a united front to OPEC. Instead, they are pursuing separate and often conflicting national policies, three of the worst offenders being the United States, Britain and France. The United States virtually doubled its importation of oil between 1973 and 1976, while that of most Western European countries remained constant or even declined. Oil imports into the United States in 1978 were 29 per cent higher than in 1975, and 46 per cent of the total volume of oil imported came from the Arab oil states, an increase from this source of 83 per cent over the previous year. The picture did not alter appreciably in 1977 and 1978. While some of the oil was acquired to build up a strategic oil reserve, too great a portion of it was simply consumed in profligate domestic use. It is really little short of scandalous that the United States should consume so disproportionate a share as she does of the oil produced in the world each year, and it is equally reprehensible that as the senior partner in the Atlantic Alliance she should have ignored the economic and strategic interests of Western Europe in committing herself to a comprehensive arrangement with Saudi Arabia over oil, the implications of which may well prove formidable. Britain likewise has shown a cynical indifference to the welfare of her European partners and allies by the restrictive practices she has followed with respect to the extraction and disposition of oil from the North Sea fields, and by insisting upon the maintenance of a substantial minimum price for it. It is wholly against the interest of Western Europe, and still more of that of the poorer countries of the world, that oil prices should remain at their present high levels.

OPEC is not a monolith. Its thirteen members—Algeria, Iraq, Kuwait, Libya, Qatar, Saudi Arabia, UAE, Persia, Nigeria, Indonesia, Venezuela, Ecuador and Gabon—all have divergent ambitions and requirements; none is the natural partner of the others, not even its Arab members. The very diversity of its membership, and the inevitable tensions that will arise now that the OPEC governments have taken full control of oil production, make the cartel vulnerable to disruption. Until recently the Western oil companies have served as a buffer to reduce or absorb potential causes of friction among the cartel's members. They still serve this function, although to a diminishing extent. They could, if they wished, abandon it altogether. As the natural antipathies among OPEC's member governments assert themselves, which they are bound to, the façade of unity will crack, particularly among the Middle-Eastern states. The entire course of Middle-Eastern history testifies to such an outcome. The day when the cartel disintegrates, however, will not be hastened by the Western powers continuing to adopt towards OPEC the posture of the rabbit faced with the stoat. If they act instead in unison to exploit the organization's patent vulnerability, using the diversity of economic and political weapons at their disposal and playing upon the antagonisms that divide OPEC's members, they will accomplish both the break-up of the cartel and their own release from financial bondage.

About the Author

Professor John Barrett Kelly was one of the foremost commentators on the Middle East, and noted for his independence of mind; along with Bernard Lewis, PJ Vatikiotis and Elie Kedourie he was one of the so-called "Gang of Four," pre-eminent scholars in the field who believed that Western policy towards the Arab world was distorted by sentimental illusions—notably, that it mistook the tyranny imposed by Arab nationalist regimes for progress.

As such Kelly was occasionally accused of being pro-Zionist. That was a simple error. He was critical of both Arab and Israeli actions at different times. His real admiration was for the British imperial servants, generally in the India Office, who had brought stability and genuine progress to Arabia and the Gulf. His real contempt was for the British and American governments who had appeased weak anti-imperial challengers, betraying their own diplomats, their sheikhly regional allies, and the subjects of repressive Arab rulers in turn.

Despite his distaste for Arab nationalist dictators, he was no supporter of the recent Iraq War. In fact, he was a strong critic of both the military campaign and of Tony Blair's statesmanship in general.

He took the view that the war had been embarked on almost frivolously, with neither a clear justification in terms of British or Western interests nor a clear idea of how its outcome would advance them. He saw it as an expression of a messianic thoughtlessness on Blair's part—and, in some respects, as the fitting climax to decades of Western policies based on fanciful illusions about the Arab world.

He did at various times, however, have some measure of influence over those policies; first over British strategy in the Arabian peninsula in the 1950s and 1960s, and then, after a move to Washington, over American Middle Eastern policy in the 1980s.

That influence came after Kelly, a professional historian, published his second book—*Britain and the Persian Gulf 1795-1880* (1968)—which established him as the leading academic authority on the history of the region. At that time his detailed knowledge of border disputes and maritime treaties in the Gulf led to his advice being sought both by the Foreign Office and local sheikhdoms.

But his robust belief that the Gulf benefited greatly from a stabilising British military and political presence ensured that he would exercise less and less influence over British policy as London relinquished its role east of Suez in the 1970s. For their part, however, local emirates continued to seek his advice and support and to relish his deep knowledge of their own histories.

Kelly was born in Auckland, New Zealand, on April 5 1925, the son of a chemist. When John was two years old his father died, and he was brought up by a succession of nuns and aunts while his mother worked as a hotel receptionist.

She scraped together enough money to send him to Sacred Heart College, the renowned local Catholic boys' school, where he showed early promise as a scholar. He went to University College, Auckland, aged 16, reading Geology before switching to History and Literature.

In 1943, when he was 18, Kelly tried to enlist in the Royal New Zealand Air Force, but his poor eyesight let him down. He had asked a friend to memorise the eye chart, but when he went in for his medical and reeled off the letters before him, he was pronounced unfit. The doctor had switched the chart.

Instead Kelly spent his summers during the war working on the docks in Auckland and helping to build aerodrome hangars for the American Air Force, which had bases in northern New Zealand for its island-hopping campaign in the Pacific. After the war he qualified as a schoolteacher and taught until 1951 in schools in New Zealand, Queensland, England and Egypt. It was in Alexandria that he met and married Valda Elizabeth Pitt – he was teaching at the British Boys' School and she at the English Girls' College.

His experience of Egypt at the end of King Farouk's reign sparked a lifelong interest in the Middle East. He would quote Talleyrand to describe life in postwar Alexandria—those who never experienced it had no idea of "la douceur de vivre."

Returning to England, and disillusioned with teaching, he decided to sit for a higher degree. Since the Auckland BA was not recognised by

London University, he had to pass papers in Latin and Anglo-Saxon and Medieval History, under the stern but kindly eye of Professor Bindoff of Queen Mary's College, London, in order to qualify for a London University BA.

He was then accepted by Professor William Norton Medlicott to take an MA at the LSE. Realising Kelly's potential, Medlicott encouraged him to do a PhD on Britain and the Persian Gulf, which was to become his field of expertise.

After receiving his doctorate in 1956, Kelly became a research fellow at the Institute of Colonial Studies at Oxford University until 1958, under the guidance of Sir Reader Bullard, British Ambassador to Iran during the Second World War, and a British minister to Saudi Arabia in the 1930s. It was with the encouragement of Bullard, who was to become his mentor, that Kelly made his first trip to the Gulf in 1957.

He visited Iraq in the dying days of the Hashemite regime and then flew on to the Trucial Coast—known in the 19th century as the Pirate Coast, and now forming the United Arab Emirates. The only Europeans in Abu Dhabi at that time were either oil men, diplomats or soldiers.

The British political officer introduced him to Sheikh Shakhbut before taking him to see his brother, Sheikh Zayid. Kelly was to form a firm friendship with both men, which was to survive the political turmoil in Abu Dhabi in the following two decades.

He paid a particularly instructive visit to the Buraimi Oasis, from where British-officered Trucial Scouts had ejected an American-backed Saudi force (engaged on an oil-grabbing mission) in 1955. He and the political officer, Martin Buckmaster, soon picked up signs that the Saudis were retaliating by stirring up the tribes of inner Oman with arms and money. Kelly passed this information on to the British political resident in Bahrain, Sir Bernard Burrows, who discounted it, coming as it did from a Gulf novice.

Burrows returned on leave to London, only to be called back to the Gulf in a hurry in July 1957 when the Imamate rebellion broke out in Oman. Kelly's first publication, written for Chatham House, was a paper on the revolt.

His growing expertise on the tribes of Eastern Arabia was soon in demand by the Foreign Office, which hired him to advise on the long-disputed boundaries between the Trucial sheikhdoms, Oman and Saudi Arabia. His first book, *Eastern Arabian Frontiers* (1964), was based on this work.

In the meantime he had left Oxford, partly out of distaste at the academic milieu of the newly-founded Middle East Centre at St Antony's College. After expressing concern at a dinner about the tenor of the reports on Middle Eastern politics from Kim Philby, the spy who was then *The Economist's* correspondent in Beirut, Kelly was told that "he was not fit to clean Philby's boots."

He left for a series of teaching posts at Wesleyan College in Delaware, Ohio; the University of Michigan at Ann Arbor; and the University of Wisconsin at Madison, where he became Professor of Imperial History and published his magnum opus, *Britain and the Persian Gulf, 1795-1880.*

As Britain withdrew from Aden in 1967 and prepared to withdraw from the Gulf in 1971, Kelly left academia and became an adviser to Sheikh Zayid of Abu Dhabi on the issue of its disputed frontiers with Qatar and Saudi Arabia. Coming up against the increasingly pro-Saudi alignment of both Britain and America, Kelly fought hard to make the best case for Abu Dhabi's retention of the Khawr al-Udayd inlet on the marches of Qatar.

This was coveted by the Saudis as an outlet to the lower Gulf. In addition, they sought to control the tract of desert south of the Liwa Oasis, which contained the newly-discovered Zarrara/Shaiba oilfield, then the largest strike in the world.

In the end Kelly was thwarted by the murky compromises of Arab and international politics. This experience left him more convinced than ever that Britain's hasty withdrawal from the Gulf had destabilised the region, leaving the smaller states prey to the territorial ambitions of their larger neighbours, Saudi Arabia, Iraq and Iran, and the West open to oil blackmail, a view later vindicated by events.

This opinion was not popular in Whitehall or the City, where eyes could appear more firmly fixed on recycling the flow of petrodollars through arms sales and lavish infrastructure projects. But it seemed to find a ready audience with Margaret Thatcher, then leader of the opposition. Further encouraged by Elie Kedourie and David Pryce-Jones, Kelly outlined his stance in his most accessible book, *Arabia, the Gulf and the West* (1980).

This publication made a great impact in Washington, where the incoming Reagan administration was searching for a new, more robust policy in the Gulf. As a visiting research fellow at the Woodrow Wilson Centre and the Heritage Foundation in Washington in the early 1980s, Kelly's advice on the region was sought by administration officials, senators, congressmen, journalists and think-tanks. He was directly involved in lobbying against the sale of AWACs early-warning aircraft to Saudi Arabia, arguing that it would further destabilise the region. But as Saudi influence grew in Washington with Reagan's forging of an informal alliance with the kingdom, Kelly's influence inevitably declined. His prescient warnings that Saudi money was being used to establish an international network of Muslim fundamentalists were thus largely ignored.

Subsequently, he advised the government of Oman on its disputed frontiers with Saudi Arabia and South Yemen, paying trips to inner Oman, Dhofar and the Masandam Peninsula.

When not advising governments, Kelly beavered away in the National Archives in Washington and the Public Record Office in London, collecting material for a book on Anglo-American relations with Saudi Arabia from 1926 to 1956, which he was never to complete.

Kelly left Washington in 1988 and the following year retired with his wife to south-western France. Although keeping up with events in the Middle East, and being asked on innumerable occasions to return to the Gulf and Washington, he preferred a quiet existence of reading and reflection. He kept himself fit playing tennis until his last years, despite his poor eyesight.

A man of great courtesy, he established for himself and his family a life of some style, though without extravagance, and was himself always immaculately turned out, with an unhurried manner which perfectly suited his innate conservatism. He recalled in retirement the prediction of his French Jesuit teacher in Auckland that he would end his days in France, a country that he always loved.

John Barrett Kelly died on August 29, 2009.

This volume was edited by his son, Dr Saul B. Kelly, a Reader in International History in the Defence Studies Department of King's College, London at the Joint Services Command and Staff College, which he joined in September 2001. Publications include *War and Politics in the Desert*, (Society for Libyan Studies, 2010) *The Hunt for Zerzura: The Lost Oasis and the Desert War* (John Murray, 2002); *Cold War in the Desert. Britain, the United States and the Italian Colonies, 1945 52* (Macmillan, 2000); Co-editor with A. Gorst, *Whitehall and the Suez Crisis* (Frank Cass, 2000).

INDEX

A

Abu Dhabi, 13, 191, 263-264, 270, 299, 307, 312, 327-331, 333, 335-337, 343-344; Shaikh Zayid bin Sultan Al-Niyayan 13, 343-344

Abyssinia (Ethiopia): 84-85, 91-92, 94, 100, 103, 109-110, 112, 117, 120-121, 128, 193, 273, 283-284, 314; Massawa, 104, 108-111, 117; Shoa, 104-105, 109-110, 112

Aden, 25-41, 60, 71, 74, 76, 91, 97, 105, 108-111, 116, 120, 129-133, 145-146, 171, 174-175, 178, 188, 192-194, 197-198, 201, 204, 211-212, 252, 262, 273, 275, 278, 281-285, 288, 297-298, 308, 310, 344; Al-Asnaj, Abdullah, 33-36; Front for the Liberation of South Yemen (F.L.O.S.Y.), 131-133, 281; National Liberation Front (N.L.F.), 131-133, 281-282; protector-ates, 25, 26, 29, 31, 33, 35, 41, 116, 131, 145, 192, 197, 211, 281

Afghanistan: 22-23, 177, 258, 264, 273, 287, 303, 305, 312, 314-315; Kabul, 130, 287, 315

Algeria, 136, 268, 278, 300, 328, 330, 334-336, 340

Amery, Julian (Conservative M.P.), 13, 193-194

Arab: cause, 16, 59, 221, 248; history, 59, 61, 63, 70, 77, 82-83; -Israeli con-flict, 56, 141, 155, 159, 161, 170, 180, 182-184, 221, 243, 248, 319, 336;

nationalism, 16, 28, -29, 31, 45, 71, 123, 181, 192, 211, 244; politics, 16, 21, 46, 81-82, 140, 148; slave trade, 9, 18-19, 84-89, 91-93, 95-103, 105, 107, 109-121, 166, 214, 254, 264, 275, 299, 304

B

Bahrain, 90-91, 101, 103, 107, 111, 116, 167, 196, 234-236, 264, 271, 299, 301, 307, 310, 343

Balfour, Arthur (Sir), 42, 57-58, 60, 82, 182, 214, 225, 264-265, 279, 287, 296, 312, 317

Boustead, Hugh (Sir), 191-193, 195-196, 210

Britain: Aden and South Yemen, 26, 29, 30-33, 41, 174, 211, 281-282, 344; Afghanistan, 314; Arabia, 74-75, 77, 216, 291, 294-295; Arabs, 59-61, 71; East Africa, 19, 97, 114, 121, 254; Egypt, 125; Empire, 15, 18, 26, 40, 232, 261; France, 44, 57-58, 97, 173, 181, 213, 224, 228, 242-243, 248, 250, 265, 275, 309, 321, 323, 325, 339; Gulf, 13-14, 26, 102, 167, 263-264, 296-297, 299-304, 309, 325; India, 9, 14, 98, 176-177, 179; Israel, 23, 59; Middle East, 43-46, 141, 174, 182; Oil, 172, 225-226, 268-269, 310, 340; Ottoman Empire, 64, 176, 185-186; Royal Air Force (R.A.F.), 63, 194, 237-238; Royal Navy, 98, 101, 103, 115, 121, 191, 225; United States, 22, 161, 173, 213, 265, 275, 309, 321, 323, 339, 344-345

British Petroleum (BP, formerly Anglo-Persian Oil Company, APOC), 167, 225, 227, 235-236, 268

C

Chatham House (Royal Institute of International Affairs), 15, 41, 49, 60, 147-148, 154-155, 343

China (Chinese), 128, 136, 200, 206, 208, 280-282

Christian, 16, 19, 21, 68, 85, 94, 104-105, 109, 113, 118, 120, 170, 184, 229-230, 253-254, 258, 274, 324

Churchill, Winston (Sir), 43, 45, 238

Clayton, Gilbert (Sir), 72-76, 186

Colonial Office, 27-28, 32, 34, 43, 45, 217

Cox, Percy (Sir), 43, 73, 164, 216

Cuba, 200, 205, 281, 283

Curzon, George Nathaniel (Lord), 45, 57-58, 232, 296

E

Encounter, 7, 16, 19, 262, 277

Egypt: 10, 27-28, 30-31, 33, 35, 40, 53, 59, 63, 72, 77-80, 82, 84-85, 98, 108-109, 112, 114, 117-120, 122-123, 125-128, 131, 151-152, 158-159, 161-162, 178, 181, 185, 203, 239-249, 251, 254, 278, 297, 300, 342; Cairo, 27-32, 34-36, 42-43, 50-58, 64, 71-73, 111, 123-124, 127, 129, 185-186, 192, 196,

203, 244, 288; Suez Canal, and Zone, 27-28, 52, 116, 123-125, 161, 239, 240, 243

F

Foreign and Commonwealth Office (FCO, formerly Foreign Office, FO), 13, 21, 43, 45, 58-59, 61, 64-66, 73, 87, 93, 114-115, 122, 128, 148, 155, 178, 180, 182, 186-187, 194, 197, 218, 225-227, 261, 290, 294, 298-301, 343

G

Geyl, Pieter, 13-14

Gibb, Hamilton (Sir), 15, 256

H

Halliday, Fred, 144-146, 202, 206-209

Heath, Edward (Sir), 298, 300-301

Heikal, Mohammed Hassanein, 249, 251

Hijaz, 43, 45, 62, 64-66, 73, 75, 96, 108-111, 113-114, 116, 118-120, 178, 185-186, 273; Jeddah, 91, 96, 108-112, 114, 117-119; Madinah, 111-112, 118; Mecca, 58-59, 63-64, 72, 111-112, 114, 118, 120, 147, 172, 178, 181, 185, 258, 275, 292, 309; Al-Hashimi, Sharif Husain ibn Ali, 62-66, 72, 75, 147, 181-182

Hormuz, Strait of, 22, 167-168, 264, 299, 315

Horn of Africa, 23, 84, 91, 117, 120, 194, 283

I

India: 9, 14, 43, 45, 52, 61, 63-66, 71, 73, 78, 84-87, 91-92, 98, 100, 103, 109, 122, 115, 136, 176-179, 186, 188, 190-192, 196-197, 202, 217, 238, 253, 255, 296, 298-299, 303-304, 307, 315, 341; Bombay, 87-88, 91-92, 97-98, 100-101, 103, 105, 107, 110 ; Hyderabad, 92, 189-190

Indian Ocean, 9, 18, 84-85, 87, 89-91, 93, 95, 97-99, 101, 103, 105, 107, 109, 111, 113, 115, 117, 119, 121, 287

Ingrams, Doreen and Harold, 27, 76, 189-192

Iraq (Mesopotamia): 16,22-23, 43, 45-46, 51-52, 58, 62, 66, 73-77, 80, 84-85, 95, 98, 101, 112-113, 122, 149, 151, 158, 160-162, 166, 173-174, 186-187, 203, 216, 225-228, 248, 258, 264, 268, 271, 273, 278, 285, 287, 299-301, 303, 310, 313-314, 316, 326, 328, 330-331, 335-336, 340-341, 343-344; Baghdad, 16, 50, 52, 54, 75, 80, 95-96, 101, 108, 124, 129, 148-149, 158-159, 166, 178; Basra (Bussorah), 90-91, 101-102, 148, 203, 225

Iran (Persia): 19, 22-23, 84-85, 93, 95, 101, 103, 110, 112, 116, 140, 144, 155, 158, 162, 165, 167-168, 170, 173, 225, 227, 235-236, 258, 262-266, 270-272, 274-275, 285, 287-288, 296, 299, 301-307, 309, 311, 313-317, 321, 327-329, 331, 334-335, 340, 343-344; Bushire, 90, 91, 96, 110-111; Khomeini, Ayatollah, 255-256, 258, 306; Tehran, 20, 23, 93, 95-96, 102, 254, 265, 269, 291, 302, 321, 325, 329

Islam, 10, 15, 22, 64-65, 79, 82, 85, 87, 94-95, 104, 116, 120, 139, 145, 163, 170-172, 177, 180, 183-184, 209, 212-214, 221, 253-259, 266, 272-276, 279, 290-292, 323-324

Israel: 23, 38, 48-49, 59-60, 81, 124, 128, 141, 151-152, 156-162, 170, 181, 183-184, 197, 220-221, 239, 242-243, 247-248, 260, 295, 297, 310, 313; Zionism, 151-152, 181, 198, 204, 261

J

Japan, 169, 173, 190, 222, 264, 269, 285-286, 302, 311, 314, 325, 331

Jordan (Transjordan), 45, 74-77, 217

K

Kedourie, Elie, 15-18, 23, 60-61, 66, 80-81, 135-139, 147-148, 185-187, 341, 344

Kelly, J.B. (JBK), 2-3, 7, 13-24, 90, 175; *Arabia, the Gulf and the West*, 5, 18, 20, 22, 24, 344; *Britain and the Persian Gulf, 1795-1880*, 90, 103, 342-344; *New Zealand*, 14, 16, 342

Kissinger, Henry, 265-266, 272, 302

Kuwait, 10, 50-52, 76, 90-91, 102, 107, 112, 116, 151, 162, 196, 202-204, 206, 211, 234-236, 264, 271, 279, 299, 301, 310, 312, 316, 326-328, 331, 340

L

Labour (British party and government), 13, 21, 31, 33, 35-36, 40, 89, 294, 297-298

Lawrence, T.E., 43, 74, 187, 231-232, 237-238

Lebanon, 10, 21, 160, 162, 183, 214, 229-230, 324; Beirut, 151, 153, 197, 204, 229, 344

Libya: 167, 211, 255, 258, 264, 269, 282, 300, 324, 328, 330, 336, 340; Qaddafi, 255, 269

Little, Tom, 25, 29, 71, 130, 164

Lloyd, Selwyn, 124, 241-243

M

Macaulay, Thomas Babington, 9, 13-15, 17, 19, 21-23, 273

McMahon, Henry (Sir), 17, 42, 63, 181, 185-187

Mediterranean, 54, 85, 98, 114, 118, 186, 246, 287, 296

Middle East, 7, 9-10, 14-17, 20, 22-23, 26-27, 40, 42-43, 46-51, 53-55, 57-58, 62, 64, 77, 80-82, 93, 122-125, 127-131, 133, 136, 140-143, 147-149, 151, 154-165, 169, 171-172, 174, 176, 180-184, 192, 194-195, 198, 200, 214, 220-221, 223-224, 227, 230, 232, 242, 244, 251-252, 255, 257-257, 262-263, 268, 270, 277-280, 285-287, 295-296, 300, 308, 312, 314, 322, 324-325, 327, 333, 341-342, 344-345

Mitchell, Colin, 25, 38-40, 131

N

Nasser, Gamal Abdul, 21, 27, 30, 35-37, 51-53, 60, 81-82, 123-126, 151-152, 158-159, 162, 192, 198, 239-240, 242-252, 297, 301

Nixon, Richard, 265, 298, 302

O

Oman: 196-196, 200-206, 211, 262-264, 270, 276, 288, 299-301, 307-308, 310, 343, 345; Muscat, 86-87, 90, 97-98, 103, 107, 110-111, 114-116, 196, 202; Dhufar, 145, 168, 197, 201-208, 210-212, 217, 262-264, 273, 281, 284, 288, 303; Popular Front for the Liberation of the Arab Gulf (P.F.L.O.A.G.), 205-210, 212

OPEC (Organisation of Petroleum Exporting States): 10, 22, 171, 173-174, 213, 220-223, 265, 267, 269-270, 311-313, 316-320, 325-337, 339-340

Ottoman Empire (Turkey), 15, 42, 45, 57-58, 62, 64, 66, 74, 99, 102-103, 111, 114, 118, 137, 141, 158, 162, 176-178, 182, 185, 191, 225-227, 296, 302

P

Pakistan, 158, 195, 253, 274, 296, 302

Palestine: 38, 43, 45, 57-59, 61, 73, 80, 144, 150-152, 155-156, 161, 180-183, 186-187, 198, 248, 260-261, 271; Palestinians, 21, 56, 183, 214, 229-230, 271; Popular Front for the Liberation of Palestine (PFLP), 144, 150, 152, 183, 198, 205; Habash, George, 150-

152, 180, 197-198; Haddad, Wadi, 150-152, 197; Hawatima, Nayif, 150, 152, 184, 198-199

Persian Gulf: 5, 9, 11, 13-14, 18, 20-24, 32, 74, 77, 84, 86, 89-92, 95, 98, 100-103, 105, 107-111, 115-116, 118, 144, 163-175, 177-178, 186, 192, 194, 197, 202, 204-206, 234-236, 262-276, 279, 281-285, 287-289, 294, 296-314, 321-322, 324-325, 327, 330, 337-338, 341-345; Abu Musa and Tunbs, islands, 167, 264, 299

Philby, Harold St. John Bridger, 10, 65, 215-218, 344

Portugal (Portuguese), 19, 85, 116, 285, 303

Pryce-Jones, David, 5, 7, 22, 344

Q

Qatar, 116, 217, 271, 299, 307, 310, 340, 344

R

Reagan, Ronald, 15, 24, 344.

Red Sea, 9, 18, 22, 74, 84-87, 89-91, 93, 95, 97-103, 105, 107-121, 267, 283, 285, 287-288

S

Sadat, Anwar al-, 51, 239-241, 247, 249

Saudi Arabia: 19, 22-23, 144-145, 158, 160, 162-163, 167-168, 170, 175, 194-195, 203, 215, 223, 256, 263, 265-267, 269-273, 275, 278-279, 284, 290-294, 297, 299-301, 307-311, 316-320, 322-323, 327-328, 330-331, 333-337, 340, 343-345; Najd, 58, 62, 65, 75-76, 112, 201, 216, 264; Al-Saud, Abdul Aziz ibn Abdur Rahman (King) , 62, 64-65, 71-73, 75-77; Al-Saud, Faisal ibn Abdul Aziz (King), 173, 222-223, 256, 264, 279, 291, 297, 299; Arabian-American Oil Company (ARAM-CO), 218,266-268, 270, 308-309, 325, 333, 335-338; Hasa, 116, 234-235, 263, 273; Rub al-Khali, 201, 218, 263; Wahhabi, 256, 266, 275, 291-292, 307

Shah of Iran, 9, 19, 21-23, 95-96, 98, 101-103, 116, 165-168, 170-174, 220-223, 262, 264-266, 270, 274-275, 299, 301-306, 312-313, 317, 322, 328

Shatt al-Arab, 91, 166, 264

Shi'i/Shi'a, 23, 95, 168, 255, 258, 272

Smiley, David, 193-196, 210

Somali Coast: Berbera, 91, 104, 107-110, 117; Zeila, 104, 107, 109-110, 117

South Arabia, 10, 25-28, 30-32, 34-41, 71, 84, 115,122, 129-133, 146, 164, 188-189, 191-193, 195, 197, 199-201, 203, 205, 207, 209, 211-212, 262-263, 281-282, 297, 310

South Yemen: 22-23, 35, 37, 41, 145, 152, 163, 193, 198, 201, 206-207, 210-211, 258, 281-284, 301, 310, 314, 345; Hadramaut (Hadramis), 109-110, 115, 188-193, 199-202, 204, 211, 283-284, 288; Mahra, 188, 201, 204, 209; Mukalla, 188-191, 193, 195, 206, 283; Qu'aiti, 189, 193, 195

Soviet Union (Russia), 15, 22, 40, 51, 98, 102, 156-159, 166-168, 177, 191, 200, 206, 211, 216, 220, 240, 248, 251-252, 258, 263-264, 273, 276-289, 296, 301, 303-306, 309, 312-315; Moscow, 51-52, 127-128, 196, 210, 265, 282, 305, 310 312

Standard Oil Company of California, 235-236, 307-308, 312, 333

Sudan: 72, 104, 117, 119, 124-125, 162, 191, 254; Suakin, 105, 111, 117

Sykes-Picot agreement (1916), 42, 44, 59, 66, 182

Syria: 30, 43, 58, 74-75, 80, 84, 112, 118, 151-152, 158-162, 178, 186-187, 202, 228, 231, 248, 278, 314, 331; Damascus, 59, 111, 152, 197, 231-232

T

Thatcher, Margaret, 23, 344

The Daily Telegraph, 7, 17, 20-21, 23, 165, 194, 220, 229

The Economist, 15-18, 23, 70, 258, 272

The Financial Times, 22-23, 291, 322

The New Republic, 7, 18, 41, 253, 281, 290

The Observer, 23, 128, 182, 260

The Sunday Telegraph, 7, 17, 23, 185, 213, 229, 231, 237, 239, 241, 251, 260, 274

The Times, 17-18, 20-23, 54, 67, 83,

133, 291, 293, 322, 323

The Times Higher Educational Supplement, 7, 17, 144, 150, 244, 322

The Times Literary Supplement (TLS), 7, 9, 15-18, 20, 23, 56- 63, 65-71, 73, 75, 77-83, 180, 224

Toynbee, Arnold, 15, 60, 187

Trevelyan, Humphrey (Lord), 122-127, 129-133

Trevaskis, Kennedy (Sir), 25-31, 33-37, 40-41, 130

U

United Arab Emirates (Trucial, Pirate, Coast), 90, 115, 168, 194, 264, 271, 276, 299, 301, 307, 343; Sharjah, 167, 194; Ras al-Khaima, 110, 167

United States, 14-15, 19, 22-23, 57, 142-143, 155, 156-157, 159-162, 169, 172-173, 180, 183, 194, 213, 222, 225, 235, 242, 252, 263, 265-269, 272, 274-275, 282, 286, 293, 301-306, 308-310, 321, 323, 325, 334, 337, 339, 345; Senate, 265-267, 272, 312, 333, 335; State Department, 242, 262, 265-267, 269-270, 272, 308

V

Vatikiotis, P.J., 16, 18, 80-81, 140, 244-249, 341

W

Western world, 5, 7, 9, 11, 14-16, 18-22, 24, 26, 28, 30, 32, 34, 36, 38,

40, 44, 46, 50, 52-54, 56, 58, 60, 62,
64, 66, 68, 70, 72, 74-76, 78, 80, 82,
84, 86, 88, 90, 92, 94, 96, 98, 100, 102,
104, 106, 108-110, 112, 114, 116, 118,
120, 124, 126, 128, 130, 132, 134-136,
138, 142, 146, 148, 150, 152, 156-158,
160, 162, 164-175, 178, 182, 184, 186,
190, 192, 194, 196, 198, 200-202, 204,
206, 208, 210, 212-214, 216, 218,
220-222, 224, 226, 228, 230, 232, 236,
238, 240, 242, 244, 246, 248, 250,
252-258, 262-264, 266-276, 278, 280,
282, 284-289, 291-294, 296, 298, 300,
302, 304-306, 308, 310-314, 317-340,
342, 344

Y

Yamani, Shaikh Zaki Al-, 22, 222,
316-320, 332-336

Yemen: 27-34, 71, 74, 76, 91, 107,
109-112, 116, 120, 132-133, 145,
162-163, 178, 186, 193, 199-200, 211,
247-248, 273, 278-281, 284, 297, 308;
Hodeida, 91, 109, 110-111; Mocha,
91, 109-110

Z

Zanzibar, 19, 85-92, 97, 100-102,
110-111, 114-116, 120

CPSIA information can be obtained at www.ICGtesting.com
Printed in the USA
LVOW13s0408190314

377989LV00004B/8/P